Mother Leakey and the Bishop

Mother Leakey and the Bishop

A GHOST STORY

PETER MARSHALL

OXFORD
UNIVERSITY PRESS

OXFORD
UNIVERSITY PRESS

Great Clarendon Street, Oxford OX2 6DP

Oxford University Press is a department of the University of Oxford.
It furthers the University's objective of excellence in research, scholarship,
and education by publishing worldwide in

Oxford New York

Auckland Cape Town Dar es Salaam Hong Kong Karachi
Kuala Lumpur Madrid Melbourne Mexico City Nairobi
New Delhi Shanghai Taipei Toronto

With offices in

Argentina Austria Brazil Chile Czech Republic France Greece
Guatemala Hungary Italy Japan Poland Portugal Singapore
South Korea Switzerland Thailand Turkey Ukraine Vietnam

Oxford is a registered trade mark of Oxford University Press
in the UK and in certain other countries

Published in the United States
by Oxford University Press Inc., New York

© Peter Marshall 2007

The moral rights of the author have been asserted
Database right Oxford University Press (maker)

First published 2007

British Library Cataloguing in Publication Data

Data available

Library of Congress Cataloging in Publication Data

Data available

Typeset by SPI Publisher Services, Pondicherry, India
Printed in Great Britain
on acid-free paper by
Clays Ltd, St. Lves plc

ISBN 978-0-19-927371-3

I

For my Mother

Preface

> I know it is a matter of very little credit to be a relator of stories, and I of all men living, have the least reason to be fond of the employment. For I never had any faculty in telling of a story, and have always had a particular indisposition and backwardness to the writing of any such. But of all relations of fact, there are none like to give a man such trouble and disreputation, as those that relate to witchcraft and apparitions . . . [1]

These words were written by the Anglican clergyman Joseph Glanvill shortly before his death in 1680. As a university-based historian, who has tended in the past to write on large and 'respectable' academic themes, I now feel I know exactly where Glanvill was coming from. Historians, like Anglican clergymen, do not usually think of themselves as story-tellers. Yet the book I have spent the last few years researching and writing, the book you now hold in your hands, is an example of that least respectable of narrative forms, the ghost story. It is perhaps more accurate to say that it is a story about stories about ghosts, a study of how a particular English folk legend came into being, of what it meant to the people who told and retold it, and of what it can tell us about the times through which they lived.

Though they do not often admit it, all history books contain within them the story of how and why they came to be written. The experienced tracker can usually reconstruct the author's progress through libraries and archives, as well as make informed guesses about how decisions were reached to arrange and present the resulting material. In my own case, I have thought it best to be more transparent than is customary about the genesis and creation of my text. *Mother Leakey* is a book that came about by accident, as well as a tale that has grown considerably in the telling. It began like this. In the spring of 2001 I was invited to speak at a conference at the University of Durham on the theme of 'early modern [i.e. sixteenth- and seventeenth-century] ghosts'. This was a recent but keen research interest of mine; I was in the process of writing a book on attitudes towards the memory of the dead in Reformation-era England, in which there was to be a chapter on spectres and spirits.[2] A brief footnote in a pioneering study of the topic—a section in Sir Keith Thomas's *Religion and the Decline of Magic*—had already alerted me to the existence of an interesting-looking, but apparently little-known document, concerning the reported appearance of a ghost in south-west England in the late 1630s. The supposed haunting took place in the town of Minehead in Somerset, a place I had heard of, but never visited nor knew much about. When I checked out the original manuscript in the Public Record Office in London (now the National Archives), I discovered that it comprised a set of depositions, or witness statements, which seemed to me to supply the ideal subject matter for a short conference paper. The depositions brimmed with illuminating period detail, and they contained several vivid accounts of where and when the alleged apparition was reported to have appeared, of what it had said and done, and of what it had looked like.

Less than a week before the talk was due to be delivered, I made a snap decision to try to supplement the rich material I already had at my disposal, and set off on a day-trip to the Somerset Record Office, situated in the county town of Taunton, about twenty-five miles to the south-east of Minehead itself. I hoped that from other records held there it might be possible to find out more details about the lives of some of the people mentioned in the depositions. In the event, I was not disappointed, and some of the fruits of that first research trip are on display in Chapter 1. As I prepared to finish up for the day in the book-lined surroundings of the manuscript search room, I chanced upon a useful-looking volume entitled *Minehead in the County of Somerset: A History of the Parish, the Manor and the Port*. This had been published at Taunton in 1903 by the Reverend Frederick Hancock, who was then vicar of the nearby parish of Dunster. His book, a monument to solid Victorian scholarship, provided me with rather more information than I had bargained for. Not only did

Hancock supply a full printed version of the depositions I had already laboriously transcribed from the seventeenth-century original, but he introduced them with a cheerfully oblivious reference to 'the famous Minehead ghost story, immortalised by Sir Walter Scott'. As someone who regarded himself as the discoverer of an archival gem virtually unknown to previous scholarship, this came as something of a shock, to put it mildly.

It was too late to do much to save the conference paper. But over the next few months I became increasingly obsessed with trying to pin down exactly how it was that the Minehead ghost had come to the attention of Scotland's greatest romantic novelist, and why the tale was evidently still familiar, three-quarters of a century after his death, to the reading public of Edwardian England. What I began to discover was that the depositions in the Public Record Office represented only the tip of an iceberg of rumour and scandal, and that the case had ramifications far beyond the day-to-day concerns of the inhabitants of a little Somerset seaport, and indeed far beyond the time in which they themselves had lived.

There was, in fact, a second story, hidden inside the folds of the first. It concerned an English clergyman, who rose from obscurity to become a bishop in Ireland, and then suffered a spectacular fall from grace. It soon became clear to me that the ghost in Minehead was thoroughly and intimately connected, though not in an entirely straightforward way, with a notorious clerical scandal. The humiliation of the bishop came, moreover, at a moment of acute historical importance, occurring right on the eve of the civil wars which engulfed both Ireland and England for most of the 1640s. His predicament was rooted in personal failings, but it was also hugely political. Examining the case seemed to offer the opportunity to say something about the relationship between English and Irish affairs in these crucial years, and to think about how a 'British dimension' might influence our understanding, both of political culture as a whole, and of individual life experiences.[3] At the same time, the close association of a ghost with a high-profile political and ecclesiastical scandal invited some serious reflection on the continuing significance of 'supernatural' events at a time of changing attitudes towards the design and workings of the created universe.

Yet as I continued to work on the materials relating to the case, I became increasingly convinced that perhaps its most interesting and significant aspect was the way it seemingly refused to remain fixed in its original historical location. Over the course of the three centuries and more following the ghost's first appearances in Mine-head, the story—or rather the two interweaving stories—did not simply fall asleep to await the modern historian's awakening kiss. Rather, they demonstrated a recurring and disconcerting capacity to get up and walk about, in the process often acquiring new sets of meanings, and illuminating for us some of the cares and concerns of new sets of actors on the historical stage. In other words, long before my own moment of epiphany in the Somerset Record Office, the stories of Mother Leakey and the bishop had already become part of a revealing conversation between the present and the past. I wanted to trace how this had happened, and what this single episode might have to say about how history is remembered and used in successive ages.

It soon became clear to me that, in order to make any sort of sense out of this, *Mother Leakey* was going to have to be a rather different kind of history book. Historians, or at least those of us who can tear ourselves away from Henry VIII and Hitler, quite often employ small incidents, and the lives of obscure individuals, as a means of opening up aspects of the wider culture which surrounds them at a particular moment. There is much of that technique in the pages that follow. But at the same time, the peculiarities of the evidence in this case, and (as you will see in due course) the peculiar way in which the full range of evidence about it came to light, also offered the opportunity to attempt something else: a rare insight into the process of historical memory as a dynamic entity, a glimpse through a narrow window into how both oral tradition and written history are created and recreated over time.

And also, to be frank, I wanted to tell the story in what I hoped would be a fresh and exciting way. 'Narrative history' has for some time been back in vogue among professional and academic historians—among the wider reading public it had of course never actually gone away. Philosophers and theorists will argue endlessly about whether it is ever really possible to tell 'true stories' about the past. Most practising historians think that it is, so long as an attempt is made to observe the rules. Historians are not allowed to make things up, to suppress inconvenient facts, or to fail to follow up relevant sources of evidence or obvious lines of enquiry. Yet even the strict observance of these criteria usually leaves a huge degree of artistic latitude in the historian's hands. It is seldom, if ever, a case of just laying out the facts in the logical and appropriate order, with an occasional seasoning of wise historical analysis. Indeed, though the point is not often explicitly trumpeted outside of specialist circles, the value and meaning of all historical writing is fundamentally determined by the way historians encounter their material and then choose to tell their tales about it.

In the course of writing this book, therefore, I decided early on not to attempt to disguise from readers that my own account is bound to be a creative exercise, a kind of story or narrative. To allow the point to emerge more clearly, I have allowed myself freely to use some of the terminology and techniques of imaginative literature—prologue, interludes, epilogue.[4] Furthermore, to assist orientation, the book is prefixed, like a play or a Russian novel, with a full 'cast of characters', to which readers can refer later when they feel the need to do so. Historical texts usually aspire to be swans gracefully gliding towards their destinations, their authors' frantic paddling hidden discreetly beneath a calm surface. I decided that I wanted to introduce into the way this book is ordered and paced something of what a historian's voyage of exploration can actually feel like. In preparing it, I have consciously replicated some sense of the pattern of discoveries—at times unexpected, at times frankly disconcerting—which I encountered in the course of my research. There will be a few shocks, twists, and turns, and moments where readers will be asked to revisit ground they have already traversed, or to reassess what they thought they already knew—just as I found myself having to do more than once in the progress of my investigation. Because a central theme is the relationship over time between two sets of stories—that of Mother Leakey and that of the bishop—there are sections where one or other of the threads slips into the background for a while, and may appear to have been lost sight of. Here your patience is asked for: the past haunts the present in unpredictable ways, and what goes around eventually comes round again.

The researching and writing of this book has been a kind of journey, and I have found myself having to ask a good many people for directions along the way. I have been exceptionally lucky in the extent to which leading historians of Ireland have welcomed an at times confused interloper onto their home territory, and have resisted the temptation to tell him, like their proverbial countryman, that 'if I wanted to get to Dublin, I wouldn't have started from here'. Copies of important articles, and many emails of sage advice, have made their way to me from Alan Ford, Clodagh Tait, Raymond Gillespie, and John MacCafferty. In addition, Ray and John provided me with much-needed orientation, and much-appreciated hospitality, during two memorable trips to Dublin. The doyen of seventeenth-century Irish historians, Professor Aidan Clarke, has over the past couple of years been particularly generous in sharing with me his unrivalled knowledge of the career of Bishop Atherton.

For many other references, pointers, and incidental kindnesses, I wish to express my thanks to Toby Barnard, David Como, Will Coster, Margot Finn, Tom Freeman, Bruce Gordon, Cynthia Herrup, Roxanne Grimmett, Trevor Johnson, Kate Jones-Davies, Alan James, Beat Kümin, Angela McShane, Michael Mendle, Anthony Milton, Helen Pierce, Sarah Richardson, Penny Roberts, Lynn Robson, Bill Sheils, and Alison Shell. My friend and colleague Steve Hindle was present at the book's conception—that momentous visit to the Somerset Record Office—and he has kept an avuncular eye on it since. While these specialists were helping me to tune the engine, the story of Mother Leakey and the Bishop was also being road-tested between 2001 and 2006 on more general audiences: at the Universities of Durham, Nottingham, Sheffield, Cambridge, Aberdeen, Oxford, York, Warwick, Sussex,

Bristol, Exeter, and University College, Dublin. On each of these occasions I learnt as least as much from the other participants as they did from me. I am particularly grateful to Eric Carlson, who arranged for me to address a lively Halloween audience at Gustavus College in St Peter, Minnesota, on the eve of the fateful US election of 2004.

Various institutions deserve an honourable mention, not least the archives and libraries from which the raw materials of my text have been quarried. I am as ever grateful to the staffs of my familiar haunts—the National Archives in London, the Bodleian and British Libraries, and the library of Warwick University. I must also thankfully record the unstinted assistance I received when venturing further afield: at Trinity College, Marsh's Library, the Representative Church Body Library, and National Library of Ireland in Dublin; at the Somerset Record Office in Taunton, and North Devon Record Office in Barnstaple; at Dr Williams' Library in London; at Chatsworth House in Derbyshire. Writing the book would not have been possible (or at least it would have been very much slower) without the receipt of a research grant and a period of funded leave from university teaching and administration. I am grateful to the members of the history panel of the Arts and Humanities Research Council for agreeing that a project on ghost stories and disreputable clergymen might be a worthy recipient of public money.

Above all, I owe a special debt of gratitude to the loyal band of friends who have read the entire text of the book in draft: Trevor Burnard, Bernard Capp, Rebecca Earle, Sasha Handley, and Alex Walsham. Between them, they have saved me from many errors, venial and mortal, and have encouraged me to sharpen up and clarify my ideas about what I thought I was doing. The final version has also benefited from the thoughtful and supportive comments of two anonymous readers for Oxford University Press. At the Press, Ruth Parr's initial enthusiasm for the project has been smoothly complemented by the professionalism and cheerfulness of Luciana O'Flaherty and Matthew Cotton.

There are important domestic debts to acknowledge too. While my historical and cultural interests have wandered wildly off their preordained course in the last few years, my loved ones, Ali, Bella, Mimi, and Kit, have helped to keep my life on the straight and narrow. They have indulged my preference for the seventeenth over the twenty-first century, *ma non troppo*. Finally, the person to whom the book is dedicated has encouraged and supported me for, quite literally, more years than I can actually remember.

P. M.

June 2006

Contents

Note to Readers

Full details of sources cited in the endnotes are to be found in the bibliography, where (unless otherwise noted) place of publication for all works is London. All dates before September 1752 are in the Old Style (Julian Calendar); thereafter, in familiar New Style, though the year throughout is taken to begin on 1 January. I have modernized the spelling of quotations from original documents.

Abbreviations

BL	British Library
Bod.	Bodleian Library, Oxford
CSP	*Calendar of State Papers*
NLI	National Library of Ireland, Dublin
NDRO	North Devon Record Office
ODNB	*Oxford Dictionary of National Biography*
RCB	Representative Church Body, Dublin
SP	State Papers
SRO	Somerset Record Office
TCD	Trinity College, Dublin
TNA	The National Archives

List of Illustrations

PHOTOGRAPHIC ACKNOWLEDGEMENTS

Hilary Binding, from H. Binding and D. Stevens, *The Book of Minehead with Alcombe* (Halsgrove, 2000): 17; the British Library: (E.165 (i)) 110, (Cup.363.gg.31.(4)) 248, (c.108.cc.6) 254; the Burke Library at Union Theological Seminary, Columbia University Libraries: 208; the Syndics of Cambridge University Library: (Syn.7.60.55) 51, (L.7.8) 65, (HIB.7.641.4) 110, (HIB.7.641.123) 127, (XIV. 24.54) 159, (Dd*.5.22(G)) 211; Peter Marshall: 267

Cast of Characters

Adair, Archibald	Bishop of Killala and Achonry, 1629–40; Atherton's successor at Waterford.
Addison, Joseph	Author and Whig politician (1672–1719); co-founder of *The Spectator*.
Alcock, Alexander	Anglican clergyman; chancellor of the diocese of Waterford and Lismore in 1710.
Atherton, Joan	Eldest daughter of Mother Leakey; wife of John Atherton.
Atherton, John	Son-in-law of Mother Leakey; vicar of Huish Champflower, 1622–36; bishop of Waterford and Lismore, 1636–40.
Aubrey, John	Antiquarian writer and member of the Royal Society (1626–97).
Benbow, William	Printer and political radical (b. 1784); author of *The Crimes of the Clergy*.
Bernard, Nicholas	Dean of Ardagh in Ireland; author of *The Penitent Death of a Woeful Sinner* (1641).
Betty, Mrs	Supposedly daughter of the town clerk of Barnstaple, *c.*1639. See Lane, Robert.
Boyle, Michael	Bishop of Waterford and Lismore, 1619–35; kinsman of the earl of Cork.
Boyle, Richard (first earl of Cork)	Landowner in Ireland, and chief justice and lord treasurer there; John Atherton's nemesis?
Bramhall, John	Bishop of Derry, 1634–60, and archbishop of Armagh, 1660–3; protégé of Sir

	Thomas Wentworth, and leading Laudian churchman in Ireland.
Brereton, William	A Cheshire gentleman (1604–61); keeper of a travel journal.
Browse, Nicholas	Vicar of Minehead, 1585–1634.
Butler, Piers	Irish landowner and son of Lord Cahir; in dispute with Bishop Atherton over land.
Byam, Henry	Rector of Luccombe, Somerset; interrogates Elizabeth Leakey about the ghost in 1636.
Carte, Thomas	Anglican priest and Jacobite sympathizer (1686–1754); defender of John Atherton.
Castlehaven	See Touchet, Mervyn.
Chamberlain, (?James)	Apprentice to the town clerk of Barnstaple *c.*1639, and steward to John Fortescue of Spriddlestone; supposed recipient of spectral messages.
Charles I	King of England, Scotland, and Ireland, 1625–49.
Child, John	Bishop Atherton's steward at Waterford, and accuser at his trial.
Clotworthy, Sir John	Presbyterian Landowner in Ireland and member of the Long Parliament; enemy of Wentworth and Laud.
Coke, Edward	English legal official, and writer on judicial matters; died 1634.
Cork	See Boyle, Richard.
Curll, Edmund	Grub Street printer, pamphleteer, and pornographer; publisher of *The Case of John Atherton* (1710), and *Some Memorials of the Life and Penitent Death of Dr John*

	Atherton (1711), which contains *A true and amazing relation* of Atherton's crimes.
Dunton, John	Bookseller, printer, and prolific Grub Street writer (1659–1732); author of *Athenianism* (1710), where *The Apparition Evidence* is first published.
Fluellin, Eleanor	Maidservant to Elizabeth Leakey; claims to have seen the Minehead ghost, and interrogated by JPs.
Glanvill, Joseph	Anglican clergyman and collector of ghost stories (1636–80).
Heathfield, John	The curate of Minehead in 1636; questioned by JPs over his claim to have seen the ghost.
King, John	Rector of Chelsea; defender of Bishop Atherton and author of *The Case of John Atherton . . . Fairly Represented* (1710).
Knill, Lordsnear	Widow of William Leakey (Alexander's brother), remarried to John Knill; resident of Barnstaple, and possessor of a golden chain.
Lane, Robert	Town clerk of Barnstaple, 1628–53. Brother of Mother Leakey?
Langstone, Elizabeth	Former servant to Mother Leakey; claims to have seen her ghost in Minehead in 1636, and examined by JPs.
Laud, William	Archbishop of Canterbury, 1633–43; a favourer of the 'beauty of holiness', and resolute enemy of puritans.
Leakey, Alexander	Mother Leakey's eldest son; a merchant and shipowner of Minehead.
Leakey, Elizabeth	Alexander's wife; supposed recipient of secret messages from the ghost.

Leakey, John	Alexander and Elizabeth's teenage nephew; dies in suspicious circumstances in 1635.
Leakey, Lordsnear	See Knill.
Leakey, Susan (aka Old Mother Leakey)	A widow of Minehead in Somerset; later, a ghost.
Leakey, Susan	Her younger daughter.
Leakey, William	John Leakey's deceased father; Alexander's brother.
Loftus, Adam (Viscount Loftus of Ely)	Chief justice and lord chancellor of Ireland; John Atherton's first patron in Ireland.
Lynch, John	Irish Catholic priest (d. *c.* 1677); author of *Cambrensis Eversus*, and originator of a myth about John Atherton.
Milles, Thomas	Bishop of Waterford, 1708–40; a high Tory, and defender of Atherton.
More, Henry	Cambridge philosopher and theologian (1614–87); collaborator with Glanvill in the compilation of supernatural phenomena.
Naylor, Robert	Dean of Lismore; a cousin and ally of the earl of Cork.
Oldys, William	Antiquarian writer (1696–1761); Atherton's biographer in the *Biographia Britannica*.
Phelips, Sir Robert	Somerset landowner and politician; one of the commissioners of February 1637.
Piers, William	Bishop of Bath and Wells (Somerset) from 1632; investigates Minehead ghost in 1637.

Pym, John	Opposition leader in the Long Parliament; chief prosecutor at Wentworth's trial.
Quick, John	Presbyterian minister (1636–1706); author of *The Apparition Evidence*.
Radcliffe, Sir George	Councillor in Ireland, and Wentworth's legal adviser.
Sacheverell, Henry	Oxford clergyman and High Church propagandist; subject of a famous trial (1710).
Scott, Sir Walter	Scottish novelist and poet (1771–1832); author of *Letters on Demonology and Witchcraft* (1830).
Steele, Richard	Irish-born writer and politician (1672–1729); founder of *The Tatler* and *The Spectator*.
Strafford	See Wentworth, Thomas.
Swift, Jonathan	Dean of St Patrick's, Dublin; author of *Gulliver's Travels* (1726).
Touchet, Mervyn (earl of Castlehaven)	Nobleman executed for sodomy in 1631.
Ussher, James	Archbishop of Armagh, 1626–56; a 'moderate' Calvinist, and opponent of Wentworth and Laud.
Walley, John	Steward of the earl of Cork's Lismore estates; bitter enemy of Atherton.
Wandesford, Sir Christopher	Lord Deputy of Ireland, 1640; ally of Wentworth.
Ware, Sir James	Irish auditor-general, diarist and historian; author of a history of the bishops of Ireland (1665).

Wentworth,   Lord Deputy in Ireland, 1633–40; ally of
Sir Thomas (earl of Archbishop Laud, and leading minister
Strafford)   of Charles I; patron of John Atherton.

Wood, Anthony   Oxford antiquarian; author of *Athenae Oxonienses* (1691–2).

Prologue

A Haunting in Minehead

OCTOBER, 1634. Susan Leakey, widow, of Minehead in the County of Somerset, lies in a chamber in the house of her son, Alexander, a once-prosperous merchant and ship owner of the town. She knows that the bed she is lying in will be her deathbed, and she prepares herself for the coming and inevitable end. With effort, she declares before witnesses what her will is for the disposal of her worldly goods, the burial of her mortal body, and the destiny of her immortal soul. Death comes for Mother Leakey in the first days of November, and on the fifth, a day when the nation is as usual celebrating its deliverance from the treason of Gunpowder Plotters, she is buried in accordance with her wishes in the graveyard of the parish church of St Michael's. During the ceremony, as the earth is cast upon her body, comforting words from the Book of Revelation are ordained to be read to the assembled mourners: 'Blessed are the dead which die in the Lord. Even so sayeth the Spirit, that they rest from their labours.' But for this particular old woman there was to be no blessed rest, no smooth passage to the life eternal. Instead, the household and neighbourhood she left behind her were soon to be thrown into confusion, convulsed by rumour, revelation, and reports of revenance—the return of the dead to haunt the places, and unsettle the plans, of those still living on this earth.[1]

Although it was unsought for, and unwelcomed when it came, the ghost of Mother Leakey was not entirely unexpected. The mistress of the house where Susan spent her last weeks was Alexander's young wife, Elizabeth, and—in the way of such things—there had been friction between the two women of different generations required to live under the same roof. From her sickbed, Susan had threatened her daughter-in-law that 'she would come again after her death'. Elizabeth was a quick-witted person, and not easily cowed or intimidated. She snapped back: 'What, will you be a devil?' The reply was an ill-omened one. 'No, but I will come in the devil's likeness.'

The first sign that Mother Leakey's spirit was not at rest came about six weeks after the burial, in mid-December 1634. 'There was a knocking and noise in the chamber and about the bed, which went away like a drove of cattle.' After this ominous portent, all was quiet until about the anniversary of Susan's death the next year, when a much more shocking event took place. Alexander's nephew, the 14-year-old John Leakey, was staying with his relatives in the house. The boy fell ill, 'and died of a languishing disease'. But this tragedy was not, it seemed, any natural event, nor yet a straightforward expression of an inscrutable divine will. In the time of his sickness, John complained 'that he could not be quiet for his grandmother'. As the boy lay dying, he cried out that 'he saw the devil'. Some that viewed the body were able to discern black marks spaced around the dead child's neck.

Thus far, there had been signs and forebodings, but no visible manifestation of a troubled spirit. One evening towards the end of March 1636, however, Elizabeth Leakey went up to her chamber to bed, a book (she remembered) clasped in her hand. There she beheld something in the shape of her mother-in-law, sitting in a chair 'in her full proportion, and in her usual apparel'. Elizabeth was understandably 'much astonished' at this sight, and for a quarter of an hour she simply stared at the apparition, unable to speak to it, until it finally vanished from her sight with a mighty groan. Downstairs in the kitchen, the maidservant heard the noise and rushed up to ask her mistress if all was well, but Elizabeth held her counsel. She did the same an hour or so later when her husband returned home from work. As they lay in bed together, Elizabeth's sighs prompted Alexander to ask what was ailing her, but she said nothing. Elizabeth knew her husband to be a 'fearful' man, and she reflected that it was perhaps kinder to keep silent: it was, after all, his mother who had made this aberrant appearance. There was, however, one person in Minehead in whom she was prepared to confide. A day or two later, the curate, the Reverend John Heathfield, was visiting the house, and Elizabeth told him all. She asked him what the strange apparition might mean, and requested him to seek out expert theological advice, to 'put the case to some divines'. Heathfield was a man of sense. This vision, he told her, 'was nothing but her fancy'. The Leakeys had worries and burdens to bear; undoubtedly, 'her head was troubled with her crosses'. He said nothing to anyone else about the matter, though; at least, not until after the ghost had revealed itself to him also.

On 16 October 1636 (Heathfield was quite certain about the date), the curate attended a great christening feast at the home of one of his parishioners, and on the way back he decided to call in at the house of his friend Alexander Leakey. There may well have been more drinking, for at about nine in the evening, Heathfield opened the kitchen door and 'went forth to make water'. As he turned to come back in again, he found the apparition of old Mrs Leakey standing within four feet of him. She was, as before, in her usual apparel, 'to wit, in a black gown, a kerchief, and a white stomacher [an ornamented covering for the chest and bosom]'. Heathfield was able to see 'the shape of her face and very countenance' by the light thrown from a candle upon the table within the kitchen. The minister was, it hardly needs saying, 'much affrighted' and he left the house in a hurry. A couple of days later, when Elizabeth asked him why he had departed so suddenly, he told her what he had experienced, and she confessed that she herself had seen the apparition 'go forth after him'.

It was about now, around the second anniversary of Mother Leakey's death, at the season of Halloween 1636, that the ghost began to become more daring and profligate in its appearances. The next to see her was the Leakeys' maid, Eleanor Fluellin, who had lived in the house only since May 1636, and thus had not known Susan Leakey during her lifetime. Going into her mistress's parlour at about eight in the evening 'to do some business there', Eleanor saw a shape standing before her. It was a woman with a pale wrinkled face, dressed, as usual, in 'black gown, white stomacher of shag, and a kercher on her head'. Its business, however, was clearly not with the Welsh maid, and the spirit vanished suddenly, leaving Eleanor 'much abashed'. Elizabeth too saw the ghost again at around this time, not in the house but at one of her husband's storehouses on Minehead Quay, quite early in the morning. She did not see the apparition's face, but 'only her back parts'. Perhaps suspecting some piece of trickery, Elizabeth locked the door and hurried home to look in her mother-in-law's chest. There she found the old lady's clothes undisturbed, just 'as she had laid them up'. Still she said nothing about it to her husband.

A couple of weeks later, in mid-November, Elizabeth had a third encounter with the apparition, and a much more decisive one. It was about nine in the morning. Alexander was away at Weymouth on business, and Elizabeth was in one of the rooms of the house 'making herself ready and handsome to go abroad'. It was a small chamber, 'there being but only room enough between the bed and the wall for one to go that way'. As she prepared to leave, Elizabeth thus found her way blocked by the looming spectre of old Mrs Leakey. Just as the curate had been a few weeks earlier, she was 'much affrighted' at the sight. But this time she managed to find her tongue, and a short but momentous conversation took place between the young mistress of the house and her husband's deceased mother. Downstairs, sweeping the hall, Eleanor Fluellin heard her employer talking with someone in the chamber above. But when she endeavoured to ascend to investigate, she found herself rooted to the spot, 'not able to go up above two steps'. Her mistress came back down, and she sat 'sad and melancholy by the fire' for two hours after, but she did not reveal to Eleanor what had transpired. Among the living, only Elizabeth was privy to the exchange in the upper room, though later she would tell others what had been said, or at least, part of it.

The younger, and living, woman spoke first: 'In the name of God, do me no hurt!'

GHOST: I cannot, God is with thee.
[*The apparition's eyes do not move; it stands completely still in the same place.*]

ELIZABETH: In the name of God, what would you have? Is there any thing left undone in your will that I can do for you?

GHOST: Go to Lordsnear [another daughter-in-law, living at Barnstaple, Devon] and deliver her a bond, and ask her for a chain of gold. And give up the bond and deliver the chain to Alexander.

ELIZABETH: In the name of God, if there be any thing else, tell me that I may be quiet, and I will do it.

GHOST: Go to Joan Atherton [Mother Leakey's daughter] in Ireland, and tell her these and these things [*sic* in the manuscript]. Bid her do them, and see you see them done.

ELIZABETH: Good Mother, tell me whether you be in heaven or in hell!

[*The apparition groans and vanishes from sight.*]

This was the last occasion on which Elizabeth saw the apparition, and the one and only time it spoke to her. She insisted that it 'spake distinctly, and in her mother's usual voice when she was alive'. Now, at last, Elizabeth was prepared to tell her husband everything that had been happening. As they discussed the matter between them, they found themselves coming to a very disturbing conclusion. For the appearance of the ghost was but the latest of a series of misfortunes to befall the couple. Alexander had had 'great losses of late by sea', too great, perhaps, to be explained by purely natural causes, especially in view of the supernatural events now unfolding within his own household. He and his wife began to harbour the suspicion that behind all these happenings lay the shadow of a heinous crime, witchcraft. Furthermore, they suspected a woman of being the witch. Elizabeth would later be given the opportunity to name her to the authorities, but she dared not do so, for fear of reprisal.

From this point on, the Leakeys clearly began to talk. For by the end of 1636, the appearances of the old lady were no longer a purely domestic affair, but had become a local *cause célèbre*: all of Minehead was buzzing with rumour and report. One who heard the news that the ghost had 'personally appeared unto diverse people' was Elizabeth Langstone, a former servant of old Mrs Leakey. Whether out of affection, or from some other motive, she wished that she might see her also. On Christmas Eve of that year, her wish was realized. As she sat with four children by the fire in her house, 'there suddenly appeared unto her a strange vision'. It was in the shape of a little child 'shining very bright and glorious'. Like the others to have seen the spirit, Elizabeth Langstone was 'troubled' and 'affrighted'. But presently the apparition began to speak to her, 'in a small and shrieking voice, sounding as if it had been afar off':

GHOST: I would gladly see my daughter.

LANGSTONE: Do you mean your daughter Lordsnear?

[*Ghost makes no answer, then asks another question.*]

GHOST: Do you see my golden chain?

LANGSTONE: The Lord bless me from you, I never saw nor had to do with your golden chain!

GHOST: The Lord is with thee, I cannot hurt thee.

[*The ghost then departs through the locked door, leaving a trail of light about the house, and transforms back into 'the wonted form and shape' of Mother Leakey.*]

At least two other residents of Minehead were reported to have seen the ghost at about this time. One of them was a man named Garland, a sailor in one of Alexander Leakey's barques, who was also supposed to have heard the apparition speak. The other was just passing through, 'an Italian mountebank', by the name of Loncatelli. After this brief mention, he disappears from history, and has no further part to play in our narrative.

🙢🙠

Everything that you have just read is, of course, a story. It was originally told (in more or less this form) by a small group of people in Somerset at the start of 1637. It may have been a true, or partially true, account of their actual experiences, or it may have been an elaborate and deceptive fiction. I have reproduced it in detail here because it is my own story's natural starting point: the first of many recorded stories, or narratives, that over the decades and centuries would come to weave themselves around the unlikely figure of Old Mother Leakey. It is from this uncertain anchorage that we are to embark on a journey in search of understanding, setting off in the hope of establishing some meaningful connections with the lost people of that strange, ghostly never-world, whose presence we regularly sense, but whose precise geography inexorably eludes us: our society's vanished past. The journey will take us to some unexpected places and some unlikely conclusions. But it begins here, on England's western seaboard, in the middle years of the reign of King Charles I, and with the categorical findings of an official investigation.

1

The World of the Leakeys

I n February 1637, three important and powerful men sat and listened to the tale you have just read, or to something very similar, and decided that they did not believe a word of it. There was a ghost story, but there had been no actual ghost: 'we are yet of opinion and do believe that there was never any apparition at all, but that it is an imposture, devise, and fraud for some particular ends, but what they are we know not'.

It had been a long and not entirely satisfactory day for this trio of local grandees, whose names were Phelips, Piers, and Godwyn. Sir Robert Phelips was a landowner of substance, and a political mover and shaker: a former MP for Somerset, and a former Deputy Lieutenant and sheriff of the county. William Piers was a churchman, bishop of the diocese of Bath and Wells, in which the town of Minehead was situated. The Reverend Paul Godwyn was one of his leading clergymen, and the son of a former bishop. The three were thrown together on this occasion by a shared responsibility: they were all justices of the peace. In Somerset, as in every English county at this time, the JPs were the essential (and unpaid) workhorses of local government. They presided over the trials of petty criminals at quarter sessions, they regulated markets and prices, they supervised the poor law, and granted or withheld licences to the proprietors of alehouses. But at the start of 1637 this small subsection of the 'county commission' of justices had been handed a much more unusual assignment. They had been ordered by King Charles I's privy council in London to investigate the rumours about the appearance of a ghost. We do not know exactly where their examinations were held: it may well have been at Minehead itself, or perhaps a couple of dozen miles to the south-east, in

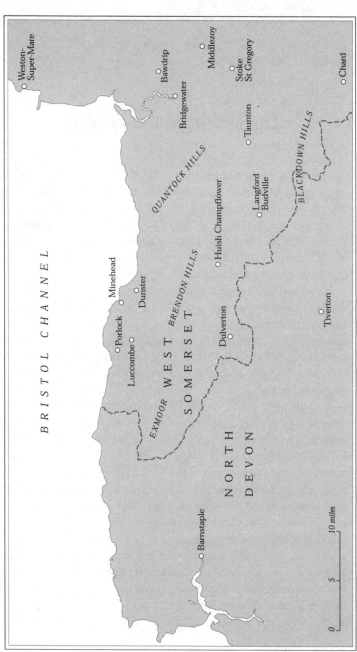

1. The world of the Leakeys: West Somerset and North Devon, c. 1630

the market town and local administrative centre of Taunton (see Figure 1). Over the course of the day, however, Phelips, Piers, and Godwyn heard evidence from four witnesses who claimed to have seen the apparition: Elizabeth Leakey (whose testimony was by some way the fullest) spoke first, followed by John Heathfield, Elizabeth Langstone, and Eleanor Fluellin. All their statements, along with the justices' own damning assessment, were received by the authorities in London on 24 February 1637.[1] The JPs had wanted to hear from other witnesses too, but found themselves thwarted. The sailor Garland was away at sea, while the mysterious Italian, Loncatelli, 'is gone from that town a good while since, we know not whither'. More frustratingly still, Alexander Leakey himself could not be brought to testify. He had been sent for on two occasions. The first time he claimed to be ill of the gout; on the second he simply absconded from home 'for fear of executions, which (as we are informed) are set out against him'. In other words, Alexander feared that the official messenger was a court officer sent to seize his property for non-payment of debt. Despite this regrettable lack of complete comprehensiveness in their investigation, the justices felt emboldened to append to the witnesses' statements 'such observations as we have made upon the same, and other circumstances incident to this business'.

Piers, Godwyn, and Phelips were men of their time, and as such, they were unlikely to have believed that all reports of supernatural apparitions were simply frauds and inventions. But they were undoubtedly convinced that this one was. In a ruthlessly forensic manner, their report dissected the testimony. It also mercilessly discredited the witnesses, seizing on inconsistencies and implausibilities, and impugning their motivation. The justices have the advantage of us here, for at least two of the witnesses (Elizabeth Leakey and Elizabeth Langstone) had been examined on a previous occasion, and the JPs evidently had in front of them a record of this earlier interrogation to compare with what they were now hearing for themselves. It had been carried out no more than a few weeks earlier by 'Mr Byam, a grave minister near Minehead'. This was Henry Byam, rector of the neighbouring parish of Luccombe, a graduate of Exeter College, Oxford, scion of a remarkable clerical family, and occasional presiding judge in Bishop Piers's own church court. The absence of Minehead's own Church of England minister from all these proceedings is accounted for by the fact that he had recently passed away. Having served as vicar for nearly half a century, Nicholas Browse died in December 1634, at the venerable age of 83. His successor seems to have spent much of his time away from Minehead, his duties fulfilled by the recently appointed curate, Heathfield, who was, to put it mildly, somewhat implicated in the affair.[2]

In the course of the proceedings in February, Elizabeth Leakey's statement in front of Mr Byam was 'often read to her and vowed by her to be the truth'. Nonetheless, she was soon caught out in a series of minor but revealing circumstantial contradictions. To the rector of Luccombe she had said that the third and last time she saw the apparition was in her husband's storehouse, but in her later testimony the fateful encounter took place in her chamber. Perhaps more importantly, Elizabeth's earlier version of the death of young John Leakey had taken a decidedly more graphic form. She had said that the boy 'did often complain that his grandmother did trouble him and pinch him, and take him by the neck, and did almost choke him', adding that 'after he was dead the print of a hand was seen in his neck'. Later, however, Elizabeth denied that there was any 'print of a hand to be seen about the throat of the child', referring only to his being 'somewhat black . . . about the neck, as some said that saw him'. A striking physical detail like this was easily susceptible to confirmation or contradiction by other witnesses, which may explain why Elizabeth chose to withdraw it. In their summing up, the JPs noted that Elizabeth told them she had been at Bristol when the child died, and had got her information from Mrs Kirry, her neighbour and sister-in-law. This lady was often with the child, and had been present when he died. With commendable thoroughness, the justices had summoned Mrs Kirry in front of them, 'who upon her examination before us denies all this, and sayeth that the child died of a consumption'.

There were suspicious disparities in the accounts of the other witnesses too. Elizabeth Langstone 'hath varied remarkably three times in her report of this business'. To Henry Byam, she confessed that the apparition opened her door and came to her on Christmas Eve, but she made no mention of its taking the form of a little child. She had apparently given yet another version of the incident to Elizabeth Leakey at Minehead, recounting how Old Mrs Leakey had appeared to her 'in the shape of a little woman without arms'. As to Eleanor Fluellin, no previous report had mentioned her seeing the apparition at all. Indeed, during Byam's examination, Elizabeth Leakey 'did positively affirm upon question that her maid Eleanor had never seen it'. The justices therefore concluded that Eleanor's story had been concocted after the fact, and that 'there is no truth to be given to her report'.

Yet even without this effective cross-checking against the record supplied by Mr Byam, the justices had reason to feel unimpressed by the cogency of the account they had heard. Almost certainly, they made sure that the witnesses were heard separately, and there was more than one glaring anomaly to be found between the testimony of young Mrs Leakey and that of the curate Heathfield. According to Elizabeth, the apparition had been a silent presence on the first occasion it appeared to her in her chamber. But Heathfield recalled the matter differently. When Elizabeth came to see him to seek his professional counsel she had told him about the ghost 'bidding her go into Cambridgeshire and fetch home her grandchildren'. The plural here may be a scribe's error, for in their summing up the JPs clarified the point. The apparition had supposedly told Elizabeth to 'go into Cambridgeshire and fetch home Susan's child, meaning her grandchild'. As we have seen already (p. 3), Heathfield also claimed that Elizabeth told him she had seen the apparition follow him out of the Leakeys' house, whereas only three sightings were mentioned in her own evidence. There was also the curious matter of the message the ghost had entrusted to Elizabeth to deliver to Alexander's sister, Joan, in Ireland. The justices naturally demanded of her what the message was, but she refused to reveal it, saying that 'she will not reveal it to anybody but only unto the king, and not unless he command her so to do'. Elizabeth had added, gratuitously but loyally, that 'he is a gracious king'. It appeared that the apparition had not specifically commanded her to conceal the contents of the message, but she was nonetheless determined to do so, fearing that its publication 'may be hurtful to Joan Atherton and her husband'. Elizabeth told her interrogators that she was preparing to go over to Ireland in the spring, and carry out her promise to the spectre.

In the mean time, however, there was the curious business of the golden chain, 'mentioned so often by the supposed apparition'. There was clearly some further pressing on this point, either by the Reverend Henry Byam, or by the justices themselves. It emerged that the chain was worth not much more than thirty shillings, and that Elizabeth had claimed not even to know of its existence before the ghost had commanded her to requisition it from her sister-in-law, Lordsnear. 'How should I know you had a gold chain, if the apparition had not told me so?' Again, the authorities had done their business, for testimony about the chain had been solicited in Barnstaple from Lordsnear herself. She affirmed that it was public knowledge that such a chain had been sent to her husband William Leakey from the Bermudas, and that it had been seen not just by old Mrs Leakey but by Alexander. Alexander had surely described it to his wife and, once again, Elizabeth seemed to her examiners to be dissembling and deceiving them.

By the end of the day's proceedings, Elizabeth Leakey had undoubtedly made an impression on the justices, though not the one she probably wanted to make. They found her to be 'an understanding woman, but bold and subtle enough'. Their judgements on the other witnesses were less flattering still. The curate John Heathfield was in their opinion 'a very phantastical man', and they noted that he was a friend to Alexander Leakey and his wife. The Welsh maid, Eleanor Fluellin, was 'a wanderer, and … a fit instrument to report anything that is put to her'. As for Elizabeth Langstone, the justices were credibly informed that 'she is a very silly and poor woman, and very often distempered with drink'. She 'doth not know what she sayeth'. No credit was to be given to the claims of the Italian Loncatelli, 'the report of whose seeing the apparition comes to us at the second hand'. Nor did the judges consider it worth pursuing evidence from Garland the sailor: 'he is an idle fellow, and is employed by Mr Leakey'. In short, the whole business of the apparition was nothing less than a knavish conspiracy, orchestrated by Elizabeth Leakey with the at least tacit consent of her husband, and the assistance of a small circle of friends and dependants. But what purpose was it all supposed to serve? As to this, the admirably perspicacious trio of justices were apparently without a theory, or at least one that they were prepared to commit to paper.

We begin, then, with a story which appears to be untrue, told to us by people about whom we still know very little. It looks like an unpromising start for a book, and a difficult brief for the historian writing it. What is more, the question we would probably most like to ask at this stage is simply not susceptible of a definite answer. We will never know for certain whether Elizabeth or any of the others really believed that they had seen and spoken with Mother Leakey's ghost. If they cynically made up the story, this was something to which they never confessed. And yet, this is not the only question worth thinking about here. The fact is that four apparently sane witnesses (one of them a clergyman) swore under oath to have had dealings with the spirit of a dead person, and this represents a provocative challenge to our modern way of seeing the world. In the Prologue, I described the claims of these Minehead people as 'a story'. In fact, historians of this period increasingly recognize that practically all witnesses in legal proceedings were in one sense story-tellers, using established moral conventions and the familiar rules of narrative and plot to place themselves and their case in the best possible light. A distinguished scholar of sixteenth-century France writes of 'fiction in the archives', something which we must learn to recognize and seek to decode. At the same time, it is clear that the 'fictions' of the courtroom had to be thoroughly plausible ones in order to deliver the desired results, and this means that they have the ability to offer unrivalled insight into attitudes, values, and usually unspoken assumptions about the world. In other words, lies have the capacity to reveal important truths about the peoples and societies of the past. It is a sobering thought.[3] We can, then, fairly and legitimately regard the Minehead testimony of 1637 as a kind of open window onto a lost landscape of meaning. But from the outset, it is also something else: a puzzle and a mystery, which challenges us to see whether we can do any better than the Somerset JPs in pinning down the precise 'ends' to which it was all directed. Who were these people, what were they trying to achieve, and (assuming it was all an imposture and device) why did it seem to them that a ghost was the best instrument to help bring those objectives about? To begin to answer any of these questions, we have to attempt to reconstruct a world, albeit a small and bounded one, the world in which the Leakeys and their neighbours lived, moved, and had their being.

The Somerset town of Minehead in the early seventeenth century was (and still is today) dominated and defined by two fixed topographical features: the hill and the sea. The place in fact acquired its name from the Welsh and Old English words for hill or mountain (*mynnyd*, *myned*), and it grew up over the course of the Middle Ages in the protective shadow of the North Hill, a promontory rising sharply some 900 feet from the grey waters of the Bristol Channel. An observer in the mid-sixteenth century captured the look of the place in a crisp thumbnail sketch: 'the fairest part of the town standeth in the bottom of a hill. The residue runneth up along the hill, in the top whereof is a fair parish church ... The pier lieth at the north-east point of the hill.' That pier supplied the little town with its real *raison d'être*. Between 1609 and 1616 it was extensively rebuilt, at 'great and extraordinary charge', by the local lord of the manor, George Luttrell, with the aim of providing sheltered harbourage for dozens of ships and boats (Figure 2). As a result, trade and prosperity increased and the town grew. Many new houses were constructed, both along Quay Street running down from the pier, and in the smart 'lower town' to the south east of the hill. Two visitors recorded their impressions of Minehead in 1633–4, the last year of Susan Leakey's life. One was the Cheshire

2. Minehead quay and harbour: a photograph taken in *c.* 1900, though the scene may not have looked so very different in 1630

gentleman, William Brereton, returning from a trip to Ireland, who thought it 'a long straggling-built village', though he admired the 'high strong pier, and a good, wide, open haven'. The antiquarian writer Thomas Gerard similarly focused on the harbour, and on its commendable suitability for 'ordinary barques'. It was a place 'much frequented by such as pass to and from Ireland as being most fit for the loading and unloading of such commodities as are transported to and from that kingdom'. This Anglo-Irish trade was precisely the business in which Alexander Leakey was engaged. We do not know where in Minehead he and his family lived, but the storehouse where Elizabeth claimed to have seen the ghost was surely on or by the quay, and her husband's house was said to be no more than a furlong (one eighth of a mile) away.[4]

What more, then, can we discover about Alexander Leakey, his calculating wife, and his soon to be infamous mother? As all amateur genealogists are aware, the logical place to start is with the parish register, a document which from 1538 onwards all English parishes were required to keep, in order to supply a permanent record of births, marriages, and deaths (or, more accurately, of baptisms, marriages, and burials). The register of St Michael's, Minehead, strongly suggests that the Leakeys were not indigenous to the town, for it contains no record of the marriage of Alexander's parents, of his own baptism, or of those of any of his siblings. Mother Leakey herself appears in the register only once, in an entry reading 'Anno Domini. 1634. Susan Leekey, widow, buried ye vth November.' The entries in parish registers are in any case usually no more than signposts, little milestones for the life journeys of the ordinary people of the past. If we wish to draw more detailed maps, we are usually better off with wills, documents that are often teeming with particulars of property and bequests, and informative lists of beneficiaries and witnesses. Wills were almost invariably made on the deathbed itself, part of the ritual of preparing for the end. The majority of seventeenth-century Englishmen, however, never made a will, and Alexander Leakey does not appear to have done so on his death in 1643. Women were still less likely to leave a will, as any substantial goods held by a married couple were legally the property of the husband. The exceptions were widows with property of their own to bequeath, as of course Susan Leakey was. In her statement before the Somerset justices in February 1637, Elizabeth Leakey claimed that her mother-in-law had indeed made a will: 'and left her [Elizabeth's] husband some household stuff which she had to the value of twenty pounds, and a bond of twenty pounds due from Mr Atherton, and a bond of twenty pounds due from William Leakey of Barnstaple, deceased before her'. To be able to assess whether this was an accurate summary, we would naturally have to consult the document itself. Alas, in May 1942, the German airforce mounted a ferocious raid on Exeter and in the process blew up the Probate Registry, where the testamentary records for the diocese of Bath and Wells were stored. The registered will of Susan Leakey, along with countless others, was destroyed in the fire.

Yet, just occasionally, dead ends in historical research turn out to be breathing still. Months after I had given up any hope of seeing

Mother Leakey's will, I discovered that in 1889 a local antiquarian had unearthed it in the Taunton Probate Office, and that a transcription of it had been published in a Minehead newspaper. It is a remarkably short and unimposing document:

> The will nuncupative of Susan Leakey, of Minehead, in the county of Somerset, made about the first of December, 1634. Imprimis, she bequeathed her soul into the hands of God and her body to Christian burial in the church or churchyard of Minehead aforesaid. Item, her goods and chattels she gave unto Alexander Leakey the younger, whom she made her sole executor. Witnesses: Sarah James, Alice Jeny.

There are several odd features here. In the first place, the date, 'about the first of December', cannot be correct, and is surely a copyist's error for 1 November. In the second place, there are the obvious divergences from Elizabeth Leakey's account of her mother-in-law's wishes: no itemizing of household stuff, no mention of bonds. Even the sole beneficiary was not the same, for 'Alexander Leakey the younger' was not Elizabeth's husband, but her son, a small infant in 1634 and a curious choice to be made the executor of a will. There is also that abrasively technical term, 'the will nuncupative'. Seventeenth-century wills were rarely written by the testators themselves, more usually they were dictated from the sickbed to a scribe—a local minister, notary, or literate layman. The scribe would read the document back to its author to verify its accuracy, and the names of witnesses were added, people who could if need be later testify to the authentic recording of the testator's wishes. But death at this time was often an impatient visitor, and was not always prepared to wait for these niceties to be performed. When a competent scribe could not be summoned in time, a purely verbal or 'nuncupative' testament was accepted as valid by the church courts, which had the responsibility for recording and validating wills. Witnesses would attest to its substance, and the will would be registered in the usual way. Needless to say, due to the uncertain circumstances of their production, nuncupative wills were disproportionately likely to be the focus of contestation and dispute.

We know, then, that Mother Leakey probably died rather suddenly, and that after the conventional pieties of bequeathing her soul to God, and her body to the ground, she simply left all her worldly possessions to her grandson. We can form a clearer idea of what those possessions actually were thanks to another fortunate survival. Before a will could be proved or 'probated' by the local church court, the executors were required to draw up a true inventory of the possessions of the deceased. The probate inventories for the diocese of Bath and Wells were archived separately from the wills, and thus escaped the unloving attentions of the *Luftwaffe*. The inventory of 'the goods, debts and chattels of Susan Leakey of Minehead, widow, deceased' was drawn up by Robert Tristram and John Kerry on the last day of December 1634. It was exhibited, along with the will, before the church court at Taunton on 20 March 1635 where the administration of the estate was granted to Alexander Leakey senior, during the minority of his son. The inventory runs to twenty-three entries, goods with an impressive total value of £71. 7s. 20d. Sadly, it does not itemize separately the kerchief, black gown, and 'white stomacher of shag' which the witnesses swore they had seen the ghost wearing, mentioning only Mother Leakey's 'living apparel'. But it did specify that when she died she was owed the fairly substantial sum of £39 in debts. Next to this, the compilers of the inventory made the troubling note: 'whereof much dispute'. We know that widows in the seventeenth century often inherited respectable amounts of ready cash, and that a good number of them were thus in a position to set themselves up as small-scale money-lenders. It looks as though Susan Leakey had decided to follow this path, or at any rate that she was in the business of granting credit to members of her family.

If the debts were causing dissension, there was likely a crucial point at issue: had the loans been secured by the signing of bonds? These were legally binding documents setting out the terms of the loan, and usually specifying that the borrower was to pay a larger sum than the actual amount owed if he or she failed to fulfil the original agreement on time. According to Elizabeth Leakey's sworn testimony, her mother-in-law had made a will mentioning two bonds to the value of £20. One of them had apparently been signed by her daughter Joan's husband, Mr Atherton, and the other by her own son William, whose widow in Barnstaple, Lordsnear, was currently in possession of the celebrated golden chain. As we have seen (p. 5), the ghost instructed Elizabeth to present the bond for repayment to Lordsnear at the same time that she was to yield up the chain.[5] At first glance, therefore, it looks as if Elizabeth was taking action to safeguard and shore up her young son's legacy by calling in her mother-in-law's debts, and staking a claim to a valuable family heirloom. The ghost, it seems, was playing a float-on part in that most regular and mundane of family dramas in this or any other age, a disputed inheritance. Yet as we shall see in due course, there was considerably more than this at stake in the strange appearances of Old Mother Leakey.

In the meantime, let us continue with our genealogical detective work. Leakey was a fairly common Somerset name at this time: there were Leakeys to be found in at least fourteen parishes in the county on the eve of the English Civil War. Yet a couple of brief entries in Susan's inventory provide some helpful clues about her earlier life. There was, for example, a 'spruce chest' in the Exmoor village of Huish Champflower, as well as a table and other household stuff at Bridgwater, West Somerset's other significant port town. Susan Leakey, we can establish, had lived in both places before coming to Minehead (see Figure 1). Frustratingly, it has not been possible to find any record of Susan's marriage or of Alexander's baptism, but the family were clearly living in Bridgwater around the turn of the seventeenth century, for the Bridgwater parish register shows that six of Alexander's siblings were baptized there between 1588 and 1600. Two of them, a boy and a girl, did not survive past their first birthdays, and another son, John, died in his early 30s in 1619. Of the remaining children, William was born in 1590 and, as we know already, eventually married a girl blessed with the peculiar name of Lordsnear. They moved to Barnstaple, but must have been resident in Minehead in the early 1620s, for a son, another John, was born to them there in April 1621. This was the boy whose premature death in 1635 was attributed to the malevolent intervention of his deceased grandmother. William himself must have died before June 1630, when Lordsnear was remarried to a Barnstaple man named John Knill. Alexander's other siblings were two girls, Joan and Susan, born in March 1595 and February 1600 respectively. Both of them have important parts to play in this story before it is done.

Nothing can be said for certain about the father of all these children, though it seems very likely that Old Mother Leakey's husband was yet another John Leakey, an apparently respectable fellow of the 'middling sort' who was a churchwarden of Bridgwater in 1605, and by the following year was serving as bailiff of the borough. The last set of bailiff's accounts he presented was for 1613, which may mean that he died in that or the following year. The possibility is reinforced by a hiatus before the accounts restart in 1615, and by a curious case brought to the attention of the Somerset JPs in 1614. Charges had been brought against Joseph Jackson, apparitor, for misuse of his authority. Apparitors were the minor officials employed to serve citations and report offences to the church courts, bodies which exercised jurisdiction over a wide range of moral offences. Jackson was accused of taking bribes and extorting money from people in the parish of Stoke St Gregory, a few miles to the south of Bridgwater. One of the claims was that he had taken 3s. 8d. from Nicholas Luscombe in return for keeping quiet about the fact that Luscombe had been summoned to the court at Wells 'upon a crime that was between the Widow Leakey and him'. The nature of the crime, whether sexual or otherwise, remained unspecified. Conceivably, this may be a different Widow Leakey. But there is no doubt about the identity of the 'Susan Leakey of Bridgwater' who was summoned before the church court in November 1618 for physically shutting Sarah and Mary Coorte out of their pew in the church, and for using 'quarrelling, brawling and scolding speeches' to make clear to Mary that she was not welcome to sit there. Since where one sat in church reflected one's status in the community, 'pew disputes', of varying degrees of ferocity, were common in seventeenth-century England. (Minehead itself was wracked by a contentious pew dispute in 1628.) Widowhood was a time when one's established status was likely once more to start seeming insecure, and this may have provoked Susan towards aggressive action in defence of her perceived rights. Taken together with the deathbed threats supposedly uttered to her daughter-in-law, Elizabeth (see p. 2), there seems to be something of a pattern emerging: Mother Leakey was a woman given to assertively strong-minded and, at times, frankly anti-social forms of behaviour.[6]

What, however, of her son Alexander? He was the head of the household at the centre of the supernatural happenings of 1635–6, yet he appears to be a curiously off-stage presence while they were taking place. We do not know when precisely Alexander transplanted himself from Bridgwater to Minehead, a move that took him twenty miles or so along the Bristol Channel coast. But he was evidently well-established in his new home by 1620, when he was called upon to serve as a churchwarden for the parish of St Michael. (This was a responsibility assumed in turn by the respectable householders of the community.) The previous year he had married a woman by the name of Alice Kirry, though the marriage was to last less than a year, prematurely dissolved, as so many seventeenth-century unions were, by the death of a spouse. Alice was buried on 28 May 1620, just ten months after her nuptials. There is no record in the register of Alexander's second marriage to Elizabeth, but it must have taken place in or before 1628, for a son with the family name of John was buried in the parish in early March 1629. Another son, Alexander—the beneficiary of his grandmother's munificence—was born in May 1632. Though no issue seems to have survived from Alexander's first marriage, good relations were evidently maintained with Alice's kinsfolk. The John Kerry or Kirry who made the inventory of Susan Leakey's goods in December 1634 was a ship's captain, and in all probability Alexander's former brother-in-law. Most likely he was married to the Mrs Kirry, whom Elizabeth called her sister-in-law, and who, as we have seen (p. 12), was often in the Leakeys' house and was with young John Leakey when he died in 1635 (see Figure 3).

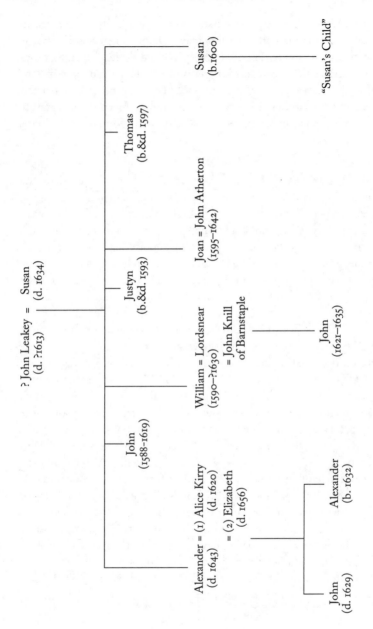

3. The offspring of Old Mother Leakey

Alexander appears to have been a solid and respected member of Minehead's tight-knit maritime community, though he was not a dominant figure within it. He could not compete, for example, with the largesse of the master mariner, Robert Quirke, who in 1630 presented the town with a set of almshouses for the poor in thanksgiving for safe deliverance from a storm, and who in 1634 and 1637 gifted to the church a set of fine painted boards with texts of the Creed, the Ten Commandments and the Lord's Prayer. Nonetheless, the customs records of the port for the later 1620s and early 1630s supply us with a picture of a man for whom business was blooming. Alexander's goods sailed in and out of the port on board the *Charity*, the *Godspeed*, the *Blessing*, the *Emmanuel*, the *Jane*, and (appropriately) the *Elizabeth*. He transported timber and tar along the coast from Bristol, but he also did business further afield, bringing in salt, wine, and vinegar from the Breton port of Morlaix in 1634, and sending back tallow and coal. His main traffic, however, was with southern Ireland and the port of Youghal (pronounced 'Yawl') on the north-eastern edge of County Cork. From Youghal, Alexander imported large quantities of Irish wool, destined for the cloth-producing towns of Somerset and Devon: Dunster, Dulverton, Taunton, Tiverton, or Exeter. Back to Ireland, he exported wheat, barley, and beans, as well as lower bulk luxury goods, such as the 'two barrels and nine firkins containing mercery, grocery, and haberdashery wares', on which he paid his duty in May 1629.[7]

The number of commercial pies into which Alexander Leakey's fingers extended suggests that it would be a mistake to underestimate the inhabitants of seventeenth-century Minehead. We should not minimize the extent of their connections with a changing wider world, or the degree to which its social, political, and religious tensions might impinge upon their lives. In some ways, of course, the world of the Leakeys was a very small one, bounded by the common interests and provincial outlook of the West Country ports of Minehead, Barnstaple, and Bridgwater. Its immediate horizons were defined through a series of local family migrations between these modest and neighbouring places. Minehead itself looks the part of a rural backwater. Culturally and geographically, it was light-years away from London, and, thanks to appallingly poor roads, it was fairly inaccessible overland even from the regional capital, Bristol. Yet while undoubtedly remote from England's centres of culture and governance, Minehead was not an entirely introspective and isolated place. Indeed, its location on a seaboard facing simultaneously north and west endowed its inhabitants with an outward-looking mentality, and gave the place something of the feel of a frontier town. This was underlined by its interesting mix of peoples. Across the waters of the Bristol Channel, south Wales was only a short sea journey away, and the Leakeys' maid, Eleanor Fluellin, was only one of many Welsh people who drifted to Minehead in search of employment. The regular commercial traffic with the ports of south-east Ireland also ensured a circular flow of people as well as goods. Already in the mid-sixteenth century, the town was reported to be 'exceeding full of Irishmen', and this had not changed a century later, with traders like 'Michael MacMahoone' paying their dues on Minehead quayside in the 1630s. The visitors were not always welcome ones. From time to time the English authorities worried that Somerset was being invaded by hordes of 'Irish rogues and vagabonds', and orders would be issued to deport them, usually via Minehead itself. Throughout the 1620s, it was a regular local complaint that this obligation had placed the constables of the town at 'intolerable charges'.

Government directives of a more ambitious kind brought the merchant community of Minehead into unwelcome contact with other types of foreigner too. Charles I's decisions to go to war with first Spain (1625) and then France (1627) opened Somerset shipping to the attentions of Spanish and French privateers, and prompted the merchants of Minehead and Bridgwater to petition the King for permission to arm a ship to safeguard the Irish trade. In 1627 two Minehead captains were themselves issued with 'letters of marque' to operate as state-sponsored pirates against enemy shipping. This was an age, not entirely unlike our own, where national and ethnic distinctions were given shape and sharpness by religious difference. While England was a firmly Protestant kingdom, France and Spain were the pre-eminent Catholic powers of Western Europe. The Irish too were in the main still 'papists', in obstinate defiance of the wishes of the governing English regime there. When an Irish priest landed at Bridgwater in 1639 he was arrested and closely interrogated by the borough authorities. There were some home-grown papists too, Englishmen and women who had never reconciled themselves to the rejection of the authority of the pope, though there seem to have been rather fewer of these in Somerset than in many other English counties.[8]

But it was divisions among those attending the *same* church which supplied much of the heat for local politics at this time, and which most obviously linked the doings of the Leakeys and their neighbours to the concerns of a larger world. In 1618 the vicar of Minehead, Nicholas Browse, delivered a hot and provocative sermon. He complained there were too many Welshmen in the town, and dismissively he 'called them Calvins'. A couple of years earlier, Browse himself had been slandered by one of his parishioners, who addressed him abusively as 'papistical knave, ass, and dunce'.[9] The insults reflected the spilling over of long-standing tensions within English society, tensions about what it meant to be a good Christian, a good Protestant, and a good neighbour.

This requires a brief historical excursus. At the time of Mother Leakey's burial in 1634, that epochal event which we call the English Reformation was almost exactly a hundred years old. It had begun with Henry VIII's faltering attempts to get the pope to annul his marriage to Catherine of Aragon, but it had turned by the time of his death in 1547 into a full-scale religious revolution. For centuries, the good folk of Somerset, like people across Western Europe, had been taught to believe that their best hope of salvation lay in leading a good life, and trusting in the range of sacraments and ceremonies supplied by the Catholic Church. Once a year, they confessed their sins to a priest, and were assured of God's forgiveness. Week on week, they attended the mass in their parish church, a service during which Christ became, in the form of bread and wine, as truly present as he had been on the cross of Calvary. They prayed in front of statues of the saints, and petitioned them to assist their plans and heal their ailments. When guilt or piety moved them, they gave alms to the poor, or went on pilgrimage to the great monastic houses, where relics and images of the saints were housed in reverential splendour.

But the Protestant reformers who influenced Henry VIII, and held even more sway with his precocious son Edward VI, regarded all this as so much flummery and superstition. There was no salvation to be found in 'good works', but only in placing one's faith in the once-for-all sacrifice of Jesus Christ. That saving faith could only be produced and nurtured from one source: the words of the Bible, which needed to be preached freely from pulpits, and translated into English for ordinary people to read. An attempt to thwart all this by Henry's Catholic daughter Mary I had been ended by her premature and childless death in 1558: a clear judgement of God. But in the opinion of many, the Reformation had simply stalled after the accession of Mary's Protestant half-sister Elizabeth I, and God's work had been left half undone. True, the Elizabethan 'Settlement' of 1559 had finally swept away the rotten pillars of medieval Catholicism: the authority of the pope, monasteries, the Latin mass, and the shrines and images of the saints. But it had kept in place the basic structures of the old church—bishops, cathedrals, and church courts—as well as watered-down versions of some of its rituals and ceremonies. Ministers were still required to wear a special vestment or surplice to celebrate the communion, for example, and they were ordered to use the sign of the cross when baptizing children.

Such compromises with the past were doubtless comforting to many, but they were anathema to a wide swathe of ministers and laymen, who believed that in order to avoid God's future displeasure every remnant of 'popery' had to be swept out of the Church of England. Their enemies mockingly called them 'puritans', suggesting an obsessive and hypocritical concern with purity of life and doctrine. They called themselves, with no discernible trace of irony, the 'godly'. Puritans were people driven by a vision of doctrinal and moral reformation, of a Church purged of its popish vestiges, and of a populace leading strictly ordered lives in accordance with the mandates of scripture. But behind the public preaching and campaigning lay an intensely personal concern with the eventual destiny of the individual soul. By the end of the sixteenth century, most English Protestant theologians had come to endorse the doctrine of predestination. This was the idea that, even before the creation of the world, and irrespective of human merits, God had determined which souls were going to enjoy eternal bliss with him in heaven, and which were to endure eternal torment with the devil in hell. The Catholic belief that humans could influence the decision through the performance of good works and the exercise of 'free will' was seen as a perverse distortion of the teaching of the Bible. Many Protestants (including a good number of the bishops) thought it was best, however, to get on with the business of trying to lead a good life without agonizing too much about predestination. It was an inscrutable divine decree, something over which one exercised absolutely no control, and of which one could possess no privileged inside knowledge. But puritans thought differently. Not only did they nurture an intense reverence for the continental theologian, John Calvin, who had most clearly formulated the doctrine (hence Vicar Browse's jibe), they also exhibited a pressing desire to feel some degree of certainty about whether or not they were members of 'the elect'. Though good works could not earn one a place in heaven, it was only to be expected that the 'fruits' of God's positive choice would be discernible in the lives of the chosen. Puritans obsessively scrutinized their own behaviour for encouraging signs of 'election', and were inclined to regard conspicuous failings in others (drunkenness, fornication) as pointers to impending damnation. It goes without saying that there was the potential here for a deeply divisive approach to the business of social relations, fertile space for the ultimate 'us and them' mentality to grow, ripen, and fester.

By the early seventeenth century, puritanism had put down deep roots in the maritime communities of Somerset and Devon. Barnstaple in particular was fast acquiring for itself the reputation

as a haven for 'godliness'. Here, as in a scattering of other places, the
puritan presence manifested in a particularly sharp symbolic way.
In choosing names for their children, some puritan families began to
reject traditional Christian names (associated with Catholic saints)
in favour of Old Testament characters and newfangled epithets
descriptive of Christian virtues. The movement began locally in
1599, when the town schoolmaster requested the vicar to christen
his child 'Do Well'. The baptism section of the Barnstaple parish
register bears witness to a subsequent crop of names drawn from the
Old Testament, as well as such new mintings as 'Lovewell', 'Pente-
cost', and 'Temperance'. The fashion struck more conservatively
minded Protestants as divisive and absurd. In 1593, the future archbishop of Canterbury, Richard Bancroft, mocked 'these new names
and fancies', and in 1605 the historian William Camden dismissed
them as the products of 'some singular and precise conceit'. Along
with More-trial, Joy-again, Sufficient, Free-gift, and Tribulation,
both Bancroft and Camden picked out 'The-Lord-is-near' as an
egregious example of such nominal excesses. Alexander Leakey's
sister-in-law, Lordsnear Knill, the mistress of the golden chain,
was thus, willingly or not, a conspicuous standard-bearer for a
reforming movement. It is quite possible that her marriage to John
Knill in June 1630 was attended by a puritan minister named William
Crompton, for a month afterwards Crompton preached at the
nuptials of another Barnstaple couple. He later published his
sermon, replete with godly exhortations and pearls of domestic
wisdom ('a wife is like a ship; well-steered she goes smooth').
Crompton was employed by the town corporation of Barnstaple as
a lecturer, that is, a minister whose principal responsibility was to
supply additional sermons—in the eyes of puritans, the most worth-
while activity any clergyman could undertake. He soon fell out with
the new vicar of the town, Martin Blake, who in 1630 reported him
to the authorities for failing to wear the required surplice while
reading services from the Book of Common Prayer.[10]

   This little local tremor was symptomatic of tectonic plates
starting to shift in the wider religious and political geosphere.
During the last years of Elizabeth I, and particularly under her

successor James I, puritans and more conservative Protestants had found ways of rubbing along with each other, something made easier by their shared and zealous antipathy to all forms of Catholicism, both at home and abroad. Full conformity—over matters like a conscientious refusal by ministers to wear the surplice—was seldom pushed to breaking point by the bishops. But when James's highly strung and high-handed son Prince Charles succeeded to his father's throne in 1625, momentous change was soon in the air. The new king began to surround himself with ecclesiastical advisers who were overtly hostile to puritanism, men who saw ceremony and ritual not as embarrassing or dangerous leftovers from the Catholic past but as powerful expressions of authentic Christian faith. Their slogan was 'the beauty of holiness'. Some of the King's favoured theologians even started to question the hallowed doctrine of predestination itself, and to find a place for man's free will to accept or reject God's offer of salvation. These thinkers were known as 'Arminians', after the dissident Dutch churchman, Jacob Arminius, who had caused a furore over the issue in his home country a couple of decades before.

Without a doubt, the brightest star in the new firmament was William Laud, a clothier's son from Reading. At the start of the reign Laud was bishop of the modest Welsh diocese of St David's. In 1626 he was promoted to the Somerset bishopric of Bath and Wells, in 1628 to the prestigious see of London, and in 1633 to the archbishopric of Canterbury. Laud's protégés, 'Laudians', were soon enjoying a virtual monopoly of appointment to bishoprics and other high church offices. One of the most zealous of them was a man whose acquaintance we have made already, William Piers. Piers was nominated as bishop of Bath and Wells in November 1632, and soon instigated a campaign to suppress puritan lectureships across his diocese. As a former holder of the bishopric himself, Laud kept a close and benevolent eye on the process. Yet in the midst of these important matters, Bishop Piers's 1637 report about the apparition at Minehead was studied carefully by William Laud. For reasons which only gradually became apparent to me, and which we will set to one side for the moment, the archbishop of Canterbury had lately developed a rather more than passing interest in the family of Susan Leakey.

Archbishop Laud's campaigns to restore the beauty of holiness ran up against some firm resistance, and not just from die-hard puritans. To many, it seemed that several aspects of his programme possessed little to distinguish them from popery itself. Two occasions of disharmony resonated particularly loudly in Somerset in the early 1630s. A central item of Laud's agenda was to elevate the dignity and importance of the communion service, over and against the sermon, as the focal point of Christian worship. To this purpose he wished to see the tables at which communion was celebrated removed from their functional location in the main body of churches, and restored to their traditional position at the far east end of the chancel. Here they were to be separated off from the less 'sacred' areas of the church by sets of enclosing rails. Such arrangements were widely associated with the settings for the medieval Catholic mass, a suspicion which was reinforced by the provocative habit among Laud and his supporters of referring to the communion table as the 'altar'—this was the term favoured by papists. After a test case in London in 1633, an order went out for all parishes to rail their communion tables and to place them in an 'altarwise' position. Many communities resisted, but the most famous of all refusals was in the east Somerset parish of Beckington in the summer of 1635. The obstinacy of the churchwardens there required Bishop Piers first to excommunicate and then to imprison them, provoking a riot in the parish in the meantime.

The puritans, however, were not invariably on the defensive in these years. In 1632 the judges who rode the 'western circuit' hearing criminal cases at the assizes issued an order prohibiting wakes, revels, and 'church ales' right across Somerset. These were communal parish celebrations, usually held on a Sunday near to the feast day of the saint to whom the church was dedicated. Puritans intensely disliked them because they involved drinking and disorderly conduct, and because they seemed to contravene the (fourth) commandment to keep the Sabbath day holy. Laudians, by contrast, regarded them as legitimate occasions of harmless entertainment, and as a desirable bond of social cohesion. Bishop Piers himself vehemently denied that church ales created disorderliness; rather they increased levels of attendance at church in the morning, and were an instrument for the relief of the poor and for 'the increase of love and charity'. Minehead's 'patronal' day was 29 September, the feast of St Michael and All Angels, and in March 1632 a copy of the judges' prohibition was sent to Nicholas Browse, ordering him to read it in church on Sunday so that 'your parish may have notice hereof before the day of your wonted revel'. The aged vicar was no friend of puritanism, and he must have announced the order through gritted teeth. But the pendulum of policy was soon to swing back again: the presumptuous judges were brought to task by Laud, supported by Piers and (for political reasons of his own) by Sir Robert Phelips, who had earlier been a vocal critic of royal policy. In October 1633, King Charles reissued an earlier declaration of his father's, the so-called Book of Sports, which declared that there could be no reasonable objection to 'lawful recreations upon Sundays after evening prayers ended'.[11]

It would appear, then, that the provincial milieu of the Leakeys, for all its apparent isolation, was in fact connected in all sorts of ways to the affairs of the world outside, and even found itself on the frontline of some of the principal controversies of the day. Remarkably, the little Somerset port of Minehead was also situated on another crucial political and religious frontier: that with the Islamic world. Throughout the seventeenth century and beyond, sailors operating out of the Devon and Somerset ports ran the risk of capture and enslavement at the hands of pirates ranging from their bases at Algiers, Tunis, and Tripoli on the North African 'Barbary Coast'. Two barques leaving Minehead with passengers for Ireland in 1634 were taken by Barbary Corsairs in the Bristol Channel, and around the same time Islamic raiders seized captives from coastal settlements near Weston-super-Mare. A few years before this, a young sailor on a ship out of Minehead had been captured and taken as a slave to Algiers, where he abandoned Christianity, adopted the religion of his masters, and took service on a Turkish vessel. But there was to be an extraordinary sequel, after his ship was seized by an English man-of-war. The youth was sent back to Minehead, and on 16 March 1628 was made to do public penance for his apostasy in the parish church of St Michael's. The event was accompanied by two long-winded and (in today's terms) extremely 'islamophobic' sermons, in the course of which the boy was particularly berated for his adoption of 'Turkish guise', with shaven head and turban. One of the preachers was none other than Henry Byam, the same minister who a few years later would interrogate Elizabeth Leakey about her supposed visions of her deceased mother-in-law. In all probability, Elizabeth and Alexander Leakey were sitting in the congregation as this poor 'relapsed Christian' was readmitted to the fold of the Church. If so, along with the other ship masters and merchants in the church, Alexander may well have sat up in his pew as Byam addressed his closing remarks directly to 'you that go down to the sea in ships, and occupy your business in great waters (for the state of the world cannot stand without buying and selling, traffic and transportation)'. Mariners were to remember, however, that 'the grave is always open before your face, and but the thickness of an inch or twain that keeps you from it. One breath, flaw, gust, may end your voyage.' Yet the dry world itself was also full of dangers. The apostle Paul survived a shipwreck, but was then bitten by a viper on the shore (Acts 28: 3): 'if all the dangers of the sea quit you, yet a mischief from the land may overtake you'. There was no other remedy for misfortune, but to fall back on 'your first love, the God of love, your blessed Saviour'.

In the spring of 1628, with his trade ventures thriving, and his new or impending marriage to a clever young wife the toast of Minehead quayside, Alexander Leakey could afford to nod gravely at the airing of such sonorous pieties. But within only a few short years he must have begun to wonder if the viper of misfortune had marked him out for special and severe punishment. His mother's death was hardly a tragically premature one, but her affairs had been left in a decidedly uncertain and contentious state. His teenage nephew had died, horribly, under his roof. Moreover, his business had fallen into serious trouble, and he feared arrest for debt. It is striking that no record of any commercial transactions undertaken by Alexander can be found in the Minehead port books for 1635 and 1636. As Elizabeth confessed to the justices in early 1637, her husband 'hath had great losses of late by sea'. Whether these losses were due to violent storms, to daring North African pirates, or to some other cause, we cannot at this remove say. But the Irish Sea trade could be a distinctly treacherous one. Only a couple of years before, another Minehead importer of Irish wool, John Walter, claimed to have lost property to the value of £800 thanks to 'the unmerciful violence of storms and tempest at sea'. He was now reported to be 'miserably impoverished and utterly decayed in his estate'.[12] Like Walter, Alexander Leakey had become a man on a downward social trajectory. In 1624, judging from his position on the lay subsidy roll or tax assessment for Minehead, he seems to have been the sixth wealthiest inhabitant of the town. By 1642, a year before his death, his assessment placed him at number 120, out of 195 taxpayers in the borough. We are familiar enough with financial ruin and insolvency. But the way that Alexander and Elizabeth sought to make sense of their troubles, and perhaps to reverse them, is a reminder that the Leakeys of Minehead, like all the people of seventeenth-century England, also inhabited another world, one whose formidable gates, for good or ill, are firmly closed to us today. This was a world in which unseen forces battled for control of human hearts, and in which signs and portents of various kinds pointed to the presence of deeper spiritual realities which undergirded the physical universe. In the face of relentless questioning from the justices, Elizabeth Leakey only ever offered one direct explanation for why she thought their lives had been convulsed by the visitations of an unquiet spirit: 'her husband and she suspect all this to be witchcraft'. In order to understand why the story of the Minehead haunting may have seemed worth telling, and what it may have meant to those who first heard it, we must attempt to scale those locked gates, and enter imaginatively into the strange pastures of a different world. This was a world in which the dead might have their reasons for appearing to the living, in which a curse could be more than simply an angry word, and in which a message from beyond the grave could attract even the anxious attention of bishops and kings.

2

The Leakeys' Other World

ON 25 July 1634, the English gentleman Sir William Brereton boarded ship at Waterford in Ireland, and, after 'a quick, pleasant, and dainty passage', reached his destination of Minehead in Somerset a mere twenty-six hours later. Unlike the voyage itself, the landing proved bothersome. The passengers had to be put ashore a mile from the port in the ship's long-boat, 'wherein we were more tossed, and in more apparent danger than in all the passage, the waves swelling and being mighty high and great'. Brereton was returning home to Cheshire after an extended tour of the Low Countries and Ireland, and he did not dawdle in Minehead. He lodged overnight at the Angel (price 6d.) and was on his way. Yet in his travel diary he took time to note something interesting he had picked up from the locals. The place where he and his companions had landed was near to a house 'which is said to be enchanted, wherein none dare lodge in the night, so it is not inhabited'. There was an orchard here, 'well furnished with apples', where a number of boys were to be found congregating. This led Brereton to conclude whimsically that it must be a place 'which the fairies sufficiently guard in the night time'.[1]

This little incident prompts a couple of immediate thoughts. It would appear that Alexander Leakey's was not the first or only haunted house in the immediate vicinity of Minehead. It also looks as though the attitude of the Somerset JPs towards Elizabeth Leakey's stories was not a unique example of cool rationalism in a superstitious age. Brereton's casual condescension towards the local belief reinforces an impression that seventeenth-century people, or at least educated people, were by no means indiscriminately credulous. They exercised judgement about supposed manifestations of the supernatural, and were quite capable of looking and sounding extremely sceptical.[2] Yet we should hesitate before concluding from this that something called 'popular culture' and something called 'elite culture' must have been in consistent opposition to each other over these issues. After all, one of those claiming to have seen the Minehead ghost was a university graduate and a minister of the established Church of England. The very fact that the case was being investigated suggests that the religious and state authorities did not view such claims as mere harmless superstitions. And indeed, some aspects of the case made it far from harmless for all concerned in it. A child had died, and his aunt and uncle had alleged that witchcraft was the proximate cause.

Witchcraft was an area of 'popular' belief which the ruling elites took very seriously indeed. Acts of Parliament in 1563, and again in 1604, made the invocation of evil spirits, or the use of 'enchantments, charms and sorceries' to kill or harm, into felonies, punishable by death. There was no frenzied 'witch craze' in later sixteenth and early seventeenth-century England, such as occurred at certain times and places in continental Europe. Nonetheless, several hundred women (they were nearly always women) were tried and hanged in these years because their neighbours suspected them of 'maleficium', of using evil magic, and invoking the help of the devil, in order to cause them harm. Somerset was not top of the league of witchcraft prosecutions in the reigns of Queen Elizabeth and James I (that dubious honour went to Essex), but fears and suspicions periodically surfaced in the towns and villages of the county. In February 1616, for example, Robert Tucker of Tintinhull in south Somerset complained to the courts that his wife Hester 'has many ways abused him, using means to find out a witch to bewitch him'. At Frome Selwood in 1612, a woman called Mary George had managed to find a witch, Agnes Pillis, and wanted her to arrange the deaths of men to whom she owed money. At Henton near Wells in 1613, Elizabeth Busher was reputedly a practitioner of witchcraft, and at Babcary in 1612, three members of the same family—Mary, Elizabeth, and Ancarett Lynge—were all 'vehemently suspected' of being witches. Still closer to home, witchcraft had been discovered in Susan Leakey's Bridgwater in 1609. Earth from under a gallows had been burned together with a bone stolen from the town cemetery, and the ashes were scattered in an orchard belonging to William Decon, so that he would marry Margaret Bridge, or otherwise die. At Taunton in 1626, Edward Dynham claimed to have been told by mysterious voices that he was bewitched, and to have been given a description of the witches: 'a woman in green clothes and a black hat with a long poll, and a man in a grey suit with blue stockings'.[3]

Alexander and Elizabeth Leakey believed, or claimed to believe, that they were the victims of witchcraft. They suspected a woman, but Elizabeth said she 'dare not yet tell her name, for fear she [Elizabeth] should be troubled'. In early seventeenth-century England, accusations of witchcraft did not erupt hysterically out of nowhere, upon the occurrence of any unforeseen misfortune. They were often the product of a long and festering history of suspicion and bad feeling among neighbours. The evidence of cases which reached the courts suggests that accused women had usually built up a reputation as witches over years, sometimes decades, before the authorities officially became involved. We can infer from this that concerns about witchcraft were more widespread than its (relatively rare) prosecution in the courts might casually suggest. People seem to have held off reporting suspected witches until some crisis finally tipped the scales. The explanation is probably not to be found in indifference, or in some degree of grudging tolerance—even though some accused witches undoubtedly did practise as white witches or 'cunning women', offering magical cures and a range of other useful services (the Decon case, cited above, shows how white 'love magic' and black necromancy could sometimes merge into each other). The business of taking anyone to court in the seventeenth century was risky and uncertain, and likely to be expensive. If the accused was acquitted (and contrary to popular belief, this did often happen in witchcraft cases) then an accuser might well find him or herself in court, charged with slander. In March 1636, a couple of weeks before Mother Leakey's first posthumous appearance in Minehead, a poor widow called Elizabeth Stile was found not guilty of witchcraft at the

Somerset assizes at Chard. The judges waived the usual costs to allow her to bring an action against her accuser, Nicholas Hobbes. There was also the more immediate danger of unofficial revenge, through natural or unnatural means.[4]

Taking their story at face value, then, there were good reasons for the Leakeys to exercise caution. But why should they expect anyone to believe that they were bewitched in the first place? There were a couple of ways in which Alexander and Elizabeth could plausibly claim to be the victims of *maleficium*. No one of course supposed that all losses at sea were the result of dark magic, but manipulation of the elements was something which witches were both willing and capable to attempt, or so maritime communities were prone to believe. Such wickedness is enacted on stage in the early seventeenth century's most famous representation of witchcraft, when the three witches of *Macbeth* plot their revenge on a sailor's wife who refuses to share her chestnuts. His barque is to be endlessly tempest-tossed, the evil spell requiring 'a pilot's thumb / Wrecked as homeward he did come'. The other clear indication of the presence of witchcraft was the fate of young John Leakey, who died, readers will remember, crying out that his grandmother was throttling him. A number of witchcraft cases in this period involved 'spectral bewitchment', a vision of the spell-casting witch combined with a physical or at least physiological assault on the victim. In Yorkshire in 1650 a young girl complained to her mother that in the depths of the night a named witch 'came in at a hole at the bed's feet and... took me by the throat'. In Northumberland in 1653, another sick child cried out to her father that Margaret Stothard was 'pressing out her heart' and she feared it would break her back. Like John Leakey, the girl died. These were, quite literally, nightmares, a word whose original meaning betokened an evil (female) spirit creating a feeling of suffocation in its prey during sleep. As in the Minehead case, such supernatural attacks could leave real physical traces. In James I's reign, the body of an alleged victim in Buckinghamshire was found to be covered with bruises when it was laid out.[5]

Beliefs about witchcraft, then, supply a ready-made box into which Elizabeth Leakey's testimony can be placed. But as we think about it more, the fit is not a particularly comfortable one. In these other cases it was a spectral vision of a living witch, not the apparition of a deceased relative, which produced the 'nightmare'. Significantly, no formal charges of witchcraft seem to have been made in connection with the Minehead happenings. There were some important connections between witchcraft and ghosts. In the view of Protestant theologians, the archetypal act of witchcraft was an incident described in the Old Testament, in the first book of Samuel. At the request of bad King Saul, the 'Witch of Endor' had attempted to summon up the spirit of the dead prophet Samuel (more on this shortly). But in cases which were actually brought before the courts, reported apparitions of the dead are extremely rare. The witches in *Macbeth* might have paraded the spirits of kings and the murdered Banquo before the usurping Scots monarch, but most ordinary English witches were too busy killing cattle, blighting crops, and causing sickness in their neighbours to bother themselves with such grandiose gestures. Intellectuals were undoubtedly more concerned than ordinary people were about the precise details of the pacts witches supposedly made with the devil. But there was a fair degree of consensus across society about what sort of creatures witches were, what sort of things they did, and how they were best to be dealt with. It is conceivable that Elizabeth Leakey threw in the allegation about witchcraft as a diversionary tactic, after she was brought to account by the authorities for the rumours and reports she had evidently been assiduously spreading. For her narrative was not at heart a tale about witches, but a story about ghosts. And in the early decades of the seventeenth century, attitudes towards ghosts were much more theologically fraught and morally complicated than those surrounding witches. Witchcraft, all could agree, was the straightforward service of the devil. Ghosts, on the other hand, raised profound and perplexing questions about God's ultimate plans for the human race.

In 1635, far away from the happenings in small-town Minehead, a London publisher brought out a massive theological compilation,

The Workes of that Famous and Worthy Minister of Christ... Mr William Perkins. Perkins, who had died thirty years before, was Elizabethan England's premier Calvinist theologian, an inspiration to puritans and a terror to his Catholic adversaries. One of the reprinted works in the volume was called, by happy coincidence, *A Golden Chain.* Its subject matter, however, had nothing in common with the gewgaw causing contention between Elizabeth Leakey and her Barnstaple sister-in-law. To Perkins, the chain was a metaphor for the harmony and perfection of God's ordering of the universe, and in particular, for the doctrine of predestination (see p. 29). A central theme of the work, therefore, was the fate of the human soul after its separation from the body. Perkins had some especially stern words for those who believed that departed souls 'wander here on earth among men, and oftentimes appear to this or that man'. This was, he admitted, widely believed among 'the common people'. But it was an ignorant and heretical opinion, 'for not all the witches in the world, nor all the devils in hell are able to disquiet the souls of the faithful departed, which are in the keeping of the Lord without wandering from place to place'. As a stalwart upholder of predestination, it was quite clear to Perkins that the souls of the dead were either immediately transported to heaven, there to remain in endless bliss, or were sentenced to eternal, inescapable torment in hell. There was, he added, 'no third place of abode mentioned in scripture'.

This last comment helps us to understand why Protestant preachers and theologians of the time, virtually without exception, refused to entertain the possibility of ghosts of the dead appearing to the living. It was a seductive opinion, but a dangerous one. For in the minds of reformers, it was indelibly associated with a banned Catholic dogma, the Roman Church's teaching about the 'third place' of purgatory. We do not need to detain ourselves overlong with the finer points of this doctrine, though historians now increasingly recognize how important belief in purgatory was to English society in the years before the Reformation. The teaching developed in the early Middle Ages to give shape to a common-sense perception: that most Christians were neither good enough to merit immediate reward in paradise, nor wicked enough to deserve endless punishment in hell. Purgatory squared the circle, making it possible for people other than saints and martyrs eventually to find their way into the kingdom of heaven. Meanwhile, any sins they had not managed to atone for during their lifetime would be 'purged' in the intermediate destination of purgatory. In countless sermons and devotional books, purgatory was imagined as a place of fire and pain, where the experience of one's stay might be compared to thousands of years.

Protestants loathed purgatory. As we have just seen, they thought there was no evidence for it in the Bible. They also thought that it took away from the unique importance of Christ's suffering and death. Had Jesus really died freely to redeem mankind, if his efforts needed supplementing with top-up fees exacted in the fires of purgatory? What is more, Protestant reformers accused the Catholic clergy of cynically operating a 'purgatory industry' for their own institutional and individual benefit. It had long been believed that, just as the saints in heaven could intercede with God for people on earth, the living could assist the souls in purgatory through their prayers, alms-giving, and other good works. In particular, the saying of masses was considered a powerful means of shortening a soul's sojourn in purgatory; the more masses the better. Huge numbers of late medieval English people left lands and money to the Church in return for such 'intercessory' masses. Purgatory was officially abolished in England during the Reformation of the mid-sixteenth century, when the official articles of the Church condemned it as a 'fond [i.e. stupid] thing vainly invented', and the government dissolved all the chantries (the institutions which performed the saying of masses and prayers). Yet a generation and more later, Protestant pastors still worried that the idea of purgatory might linger in the dark corners of people's hearts.[6]

What, you may be asking yourself, did any of this have to do with ghosts? Before the Reformation, ghost stories in England were often circulated or recorded by the clergy, and they were usually tales of souls returning (temporarily) from purgatory, either to warn friends and kinsfolk not to emulate the sins for which they were now paying the price, or to request special masses to be said for their quiet repose. There was sometimes a satisfying 'before and after' effect, with apparitions initially presenting a smoky and blackened visage and, after the appropriate rituals had been performed, reappearing in pristine white to signify their happy state in heaven. The duty of praying for the dead was particularly brought to people's minds in sermons and services at the beginning of November, where the Church had instituted two important consecutive holy days. These commemorated 'All Saints' who did not have their own individual feast, followed by the still humbler 'All Souls' on 2 November. On the night of 31 October, the eve of the feast of All Hallows (Halloween), parishes traditionally rang their church bells on behalf of the departed. Unsurprisingly, the spirits of the dead were believed to be particularly likely to appear and press their claims around this time. To the consternation of the Protestant bishops, some parishes were still ringing at Halloween well into the 1580s. Many years after that, Elizabeth Leakey claimed to have seen her mother-in-law's spirit 'about All Hallowtide'. It is also interesting that Elizabeth Langstone saw the apparition on Christmas Eve, for this too was a long-established moment of 'slippage' between the parallel worlds of living and dead, a time when souls were granted day-release from purgatory in celebration of their saviour's birth.

To Protestants, purgatory simply did not exist: it was an invention, a fraud, and a fable. It followed that appearances of ghosts were similarly fraudulent, and it became an article of faith among reformers that for centuries friars and monks had staged histrionic hauntings to induce credulous believers to part with their cash. With the advent of true religion, however, such wicked nonsense would finally come to an end. 'The gospel has chased away walking spirits', rejoiced one of Queen Elizabeth's bishops—rather prematurely, as it turned out. For the gospel had not managed to dig up the roots of Catholicism itself. A faithful remnant of English Catholics resisted both threats and blandishments to attend the services of the new Church of England (or they attended sullenly, intermittently and reluctantly). From the mid-1570s onwards, these 'recusants' were ministered to by priests who were trained on the continent, and who risked death by returning to their homeland. Among English Catholics, ghost stories continued to circulate, and to perform their traditional function of publicizing the reality of purgatory. In one account of 1612, emanating from a Catholic household in Lancashire, the soul of a troubled priest reappeared in the form of an innocent child after reparations had been made for his wrongdoing. (Remember that Mother Leakey's spirit appeared to Elizabeth Langstone 'in the shape of a little child'.) Protestants meanwhile suspected that the papists were still up to all their old tricks. In 1624, for example, a Protestant pamphleteer accused Jesuit priests in London of staging apparitions to convert gullible young women and get their hands on their inheritances. Small wonder, then, if a popish connection was one of the lines of enquiry the Somerset JPs thought of pursuing into the Minehead haunting. It must have struck them that the curate John Heathfield responded noncommittally to their questions about Mother Leakey's religious allegiances. The old lady 'was for ought he knew a Protestant, for she came ordinarily and duly to church'.

Yet as far as we can tell, the Leakeys were not Catholics, and none of the principals in the case were ever among the tiny handful of Minehead folk reported in these years for not coming to receive the communion at Easter time. In any case, belief in ghosts was by no means confined to the small Catholic minority: most commentators agreed with Perkins that it was simply endemic among 'ignorant persons'. Nor could the number of reported sightings all plausibly be ascribed to the deceptions of Jesuits, however busy, devious, and sinister Protestants imagined them to be. Some reported 'apparitions' were, it was agreed, undoubtedly the product of overactive imaginations, of howling winds, creaking floorboards, and mooncast shadows on churchyard walls. But nearly everyone who thought about the matter agreed that some appearances of spectres seemed to be objectively 'real', and these had to be accounted for. The Elizabethan translator of a Swiss treatise on ghosts and spirits conceded that there were very many people, 'even nowadays, which are haunted and troubled with spirits'. The key question: what could such spirits actually be?

The official answer was arrived at by a process of elimination. There was no purgatory from which souls could return, no possibility they could escape from hell, and no conceivable reason why they should abandon their reward in heaven to wander around on the earth. Apparitions then could not be human souls, and it therefore followed that they had to be visible manifestations of either good or evil spirits—the angels or demons who thronged the universe doing the bidding of their respective masters, God and the devil. It was naturally more comforting to believe that they were angels than demons. At Launceston in Jacobean Cornwall, Sir Thomas Wise encountered a woman in shimmering white standing at the foot of his bed, and was later reassured by a local archdeacon that he had seen 'an angelical apparition'. Yet this was a minority opinion among the theological experts. Angels had frequently appeared in biblical times, but the need for an 'age of miracles' had long since passed, since the Bible itself contained all the truths that it was necessary for Christians to believe. It was not inconceivable that angels might still occasionally appear carrying a particular message from God. But why would they assume the appearance of a recently deceased person? Nor was it thought at all likely, the Launceston case notwithstanding, that an angel would ever appear in the form of a woman. This left a starker and unsettling probability: that many 'ghosts' were in reality deluding demons, or even the devil himself. The Bible taught (2 Cor. 11: 14) that Satan had the power to transform himself into 'an angel of light', and what better disguise could there be for deluding and misleading the unwary than the similitude of a departed friend or neighbour? The story of the Witch of Endor in the first book of Samuel was grist to the mill here. The standard Protestant interpretation of this passage was that the witch had simply deluded herself into believing she had raised the spirit of Samuel, when in fact it was the devil who appeared in Samuel's guise, and encouraged Saul to fall down in worship before him.[7]

Angel or demon? 'Spirit of health, or goblin damned?' If the dilemma sounds familiar, it is because William Shakespeare used it as the hinge on which to hang the plot of his greatest play. Hamlet (and with him the audience) remains throughout uncertain as to whether the apparition commanding him to seek revenge upon his Uncle Claudius is really the spirit of his murdered father, condemned 'to fast in fires / Till the foul crimes done in my days of nature / Are burnt and urged away'. Or, conversely, whether 'the spirit that I have seen / May be the devil, and . . . abuses me to damn me'. But it was not just on the London stage that such a predicament might present itself. When Susan Leakey threatened to return after her death, her daughter-in-law's retort could hardly have been more impertinently pertinent: 'What, will you be a devil?' (p. 2). There is no doubt that Elizabeth Leakey was familiar with the official Protestant line on ghosts, the one she must have supposed her examiners to hold. The old lady's rejoinder is also intriguing: 'No, but I will come in the devil's likeness.' This need not make us think of horns and a tail, for evidence from seventeenth-century witchcraft trials suggests that when the devil visited his servants he could adopt a variety of plausible forms: 'the shadow of a man', 'a handsome young gentleman with yellow hair and black clothes', 'in the shape of a proper gentleman, with a laced band, having the whole proportion of a man'. Sometimes it was only the cloven foot that gave away his true identity.[8]

Critics sometimes ask whether the apparition of Old King Hamlet was intended to be understood as a 'Catholic ghost' or a 'Protestant ghost' (i.e. a devil). Yet the same question will not take us very far towards making sense of the Minehead haunting. Though aware of what the orthodox Protestant position was, all of the witnesses seem in the end (like Hamlet) to have rejected it; to have taken the apparition at its own word, and to have accepted it for what it claimed to be—the spirit of the old lady. 'Good Mother, tell me whether you be in heaven or in hell', Elizabeth is supposed to have asked. Yet there is no suggestion of a third possibility here, and indeed (other than the seasonal timing around Halloween) there is nothing identifiably Catholic about the haunting at

all—no talk of masses and prayers, or of souls languishing in purgatory. One result of the Reformation, of course, was a good deal of
theological fusion, and confusion, at the popular level of society. But
another possibility here is that the stories about Old Mother Leakey
drew on very deep wells of belief about the expected behaviour of
ghosts and revenants, beliefs which were in large measure independent of the formal theologies of either Canterbury or Rome.

The ghosts of the modern heritage industry are the ancient fixtures
of the stately homes circuit: long-deceased and often anonymous
chain-clankers and head-carriers. But the ghosts encountered by
our sixteenth and seventeenth-century forebears were usually very
different from this. They were nearly always the recently dead, still
clearly remembered in the communities which they had inhabited
in life, and which they now traumatized in death. The return of the
dead—revenance—was not a frequent occurrence in this society;
there was no expectation that the quiet rest of the great majority of
departed Christians would ever be thus disturbed. Yet one common
factor in both medieval and post-medieval ghost narratives was the
failure to make a 'good death'. Likely candidates for revenance were
those who had suffered a sudden or violent end: suicides, executed
criminals, or (like Hamlet's father) the victims of murder. By
contrast, the 'good death' was not, as we would have it nowadays,
a swift and painless one, but one in the course of which the loose
ends of life, spiritual and social, had all been tied up. The ideal was
to make peace with God and neighbour, and to shine as an example
of Christian fortitude in the face of physical suffering. We can find
a model in the account of the last hours of Elianor Evelyn, mother
of the famous diarist John, who died in Surrey in September 1635.
She summoned her children around her, and issued them each with
pious instructions and a memorial ring before commending them to
her husband's care. She urged him to bestow charity on the poor
rather than splash out on a lavish funeral, and then resigned her soul
to God 'with elevated heart and eyes'.

We can imagine a rather different scene unfolding ten months
earlier in the quayside house at Minehead. There were unresolved

tensions between the dying woman and her relatives, and when the end finally came it seems to have been too sudden for the making of a written will or, perhaps, for the making of proper amends to kin and Creator alike. The troublesome dead tended to be people who had been troublesome in life, and we know that Susan Leakey had on occasion quarrelled violently with her neighbours (p. 22). In a number of ways, she fitted the pattern of the difficult and dangerous dead, who were widely believed in European folklore to want to seize a companion, like poor John Leakey, from among the ranks of the living. The ghosts of those who suffered a 'bad end' were seeking what we might today call 'closure'. Those whom they haunted had no less of an interest in righting the wrongs and redressing the imbalances that had led to such disrupture in the fabric of life and death. Elizabeth Leakey asked the ghost what she needed to do 'that I may be quiet', and whether there was 'any thing left undone in your will that I can do for you'.

Like the other witnesses, Elizabeth was well aware that there was a proper procedure, a kind of safety code, for interacting with a spectre. 'In the name of God', 'the Lord bless me from you': these phrases came naturally to their lips in their supposed exchanges with the ghost. Sir Thomas Wise had similarly challenged the spirit in his Cornish bedchamber 'in the name of the God of heaven to come no nearer'. Protestant authorities advised that people confronted by an apparition should make just such a simple declaration of faith, though they also insisted that on no account should one enter into conversation and communication with such spirits. This was an injunction prudently observed by Wise, but spectacularly disregarded by Elizabeth Leakey and Elizabeth Langstone. The etiquette for addressing spirits was sufficiently well known for it to be satirized in a late sixteenth-century parody called *Tarleton's News out of Purgatory*. When the narrator meets the ghost of the actor Richard Tarleton, he starts back, crying '*In nomine Jesu*, avoid, Satan, for ghost thou art none, but a very devil. For the souls of them which are departed ... never return into the world again.' But this tirade signally fails to impress the ghost, who responds wearily, 'Oh, there is a Calvinist'.[9]

There was, in other words, no absolute consensus around what to believe about ghosts in early seventeenth-century England, just as there was no absolute certainty about what one might look like. The modern cliché about ghosts and white sheets probably has its origins in this period, as to many people it seemed logical that apparitions of the dead would manifest themselves wearing the cloth burial shrouds in which they had been interred. They may often have appeared like this in the theatre, for *A Warning for Fair Women*, an anonymous play written about the same time as *Hamlet*, was already mocking the tradition of bringing on stage 'a filthy, whining ghost, / Lapt in some foul sheet', screaming for revenge 'like a pig half-sticked'. Later in the century, an author referred to 'the old fashions of ghosts' as 'always the same: a winding-sheet with two knots, and a taper in the spirit's hands'. This was how an apparition was depicted in an early seventeenth-century sketch made on the blank title leaf of a copy of a *Treatise of Specters* (Figure 4). Mother Leakey, by contrast, appeared in her ordinary apparel, no doubt so that there could be no uncertainty about her identity. But what ultimately was that identity? The Protestant theologians' clear, hard stance on this question was familiar enough in the parishes, but ordinary people were not entirely persuaded. Perhaps this was because of the strength and resilience of traditional beliefs, or perhaps because it was simply too cruelly counter-intuitive to insist that every attempt of departed souls to contact living relations was in fact a subtle ruse of Satan. Making the idea seem more implausible was the fact that much of the actual activity of ghosts appeared to involve the detecting of crimes and righting of wrongs. And even among the Protestant clergy themselves there was no absolute adherence to the party line. A story circulating in Oxford in 1627 led the minister and Queen's College fellow, Thomas Crosfield, to note in his diary: 'the question disputed whether spirits really and substantially appear, i.e. the ghosts of the deceased'. The Reverend John Heathfield's first instinct had been to regard Elizabeth Leakey's visions as the product of melancholy and stress, rather than as a delusion of the devil. But later he too beheld what he was not embarrassed to call 'the apparition of Old

4. How an early seventeenth-century reader imagined (remembered?) a ghost. From a copy of Pierre le Loyer's *A Treatise of Specters* (1605)

Mrs Leakey', though he was careful to protest that he had 'said nothing, nor the apparition to him'. Everyone who thought about the matter was agreed, however, that the presence of an apparition—whether angel, demon, or unquiet soul—must signify *something*. It was a portentous event, and not an experience anyone could go through lightly. All four of the Minehead witnesses spoke of the fear they had felt in the presence of the apparition. 'It is natural unto us', observed one theological expert, 'to be amazed with fear when we see such things'. Yet to encounter a spirit in human shape was bound to be an occurrence with a meaning and a message, and not just a random hazard of nocturnal wandering.

The purposes for which ghosts returned to this world were many and various, particularly after the abolition of purgatory had removed their previous taste for masses and prayers. Two other West Somerset cases from the years of Mother Leakey's widowhood illustrate the range of possibilities. In 1613, in the village of Kingston near Taunton, a man confessed to the unsolved murder of a rich widow, after discovering 'that the ghost of the woman he had slain was continually before him, so as his very life was burdensome to him'. Nine years later, in the summer of 1622, another haunting was reported in the village of Middlezoy outside Bridgwater, where Thomas Whyn was telling anybody who would listen to him that the ghost of Christian Godfrey had recently appeared to his daughter Joan. Christian had announced that she was in hell, 'and that it was a good thing to go to heaven', though she knew the names of a number of Middlezoy residents who would shortly be joining her in the lower place. Yet the mainspring of this reported haunting turned out to be almost comically commonplace, the cause of Christian's eternal damnation a piece of alleged petty larceny. She could not be at rest, Whyn supposed, 'until she came and tell me of a plank which was in a buttery, and that plank I will beswear was my own'.[10] Where then should we position the appearances of Mother Leakey on this spectral spectrum? We are perhaps likely to think that they belong closer to the ridiculous than to the sublime end of it, even allowing for the fact that a golden chain from the Caribbean was a marginally better reason for disturbing the sleep of the dead than a plank of wood in the buttery.

Yet we are surely missing something important here, and alert readers will already have noticed what it is. What about the message that Mother Leakey commanded Elizabeth to carry personally to her sister-in-law (Mother Leakey's daughter) in Ireland? A message that was potentially harmful to the recipient, Joan Atherton, and to her husband, if knowledge of it was to leak out. A message whose contents Elizabeth Leakey refused to divulge either to the Reverend Henry Byam or to Bishop Piers, and which she would hesitate to reveal even to the King himself, 'unless he command her so to do'. I confess that when I first began to work on this material I did not know quite what to do with this strand of the investigation, and so I put it mentally on one side while I focused on the apparent 'function' of ghost beliefs in regulating the smooth transfer of property from one generation to the next. Yet the Leakeys belonged to a culture that took supernatural messages and warnings very seriously indeed. At all levels of early seventeenth-century society there was an intense interest in divine 'providence'—that is, in God's direct intervention in the created natural world, and in the messages he might inscribe on it for humans to read and understand. The Lord's methods were many and various—plague, fire, freak weather, strange portents in the sky, great sea creatures washed up on beaches. Apparitions too might serve as instruments of God's great justice, and it was in this way that some Protestant writers were able to square the theological circle, reconciling the evil nature of spirits with the apparently laudable ends they seemingly wished to bring about. A pamphlet of 1623 told of the son of a Wiltshire tailor who held back legacies intended for his sisters. As a result, his house was plagued with a poltergeist, and local children saw a vision of his dead father walking in the churchyard. The author hesitated to say this was a human soul, but conceded that, by God's permission, a spirit might 'assume an apparent likeness' of the old man, in order to show that 'all these things for his sake happened to the wronger'. Whenever apparitions promised to speak more directly there was an intense interest in what they had to say. After King James's eldest son Henry died in November 1612, a (probably mad) young man turned up stark naked at St James's 'saying he was the Princes ghost come from heaven with a message to the king'. Thousands of Londoners reportedly came to see him incarcerated in the porter's lodge there.[11]

There was, and still is, a world of social, cultural, and geographical distance between the gatehouse of the palace of St James's and the storehouses of Minehead Quay, between a staged apparition of the one-time heir to the English throne, and that of an obscure Somerset widow. Yet this very contrast suggests a question which I imagine many readers will have asked themselves already, and which, embarrassingly enough, I somehow neglected to pose until forced to do so by the unexpected intrusion of Sir Walter Scott (see p. ix). Why on earth were the leading justices of the county of Somerset reporting directly to the royal council in London about the fantasies and delusions plaguing the family of an inconsequential West Country merchant? To claim to have seen a ghost was not exactly a common occurrence in the mid-1630s, but nor was it so very unusual, and nor was it in itself a crime. As one historian of witchcraft has remarked, 'we are not dealing with a world in which seeing spirits or hearing voices was entirely normal and everyday, but one in which within certain limits and at certain points, it was explicable as a phenomenon of the real world rather than simply an internal delusion'.[12] In Catholic Spain at this time, the Inquisition closely monitored the beliefs of the common people, providing in the process a wonderful archive for later historians to exploit. But the church courts in England were much more concerned with getting people to pay their tithes to the clergy, and stopping them engaging in pre-marital sex. Only very rarely does 'the other world' make much of a mark on their proceedings. Claims of ghostly intervention surface very occasionally in the records of the criminal courts, but not unless some sort of serious crime was being investigated or alleged. Other than the vague hints about witchcraft, there was no direct suggestion of this in the testimony of February 1637, so what the devil was going on?

There is no simple or straightforward answer to that question, though the following chapters will do their best to supply it as fully as the evidence allows. We will hear nothing more about the golden chain, which, however much Elizabeth Leakey may have coveted it, was of very little interest to the authorities. What did interest them was the concealed message for Elizabeth Leakey's in-laws in

Ireland, Mrs Joan and Mr John Atherton, about whom we are shortly to learn a great deal more. Concealment implies a secret, or secrets. As contemporaries well knew, 'one of the things ghosts came back for was to uncover secrets'.[13] Susan Leakey took her secrets to the grave, but she did not stay with them there, or they with her. Her secrets were to cross the sea to Ireland, and in due course to play a small but demonstrable part in the collapse of a kingdom. People might tell stories about ghosts, but ghosts could also tell stories about people. They could help bring to light suppressed knowledge that had eluded other, more conventional, methods and channels of exposure. When humble and ordinary folk, ordinary women even, acted as the intermediaries of super-naturally sanctioned disclosure, the great and the good were, for once, obliged to take notice of them and listen to what they had to say. It is in pursuit of a secret, then, that we must, like the crew of one of Alexander Leakey's barques, take ship from Minehead for the east coast of Ireland. But to get a proper sense of the significance of this knowledge, we must also move quickly forward four years in time, to the final weeks of 1640, and to the scene of a shocking and violent event, one that would finally allow Mother Leakey's secrets to start explaining themselves to a watching and wondering world.

INTERLUDE
A Hanging in Dublin

DECEMBER 1640, a cold Saturday morning in the city of Dublin, the grandest place in King Charles I's other kingdom of Ireland. A coach is making its way slowly through unusually crowded streets, from the seat of government at Dublin Castle to the common ground of Oxmantown Green on the north side of the River Liffey, a place where the citizens of Dublin are accustomed 'to walk and take the open air'. There is no such innocent recreation today, however: the people milling around the open spaces to the rear of St Michan's church are starting to congregate around a scaffold which has been erected there, and they have come to see a man lose his life upon it. In Ireland as in England, hangings are common enough things. But this particular expression of the judicial severity of the state has turned into a momentous civic event. In the vicinity of Dublin Castle, a single bell, a passing-bell, tolls from the tower of the cathedral church of the Holy Trinity, commonly called Christ Church. At this eloquent signal, we are told, 'the whole town and castle so thronged, as was never the like seen, that if there had not been a coach allowed him, it would have been impossible to have gone through'.[1]

Inside the coach, five men sit side by side, grim-faced, and shielded by curtains from the peering plebians on the streets below. Two of them are there to represent officialdom, and to see the sentence of the court carried through to its fatal conclusion. There is one of the sheriffs of the city of Dublin, and the sub-sheriff of Dublin county. The third man is a minister of the Church of Ireland, there to provide spiritual succour, and to help the convicted criminal make a 'good end'. The fourth is of less account, a servant.

But the fifth has brought all the others together by the fact of his impending death. Nonetheless, he is the most loquacious of the group. Upon climbing into the coach, he had mused that 'this puts me in mind of Elijah's chariot, he was carried to heaven in'. The sight of the throng pressing around the wheels of the carriage by the gates of Dublin Castle had prompted him to tailor to the occasion the very words of St Paul (1 Cor. 4: 9), 'I am made a spectacle to men, but I hope to angels also, who are attending to receive my soul.' He passes the short journey with prayers, the singing of psalms, and reflections on the vanity of life, the separation of the soul from the body, and other earnest matters. As the coach turns right onto the solid stone edifice of Dublin Bridge, he catches through the curtains a first glimpse of the gallows ahead on the other side of the river, with the people teeming about it. Turning to the minister, he pronounces solemnly, 'there is my Mount Calvary, from which I hope to ascend to heaven'.

But as the coach arrives at its final destination, the mood of the crowd is unsettled, volatile; the officials are nervous, fearful of disorder. The convict's composure slips now, and the flow of pious consolation momentarily ceases. One of the sheriffs, trying to clear room around the hard-pressed vehicle, has laid about him with a stick: the convict's faithful footman, keeping pace on foot alongside the coach, has had his head broken, and blood is pouring down his face. His master cannot bear to see it, and begs for him to be removed from his sight. As the condemned emerges from the carriage, the people can see him properly for the first time. One witness who 'by favour...got near the gallows' has left a vivid impression for us: he was 'a proper straight person, of a brown blackish hair, about the age of fifty'. He has 'a handsome beard' and a hat upon his head. Another who was present remarks on his hands being bound, 'with a three penny cord, as a common rogue'. But this is no ordinary criminal, as all can plainly see from the long black cassock he is wearing, a garment which provides some protection from the chill winter air, if not from the persistent gnawing of an icy inner sensation. Nor is this a merely common clergyman. The man about to die is a bishop, a prince of the Church, who in a short time must ascend a ladder, allow a rope to be placed around his neck, and then be 'turned off' into darkness and death.

But before this can happen there are words to be said, an account to be offered. The speech of a condemned man is a convention of the occasion, but also a portentous thing. Last words echo in the mind, and bear the character of truth. Who would go to his maker with a lie upon his lips? Yet at first it seems uncertain that the crowd will suffer him to speak at all. As the bishop ascends the scaffold, stands by the ladder and begins his address, he is heckled by 'a fellow got up on one end of the gallows, deriding him and interrupting him'. He bears it patiently, waits for silence, and resumes:

> Gentlemen, my first salutation to you is, God bless you, and God save you, and I desire you to pray the same for me. I am, I think, the first of my profession that ever came hither to this shameful end, and I pray God I may be the last. You are come hither to see a comedy turned into a tragedy, a miserable catastrophe of the life and actions of man in this world...

A comedy and a tragedy. The life and actions of John Atherton, distinguished brother-in-law to Alexander and Elizabeth, and son-in-law to Old Mother Leakey, were by the standards of any age, quite extraordinary ones. The story of how he came to his 'shameful end' on a gallows outside Dublin is what will occupy us on the next stage of our journey. It will also start to reveal how apparently disconnected spheres—the small world of the Leakeys, and the large world of Archbishop William Laud—embarked on a course of convergence with each other, with eventually explosive and fatal results.

3

The Devil Let Loose off his Chain

I N the summer of 1629, five years and more before the chain of events set in motion by the death of Susan Leakey, a Somerset clergyman took ship for Ireland, where he had hopes of bettering his prospects. John Atherton was at that time a mature man of 31, and had been an ordained minister in the Church of England for almost eleven years. His professional rise up to this point had been, if hardly meteoric, at least solidly upwards. The decision, in mid-career, to set an oblique course and to continue to pursue it in the Church of Ireland requires explanation, though it was not quite as eccentric as it might sound. A steady stream of English clergymen in these years were choosing to emigrate there. Yet behind each such departure, as behind every exercise of human choice, there lay a story—or a story can be inferred, fashioned, or imagined. A full range of theories as to what it was that impelled Atherton to leave his native Somerset only emerged into the realm of public discussion years after the event itself, so we will pass over them for the moment. It was, in fact, events in Ireland itself that would, in December 1640, bring John Atherton to his strange and violent death at the end of a rope, but a full explanation of that remarkable occurrence will nonetheless require us to come back, in due time and order, to the Bristol Channel coast, the world of the Leakeys, and a set of secrets from beyond the grave.

John Atherton was born in the closing years of Queen Elizabeth's long reign, in 1598. Like many of the clergy of pre-Civil War England, he was himself the progeny of a parsonage. His father, also John Atherton, was rector of Bawdrip, a rural parish four miles outside Bridgwater. His parents had in fact married in Bridgwater in February 1596, at a time when the Leakeys were prominent residents of the town, so connections between the families may well have been long-standing. The elder Atherton died in July 1609, and four months later John's mother Joyce remarried. John was clearly an able youth, going up to Gloucester Hall, Oxford, in October 1617, and, remarkably for one so young, taking the degree of BA there later that year. In March 1618, still probably short of his twentieth birthday, he was licensed as a preacher by the then bishop of Bath and Wells, Arthur Lake. In September the following year he was ordained a priest of the Church of England. In June 1620, Atherton began exercising his priestly functions for the first time, when he was appointed curate of the little parish of Huish Champflower, nestling at the foot of the Brendon Hills between Taunton to the south-east, and Minehead to the north (see Figure 1). Somehow, Atherton managed to combine his curacy with the furtherance of his Oxford education, gaining his MA (the passport to any serious advancement in the Church) at Lincoln College in June 1621, along with a growing reputation as a smart young lawyer, an expert in the 'canon law' of the Church.

It is now that the twin stories of my title, those of Mother Leakey and the Bishop, begin meaningfully to intersect for the first time. Shortly before his appointment as curate, Atherton had married Joan Leakey, eldest daughter of Susan Leakey of Bridgwater. His widowed mother-in-law, and his unmarried sister-in-law, Susan, were either already living in Huish, or moved there along with the newly-weds. Whether it was a love match, we cannot presume to say. It may have been, for by marrying, Atherton disqualified himself from the fellowship at Lincoln which seemed the obvious next step for an ambitious clerical graduate. But the young couple were not required to live on love and air, or on the meagre sustenance of a curate's stipend. In 1622, the living of Huish fell vacant, and on 16 July Atherton was instituted as rector there. The chronology of all this is suspiciously convenient. The right to promote a clergyman to a parish living or 'benefice' in this period was effectively a piece of property, vested in a range of clerical and lay patrons. Atherton was appointed to the parish by a kinsman, Philip

Atherton, who was exercising a right of presentation *pro hac vice* (for this occasion) under a grant from the actual patron, Sir Maurice Heale. There is no suggestion in the records that the previous holder of the post had died, though he had been rector there for over forty-five years. It looks rather as though the aged incumbent had been enticed to resign, and the patron persuaded to sell the 'right of next presentation' to make a berth for the newly married young clergyman. It was a comfortable berth too. The tithes on agricultural produce payable to their rector by the parishioners of Huish produced an annual income of around £130, far above the average for a Somerset rectory at this time. It was just as well. The marriage produced five daughters over the next few years. The eldest, Joan, was named for her mother, and the second (born in September 1621) was christened Susan, like her aunt and maternal grandmother. Sarah, Agnett, and Christian followed. As we know already, from the cryptic testimony of their grandmother's ghost, wife and family accompanied Atherton when he suddenly abandoned his ministry in rural Somerset for a new life in Ireland.[1]

In many ways, Ireland in the early seventeenth century was much what it had been since the English had begun intruding there nearly five centuries before. At once a near neighbour, and a land apart, it was a place of dreams (of wealth, of spiritual mission) for some, of disillusionment and loss for others. In name Ireland was a kingdom, and constitutionally a miniature replica of the English state, with its own parliament, privy council, law courts, and county commissions of the peace. But in reality it was a colonized land, home to a complex and unstable ethnic and religious mix, and a sad and violent recent history of war and rebellion. No act could be passed by the Irish parliament without prior approval from the King in London, and from the King's representative in Ireland, the Lord Deputy in Dublin. At the time of Atherton's arrival, the responsibilities of this post were being jointly and uneasily exercised by the two chief justices: Adam Loftus, first Viscount Ely, and Richard Boyle, first earl of Cork.

If some aspects of Ireland's condition were bred in the emerald bone, much had also changed within the span of living memory. Both Loftus and Boyle were leading representatives of the 'New English', the group which, from the time of Elizabeth I, had dominated the government and economy of the island. These settlers had acquired tracts of land at the expense of the native Irish, who were unable to demonstrate any formal 'title' to their estates which would satisfy the anglophone courts. New English numbers were increased by the policy of 'plantation', which gave Protestant settlers land in return for militia service. The New English were marked out by their language, and also by their religion, which often had a markedly puritan tinge. This was even more the case with the Scots settlers who took part in the Jacobean plantation of Ulster.

Nearly all the settlers manifested a profound hostility towards the language, customs, and culture of the Gaelic-speaking Irish population. These were often regarded as 'savages', differing little from the peoples which more intrepid emigrants were now encountering on the far side of the Atlantic. The antipathy was religious as well as ethnic, for the Protestant Reformation had simply failed to take root in Ireland in the way it had done in Scotland or Wales. Despite the official proscription of the mass and Catholic clergy, a self-confident Roman Catholicism was by the seventeenth century resurgent throughout most parts of the island, fuelled by the activities of the orders of friars and Jesuits. Critical to the failure of Reformation in Ireland was the attitude of the 'Old English', descendants of the Anglo-Norman settlers of the twelfth century. With few exceptions, the Old English remained Catholic, and as a result found their accustomed dominance eroded by Protestant newcomers. Yet the regime in Dublin could not govern the country without them: they continued to hold local office, attend parliament, and pay taxes to the Crown. It was to secure the flow of taxes that in the mid-1620s a series of concessions on land tenure and the exercise of religion, 'the Graces', had been negotiated with the Old English. But the status of the Graces remained uncertain. The

Protestant settlers were deeply wary of further concessions, the Old English fearful that they might be removed.

The government's tacit recognition that Catholics could not be compelled to attend Protestant services raises questions about the nature of the institution to which John Atherton was about to offer his services. The church of Ireland was the legally established religion of the land, a scaled-down facsimile of the church to be found at home in England. It had inherited the parish churches, cathedrals, and bishoprics of old Catholic Ireland. All Irish people had to pay tithes for the support of its clergy. Yet it commanded the allegiance of only a minority of the population. By the 1620s, in fact, the church had effectively given up the aspiration to convert the nation as a whole. Only a handful of dedicated eccentrics among its preachers were able or prepared to spread the gospel in the Irish language, and as a result its ministry was largely confined to the imported Protestant population. A sense of beleaguerment was added to by the financial and material condition of the church. Across Ireland, many churches lay in ruins, and the inability of individual parishes to provide sufficient support for a minister produced endemic pluralism (the holding of more than one church office). The financial problems could not simply be laid at the door of the papists, for as often as not, it was into the hands of New English settlers that lands and revenues originally belonging to the church had disappeared.[2]

Despite all of this, the Church of Ireland acted as a magnet for English clergy in these years. Early seventeenth-century Ireland was chronically short of Protestant clergymen, and places were available for almost all who sought them. Many of these clerical fortune-seekers originated from the coastal communities of the south-west of England. One was the younger brother of Henry Byam of Luccombe, whom we have already encountered interrogating Elizabeth Leakey about the appearances at Minehead. Edward Byam was a minister of unimpeachable character. But not all of the incoming priests were as reputable. According to one satirist, it was notorious that for years the western kingdom 'hath been the receptacle for our English runagates, that for their misled lives in England, do come running over'. The archbishops of Dublin and Armagh complained in 1615 that they had been forced to accept English ministers who turned out to be 'very offensive and scandalous'. One such was the fugitive puritan preacher, Stephen Jerome, who decamped to Ireland in 1622 after being caught *in flagrante* with a parishioner's wife in Newcastle. Nonetheless, he became a chaplain to the earl of Cork, and minister of a parish in County Waterford. Returning to England, he was obliged to leave again in 1626 after allegations of attempted rape from his maidservant. This proved no bar to appointment as a minister in Dublin. Small wonder if an Irish gentleman then urged that ministers in the Church 'ought to be no vomited persons out of England'.[3] Whether our John Atherton was precisely such a 'vomited person' is a very moot question.

We know that Atherton was in Ireland by August 1629, for on that date he was elected to a fellowship of Trinity College, Dublin. In January 1630, he secured a position at Christ Church, one of Dublin's two Protestant cathedrals (see Figure 5). This was thanks to the good offices of a powerful patron, the Irish Lord Chancellor, Adam Loftus. We do not know how Atherton brought himself to Loftus's attention, perhaps his expertise in canon law recommended him. At any rate, he was now firmly on the promotion ladder of the Irish Church. The post was the prebendship of St John's (prebends were the portions of a cathedral's revenues granted to the clergymen who made up the 'chapter' or governing body). Along with it came the rectorship of a city parish, the church of St John the Evangelist, within spitting distance of the cathedral itself. St John's was demolished in the nineteenth century, but in 1630 it was one of the more cheerful Irish livings for an expatriate Englishman to hold, with a respectable annual income of £60. A report in that year by the archbishop of Dublin declared that 'the most part of the parishioners are Protestants, and duly frequent their parish church'. This could (perhaps) be taken for granted anywhere in England, but in Ireland it was decidedly unusual even in the city of Dublin itself.

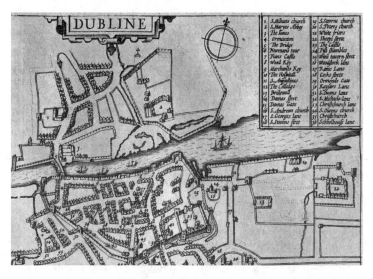

1	S.Mihans church	19	S.Stevens church
2	S.Maryes Abbay	20	S.Peters church
3	The Innes	21	White friers
4	Ormunston	22	Sheepe strete
5	The Bridge	23	The Castle
6	Newmans tour	24	Fish shambles
7	Floris Castle	25	Wolt tavern strit
8	Wood Key	26	Woodstock lane
9	Marchants Key	27	Rame Lane
10	The Hospitall	28	Cockes strete
11	S.Augustines	29	Ormonds Gate
12	The Colledge	30	Kayšars Lane
13	Bridewell	31	S.Owens Lane
14	Dames stret	32	S.Michaels Lane
15	Damas Gate	5	Christchurch lane
16	S.Andrews church	34	S.Owens church
17	S.Georges Lane	35	Christchurch
18	S.Stevens stret	36	Schholhous Lane

5. Atherton's Dublin (St John's church is no. 37), from John Speed's *Theatre of the Empire of Great Britain* (1611).

As prebendary of St John's, Atherton was not principally a parochial minister of the kind he had been in Somerset (a curate saw to the spiritual needs of the parish). Rather, he became the leading crewman in a flagship institution of the Church of Ireland, a church attempting to plot its course without coming completely adrift in a swelling sea of Counter-Reformation Catholicism. As the diocesan Cathedral of Dublin, Christ Church provided a round of liturgical services, and its pulpit was the venue for high-profile preachers. It was also the spiritual home of the English administration housed nearby in Dublin Castle. Yet the cathedral entered the seventeenth century in an weak position, with a decaying fabric, and struggling to collect rent arrears from its tenants. Chapter meetings were irregular and there was no long-term strategy for reform. This was to change with the advent of John Atherton, who became the driving force of reform after his appointment to the dormant office of sub-dean in July 1630. Almost immediately, however, a curious hiatus intervened. On 10 November 1630 Atherton was granted a licence by the chapter 'to pass over into England about some special affairs of his own, for the full term of one whole year'.[4] Whatever was accomplished during this sabbatical, Atherton's English affairs, as we shall see, were quite literally going to come back and haunt him.

Atherton's impact on Christ Church was a microcosm of larger processes at work in the world. In July 1633, a more significant English immigrant arrived in Dublin, the new Lord Deputy, Sir Thomas Wentworth. Wentworth was a close ally of the soon-to-be-appointed archbishop of Canterbury, William Laud, and a central part of his mission was to see that the Irish Church got with the programme being devised by Laud in England. The aim was to curb puritanism, and quell 'seditious' preaching, to restore the 'beauty of holiness' to the Protestant Church's buildings and worship, and to enhance the economic and jurisdictional authority of its clerical personnel. It would not be long before John Atherton flashed across the radar of the mercurial Lord Deputy. Almost from the start, their fates were linked, and they would rise, and fall, together.

The early seventeenth-century ethos at Christ Church, as of the Church of Ireland more generally, was noticeably 'godly'. It was Calvinist in its theology of grace (only the predestined would be saved); relatively indifferent to ritual and ceremony; insistent on the importance of preaching; and virulently anti-Catholic. Bright stars in the Irish Church were at something of a premium, but they included the archbishop of Armagh, James Ussher, who preached in Atherton's church of St John's in 1632, obliging the churchwardens to lay out four shillings for the hiring of seats. In the Laudian worldview, however, preaching was not enough. It stressed the importance of ceremony and ritual as means of making the lives of Christians holy. More particularly, preaching needed to take second place to the celebration of the holy communion. The controversies about the positioning and railing of communion tables that we have seen exciting passions in Somerset (p. 32) were no less acute in Ireland in these years. Yet here, Christ Church, and John Atherton, were in the very vanguard of change. In June 1633, the Irish auditor-general, and noted antiquarian, Sir James Ware, made a rather perplexed entry in his journal: 'the communion table in Christ Church was set up after the manner of an altar'. Ware left little doubt about where responsibility for this innovation lay: 'upon Sunday following...the epistle and Gospel and ten command-ments were read there by Mr Atherton'. Atherton's own church of St John's soon followed suit.[5]

Liturgical innovation at Christ Church was accompanied by a makeover of personnel. Between 1632 and 1635 every member of the chapter, bar Atherton himself, was replaced. The new arrivals were mostly Englishmen sympathetic to Laudian ideals. The most not-able of them was the Yorkshireman, John Bramhall, who became treasurer of Christ Church in 1633 and bishop of Derry the follow-ing year. Among the bishops of the 1630s, none would play a more significant role in attempting to bring the Church of Ireland into conformity with the new-look Church of England. Atherton too had a part to play on the larger national stage. In June 1634 he was chosen by the chapter to represent them at the meeting of convo-cation—the church body which met concurrently with the parlia-ment, now summoned for the first time in Ireland since 1613. In 1615, Convocation had formulated the Irish Articles, a more emphatically Calvinist statement of belief than was ever adopted in England. The 1634 Convocation, under the influence of Bramhall and Sir Thomas Wentworth, replaced these with the Thirty-Nine Articles of the English Church, and also accepted a version of the English canons of 1604, a set of disciplinary regulations which would make it easier to hound puritans from the ranks of the clergy. Atherton clearly did his bit. Bramhall praised the 'much judgement and moderation' he had displayed during Convocation's proceedings.[6]

Meanwhile, Atherton was placing the finances of Christ Church on a more sustainable footing, becoming chief enforcer of rent arrears, with authority from the chapter to use all necessary means to get defaulters to pay up. At the same time, he took steps to regulate the life of a sometimes fractious religious community, bringing in new rules to tighten discipline among the choristers and vicars choral who sang services in the cathedral. They did not always take it well. After he docked the wages of one of the vicars choral for persistent absenteeism, the man called him 'ass, idle, base and saucy fellow', and was made to beg Atherton's pardon on his knees during divine service in the cathedral. The same fate befell another vicar choral, who gave 'contemptuous and disobedient speeches' to Atherton when he rebuked him for drunkenness. Such behaviour, the chapter noted, was 'a scandal to his calling and our religion'. Few of its members could have suspected that only a few years later almost identical phrases would be used across the nation in connection with Atherton himself.[7]

While Atherton was safeguarding the interests of the cathedral in these years, he was also looking out for number one. The accumulation of offices was hardly unusual in the Irish Church, but it was pursued by Atherton with zealous tenacity. In 1634, he became chancellor of the diocese of Killaloe in the west of Ireland. He was also made rector of two parishes to the south-west of Dublin: Killaban and Ballintubber. His interest in these places was fiscal not pastoral. In 1635, he secured an order commanding the High Sheriff of the Queen's County to establish him 'in the quiet and peaceable possession of the rectory of Killaban ... and of all the tithes, lands, duties, profits and emoluments, whatsoever thereunto belonging'.

There was one valuable source of revenue, however, that Atherton had possessed long before his arrival at Christ Church, and that was his Somerset rectory of Huish Champflower. It became clear that he had absolutely no intention of relinquishing it, despite the fact that the canons of 1604 forbade ministers to hold more than one parish living, unless the two were within thirty miles of each other. Soon after his arrival at Christ Church, Atherton took steps to safeguard his Somerset nest-egg. He turned to his patron Lord

Chancellor Loftus, and in August 1632 was issued with letters of dispensation, allowing him to continue to hold a benefice in England that by law required personal residence, though the dispensation was valid for only six months. Curiously, Atherton produced it at a Christ Church chapter meeting long after its expiry, on 2 June 1634, 'and humbly besought the same might be admitted and recorded'.[8]

In all probability Atherton had become uncomfortably aware of the dim view of 'pluralism' held by William Laud, and wished to advertise some legal precedent for his (now irregular) situation. His patrons, Loftus, Bramhall, and Wentworth, were all wheeled out to petition Laud for a new dispensation, the latter arguing that if Atherton was deprived of his English benefice it would discourage other talented clergymen from seeking preferment in the Irish Church. Yet Laud was implacable. He conceded that he had 'received very good testimony' about Atherton, and of the pains he had taken to recover revenue for the Church. But if Irish churchmen were allowed to hold offices in England, the practice would most probably spread to Scotland too, 'and the Church of England made a stale to both'. In short, the squalid affair of Atherton's pluralism brought Wentworth's agenda for the revitalization of the Church of Ireland into direct conflict with Laud's concern for the integrity of the Church of England. It was, suggested the archbishop, 'to my remembrance the only thing in which your judgement and mine have differed'. Wentworth graciously gave way.[9]

There, however, the matter did not rest, and over the following months Atherton's prevarications over Huish Champflower began increasingly to irritate the archbishop of Canterbury. At first it appeared that he had agreed to resign, and had offered, via Wentworth, to secure as his successor there anyone whom Laud cared to name. Alas, it turned out to be not so straightforward. Rather than simply resign the living, Atherton travelled to England in the autumn of 1635 to try to negotiate advantageous terms. He gained an interview with Archbishop Laud, though the meeting was clearly a frosty one. 'Dr Atherton hath been with me, but so far from resigning his benefice ... all his suit was for longer time to hold it.' The promise to place the choice of successor in Laud's hands was a pledge built upon sand. It transpired that the patron had already committed the succession to another minister, and Laud was inclined to believe that Atherton already knew this when he made his 'fair offer'. More likely, Atherton had become aware of it on his arrival in England, for he sought to make the best of matters by a strategy of dubious legality and still more dubious morality. Approaching his nominated successor (who must have been unaware that Atherton was on the point of being forced to give up the post), he offered to resign immediately on condition that the candidate agreed either to pay him £300, or to marry his (presumably eldest) daughter. This was outright simony—the buying and selling of sacred things—and a besetting sin of the Christian Church ever since the conjuror Simon Magus had offered the Apostles money in exchange for their miracle-working powers. Atherton protested that there had been a misunderstanding: he had merely proposed a marriage treaty to his successor, and requested a suitable dowry. But Laud was not taken in: 'excellent honest simony', he scathingly termed it. The interview concluded with Laud sending Atherton off to his own bishop, William Piers of Bath and Wells. Whatever action Piers decided to take, Laud was nonetheless determined to 'call him to residence'.[10] We do not know whether Atherton actually visited Somerset during the fraught negotiations of September 1635, though it is quite likely that he did. If so, we can only speculate as to whether he made any contact with his wife's family in Minehead, recently bereaved by the death of his mother-in-law, and already—or so they would later claim—troubled by supernatural noises, and portents of something badly amiss.

For the moment, however, none of this was of much concern to the sub-dean of Christ Church, who was riding high in the summer of 1635. In June, Trinity College created him an honorary doctor of divinity. In December, he was promoted from sub-dean to chancellor of Christ Church. By the end of the year a still greater honour was waiting to fall into Atherton's lap. On 27 December 1635, the bishopric of Waterford and Lismore became vacant through the death of Dr Michael Boyle. Atherton was nominated to succeed him. The messy saga of Huish Champflower was now at last resolved—when parish ministers were promoted to bishoprics the right to nominate their successor reverted to the Crown. In February 1636, William Sherley was instituted as rector of Huish. He may, or may not, have been the same man to whom the living had earlier been promised.[11] But the succession to the bishopric of Waterford was no routine administrative matter, and Atherton's appointment to it came only at the end of a contentious and difficult process. For reasons which will shortly become evident, Atherton's promotion was an icon of Wentworth's entire policy for the governance of the Irish Church. For a time, it seemed to have been a triumphant vindication of that policy's priorities and methods. In the end, it was to become a ringing metaphor for their failure, and a cause of scandal and disgrace echoing across two kingdoms.

The bishopric of Waterford and Lismore (the adjacent dioceses had been conjoined in the fourteenth century) lay along the south-east coast of Ireland, between Wexford to the north-east and Cork to the south-west (Figure 6). In the seventeenth century, Lismore was an inconsequential sort of place, but the episcopal seat of Waterford had for centuries been a leading trade and commercial centre. The English traveller, William Brereton, passing through in 1634, noted it to be 'reputed one of the richest towns in Ireland'. Its ships regularly plied their trade with the ports of south-west England, Minehead among them. News of the appointment of a new bishop, and of a local boy made good in Ireland, must rapidly have crossed the Irish Sea in the early spring of 1636. It cannot be mere coincidence that its arrival in Minehead coincided precisely with the first reported sightings of the ghost of the new bishop's mother-in-law.

In the early 1630s, the diocese of Waterford and Lismore was a shadow of its former self, an archetype of everything that seemed to be wrong with the Church of Ireland. Its bishops were impoverished, having lost buildings, estates, and patronage to powerful lay

6. South-east Ireland in the 1630s

landowners. Their spiritual authority was likewise decayed. Though there were some Protestants in Waterford itself, the majority in town and county alike was resolutely Catholic. When full-scale Catholic rebellion broke out in Ireland in 1641, the town of Waterford became a centre of resistance to the English regime and, for a time, the home of a papal nuncio, who dubbed the place *Parva Roma*, a little Rome.[12]

This was still in the future when the new Lord Deputy, Thomas Wentworth, took office in 1633. Yet from the outset, Waterford loomed large in Wentworth's plans for reform. This was not because it epitomized the Catholic threat. To the mind of Wentworth, and trusted lieutenants like Bramhall, there was little point in harassing Catholics while the Church of Ireland itself was in no fit state to effect an orderly Reformation. Before that could happen, there was a pressing need to establish doctrinal and liturgical conformity among Protestants themselves, and to address the jurisdictional and financial toothlessness of the church as an institution. The rogues' gallery of Wentworth's imagination was largely peopled not with papist priests, but with divisive and seditious presbyterians, malcontents who wished to see a Church without bishops, and with 'impropriators' among the Protestant gentry—those who had contrived to get into their own hands tithes and other revenues properly pertaining to the clergy, and who often refused even to find a decent wage for a curate to serve the living.

As Wentworth viewed the matter, all these malefactions were summed up in the person of one man: Richard Boyle, first earl of Cork. Cork was the epitome of the self-made New English landowner. Son of a Kentish yeoman, he had gone to seek his fortune in Ireland in the momentous year of 1588. Through a series of astute purchases and judicious marriages, as well as an acute legal nose for the flaws in other men's titles to land, he managed to build up a huge estate. With wealth came political distinction: a knighthood in 1603, membership of the Irish Privy Council in 1613, an earldom in 1620. In 1629 Cork was appointed (alongside Atherton's patron, Loftus) as one of the Lords Justice of Ireland, and in 1631 as High Treasurer. By this time, his income was greater than that of any of Charles I's other subjects. Yet a considerable portion of this wealth had been acquired at the expense of the church, most particularly, the diocese of Lismore.

From the moment of his arrival in Ireland, Wentworth began to plot against the earl of Cork, and looked to bring him low.[13] In

January 1634 he sent Laud a detailed inventory of properties he intended to get out of Cork's hands, a list commencing with 'what his lordship has gotten forth out of the bishopric of Lismore'. He might have added that Cork's imposing castle at Lismore was actually the former bishop's palace, rebuilt with materials taken from the ruined cathedral. Cork's retention of the Lismore lands, on long leases or at nominal rents, seemed to Wentworth nothing less than 'a direct rapine upon the patrimony of the church, a coal taken from the altar'.

The implications for the actual holder of the bishopric of Waterford were made pitifully clear in a petition which the current incumbent Michael Boyle (a cousin of the earl of Cork) was induced to present to Archbishop Laud in March 1634 at the instigation of Wentworth's henchman Bishop John Bramhall. The earl held Lismore diocesan property worth £900 a year, 'fraudulently made away with by my predecessors', and had seized many parish livings. Boyle claimed to receive only around £50 a year from Waterford and Lismore combined, though the diocese was on paper worth thirty times this. He begged Laud to assist him, since 'you are now so great, and as we were at college together'. The archbishop was unmoved by the appeal to halcyon student days: his letters show that he considered Bishop Boyle a time-server, a wind-bag, and a fool. Yet he was no less indignant than Wentworth was about the underlying issue. Laud made sure that the king himself was well informed about the 'great sacrileges in that kingdom', and was dismissive of a reported offer by Cork to rebuild the cathedral at Lismore: 'I will believe it when I see it.'[14]

Already in 1634, Wentworth had formed a plan. It occurred to him that the grants and leases which Cork had acquired had been ratified only by the dean and chapter of Lismore. If the dioceses were fully united, then it could be argued that they required the consent of the dean and chapter of Waterford as well, and could be unpicked in the courts. The stratagem was at best a finely legalistic one, which showed little regard for property rights as they were understood and cherished at the time. But as Wentworth remarked to Laud in March 1635, the Church could not hope to be restored 'unless a little violence and extraordinary means be used for the raising again, as there has been for the pulling down'.[15]

This then was the context in which John Atherton found himself nominated to the Irish bench of bishops in early 1636. Having identified Lismore as the soft underbelly of Cork's hegemony, Wentworth needed a pit bull in the diocese, someone to lead the attack, and to resist being, as a previous holder of the office plaintively put it, 'boyled to death'. Atherton, the tough lawyer who had proved himself aggressively competent in his management of Christ Church's finances, seemed just the man. But the appointment did not proceed without difficulties, or without some serious soul-searching on all sides; all sides, that is, but Atherton's own.

The candidacy was first broached in a letter from Wentworth to Laud in January 1636. The vacancy at Waterford represented both opportunity and danger. The earl of Cork was reportedly willing to give £100 to set his own candidate in the diocese. It would, Wentworth reflected, be 'very difficult to find a fit man for it, considering the revenue of that bishopric is very mean'. Yet the Church needed 'a man of spirit and understanding', someone 'thoroughly to prosecute the rights thereof'. Whoever he was, he would have to be allowed to retain his current living, 'else I fear no fit and sufficient person will accept of it' (an unwelcome message for Laud to hear). It occurred to Wentworth that 'Dr Atherton, for the soliciting part, and recovering the rights of the bishopric were very fit'. But something gave him pause: 'I hold him not so fit to be the bishop.' Laud too had his doubts: 'better Dr Atherton than a worse, though, for my part, I like nothing in him at all but his soliciting part'. Other candidates were considered, but as Wentworth reflected on the matter he became increasingly convinced that Atherton was the man for the job. 'There is exception against the man, I confess', but he was the kind of character 'the deplorable state of that bishopric requires'. There would also be a delightful bonus: the earl of Cork 'will think the devil is let loose upon him forth off his chain. I will undertake there is not such a terrier in England or Ireland for the unkennelling of an old fox'. There was no gainsaying the Lord

Deputy on this matter, and Laud duly secured the appointment. Serious misgivings, however, remained: 'I confess clearly to you, since I had speech with him in England, I have no opinion of his worth or honesty. I pray God I be deceived.'

The deal was done; the bargain struck. On 5 April 1636, the King wrote to the Lord Deputy, appointing John Atherton to be bishop of Waterford and Lismore. On 28 May, in a ceremony in Christ Church, Atherton was consecrated by four of his new episcopal colleagues: Archbishop Lancelot Bulkeley of Dublin, Bishop Richard Boyle of Cork, Cloyne and Ross (another cousin of the earl), Bishop Lewis Jones of Killaloe, and Bishop John Richardson of Ardagh. Ironically enough, this was something of a roll-call of the easygoing old-style prelates whom Wentworth considered unfit for purpose in the reconstruction of the Irish Church. But with the promotion of Atherton the balance was shifting. Already the Laudians John Bramhall and Henry Leslie had been appointed to the presbyterian-infected Ulster dioceses of Derry, and Down and Connor. Over the next couple of years they were to be joined by a succession of reliably on-message advocates of the Laud–Wentworth project. The venerable Calvinist primate of All Ireland, James Ussher of Armagh, increasingly looked like yesterday's man.[16]

With Atherton installed at Waterford, the unkennelling of the earl of Cork could get properly under way. Cork had already been summoned before the Irish Privy Council in October 1634 to answer charges relating to irregularities in the acquisition of church lands. By May 1636, he had been forced to return twelve impropriations worth £500 a year, and had agreed to pay a fine of £15,000. Meanwhile, Atherton had launched no fewer than five separate suits against the earl to regain episcopal lands and impropriated rectories. By February 1637, he had recovered the site of the bishop's palace at Waterford, and was pressing ahead with the test case of Lismore. By the summer, Cork was ready to come to terms. In July, a treaty was drafted which allowed him to retain the castle and manor of Lismore, and lands of Bewley and Killomlash. In return, he agreed to surrender the manors of Ardmore, Kilbree, and New Affane, and to pay Atherton £500 to build a new episcopal residence. In August,

Wentworth confirmed the arrangement, and Laud pronounced 'the agreement between Lord Cork and the Bishop of Waterford very happily ended to the great advancement of that see'. Bramhall predicted that by the following Easter the revenue of the bishopric would have risen from the measly £50 Atherton inherited to nearly £1,000 a year.[17]

Yet, as the restoration of Waterford and Lismore continued apace, a curious matter had come to the attention of Archbishop Laud at his palace at Croydon. In early December 1636 he decided to write to Wentworth about it:

> At this instant here is great news out of Somersetshire, that one Mrs Leakey, who died about two years since, does often appear and trouble her son's house, and lately appeared to his wife, her daughter-in-law, and charged her to go into Ireland, and deliver a message to Bishop Atherton, who, they say, married a daughter of the said Mrs Leakey, and that she promised to meet her there. The message which she has to deliver to the Bishop she will not tell to any but himself, and purposes to come into Ireland on purpose for it. You may believe what you list of this; but some people, of very good quality, do affirm this, and a great deal more. But what will appear truth in the end, God knows.

The report clearly had Laud worried. The fact that people of quality were giving credit to the appearance of an apparition with secrets to reveal to, or about, a bishop of the Established Church was no laughing matter. The archbishop certainly considered it an episode of some political danger, and saw it as part of a developing pattern of subversion. He linked it with 'a notorious libel' against himself which had appeared in a recent puritan treatise against Sabbath-breaking, and with 'another in form of a curanto' (i.e. a newsletter) directed against the ultra-Laudian bishop of Norwich. He apologized to the Lord Deputy for having 'so much of this kind of stuff to write unto you', but predicted that such libels would be forerunners of still worse things if the government failed to take a firm line.

Sir Thomas Wentworth's nature was more sanguine. His inclination was to treat the matter lightly, while not altogether making light of it. 'I will enquire after Mrs Leakey and her errand, and if it be to be met with, I will learn what the devil has to say to the Bishop of Waterford, sure I am the earl of Cork wishes them together already.' This set the tone for a series of half-facetious, half-earnest exchanges about the Leakey affair which peppered the correspondence between Wentworth and Laud over the following eight months. In January 1637, Laud wrote that 'the king has commanded me to write to the Bishop of Bath and Wells to take some justices to him and examine the business'. When the examination had been sent to him, Laud promised to write again with word of 'what her errand is, if by that I can learn it'. Wentworth professed himself 'glad to understand what it is Mistress Leakey has to say to my Lord of Waterford'. The initiative, we can be fairly sure, was Laud's own, but it does seem more than likely that the rumours from Minehead had been brought to the attention of the King himself. The mystery of why the county's top justices were investigating what one historian of Somerset has called 'the most trivial and time-consuming' matter ever to be referred to their attention is starting to resolve itself. Atherton was a politically controversial and high-profile recent episcopal appointee, and one about whom Laud already had his doubts. As a former bishop of Bath and Wells (and someone who had conducted an archiepiscopal visitation of the diocese in 1634), Laud had many contacts in Somerset, and the disquieting rumours must rapidly have come to his attention. It is a small but revealing instance of how the problems of local, national, and 'British' governance might intersect, and require coordinated action.

Yet the picture remained cloudy. Laud was unable to tell Wentworth what Mrs Leakey wished to say to the bishop, though by the beginning of April he was able to update him about developments with which we are already familiar:

This I can tell you, the Bishop of Bath and Wells, and Sir Robert Phelips, and Dr Godwyn, have, by the King's command, examined that business of the apparition, and certainly it is a fiction and a practice, but to what end cannot be discovered. And the younger woman, at that part of the examination, stood still to it that she had a charge not to utter that to any but to Dr Atherton, yet to the King and him only she would tell it if he commanded. If she come over into Ireland (as she says she will), it may be that and more may be fished out of her; but a cunning young woman I hear she is, and her husband in decay. And, therefore, I doubt it may be some money business.

We can perhaps sense here the archbishop's relief that the Leakey affair now seemed to be a straightforward matter of extortion or embezzlement, with no sinister political overtones. He allowed himself a little joke: 'there is some use of the Bishop of Waterford's forty pounds per annum, which you say he has recovered, if he cannot tell otherwise what to do with it'. In July, Wentworth reported that

I have nothing more of Mistress Leakey or her familiar, but if money be that they aim at, it must be a strong and crafty devil that gets any of the bishop's purse. For money will not be thence cast out, no not without much fasting and prayer, as firmly seated there than the strongest of those devils we read of elsewhere.

This was urbane and witty, if decidedly cynical stuff. Wentworth combined (mildly affectionate?) jibes about the notorious close-fistedness of Bishop Atherton with mocking allusion to popular beliefs about witches' familiars (pet demons), as well as to the practice of exorcism of those possessed by evil spirits. By the 1630s exorcism was firmly associated with the two groups Wentworth regarded as his principal enemies in Ireland: papists and puritans. It was the latter, indeed, who utilized 'fasting and prayer', rather than set formulae, as the means of driving devils out. Laud touched on the subject just once more, in August 1637, and reheated the Lord Deputy's little joke: 'certainly that business of Mrs Leakey was a money business; and if that devil be so fast knit up in the Bishop's purse, it seems they will have but a cold pluck of it'. In any case, he concluded, 'that matter is now quite out of speech'.[18] And with that, two of the greatest men in the early Stuart state could stop having to discuss the babblings and schemings of obscure Somerset folk, and get on with the business of governing King Charles's three realms. As for young Mrs Leakey, if she did come to Ireland, either to meet with Bishop Atherton, or with the teleported spirit of her mother-in-law, the resources of the Lord Deputy do not seem to have detected it. In Ireland, of course, the resources of the Lord Deputy were very far from infinite. The actions of Elizabeth Leakey in the spring or summer of 1637 are of considerable significance for our story, but must remain, for the moment, obscure.

Bishop John Atherton can hardly have been unaware of the rumours circulating in Somerset, and now, perhaps, in Ireland, about messages for him from beyond the grave. But they did not deflect him from the courses on which he had set himself. After the (partial) victory over the earl of Cork in the summer of 1637, the campaign to restore the rights of Waterford showed no signs of letting up. The pace was quickened by the placing of reliable supporters within the diocesan administration. In the early part of 1637, Arthur Gwyn, a minister whom Wentworth had used to lever three impropriated parishes away from Cork in 1635, was created archdeacon of Lismore and successfully sued for the restoration of two more. The following year, Cork was forced to surrender his leases of twenty-eight acres belonging to the treasurership of Lismore, after Francis Kettleby was appointed to the office and began a suit for their return. In March 1638, the dispute over the Lismore lands was finally settled, with the enactment of the agreement of the previous summer. Cork punctiliously recorded in his diary the deeds—and the 'five hundred pounds in gold'—that he had personally handed over to 'the L. Bishop of Waterford' in the chapter house at Lismore. By now, Atherton had become (at least in his aggressive litigiousness) a model for other bishops to emulate, and Wentworth was keen to move him on to work his magic elsewhere. When the bishopric of Cork, Cloyne and Ross became vacant, the Lord Deputy believed that Atherton would prove 'a marvellous fit instrument to settle the bishopric... by recovering at least £800 a year to those churches'. A royal order for the translation was secured in May 1638, though Laud made clear that it was 'a business which I confess I like not', and that the King himself was beginning to demur about it. The 'Leakey business' had perhaps after all begun to cast a shadow over Atherton's prospects. In the end, a planned reshuffle of several bishops failed to materialize, and Atherton stayed where he was.

The earl of Cork was not alone in feeling the force of the bishop of Waterford's restless energy. An account of the landed income of the bishopric, compiled in 1660 by the registrar of the diocese, Joshua Boyle (another kinsman of the earl!), provides striking evidence of Atherton's tenacity in pursuit of his perceived rights. From it we learn of half a ploughland at Bishops Court, 'yielded up by Nicholas Wise'; of a ploughland at Kilronan, handed over by Sir Thomas Sherlock; of leases of lands at Keiloge and Kilmacleague, surrendered by Peter Archdeacon; of a half ploughland at Kilcarragh, disgorged by Richard Butler. Unlike previous bishops, Atherton followed through. An attempt in James I's reign to question the validity of a sixteenth-century lease of lands at Donoughmore came to nothing. But Atherton reopened the case in the court of chancery, summoning before it the present lease-holders, Piers Butler and his son Theobald, and securing a decree for its annulment. The result was the restoration to the bishopric of a litany of lands that must have been as hard for the English bishop to pronounce as they have been for modern scholars to identify: Ballyhemmikeen, Rathnetowne, Ballytonchester, Ffaren Coytie, Bregoge, Ballybegg, Cloghenm'cody. There were other leases too which, without doubt, 'John, late Lord Bishop had voided if he had lived', and several further cases proceeding in the chancery, 'abated by the said bishop's unhappy trouble'.[19]

That unhappy trouble was still unforeseen in the autumn of 1638, as the earl of Cork departed for the court in London, anxious to restore himself to the royal favour which his long-running feud with Wentworth had jeopardized. But news of the machinations of Bishop Atherton were regularly relayed to him. The most assiduous correspondents were the faithful steward of his Lismore estates, John Walley, and the dean of Lismore, Robert Naylor, a maternal cousin of the earl, and one of the few Boyle loyalists to remain in the upper reaches of the diocesan administration. His removal to the deanery of Limerick in the spring of 1640 was in his own estimation 'the Bishop of Lismore's plot', designed to enable his successor to sue for more of the earl's lands. This was after the bishop had hypocritically protested that 'it should not be in the power of the devil himself to cause any distance or difference between your lordship and him'. Walley agreed it was all Atherton's doing, and the bishop's practices provoked an outpouring of denunciation from the excitable Lismore steward: 'like hungry wolves the churchmen now look, and come round about where to snatch and catch a prey, not regarding either right or wrong'.

Walley was the earl's loyal servant, but at times insufficiently discreet in the execution of his master's affairs. After a generous reception at court in December 1638, the earl sent him an account of his triumph, but in his cups Walley boasted of Cork's English successes (and perhaps threatened comeuppance to his enemies at home). According to Cork's son-in-law, Lord Barrymore, 'the coxcomb was so drunk coming from Waterford that he read it [the letter] at Dungarvan to all the country'. What was more, 'in a drunken humour' he had given it to Bishop Atherton to read, and the bishop of Derry (Bramhall) now had a copy. Naylor added that the bishop had summoned Walley to Waterford where, 'the gentlemen of that city having warmed him with sack', Atherton prevailed upon him to hand over the earl's letter. He then immediately forwarded it to Wentworth's government in Dublin. As a result, 'whereas before, your lordship's occasions and suits went on in a calm, quiet way, new storms presently arose and every man had free access and audience against your lordship'.[20]

Between them, the dean and the steward of Lismore repeatedly warned the earl that 'the most proud and insulting bishop' was plotting to betray and undermine him at every turn. They also sought to reassure their patron that they were doing all in their power to thwart the bishop's malevolent designs. Thus when a commission was granted to Atherton to investigate the status of ancient lazar (leper) houses in Munster and Leinster, Walley activated a plan to safeguard his master's possession of the lands of the defunct Lismore lazar house: 'if I can hear of a leper in all of these parts (whereof I am diligent to inquire) I will put him into one of the two houses that are now void' (history does not record whether he was successful in his epidemiological quest). Tales were told that Atherton was plotting to get into his own hands all the 'advowsons' (rights to nominate rectors and vicars) of parishes historically in the gift of the earl of Cork. In one disputed case, Naylor (pouring oil on the fire) reported that 'his lordship's cavil (I remember) was that your honour had not given him *omnem reverentiam et honorem tanto patri dignum* (all the reverence and honour due to a father)'. Gratuitously, he added, 'such a father I think the Church of Ireland has not; we could wish him removed into Scotland'. This was a political rather than an ethnic joke, and a slightly risky one at that. In February 1638 an assembly of Scottish notables had signed a 'National Covenant' to resist Charles and Laud's attempts to introduce a version of the English Prayer Book north of the border. They resoundingly rejected episcopacy—the government of the church by bishops—in favour of a presbyterian system of self-disciplining congregations functioning under the oversight of presbyteries, synods, and assemblies. The following summer, in the first of the so-called 'Bishops' Wars', the Covenanters soundly defeated the English forces sent to show them the error of their ways.

Yet if a storm of anti-episcopal sentiment was brewing on both sides of the Irish Sea, Atherton remained oblivious to it, and continued to exercise the prerogatives of his office to the full. In December 1639, for example, Walley complained of fines of fifteen shillings and more that the bishop was imposing for the 'crime' of eating meat during Lent. There were also arguments about where the justices of the peace for the County of Waterford should meet, Atherton being determined that all jurisdiction should emanate from his episcopal seat, the town of Waterford. In 1639 there was open schism, with a rump of pro-Atherton JPs meeting in Waterford, while opponents held their sessions at Tallow, in the south-east of the county on the border with County Cork. Fines, writs, and affidavits fired in both directions, as Dean Naylor lamented that 'there is never a church or county in England [or Ireland] so out of control and disordered as this now is'.[21]

Atherton's penchant for high-handed clerical authority had one other outlet in these years. In February 1636, Wentworth reconstituted the Court of High Commission in Ireland, a body of clergy and leading laymen first established in Elizabeth's reign with special powers to help enforce the Reformation. In its 1630s incarnation, the court was predictably more concerned with the rights and privileges of the Church, and with pursuing Protestant nonconformists, particularly the presbyterians in Ulster. The fragmentary surviving records of High Commission's activities suggest that Atherton was a regular member of the court through the later 1630s. Some of the cases over which he deliberated concerned the prosecution of impropriators for defaulting over the payment of curates' salaries, others involved the punishment of sexual immorality. But the most notorious High Commission case with which Atherton was associated was a more blatantly political one. In October 1639, Archibald Adair, the Scots-born bishop of Killala and Achonry in the far west of Ireland, was summoned before the commissioners 'for certain words alleged to be spoken by him against the Scottish bishops'. His nemesis was a fellow Scot, John Corbet, an ultra-Laudian minister who had left his native land and ended up in Killala after publishing a pugnacious tract against the Covenanters. Adair made no secret of where his sympathies lay, reportedly mocking the minister as 'an impure corbie thrust out of God's ark'. (Corbie is the Scots dialect word for a carrion crow, and the allusion is to the raven which Noah sent forth from the ark in Genesis 8: 7, and which 'went forth and to until the waters were dried up'.) Worse, Adair had belittled the predicament of the Scots bishops, blaming them for the troubles there and saying 'I wish they had all been in hell'. Atherton was later reported to have been fierce in his condemnation of Adair's conduct, and the punishment when it came was certainly draconian. In February 1640, Adair was fined

£2,000, sentenced to indefinite imprisonment, and deposed from his bishopric. Appropriately enough, one of the Scots bishops he had slandered was nominated his successor.[22]

Atherton had no tears to shed for Adair, nor is it likely that he spilt many when a yet more significant figure, his former patron, Loftus, fell dramatically from favour. Loftus was a rival power broker to Wentworth, and had been living on borrowed time; there had long been complaints of corruption against him. In May 1638, he was stripped of the lord chancellorship, and temporarily imprisoned.[23] Secure in the favour of a seemingly unassailable Lord Deputy, John Atherton could look on with equanimity as the wheel of fortune turned.

The bishop of Waterford's own fortunes seemed at their zenith at the dawn of 1640, a year that would prove as momentous for Atherton personally as it would be for the British state as a whole. A parliament was summoned to commence on 16 March, and Atherton, along with the other prelates of the Irish Church, made his way to Dublin Castle to take his seat in the Irish House of Lords. On 20 March, the two houses conjoined to hear an opening speech by the newly appointed speaker of the Commons, Sir Maurice Eustace, MP for County Kildare. He began by praising Thomas Wentworth, recently promoted to Lord Lieutenant of Ireland and created earl of Strafford, as 'another *Solon* or *Lycurgus*', who had brought peace to a troubled land. Casting his eyes theatrically about the hall, Eustace lighted next on 'the glorious lights of our Church, the most reverend archbishops and bishops, who show us the true *via lactea* [Milky Way], which leads into heaven'. Shifting his metaphor slightly, Eustace went on:

> When your Lordship came first amongst us, the most of these lights did but burn dim, and many of them were like to be extinguished for want of oil ... But your lordship's first care was that their lamps, as most fit, should be trimmed and replenished, and that these lights, which show us the way to heaven, should be

placed in golden candlesticks, and so the thief which wasted the
candle was taken away.

Atherton must have preened to hear the policies with which he was
so closely associated described in such glowing (if euphemistic)
terms. But there were others who may have bristled as the enco-
mium proceeded. Among the MPs sitting for the county and
borough of Waterford in 1640 were Richard Butler, whom Atherton
had sued in 1637 for the recovery of lands, and John Power, who in
1639 had accepted an unfavourable arbitration with the bishop 'for
avoidance of suits in law'. Catholics both, Butler and Power may
have had their own opinions about Wentworth's imported Protestant bishops lighting the way to salvation. Resuming his astronomical metre, Eustace then began to praise the nobles of the land, no
longer fiery comets, but stars fixed in their sphere 'following our
Charles-Wain'. This was a clever image, and probably the starting
point for the whole wordy confection: Charles' Wain was the
contemporary name for the Great Bear or Big Dipper; a wain was
a wagon or chariot. It would, Eustace effused, be as easy to 'pluck a
star out of the fixed firmament, as to draw any of these from their
loyalty and obedience'.

Yet the conventional language of unity and deference masked a
complex pattern of factional alignments, and a political world
starting to shift on its very axis. The Irish House of Commons in
1640 contained a core 'government party', but there were numerous
other members looking to the interests of Cork or other aristocratic
leaders, as well as a sprinkling of Ulster Scots, sympathetic to the
cause of their ethnic and religious brethren in rebellion against
Charles I. Of the 240 or so MPs, around a third were Catholics,
looking to wring concessions from a weakened central government
in London. Wentworth meanwhile had been recalled to England in
the autumn of 1639. He returned briefly for the opening of the
parliament, but his brief in government was now to take charge of
the quelling of the Scottish insurrection. Irish affairs were left in the
hands of his cousin and friend Sir Christopher Wandesford, who
was installed as the new Lord Deputy in April 1640. The Scottish

crisis was the reason the Irish Parliament had been summoned into existence at all. Like its cousin, the 'Short Parliament' in England, it was supposed to supply funds for the repression of the Covenanters, and to finance the recruitment of a new Irish army for use against the Scots.[24]

Things started well enough. By 23 March, the commons had done what was expected of them and approved a bill to grant subsidies to the Crown. The following day, Atherton was one of twelve lords appointed to meet with representatives of the commons 'to congratulate their cheerful giving'. After the agreement to grant the taxes, the most immediate business was the drafting of a declaration to be appended to the Subsidy Act, professing willingness to pay out future sums, and exhorting the rebellious Scots to come to their senses. Over the week leading up to the suspension (or prorogation) of parliament on 31 March, Atherton exerted himself as a busy and loyal member of the government team, urging the peers to sign the declaration with 'no scruple', and performing useful service on the parliamentary committee on privileges and grievances. All in all, the session of March 1640 had been a great success from the government's point of view: it had 'managed' parliament, securing grants of taxation without having to make embarrassing concessions in return. Yet on the morning of the final day, one of the bishops (it is not clear which) made an egregious *faux pas*, proposing that the bishop of Killala, Archibald Adair, might be sent his writ of summons. Speaking for the government, John Bramhall was frosty in his response. Adair had been justly censured and deprived as 'a favourer of the Covenant of Scotland'. He was a man 'fit to be thrown into the sea in a sack, not to see the sun, not to enjoy the air'.[25] Yet for Atherton and for Bramhall, the days of such lordly ascendancy were fast drawing to a close. Fortuna's Wheel was turning once more.

The Irish Parliament was suspended rather than dissolved in March 1640, because the government had further business that it did not want to become entangled with the business of securing subsidies—principally, a proposal of Wentworth's for the plantation of Connacht. The cooperation seen in March was not, however, replicated in the parliament which met again on 1 June. A distinct mood of truculence prevailed, with disconcerting evidence of coordination between Old and New English opponents of the government's policies. Writs for attendance were issued to seven Old English boroughs, which Wentworth had disenfranchised in the 1630s; the bill for the plantation of Connacht disappeared terminally into a committee; another committee (with Catholic and Protestant representation) was drawn up to prepare a list of grievances against the exactions of the clergy. In short, the government had lost control of the commons, and on 17 June, only two weeks into the session, Wandesford prorogued parliament again till 1 October.

On the same day, a petition was delivered to the House of Commons. The MPs immediately established an eight-man committee to attend upon the Lord Deputy and acquaint him with its contents. The petition was, as the commons' *Journal* recorded, 'preferred by John Child against the Lord Bishop of Waterford', and the committee was to ask Sir Christopher Wandesford 'to take a course for the securing as well of the said John Child, as the said Lord Bishop, to answer the said petition and allegations, in such manner as his lordship, in his great wisdom, shall think most fit'. The diarist Sir James Ware was less mealy-mouthed in his recording of the incident: 'John Atherton, bishop of Waterford and Lismore, was accused in the house of commons by one John Child his servant to have committed sodomy with the said John Child. Whereupon the house appointed a committee to desire the Lord Deputy that both their persons might be secured till it came to a trial, lest either should escape.'[26] The world of John Atherton was about to come tumbling down, and many long-suppressed secrets would begin spilling forth into the light.

4

The Shameful End of Bishop Atherton

'**A** detestable and abominable sin, amongst Christians not to be named, committed by carnal knowledge against the ordinance of the creator, and order of nature.' This was how the eminent English jurist, one-time attorney-general, and scourge of the Gunpowder Plotters, Sir Edward Coke, described the crime of 'buggery or sodomy'. He went on to define the act as involving '*penetratio*, that is, *res in re* [thing in thing], either with mankind, or with beast'. It was for this most heinous of moral offences that John Atherton was tried, convicted, and executed in the last months of 1640. In England, sodomy had been a capital crime for more than a hundred years; Henry VIII's parliament had passed an Act in 1533 making 'the detestable and abominable vice of buggery' into a felony punishable by hanging. In Ireland, by contrast, it had been a hanging offence for only six years, after the parliament of 1634 belatedly enacted the English legislation. The timing has struck several commentators as significant. Only three years earlier, a sensational trial had taken place in England, culminating in the execution of the nobleman Mervyn Touchet, eleventh Baron Audley, and second earl of Castlehaven. The earl had committed acts of sodomy with his servants and helped one of them to rape his (the earl's) wife. Although Touchet was domiciled in England, his family's background was in Ireland, and the earldom of Castlehaven was an Irish title. The furore created by this juiciest of *causes célèbres* may have prompted the authorities to notice the deficiencies of Irish law. But it is equally plausible that the Act was passed as part of a more general policy of catch-up with the moral, social, and economic measures already on the English statute book. In addition to the sodomy legislation, the 1634 parliament passed bills concerning bigamy, usury, swearing and cursing, the regulation of alehouses, the preservation of fisheries, as well as the sonorously titled 'act concerning women convicted of small felonies'.

The notorious Castlehaven case aside, the number of persons convicted of sodomy in England or Ireland in the late sixteenth and early seventeenth centuries appears to have been remarkably small. In part at least, this was due to the difficulties of securing a conviction, or of cases coming anywhere near the courts in the first place. As a consensual sexual act between two adults, sodomy was not a crime likely to produce too many reliable witnesses, even in a world where men habitually shared beds with each other in crowded inns and servants' quarters. Since, in Coke's phrase, 'both the agent and the consentient are felons', there was clearly little incentive for the one to inform upon the other: it was a self-incriminating act.[1] All of this renders deeply perplexing the circumstances in which Atherton's steward, John Child, so publicly implicated himself in the execution of a serious felony. It was a step which was to have momentous consequences for both of the men involved, and which was to set in motion the long process of memory, reflection, and debate about John Atherton which makes it possible to attempt to write a book about him today.

In late June 1640, the revelations about Bishop Atherton landed like a hot potato in the lap of the new Lord Deputy, Sir Christopher Wandesford. A few days after Child's petition was presented in parliament, Wandesford wrote about the matter to another of the Wentworth clique, the lawyer George Radcliffe. Wandesford clearly shared our perplexity about the source of the petition: it was remarkable, he observed, that it had been 'exhibited by the party himself'. He also warned Radcliffe that 'you will, as all civil men do here, blush when you see what stuff is in it'. A week later, Wandesford reported that the bishop had been granted bail, and added wearily that 'here be few who pity him. I must watch that he have a fair and just proceeding, or else it will go the worse with him.'

While all this was happening, Atherton himself seems to have been in denial, or at least to have decided to face out the allegations with a display of maximum public insouciance. After the close of the parliamentary session, the Lord Deputy, accompanied by the bishops and lay peers, prepared as usual to attend divine service in Atherton's old stamping ground of Christ Church cathedral. It was reported that the bishop had 'fitted himself in all his pontificalibus [i.e. his episcopal robes] to give his attendance, before he has any ways cleared himself of the foul offences'. Wandesford, however, quickly sent word forbidding him to attend, and a few days later, Atherton was committed to gaol in Dublin Castle, where he remained until the commencement of his trial in November.

Through the long summer of 1640, as political storm clouds gathered on both sides of the Irish Sea, news and rumour intensified about the bishop of Waterford's alleged depravities. Someone who was taking a keen interest in the accumulating evidence of scandal and debauchery was his old foe, the earl of Cork's steward, John Walley. His letters to Cork could scarcely contain his glee at the downfall of Atherton: 'the bishop of Waterford is now discovered, and his most filthy and odious sins of sodomy and adultery laid open to the world'. Child's accusation was no longer the whole of the matter. Walley had heard of 'his sodomy with two youths that waited upon him', as well as 'adulteries and adulterate attempts', crimes 'so many and the manner so vile and detestable as no modest tongue can make relations thereof'. Old scores were clearly now being settled. As Walley put it, 'his extortions have now set open many men's mouths'. Already, the examinations into the bishop's 'wicked ways' had taken up 'six or seven quires of paper'. Yet Walley did not wish to appear too remorselessly vindictive: 'God give him grace to repent, that whether he live or die, he may become a new creature.'

Another account of the unfolding Atherton scandal was meanwhile being sent to Edward Viscount Conway, an English peer with Irish connections. His informant was the professional newsletter writer, Edmund Rossingham, who reported a rumour, circulating 'a good while', that a bishop had been arrested for 'foul offences'. Rossingham was able to confirm that it was the bishop of Waterford, 'whom a man servant of his doth accuse to have buggered him at several times', and who 'does heartily deny the charge'. Once again, the circumstances struck the observer as odd: 'his servant does as heartily accuse him, although he does well know it, that he must suffer death for exposing himself willingly to the other's filthiness'. Rossingham added that 'many other foul offences are since brought against him', including 'some adulteries and single fornications' which the bishop did not deny. It was becoming clear, in fact, that the bishop of Waterford's parallel life as a sexual predator had been an open secret in some sections of Irish society. Rossingham had heard 'that no man whatsoever was more severe in his sentence in the High Commission court in Ireland against incontinent persons than this bishop was'. Yet a man being sentenced there for fornication, 'and observing that bishop to be much more severe than all the rest of his judges' had told him to his face that he was surprised to be treated so harshly, 'the bishop himself being guilty to his knowledge of the like transgression'. There was talk of a bawdy house, and of a shilling given to a wench, 'which wench his lordship took from him for his own use'. Swift action had been taken to preserve Atherton's reputation: the man was punished by the court of Star Chamber 'for scandalising a judge in a court Christian'. But whispers and innuendo would surely have been stirred up, perhaps confirming what many already knew or suspected.

Atherton's arrest in June 1640 in fact opened a floodgate of accusations. In August, Walley told Cork that 'each day doth produce more matter against him'. There were now reports of 'his adulteries with married women, single women and young girls, besides other most shameful and odious abuses to honest women', all becoming 'so innumerable as the examinations taken thereof will make a large volume'. Adultery with married women was not of course a capital offence, even for a bishop; it was the sodomy charge that cast the shadow of the rope. There were now two other men imprisoned under suspicion of having committed the act with him. One (presumably John Child) 'hath confessed it, and still doth justify his confession'. The other was prepared to confess only to the bishop's 'tempting and pressing of him unto it, in your Lordship's house of Lismore when he was there to present the leases to your lordship'. In Walley's opinion, Atherton was now as good as dead or, if he did manage to escape with his life, 'he cannot expect to be restored in the Church'. It was time to plan ahead for a more congenial regime at Waterford. Walley urged the earl to take matters in hand for 'procuring some one of your own in whom you may repose'. Robert Naylor, he suggested, would be just the man. Meanwhile, Walley hinted darkly, Atherton might not turn out to be the only sodomite bishop sitting on the Irish bench: Wentworth's disciple John Bramhall 'were he put to the test, would prove as bad mettle as the other'.

Walley's distaste for bishops was well-honed: 'few of that coat be so honest'. By 1640, an anti-episcopal backlash against Archbishop Laud's policies was under way in all three of Charles's kingdoms. It was this no doubt that prompted the preaching of a sermon on 'the excellence of the order of the Church of England under episcopal government', at Blandford in Dorset, probably during the summer of that year. It is mentioned here because the preacher, William Sherley, was the man who succeeded Atherton at Huish Champflower in the spring of 1636. The occasion was an ecclesiastical visitation, or inspection of the parishes, and one of Sherley's themes was to observe how 'the ear of authority may easily be abused in her informations'. The rulers of Church and Commonwealth, he argued, must be careful 'not to account every information that rides post to them, sufficient evidence whereon to pass a sentence'. His biblical point of reference was a highly suggestive one: 'when the cry of Sodom's transgression travelled so far from earth as to heaven, the Lord seems not, at this distance, to give credit to it, but resolves to go down and see'. Was this an oblique allusion to the stories about the bishop of Waterford starting to spill out of Ireland? If so, it is a reminder of the political significance of Atherton's case, and of its potential implications for the stability of the established order.

Not all of the rumours and accusations buzzing around the imprisoned bishop of Waterford related to his time in Ireland. In the summer of 1640, a story began to surface which Atherton had managed to keep submerged for the best part of two decades. It concerned an event which may well have been the catalyst for him to seek preferment in Ireland, and be 'vomited' out of England in the first place; an event that cannot have been unrelated to the return of Old Mother Leakey, and the mysterious message supposedly imparted in a small upstairs chamber in Minehead nearly four years previously. We will simply take note of it here, and return to investigate it properly in due course. Among the 'foul offences' Edmund Rossingham had heard spoken of, one stood out as different in kind from the other fornications and adulteries: 'that the bishop hath committed incest with a sister of his wife's'. Rossingham was not certain that 'Egerton', as he managed to mangle the bishop's name, actually had a wife. But he was certain that he had been accused of incest, and that he had denied the charge.[2]

🐾

Atherton went on trial in November 1640, in the nation's premier criminal court, the King's Bench, located in the administration's command centre of Dublin Castle. We know little for certain about the trial itself, other than its verdict. The official records were lost, along with much else, when rebellion swept across Ireland in 1641. Atherton was certainly tried in front of a jury, and it seems probable that the prosecution would have been led by the Irish attorney-general. At least one of the three judges in King's Bench was part of the circle of the earl of Cork, and all of them were later praised by a nineteenth-century historian for being 'proof against all [Wentworth's] assaults . . . though honoured with hearty Castle hatred, the tyrant was afraid to remove them'. Atherton had not landed among friends.[3]

The fullest account of the trial, ironically enough, is that given to us by the prisoner himself, as part of his speech from the scaffold in December 1640. In the circumstances, we can hardly expect an unjaundiced analysis, but we can glean from it something of the demeanour with which Atherton faced his final test. Characteristically, he put up a fight. Although he had been denied counsel (something he did not believe to be legal), he had judicial wiles of his own to employ, claiming, for example, to have found an error in the indictment. There was also 'a volume of papers, which with a great deal of pains he wrote out of law books in his defence'. Atherton clearly considered the case against him to be far from water-tight. With regard to his chief accuser, John Child, he claimed he could have 'sent into England, and have had him indicted for a hand he had in a stealth there', thereby outlawing him and voiding his testimony. He could also have objected to the jury, and 'excepted against twenty at least', including the jury foreman, whom he knew to be an outlaw. By such means, he might at worst have secured a postponement of the trial. Yet he had scorned 'to stoop to such poor shifts and protractions', being full of confidence in 'the height of his spirit'. Too late did it dawn upon him that he was a man who had always placed too much trust in 'his own wit and expressions, with which till now in any thing that ever he had attempted, he had not miscarried'.

Another brief contemporary description of the trial supports the idea that the outcome was no foregone conclusion. A man called John Price, an eyewitness of Atherton's execution, tells us that there were in the end two capital charges: 'the bishop of Waterford was charged by his own servant man, and by a woman; the former, for sodomy upon him, and for a rape upon her'. Atherton had attempted to deflect the rape allegation in the almost timeless manner: 'she swore it, but God knows what she is'. As to the buggery, Child's testimony itself 'was under suspicion'. But further damning evidence had emerged during the course of the trial. There was a boy who waited upon Atherton during his imprisonment, but unwisely, the bishop had 'never cautioned him what to say, in answer to what should be put to him'. Under questioning, 'the boy owned that he had offered the like act to him'. This seems to have been enough to sway the jury, which on 27 November returned a verdict of guilty on both charges.

Looking back on these proceedings from the foot of a dangling rope, Atherton had found a kind of peace with God. But he could not bring himself to acquit everyone who had helped bring about this (to him) unexpected denouement. He owned that the jury were 'honest gentlemen and went according to their consciences', yet the evidence in front of them was not so clear-cut 'but they might have stuck at it'. The judges were at fault in denying him counsel, and 'some were hot against him', though he generously attributed this 'only to their zeal against sin'. Atherton's greatest ire was reserved for the witnesses and informers: 'they were such as eat of his bread, came daily as friends to his table'. Some of them indeed 'were at dinner with him the day before the complaint was put in against him'. John Atherton was a man betrayed by those closest to him.[4]

Was he also a man betrayed in another sense, the victim of a miscarriage of justice, perhaps even of a dark conspiracy? Several later writers would suggest so. Atherton himself does not seem to have directly claimed as much, though his gallows declaration that 'none of the Romish Church, though differing from me in points of religion, had a hand in this complaint against me', suggests he knew who his real enemies were. Here the reader might reasonably expect a competent story-teller to produce a moment of lightning revelation—an archival smoking gun or fingerprinted dagger; a trail of evidence making sense of the perplexing circumstances involved in Atherton's fall. Why did Child choose to launch his suicidal accusation against Atherton at that politically critical moment, in June 1640? Did someone put him up to it, and did he expect that he would be reprieved? If so, he was to be sorely disappointed: Child himself was hanged in the plantation town of Bandon Bridge, County Cork, in March 1641. The claim would be made later on that year that, at his execution, Child withdrew the accusation against Atherton. Was the bishop then innocent of the felony that cost him his life? Who stood to gain most by Atherton's removal from the scene; against whose name can the familiar and compelling trinity of means, motive, and opportunity most plausibly be pinned?

Alas, disappointment awaits. There is no neat resolution or dramatic closure to be had. There were, of course, countless persons, in County Waterford and elsewhere, with reason to wish the bishop ill. Even as he prepared to ascend the ladder, there was a man in the crowd 'calling out to him about some papers or leases'. There were also those who gained materially from Atherton's death. In August 1641, for example, an order of the Irish parliament reversed the chancery decree granting Atherton the town lands of Donough-more, and restored them to Piers Butler, the son of Lord Cahir. Piers and his son Theobald had been staunch opponents of the bishop's land policy in Waterford, but there is nothing to connect them directly with the complaint against Atherton in parliament. A yet more evident beneficiary of the debacle was, of course, Richard Boyle, earl of Cork. In the autumn of 1640, as Atherton languished in Dublin Castle, 'an act concerning Richard, earl of Cork, Lord High Treasurer, and John, Lord Bishop of Waterford' was hurried through the Irish parliament. Yet this Act simply confirmed the 1637 settlement relating to Lismore and Ardmore, a settlement distinctly unfavourable to Cork. Its statutory ratification looks, therefore, like a pre-emptive step by the government to secure the gains made for the church, rather than an attempt by Cork to exploit Atherton's removal from the scene. Conspiracy theories in every age thrive on the absence of real proof. Yet if, from his base in England, the earl of Cork did mastermind a conspiracy to bring down the bishop of Waterford, he covered his traces too well for us to discover them. Upon receipt of Walley's letter of 21 July 1640, Cork summarized its contents, noting the financial and estate news his steward had to impart. But his synopsis includes no mention of the revelations about the arrest of Atherton. The earl did, in his thick confident hand, inscribe 'Bishop of Waterford' in the margin of Walley's next juicy newsletter. But there is no suggestion in the surviving one-sided correspondence that he was particularly pressing his steward for details and developments. Remarkably, Cork's diary entries for December 1640 contain no notice of Atherton's execution.

It seems very unlikely, however, that Cork was simply uninterested in Atherton's fate. In September 1643, exhausted by the ongoing struggle with Catholic insurgency, his castle at Lismore besieged by rebels, and confined to a Protestant enclave around his estates at Youghal, Cork finally lay down and died. The inventory of his papers and personal belongings taken in Dublin reveals the extent to which the irksome bishop of Waterford had over several years obtruded himself into the earl's field of vision. 'My lord's sweet wood box with drawers' was, for example, found to contain 'the writings belonging to the bishop of Waterford and Lismore', as well as 'a portmanteau of the bishop's with a gown in it'. A new iron chest had inside it 'a parchment book in large folio, wherein are entered the proceedings betwixt Richard, earl of Cork, and John Lord Bishop of Waterford, for the securing of the manors of Lismore, Bewley and Kilmolash'. In the drawer of a trunk was 'the draft of some pleadings betwixt John Lord Bishop of Lismore, and Theobald Butler fitz Pierce for the lands of Donoughmore'.[5] Land, family, power: these were the gods worshipped by the earl of Cork, and the bishop of Waterford had for a time intruded on his devotions. He doubtless rejoiced in Atherton's misfortunes, and took what advantage he could. But there is no proof that he was their principal author. Perhaps there was no conspiracy at all. Atherton's appetite for boundless self-gratification was clearly a fatal flaw, and ultimately a compulsive and calamitous recklessness. The unfortunate steward John Child may have been the instrument of other forces, or he may have had vengeful personal motives of his own for the action he took. We certainly cannot say that Atherton's disgrace was not craftily engineered by his enemies, but it seems just as likely to have been a gift that fell unexpectedly into their hands. Either way, it is the use they managed to make of it which turned Atherton into a more significant figure in death than he had managed to be in life.

But we are getting ahead of ourselves again. After Atherton was convicted and sentenced, he was returned to his cell in Dublin Castle to await the day of execution. Almost immediately, he found he had a visitor: the clergyman Nicholas Bernard, prebendary of Dromoragh in the diocese of Dromore, and dean of the diocese of Ardagh. Bernard had come to help Atherton prepare for his death, to offer counsel, and to encourage signs of repentance. He is an immensely important figure in this tale, with his own influential stories to tell about John Atherton, and we will return to him in the next chapter.

Meanwhile, disgrace continued to be heaped on the bishop of Waterford's head. On 5 December, the morning of his execution, the Board of Trinity College revoked the doctorship of divinity they had bestowed in 1635. Another humiliation was planned, but in the event did not come to pass. There was to have been a ceremony of formal deconsecration, a degrading of Atherton from the priestly and episcopal orders his conduct had besmirched. Yet an unexpected and unfortunate event led to a last-minute cancellation. On Thursday 3 December, the Lord Deputy, Sir Christopher Wandesford, 'died suddenly about five o'clock in the morning of a burning fever'. As a result, when Atherton went to the gallows he was still fully a bishop—to date, the only Anglican prelate to have been convicted and executed for the crime of sodomy.

Of the execution itself, we have perhaps heard enough already. Yet we owe it to Atherton to note that he died bravely enough. Bernard states that as he ascended the ladder he said to the crowd, 'I thank God, I dread not death.' The minister claimed to have been the last to hold him by the hand, 'and to my admiration his hand shook no more than mine'. Both Bernard and Price (the other eyewitness) agree that as Atherton balanced on the ladder in the last moments, he grasped the sides of the cassock that by rights he should not have been wearing, 'lest he should seem to struggle at going off'. It was, in many of the respects by which contemporaries judged such matters, 'a good death'. But one aspect of the event remained crucially undetermined. According to Price, Atherton's last speech recognized 'that it is known to you all what is laid to my charge, and for which I received sentence of death'. He went on to declare, 'I do here before the Lord, his holy angels, and you all, own the sentence against me to die this manner of death to be just, and that I was guilty of the charge laid against me.' Yet Bernard has it that after his conviction, and again upon the gallows, Atherton 'denied ... the main thing in the indictment', adding that this 'hath been since confirmed by the confession of his chief accuser at his execution also'.[6] Whether the bishop of Waterford ever actually confessed to the crime of sodomy was to remain a matter of considerable importance over the years to come.

In both England and Ireland, the world was being turned upside down during the autumn and winter of 1640–1. In historical accounts of this process, the fate of John Atherton has occasionally been (quite literally) a footnote to the narrative, but most often it has not merited even that. Soon, of course, it was to be overtaken by much greater events: rebellion in Ireland in October 1641; civil war in England in August 1642. An occurrence which might in more settled times have held the shocked attention of the nation—the execution of a bishop for sodomy—simply fell submerged into the stream, as a confluence of still more extraordinary social and political currents produced a maelstrom of constitutional crisis, and then a torrent of war and revolution. Before these processes had reached full spate, however, Atherton was destined to achieve considerable posthumous celebrity, and to play a small but by no means negligible part in the unravelling of the established order on both sides of the Irish Sea.

A week after the hanging in Dublin, Cork's irrepressible Lismore steward John Walley was in triumphal mood, and sat down to pen another letter to his master. Echoing the biblical words of Mary and her hymn of praise in the Magnificat, Walley declared that 'it is the wrathful hand of the Almighty that casts down the proud and lofty from their seats, and exalts the meek and lowly'—though whether he saw himself, or the plutocrat earl as examples of the meek and lowly is not entirely clear. Who would have thought that Wentworth's 'tyrannising and most intemperate hand in the governance of this kingdom' would ever come to an end? Yet the Lord had restored the earl of Cork 'to the seat of honour and justice, to judge him who did thirst after your ruin'. Wentworth's confederates and lieutenants were now similarly brought low: his lawyer George Radcliffe was arrested on charges of treason; his successor as Lord Deputy, Christopher Wandesford, was 'dead even upon a sudden, not two days sick'. And then there was Atherton, who 'ended his life with a halter'. The bishop was now reduced in Walley's repertory of villainy to the status of a bit player, 'not to be ranked with the former in the power of doing ill', though he had 'as much malicious a heart as any of them'. His demise prompted the Lismore steward to pluck at a familiar string: 'a way is opened to your Lordship to have a good man placed there...I hope your Lordship will be

pleased to remember Dean Naylor'. Yet the ever-hopeful Robert
Naylor was not destined to succeed Atherton at Waterford. In the
early summer of 1641, Archibald Adair, the disgraced and dismissed
former bishop of Killala, was appointed to the diocese, with all the
charges against him ordered to be erased from the files of High
Commission (see pp. 84–5). With a symbolic resonance quite evident to all, Adair, the public face of resistance to the ecclesiastical
policies of Wentworth, had supplanted Atherton, the personifica-
tion of their worst excesses.

Before this, however, a reckoning had to be made with Wentworth himself. On 11 November 1640, impeachment proceedings
against him were begun in the English House of Lords. The
Crown's most powerful minister was to be brought down, in very
large measure because of the nature of his administration in
Ireland. In these manœuvrings Wentworth's protégé Atherton, a
man about to go on trial for his life, would play a conspicuous
role.

The background to this was the Crown's complete loss of control
of both the Irish and English parliaments, reconvened towards the
end of 1640 as a result of King Charles's total failure to crush the
rebellion of the Scots Covenanters. On 3 November, MPs gathered
in London to begin the deliberations of what would later be
known as the Long Parliament. Its members included a powerful
opposition group led by the Somerset landowner, John Pym, a man
ferociously hostile to the ecclesiastical policy of Archbishop Laud,
and the arbitrary government that seemed to have accompanied it
over the course of the 1630s. Almost immediately, the government's
opponents in the Irish commons dispatched agents to liaise with
their counterparts in England.

    In its first week, the Long Parliament decided to establish com-
mittees of the whole Commons to discuss particular grievances.
Irish affairs were rapidly pushed up the agenda, and on Saturday 7
November the House prepared to hear expert witnesses describe the
Lord Deputy Wentworth's crimes and misgovernment there. For
these purposes, Pym had a star turn up his sleeve: his brother-in-law,

Sir John Clotworthy, who sat as a member of parliament for Maldon in Essex. Clotworthy, however, was no home-grown English squire, but a New English planter (of Devon stock) from County Antrim in Ulster. He was, moreover, a presbyterian sympathizer with the Scots Covenanters, and a ferocious anti-papist, who nursed a long-standing hatred of Wentworth and all that he stood for. His wife, along with other Ulster nonconformists, had suffered imprison-ment at the orders of the Lord Deputy. His father-in-law was a close ally of the earl of Cork. Clotworthy therefore brought together in his own person a web of opposition politics spanning three kingdoms. Whether he ever directly crossed the path of Atherton is impossible to say, though he had been summoned in front of High Commission in November 1639. He certainly had no time for epis-copacy, once asking a New England pioneer if a bishop had been appointed 'for your not as yet polluted land'. A sympathetic twen-tieth-century biographer of Wentworth thought Clotworthy a 'dour and heartless man'. But Archbishop Laud's assessment seems nearer the mark: 'a firebrand brought from Ireland to inflame this kingdom'.[7]

He certainly did his best to inflame the Irish Committee when his turn came to address it on the afternoon of 7 November. We have no certain record of what Clotworthy said. The printed news-book or 'diurnall' of events in the Long Parliament reported only that he 'spake long and largely of abuses in Ireland . . . reflecting much upon the Lieutenant', though he avoided mentioning him by name. Fortunately, this synopsis can be supplemented by the evi-dence of several diaries kept by members of the Commons. These leave no doubt that, if Clotworthy avoided using Wentworth's name, he did so for rhetorical effect, inviting members to draw their own conclusions about who was responsible for the deplorable state of affairs in Ireland. The fullest account is that of the MP for Sudbury in Suffolk, Sir Simonds D'Ewes. His summary suggests that Clotworthy did not pull any punches. There were 'no small disorders' in the ecclesiastical government of Ireland: 'rake hell and you cannot find worse'. The oppressions of High Commission were a cause of much grievance, though papists were never troubled by it.

They were, in fact, permitted to practise their religion unchecked; popish monasteries and houses of religion were springing up in towns all over the kingdom. Before going on to consider the failings of secular justice and the corruption of the customs system, Clotworthy brought the first part of his oration to a close by revealing to his listeners the identity of the Irish bishop 'indicted of whoredom and sodomy'. Yet the question he wanted them to consider was this: 'who commended this whorish incestuous bishop who lay with his sister in England?' The sister, he added, had suffered punishment, but the bishop escaped. The rumour reported by Edmund Rossingham the previous summer could scarcely have been granted a more public airing. Yet this was not all. Another diarist, the Norfolk MP Sir John Holland, summarized Clotworthy's speech in only sixteen words, but in doing so surely preserves for us what must have stuck most firmly in the minds of those present: 'Bishop of Waterford, Doctor Atherton, guilty of incest and murder in England, and sodomy in Ireland.' Murder? It seems that the accusations against Atherton were escalating, and perhaps becoming wilder. Luckily, a third diarist is able to elaborate. Clotworthy told the parliamentarians how Atherton, after committing incest with his sister, 'agreed with her to murder the child, which was done, for which she suffered and he escaped'. Infanticide was a serious capital offence: was Atherton guilty of this, too? We will return to the question at the end of this chapter, but a fuller answer will have to wait, for a detailed public accusation against him was to take another seventy years to emerge into open view (see Chapter 7). And even then it remained, like so much in the case of Bishop Atherton, a murky and uncertain business.

With Clotworthy's explosive speech, we have come, if not quite full circle, then at least to a point of intersection. In November 1640, the accumulated family skeletons—metaphorical and perhaps real—of the humble Leakeys of Huish and Minehead were being paraded before the governors of the kingdom, and in the highest court of the land. This was for the express purpose of bringing down the regime's most powerful minister. Here was an extraordinary conjunction of the local and the national, of the small world of village scandal, and the grand stage of high politics, of personal secrets and public manifestos. It was the kind of awkward coupling that, for some, may have required a visitor from another world to make sense of it, but Mother Leakey herself was, for the moment, obscured from view. If Clotworthy had heard stories about a ghost, he chose not to say so. In any case, around the turn of 1641, after years of Laudian oppression, the 'godly' did not need supernatural testimonies to see evidence of God's hand at work. The Scots minister, Robert Baillie, in London as part of a Covenanters' delegation negotiating with the king, wrote home gloatingly of a growing mood of hostility to bishops in the capital: 'the episcopal clergy are made vile in the eyes of the world'. As committees sprang up to investigate secular and ecclesiastical maladministration, it seemed clear to Baillie that 'God is making here a new world'. In December, Laud was impeached and imprisoned in the Tower, where a dozen other bishops were to join him over the coming months. Meanwhile, over 15,000 Londoners signed a petition calling for the complete abolition of episcopacy 'root and branch'. The world was turning indeed, and in the eyes of godly preachers 1641 was to be 'the *mirabilis annus*', 'a wonderful year of God's mercies to England'.[8]

The trial of Thomas Wentworth began on 22 March 1641. He was escorted by the chief usher of the House of Lords, then and still known as 'Black Rod', into the special courtroom of Westminster Hall, the place where the Gunpowder Plotters had been put on trial nearly thirty-five years earlier. During the proceedings, Wentworth appeared, noted Robert Baillie, 'always in the same suit of black, as [if] in dole [mourning]'. Articles of impeachment had been prepared in November (many of them relating to his governance of Ireland), but on 23 March, the second day of the trial, the chief prosecutor John Pym produced three new charges to which the prisoner would be required to make answer. These were that he had defrauded the Irish Exchequer; that he had used the English treasury to maintain garrisons in Ireland; and that 'he had advanced popish and infamous persons, as the Bishop of Waterford and others, to the prime rooms in the Church of Ireland'. Pym reminded his audience of developments since Clotworthy had first brought the bishop of Waterford to their attention the previous November: 'Dr Atherton is not to be found now above ground, for he was hanged for many foul and unspeakable offences'. Two further examples of 'the patterns of his [Wentworth's] clergy' were felt to suffice. One was Bishop John Bramhall, 'a man that now stands charged with high treason'. The other was Atherton's archdeacon of Lismore, Arthur Gwyn, 'who about 1634, was an under-groom to the earl of Cork in his stable'. Yet he had been ordained by Bramhall, and two impropriated vicarages taken from the earl of Cork were given to him. Social as well as sexual transgressions were hallmarks of the ecclesiastical regime over which Wentworth had presided. It is striking that a thread linking all three of the 'infamous' clergymen was the offence they had given to the earl of Cork.

Later, Wentworth's turn came to address the charges. According to the hostile Robert Baillie, he 'made some apology for Bramhall, Atherton, [and] Gwyn'. In fact, ever the eloquent orator, Wentworth was considerably more expansive than this. As far as Bramhall went, he was totally unrepentant. He had indeed recommended him for the bishopric of Derry, considering him 'a very learned man', and 'a very worthy churchman'. As to Gwyn, Wentworth at first claimed never to have heard of him. 'But recollecting my thoughts, I think he was recommended to me by my Lord of D[erry]. For in matters of the Church, I did use that gentleman, and if I were to begin the world again, I would use him still, holding him a very honest worthy man.' Atherton, however, was a very different kettle of ecclesiastical fish. At the outset, Wentworth reminded his judges that bishoprics were not in the gift of the Lord Deputy, but of the King, 'and that he is not responsible for what the king doth'. Yet he confessed that Bishop Atherton was not known to his Majesty, and that he himself had recommended him for the place. 'When he befriended the Bishop of Waterford, he conceived him as a man of integrity and learning, fit for such employment. Nor was there then the least suspicion of those

monstrous impieties, wherewith he was afterwards charged.'
Wentworth pleaded with his audience to see reason:

> But suppose he had a secret fault of his own (God knows it was
> unknown to me), may not a man be deceived in his judgement of a
> man, but this shall be turned against him? It is a very easy thing for
> a man to cover his faults from the eye of the world. I thought him
> not a vicious man. He proved so, and he had his merit; he suffered
> for it. And unless I had the inspection of Almighty God, I suppose
> this cannot be laid to my charge.

This was rhetorically powerful stuff, but as we know, quite spectacularly disingenuous. Wentworth had indeed been deceived in his
judgement: his judgement that it was in the best interests of the
Church of Ireland for a 'solicitor', and a man against whom he knew
there to be valid 'exception', to occupy one of its most prominent
public positions. It had turned out to be perhaps the most spectacular own goal of his entire Irish policy.[9]

On the morning of 12 May 1641, Thomas Wentworth, earl of
Strafford, went courageously to his death, the King's faltering
efforts to save his favourite having withered in the face of his
enemies' implacable resolve, backed by the menacing presence of
huge London crowds. Cork, who had given evidence against him at
his trial, recorded in his diary that 'the oppressing earl of Strafford . . . was beheaded on the Tower Hill of London', adding sav-
agely, 'as well he deserved'. He also sent an account of the trial back
to Lismore, and received a predictably effusive response from his
servant John Walley: 'Blessed and ever happy may your Lordship be
in all things, as you have been hitherto to see the downfall and ruin
of all such as have risen up or been raised against you. It is a thing
that, duly considered, doth plainly declare it to be the powerful
work of God.'[10]

But other than his evident affection for the earl of Cork, what
message was God seeking to send his people through the upheavals
of the hour? For opposition activists such as John Clotworthy
and John Pym, the Atherton affair was highly symbolic of the

corruption of the Church of Ireland by bishops, a compelling argument for the introduction of a presbyterian system. The point was strongly made in an anonymous set of 'Observations on the Government, Status and Condition of the People of Ireland', drafted in April 1641, and probably intended for publication in that year. This document railed against the bishops for giving 'ill example to others, both by their life and doctrine'. They would do anything which would 'help them to a better bishopric'. Under their very noses, churches were falling down through neglect, yet 'they suffer hirelings and base fellows to possess preachers' places, who like dumb dogs neglect their duties'. They had 'turned Christianity in[to] state policy', making concessions to papists in pursuit of a false sense of security. The conclusion to draw from all of this? 'When bishops shall be condemned for the sin of sodomy, it is time for the church to look into and suppress them.'

This was certainly the view of one veteran agitator, the lawyer and pamphleteer, William Prynne. In 1633, Prynne had suffered the punishment for seditious libel, having his ears cropped after criticizing Queen Henrietta Maria's decision to act in a court masque. They had been properly lopped off, his nose slit, and his cheek branded, for criticism of Laud in 1637. In the heady days of 1641, Prynne became a 'root-and-branch' opponent of episcopacy, publishing a massive historical tract exposing the 'treasons, conspiracies, and rebellions' perpetrated by bishops in Britain, Ireland, and France. The late bishop of Waterford was not technically a conspirator or a traitor, yet Prynne could not resist using him to ice the anti-episcopal cake: 'not to mention the lewd, beastly, sodomitical life and most detestable actions of Atherton, bishop of Waterford in Ireland, for which he was lately arraigned, condemned and hanged as a bishop without any preceding degradation, to the great dishonour of his rochet [a ceremonial vestment worn by bishops]'. For those watching the signs of the times, there was something distinctly epigrammatic about the manner of Atherton's end. The terse diary entry of an Oxfordshire minister named Thomas Wyatt suggests something of how the attention of observers had been caught, and how the allegations of Clotworthy had acquired sacrosanct status: 'This year, 1640, one Atherton, bishop of Waterford in Ireland, was hanged for murder and incest and buggery.'[11]

The opening months of 1641 were a time of intense political manœuvring, and by the early summer the execution of Atherton was perhaps already beginning to seem like old news. Yet in July the dead bishop of Waterford was catapulted back into the limelight. The occasion was the publication in London of a short pamphlet in verse, graced with one of those helpfully informative titles characteristic of the genre: *The Life and Death of John Atherton, Lord Bishop of Waterford and Lismore within the Kingdom of Ireland, born near Bridgwater in Somersetshire, who for Incest, Buggery, and many other Enormous Crimes, after having lived a Vicious Life, died a Shameful Death, and was on the Fifth of December last past, hanged on the Gallows Greene at Dublin, and his man John Childe being his Proctor, with whom he had committed the Buggery, was hanged in March following at Bandon Bridges, condemned thereunto at the Assises holden at Cork.* This pamphlet was the first biography of John Atherton. We are obliged to look at it closely, for it ties up a number of threads left hanging in our narrative up to this point. Yet at the same time, it begins to unpick others, and it raises intriguing questions about the circulation of rumour and news at both elite and popular levels. What is more, it reintroduces the figure of Mother Leakey's ghost, and places her firmly back at the heart of our story.

We do not know who wrote *The Life and Death of John Atherton*, nor who published it. A publication date of July can be inferred from the fact that the London bookseller, George Thomason, who amassed a huge collection of pamphlets in these years, kept his acquisitions in the order he had purchased them, and topical references can be sought in the publications either side in the series.[12] The virtual collapse of government censorship in the summer of 1641 resulted in a wave of popular pamphleteering, which scholars often refer to as an 'explosion' or 'revolution' in printing: more items were published in 1641 than in any preceding year in the history of the English press (well over 2,000). These items were typically small ('quarto' rather than folio in size), short (invariably less than 100 pages, and often four or five), and cheap (ranging from 1d. to 6d. in price). The subject matter was usually political, the tone often subversive or libellous. Archbishop Laud and his clerical henchmen were a frequent target; the text was often accompanied by satirical images, depicting Laud or other bishops in a range of humiliating guises. There was a levelling consequence of this deluge of print: news and opinion was being produced and consumed by the people on a scale never quite seen before.[13] In itself, the *Life and Death* represented a tiny ripple in this great flux of criticism and complaint, but it is the current on which the next part of our story is destined to float.

If we cannot identify the author of the *Life and Death*, we can say that it was produced in a hurry, and with the expectation of a wide readership. The tract survives in at least two variant copies, with distinctively different decorative borders and title page impress (the ornamental motif placed by the printer on the front of his work). This suggests that the title was being farmed out between two print shops so that both could work on it simultaneously. It may also suggest that information had come into the author's or printer's hands which needed to be disseminated quickly while it was still agreeably topical. The work was illustrated, after a fashion. A woodcut print in the frontispiece depicts the 'shameful end' of Atherton and Child on their respective gallows (Figure 7). The picture of Atherton makes no real attempt at versimilitude. It is a bust portrait of a bishop, set in a roundel, and crudely attached to an out-of-scale rope. The main point of it seems to be precisely that it is instantly recognizable as a bishop: 'Atherton' wears the square cap, white 'rochet', and sleeveless 'chimere' that between them were the unmistakable marks of an Anglican prelate. Apart from anything else, we know of course that Atherton was not hanged in this gear, but in his more workaday cassock. The incongruity of the image may be purely pragmatic, prompted by the need to lay hands quickly on a more-or-less appropriate illustration. It seems certain, in fact,

7. Atherton's
shameful end, from
the 1641 pamphlet

8. Archbishop Laud
as the model for
Atherton, from *The
Bishops Potion* (1641)

that the woodblock in question was adapted from one providing a likeness of Archbishop Laud for another anti-episcopal tract of 1641, *The Bishops Potion*. This was itself copied from a formal portrait engraving by William Marshall, with the addition of a chain to signify the archbishop's recent incarceration (Figure 8). Yet the parsimony served a political and satirical purpose, for just as Laud was the archetype of wicked episcopacy, the conflation of his image with that of the sodomite Atherton functioned to tar all bishops with the same scandalous brush. The visual morphing of the two prelates may well strike us as a decidedly ironic touch, given how much Laud had disliked Atherton, and how hard he had tried to prevent him from becoming a bishop at all.[14]

The *Life and Death of John Atherton* opens with a conventional poetic flourish:

> Confusion give my thoughts once leave to be
> Exempted from thy lawless tyranny;
> If for the space of one poor half hour
> O give me leave to sit in quiet's bower

But the purpose of this reverie is so 'that I with patience may delineate / In lines of life this prelate's sordid state'. Almost immediately we are plunged into juicy revelations about Atherton's pastorship at Huish Champflower. Here he passed his time 'viciously', and though married to 'a handsome wife' and blessed with 'sweet children', gave himself over to deflowering virgins and defiling marriage beds. He was, moreover, a proud, impudent, and ambitious man, who sowed 'seditious strife' among his parishioners, setting 'friend against friend, husband against wife'. Though placed amongst many, 'he did live alone / And loving none, beloved was of none'. So far, so scurrilous. But the next accusation strikes an already familiar note:

> Lastly, through pride, high fare, and lustful life,
> Incest committed with the sister of his wife,
> For which he sued a pardon, and then fled
> To Ireland, where a worser life he led.

In Ireland he obtained 'by insinuation' the church of St John's, became chaplain to 'that honoured Lord and worthy peer' Viscount Loftus, and through his assistance ascended to be sub-dean of Christ Church. But Atherton proved to be 'a Judas', betraying Loftus and bringing him into disgrace with Thomas Wentworth, a man 'who brooked no rival, nor competitor'. His switch of allegiance brought him the bishopric of Waterford and Lismore, 'where he did five years lord it'. But in the interim a strange event befell:

> He surely warned was to mend his life
> By his own sister Master Leakey's wife,
> Which Master Leakey's mother being dead,
> And in her lifetime conscious how he led
> His lustful life, her ghost in ghastful wise
> Did oft appear before her sister's eyes.
> But she fear-stricken durst not speak unto it,
> Till oft appearing forced her to do it.
> Then thus she spake, 'Mother-in-law, what cause
> You from your rest, to my unrest thus draws?'
> Who answered, 'daughter, 'tis the wicked life
> Your brother leads, warn him to mend his life.
> If not, then plainly tell him 'tis decreed,
> He shall be hanged, bid him repent with speed.
> Then shall my restless spirit be at rest,
> And not till then'. Thus vanished. She addressed
> Herself for travel, into Ireland went
> With this sad message unto him was sent,
> Which how he took to heart may plain appear
> By the slight answer he returned her.
> 'What must be, shall be: if I must, I must die,
> Marriage, and hanging, come by destiny.'
> Thus scorned her counsel, sent her back, and when
> She was returned, he drew far viler than
> He was before, if viler man may be,
> For one bad act before, committed three.

The author then proceeds to enumerate, in equally execrable verse, the various sexual sins that Atherton committed in Waterford: 'a strict list being taken of each whore / he was known to use, amounts to sixty-four'. This could not be ascribed to mere frailty of the flesh, for when 'nature failed all these to please', he resorted to the use of Cantharides (the aphrodisiac better known as Spanish Fly). Rather than attempt to hide his infidelities, he boasted of them, saying that the act purified his blood. No neighbour's wife was safe from his attentions, and his tastes were catholic (small 'c'):

> Some women he did do in charity
> And some because they used good cookery,
> Knew how to please his palate as his bed,
> So that at once his corpse and lust he fed.

Nor was 'this lustful elf' above the use of low trickery to gratify his desires. One anecdote told how a man 'well known in Waterford' had approached the bishop to request a loan of £100, promising to repay it within a month. Atherton agreed to oblige him, but insisted that the man's wife be present as a witness when the sum was handed over. On their arrival, Atherton told 'the poor cuckold' that the cash prepared for him included an odd piece of gold which needed to be taken out, and asked him to go to his study to count it. For security, he would lock the door, and would wait, talking the while with the man's wife: ' 'tis granted, in his seat / The bishop mounts, and does the well-known feat.' Another ploy of Atherton's was to stay on at feasts after the guests had departed, and to request the 'goodman of the house' to go out and set the bishop's watch at his sun-dial. The householder 'proud of such favour' would happily do it, leaving Atherton to set another mechanism 'by his wife's noon-dial'.

But all of this, so the pamphlet informs us, should be seen as mere 'tricks of youth' when compared to the bishop's most heinous crime:

> Suppose a devil from the infernal pit,
> More monsterlike, than ere was devil yet,
> Contrary to course, taking a male fiend
> To sodomize with him, such was the mind
> Of this Lord Bishop. He did take a Child
> By name, not years, acting a sin so vile
> As is forenamed, this Child a proctor too.
> Nor him alone, but his parrator he must do;
> These and a thousand like these he hath done.

The accusation that Atherton had had homosexual relations with another dependant, his apparitor (see p. 22) is a new detail. But in the view of the *Life and Death*, sexual transgressions were not the sum of his wrongdoing, nor should they be taken in isolation from other, more political sins. His crimes were, quite literally, astronomical. He had done no less than endeavour 'to eclipse the sun / Of this our sky, by making Charles' Wain draw sublunary'. This was an interesting inversion of the metaphor employed by Speaker Eustace at the opening of the 1640 Parliament (see p. 86), suggesting that aggressive bishops were seeking to take away the power and authority of the King. Atherton's aim had been to subvert 'the law fundamental', and to put in its place 'Commission High, Pope's canons, Great Laud's grace'. This was a litany of grievance common to much of the growing swell of anti-episcopal agitation. But the author of the *Life and Death* does not seem to have been an out-and-out root-and-brancher. Atherton's fate was rather a warning to 'lord-like prelates' to shun all the vices which he exemplified: avarice, extortion, and pride, as well as lust, incest, buggery, and rape. Their model should be 'godly Timothy'—a reference to the list of attributes of the good bishop in the first letter of Timothy (3: 1–7), beginning, in the King James version, with the requirement to be 'blameless, the husband of one wife'. If, the pamphlet insists, prelates learnt to be 'meek like Christ your bishop, lord and king', then they would 'live beloved', not end their lives by the axe or on a rope.

There is, in this short text, a great deal for us to try to get our heads around. The overt linkage of sexual and political corruption does not perhaps occasion much surprise. But the sheer volume and range of the sexual misdemeanours ascribed to Atherton may well strike a modern reader as distinctly odd. Is it at all likely that the bishop could have been so voraciously and indiscriminately bisexual (to use a thoroughly modern term)? Would people at the time have found it in any way plausible? Perhaps the question we are asking ourselves is this: was the bishop of Waterford really a homosexual?

To make sense of any of this, we are required to make a leap of imagination, and to unthink some of the categories we habitually use to define personal sexual identity in the modern Western world. As historians have come to recognize in recent years, 'homosexual' was neither a word nor a concept familiar to the people of sixteenth- and seventeenth-century England. The terms 'bugger' and 'sodom- ite' did of course exist, but neither was simply synonymous with what we would today call homosexuality. As we saw at the start of this chapter, the jurist Edward Coke defined the offence of buggery or sodomy as acts performed 'either with mankind, or with beast'. At other times, sodomy could be used to refer to further types of 'unnatural' sexual activity, such as masturbation. In short, 'sodomy' was not homosexuality per se, but unbridled, unlicensed sexuality: debauchery. It was an unfocused, unrestrained form of desire threatening the hierarchies and boundaries that structured the society of the time: marriage, class distinction, religious order. It follows that if there were no identifiable 'homosexuals' in the early seventeenth century, there were no actual 'heterosexuals' either. It has been well said that 'there is a tendency for historians to look for homosexuals, lesbians and heterosexuals, where early modern people would see only sinners'. Sodomy was a temptation into which all potentially might be led. Yet it was a crime very rarely punished by the courts. In part, as I have suggested already (p. 90), this was due to the problems of securing evidence. But, it has also been plausibly argued, the paucity of prosecuted cases might reflect reluctance on the part of contemporaries actually to identify or 'recognize' as the vile sin of sodomy every instance of casual or affectionate same-gender sexual activity (particularly between men of equal social status). Where sodomy was legally invoked, as in the case of Atherton, or that of the earl of Castlehaven, the circumstances tended to be exceptional ones, with a broader pattern of disruption and disorder being held up for display and condemnation. The rolling catalogue of Atherton's sins outlined in *The Life and Death*—fornication, adultery, incest, rape, sodomy—may therefore have struck its readers not as a patchwork of far-fetched tabloid allegations, but as the expected pattern of the 'sodomite' who had lost all his moral and religious bearings. That it should also imply attempts to subvert the good order of the Church and the state, and that it should be associated with Catholicism (the greatest threat to both), would similarly have made perfect sense.[15]

Yet for our purposes, *The Life and Death of John Atherton* is important as much for its particular detail as for its general patterns. The author seems remarkably well informed, both about Atherton's early career in England, and about his apparently priapic reign at Waterford. We are left wondering whether he had been specifically briefed by an interested insider (Clotworthy, or one of his allies?), or whether the tract represents a collation of rumours about the bishop that had been circulating in both England and Ireland for some considerable time. If such rumours *were* circulating before Atherton's arrest in the summer of 1640, it must surely have been the reputed appearances of Mother Leakey which gave them much of their currency and colour. The pamphlet exhibits none of the scepticism expressed by Laud, or by the Somerset JPs, about the reality of the ghost's visitations, and seems to imply that its readers will happily accept the notion of a returning spirit acting as an instrument of God's providential justice. The fact that the secret revelation to Elizabeth Leakey (or a version of it at least) is at last being openly described, suggests that Elizabeth may not have been nearly as consistently tight-lipped about the matter as she was during her appearance before the justices in 1637. We also now learn that Elizabeth Leakey did after all travel to Ireland in the spring of that year, or at any rate, that she was believed to have done so. Yet the tract is also interesting for what it does not mention: the alleged infanticide of the child Atherton had conceived with his sister-in-law. The charge had been given wide circulation by Clotworthy's revelations before the Irish Committee of the Long Parliament, which may imply that the author's informant or informants came from outside the circle of opposition MPs at Westminster.

We will simply never know the particulars of how the *Life and Death* came to be conceived and produced. It reminds us nonetheless that the telling of politically sensitive stories about the doings of the great in this society was not the sole prerogative of an insider political class, but the stuff of rambunctious public dialogue, often processed within that great factory of news and report, the city of London. Yet for all that this small publication can suggest about patterns of circulation of rumour, about 'constructions' of sodomy, about the conventions of satirical print, a nagging question is likely to remain: how much of it is actually true? This is a question whose seeming naivety will make the postmodernists throw up their hands in despair, but I feel obliged to ask it nonetheless. Some of the details of the pamphlet confirm what we know already; others, such as the betrayal of Loftus, seem at the least plausible on the basis of what we have learnt about Atherton's motivation and character. But there is a significant gap in the transcript here, some pages missing from the story. We have not yet established what really happened during those early years of Atherton's career, between his appointment to the living of Huish Champflower in 1622, and his taking ship for Ireland in 1629. It is time for us to step back almost twenty years, to Somerset in the early 1620s, making use of that technique beloved of film directors and TV script writers: the flash-back. Readers may feel that I have been deliberately manipulative, holding back information that would have helped make sense of what we have learned up to this point. But historical research is a journey of unpredictable directions and diversions. Some of the revelations of 1640 and 1641 were as much of a surprise to me as they were to many of Atherton's contemporaries. They sent me back to consult once more the archives in Somerset, and readers are invited mentally to accompany me there, while our scene resets itself.

&&&

It is the late summer of 1622: King James I sits autumnally on the English throne, and plans a Catholic marriage for his son Charles. William Laud, freshly created bishop of St David's in Wales, congratulates himself on his performance in a disputation with the Jesuit, John Percy, and prepares a version of it for the press. Thomas Wentworth, MP for Yorkshire in the parliament of the previous year, is in deep mourning for the death of his wife, Margaret Clifford. John Atherton, by contrast, is not long wed, and is comfortably ensconced in the parsonage of Huish Champflower.

Atherton is no stranger to the people of Huish, having served the parish as curate since 1620. 'Served' may or may not be the apposite term: as a student in Oxford until 1621, his presence among them must have been intermittent at best. Like all ministers of the Church of England, Atherton is required by canon law to be a man of 'sober conversation': to avoid alehouses, servile labour, dicing, and card play. He is instructed to remember that ministers 'ought to excel all others in purity of life, and should be examples to the people to live well and christianly'. Inside the church at Huish, a table is mounted on the wall to spell out for the people a concrete example of Christian living. This outlines for them 'the degrees prohibited by the laws of God', within which they must not presume to seek a marital partner. These include the sister of a man's first wife. Any such union will be 'judged incestuous and unlawful'. Incest is not a civil crime in this society, but a religious one, punishable by the church courts. As the table makes clear, kinship is not just a matter of shared genetic tissue. A few years earlier, a religious writer has defined it as being 'of two sorts, by society of blood, which is called consanguinity, or by carnal conjunction of man and woman, which is called affinity'. The technical jargon of consanguinal and affinal kinship may not be familiar to all, but the point itself is well understood, for does not the book of Genesis itself teach that when a man leaves his father and mother and cleaves to his wife 'they shall be one flesh'?[16]

Perhaps we will not be surprised to learn that the new rector's pastoral relationship with the parishioners of Huish got off on a bad foot. One Sunday in the autumn of 1622, the churchwardens of the parish were waylaid in the church by Atherton's servant, Thomas Capron, who demanded that they deliver to him for his master's use any wine that had been left over from the communion service. One of the wardens, Richard Darch, objected 'that it was their custom to drink it there'. He received the ominous reply 'that there were many customs in the said parish, but he thought that some of them would be broken shortly'. The rector's servant was as good as his word. Within months, a dispute had broken out about the appointment of the parish clerk, with parishioners complaining to the authorities that he had not been properly sworn in. Parish clerks, whose duties included reciting lessons in church, and teaching the children of the parish to read, occupied an uneasy middle position between clergy and lay people. By the early seventeenth century, the right to nominate them had finally been declared to lie with the minister of the parish, but he was supposed to signify his selection to the parishioners during Sunday service. It looks as though Atherton had omitted this residual nod towards consultation with his flock, a portent of imperious clerical attitudes.[17]

And now we come to the heart of the matter. Sometime in the summer of 1622, Joan Atherton's unmarried sister, Susan Leakey, became pregnant, and was delivered of a child at around Easter 1623. Bastard-bearing was a serious business in the villages of seventeenth-century rural England. Questions of morality apart, a bastard child was a potential charge upon the rate payers of the parish. Churchwardens were sometimes not above carting heavily pregnant women across parish boundaries, so that the expense of maintenance would fall elsewhere, and midwives were encouraged to press women in pains of labour for the name of their child's father, so that responsibility, financial as well as moral, could be fixed upon him. The justices of the peace could become involved, issuing bastardy orders for the support of the child and the chastisement of its parents. In 1610 an Act of Parliament authorized them to send 'lewd women' to houses of correction for a year, and such an institution was soon established in West Somerset, in the county town of Taunton. Two cases from Huish Champflower in the decade before Atherton's arrival there offer a glimpse into a world of financial and emotional misery. In 1613, the father of Joan Cordinge's child was ordered to pay the churchwardens 6d. weekly for its support, and Joan herself was told to see it properly looked after 'or otherwise be committed to the house of correction at Taunton for a year'. In 1615, another unmarried Huish mother, Rebecca More, was not so lucky: the JPs ordered her to be sent to the house of correction, 'there to remain, be set to work and punished'.

Susan Leakey was not an impoverished and friendless maidservant or farm girl, and her drama did not play out in quite this way. For a start she left the parish, taking refuge in the house of Emmina Cookesley some nine miles to the south-east, in the parish of Langford Budville. Like Susan's mother, Cookesley was a widow. Perhaps she was a friend of the elder Susan Leakey, or perhaps someone who simply offered decent lodgings and asked few questions. But the attempt to conceal the pregnancy and birth misfired. In September 1623, the Taunton archdeaconry court took action against Cookesley for having 'received into her house a stranger named Susan Leakey', who was 'there delivered of the said child and suffered to go away unpunished'. A month later, the bishop's court took evidence from the Huish churchwardens, and heard that the court's apparitor and Huish parishioner, John Goodman, had earlier in the year gone to the house 'and there finding one Susan Leakey in bed sick, and demanding of the people of the said house what was the reason of this sickness, they answered that she . . . was there delivered of a child about Easter last'. There was a 'public fame' in the parish that a 'strange child' had been brought to their parsonage house, with Goodman telling people it was Susan's baby.

Rather than simply saying good riddance to the problem of an unwanted local pregnancy, it seems then that the villagers of Huish were taking a remarkable interest in Susan's fate; indeed they had brought it to the attention of the courts in the first place. On 23 June

1623, Susan Leakey of Huish Champflower had been cited on a charge of having committed the crime of incest with Master John Atherton, rector there and husband of her natural sister, and of having borne a child of which Atherton was believed to be the father. Atherton himself was cited before the court on the same day. The basis of the charge was the 'vox et fama' (voice and fame) of the community. This may mean that everyone in Huish believed Atherton to be the child's father, or perhaps that a smaller group of socially significant parishioners had thrown their weight behind the charge. We cannot say for certain whether Susan was ever made to undergo penance or punishment for her offence. She was certainly excommunicated, and was cited before the courts again in late October for 'standing excommunicated and aggravated'. The charge was repeated a month later, and again in December. The commonest cause for the issuing of excommunications by the church courts was the failure of the accused to show up in front of them, and it looks as if Susan had become a persistent judicial truant. What happened to her, and where did she go? Did she return to her mother in Huish, and in due course travel on with her to a new home in Minehead? Perhaps, though there is another, grimmer possibility.[18]

After his initial citation, Atherton does not reappear in the surviving disciplinary record in connection with this matter. Perhaps for absence of proof the charges were dropped and the case dismissed, though, as we have seen, *The Life and Death* suggested that he had 'sued a pardon'. The meaning of this is not entirely clear, though it may imply that Atherton had judicially purged himself, either on his own oath, or with the aid of a specified number of 'compurgators', prepared to attest to their belief in his innocence. It may also mean that Atherton's career as an ecclesiastical lawyer began with an act of egregious perjury. In any case, John Atherton did not, as the poem of 1641 implied, immediately flee to Ireland. Rather he remained in his parish for another six years. The diocesan authorities were apparently prepared to forgive and forget, but the people of Huish Champflower may not have been so understanding. Nor was Atherton himself prepared to hang his head meekly in shame, or take emollient steps to ease his relations with his neighbours. In August 1624 he sought and secured revenge on John Goodman, the parishioner who had played the major role in bringing his incest and adultery to light. Charges were brought against Goodman for a series of abuses and extortions in the exercise of his office as apparitor for the deanery of Dunster, and Atherton was the chief witness against him. On acquiring his post, Goodman had boasted that 'he would not be beholden to the clergy of the said deanery, but they would be beholden to him'. Now he was made to eat his words, sentenced to perform public penance in the parish church of Dunster 'with a white sheet upon his uppermost garment and a white wand in his hand'.

But the contest was by no means over. For in October 1627 Goodman launched a flank attack, citing the former churchwarden William Huishe before the church court for neglecting to report a series of offences committed by the rector. These included failing to recite prayers on weekdays, and being negligent in catechizing the youth of the parish on Sundays. Atherton had also allowed his horses to defile the churchyard, and had omitted to wear the prescribed surplice for saying services—a curious failing in one who was later to become such a public champion of Laudian ceremonialism (and perhaps an indication that political opportunism, rather than ideological commitment, explains his adherence to Wentworth's cause in Ireland). By now, a new reforming bishop—William Laud himself—was in post at Bath and Wells, though it is unclear whether Laud knew about the earlier charges of incest. If he did, it casts a rather different light on his reluctance to accept Atherton's nomination for Waterford, and on his swift response to the later Minehead rumours. It would also be understandable if Atherton was looking for an opportunity to make a fresh start elsewhere; equally understandable if, even after his departure, the odour of scandal were to linger in the locality, and swirl around the nostrils of those like young Elizabeth Leakey who married into the family at about this time. The parish of Huish Champflower itself was certainly left in a mess when Atherton decamped for Ireland. In September 1630, the rector was reported to the church court 'for that he is not resident', and parishioners were confused

about who was actually responsible for serving the cure: an unlicensed minister had preached in the parish church, and another
curate had celebrated communion at Christmas, but 'whether he be
licensed they know not'. Several parishioners, including Atherton's
maidservant, had failed to receive communion, and one had received not in the church, but 'privately in a home of the parish'.
Thanks to the negligence of the churchwardens, the church 'wants
whitening in the inside', and the scriptural texts on the walls were so
worn out that none could read them.[19]

What, however, of the illegitimate child itself? We may think we
know the answer to this: Atherton colluded with his sister-in-law to
murder it. Seventeen years after the alleged event, Sir John Clotworthy told shocked members of the Long Parliament that this was
an act 'for which she suffered and he escaped'. This seems to imply
that Susan Leakey had been tried, convicted, and executed for the
offence. If this were so, sentence would have been given against her
by the Crown's assize judges, who toured the country on regular
circuits to try serious crimes. Unlike incest, the murder of new-born
children was not a merely moral offence punishable by the church
courts. But here our investigation, for the moment at least, hits a
brick wall. The non-survival of all Somerset assize records from
before 1629 makes it impossible to say for certain either that such a
trial did take place, or that it did not. It is striking that the *Life and
Death*, so apparently well informed in many respects, does not make
this particular charge. Nor is there any hint of infanticide in the
ecclesiastical court material generated in 1623, other than the implicit suggestion that Goodman did not actually see the child on his
visit to the house in Langford, and the cryptic report that the child
had been taken to the rectory. Alert readers will also remember one
of the injunctions reportedly given by the ghost to Elizabeth Leakey during their fateful encounter in Minehead in 1636. According
to the minister Heathfield, the apparition had told her to 'go into
Cambridgeshire and fetch home Susan's child, meaning her grandchild' (p. 13). We cannot infer from this whether Susan was alive or
dead at the time. Nonetheless, the family version seems to give the

lie to the suggestion that the baby had been murdered. It had instead been sent away, across the country to the distant fenlands of East Anglia. But could this itself have been a spurious report, designed to allay suspicions of infanticide; or even to hold them in reserve, while a calculating scheme of blackmail unfolded itself?

Like sodomy, the infanticide of new-born infants was a difficult crime to prove in the courts. Rates of stillbirth and neonatal death were by modern (Western) standards very high in this society. Who was to say that a young infant had not died of natural causes? Indeed, if concealment was the aim, who was to say that there had been a death, or a birth, at all? In May 1624, almost exactly a year after Susan gave birth to her child in Somerset, a new Act of Parliament was passed 'to prevent the destroying and murdering of bastard children'. This declared that 'many lewd women' conceiving bastards 'to avoid their shame, and to escape punishment, do secretly bury or conceal the death of their children'. If the child's body were found, they would allege that it was born dead. To prevent this, the Act stipulated that if a woman gave birth to a bastard child, and attempted to conceal its death by secret burial or other means, she should suffer the penalties for murder—unless, that is, she was able to produce at least one witness to attest that the child was born dead. This represented something close to a presumption of guilt in cases where concealment could be demonstrated, a reversal of the usual burden of proof in English common law. Social historians now tell us that the Act was not as draconian in operation as it sounded, that acquittals and pardons were quite common. It is nonetheless notice-able that though the Act mentioned 'the procuring of others', its provisions were aimed squarely at mothers. Perhaps even more than witchcraft, infanticide was a 'sex-specific crime' in seventeenth-century England. The authors of pamphlets and moralistic tracts often portrayed it as the ultimate 'crime against nature', with nurtur-ing mother turned cruel murderess. Men were sometimes accused of participating in cases of infanticide, but were rarely convicted for it.

There were, however, exceptions to the pattern. Murder was murder. In July 1637, as Bishop Atherton was congratulating himself on his success in the Lismore treaty with Cork, a married man was hanged at Northampton for his part in doing away with his adulterously conceived child. The case is reverberant with familiar echoes. The child had been bred in incest: its mother (also hanged for her part in the murder) was the man's 'near kinswoman'. He himself was a parish clergyman, John Barker, the vicar of Pitchley near Kettering. With the help of Barker's maidservant, the parents had sought to conceal the crime. But 'God discovered the same', through the agency of a small boy who saw the servant place the tiny corpse in a hole Barker had dug in his orchard. From the gallows, the minister delivered the expected penitent declaration to the watching crowd, but he denied his guilt of the specific charge on which he had been convicted. Infanticide was, almost by definition, a secret crime, and in the minds of contemporaries its uncovering could be conceived as peculiarly dependent on divine intervention, whether God's instrument took the form of a furtive juvenile apple-scrumper or a visitor from another world. A Cheshire justice of the peace described the murder of new-born children in 1626 as 'a sin which cries for vengeance, and rather than it shall be undiscovered, God will work miracles'.[20]

A dead baby, a supernatural revelation, a succession of secret 'crimes against nature': these elements of our tale will all remain tenaciously present, as we observe the intertwining stories of Mother Leakey and Bishop Atherton start to pull away from their moorings on the harbour of documentary record, and make head-way onto a sea of memory and myth. But not all of the stories and myths about Atherton were fixated upon the themes of deviance and crime. One of the most powerful and enduring of them had a very different agenda indeed. It was the creation of the man we last observed scurrying towards the condemned cell at Dublin Castle in November 1640, after news of the bishop's condemnation was announced to the world: the dean of Ardagh, physician of the soul, and self-publicist extraordinaire, Nicholas Bernard.

5

The Penitent Death of a Woeful Sinner

O N Saturday 28 November 1640, the day after the verdict of guilty had been read against him in the court of King's Bench, John Atherton received a visitor in his cell in Dublin Castle. It was not a time for formalities or small talk, and the caller launched straight into a serious monologue concerning 'the scandal of the fact, justice of the sentence, misery of his condition without repentance'. Atherton heard him out in silence, then asked, warily, if anyone had sent him. The visitor assured him that he had come solely on his own account, whereupon Atherton grasped him by the hand and told him he was very welcome, believing he had 'no other end but his good'. He had, in fact, been advised to send for this very man, but finding him come of his own accord, he supposed him to be 'sent of God'. Atherton at once acknowledged his own 'stupidity and senselessness', and entreated his guest 'to preach the law to him, to aggravate his sins by the highest circumstances, that he might grow but sensible of the flames of hell'. The two men spoke together for nearly two hours, and as the visitor rose to leave, Atherton begged him that he would not depart the city until he had been able to leave him 'in better case'. The bishop of Waterford had exactly one week to live.[1]

Our knowledge of this encounter, like virtually everything we know about Atherton's last few days, is dependent upon one source: Nicholas Bernard's *The Penitent Death of a Woefull Sinner*, printed in Dublin in the autumn of 1641, along with *A Sermon Preached at the Burial of the Said John Atherton* (Figure 9). The work clearly struck a chord with the reading public. It was reprinted in London the following year, and a third edition followed in London in 1651, with the sermon retitled as *A Caveat to the Ministry and People*. Bernard

THE
PENITENT
DEATH
OF A
VVOEFVLL SINNER:
OR,
THE PENITENT DEATH OF
JOHN ATHERTON

Executed at D U B L I N the 5. of
December. 1640. With some Annotations upon severall passages in it.

As also the Sermon, with some further *Enlarge-
ments,* preached at his Buriall.

By *Nicholas Barnard* Deane of Ardagh
in I R E L A N D.

*Quis in seculo peccavit enormiùs Paulo? Quis in religione gra-
viùs Petro? illi tamen per Pœnitentiam assequuti sunt non so-
lum Ministerium, sed Magisterium sanctitatis. Nolite ergo
ante tempus judicare, quia fortasse quos vos laudatis, Deus re-
prehendit, & quos vos reprehenditis, ille laudabit, Primi novissimi, & novissimi Primi.* Petr. Chrysolog.

D V B L I N,
Printed by the Society of Stationers. 1641.

9. The official version, title-page of Nicholas Bernard's *Penitent
Death* (1641)

made no apology for his unadorned style, for 'the plainer it is, the more fitting a narration'. He also assured his readers that every word of it was true, as the author was one of 'whom no relation whatsoever can suspect him partial'. Since we are to spend some time with *The Penitent Death*, we have little option but to take Bernard's word for this. Like the sole survivor of a plane crash or shipwreck, he is someone whose testimony we are in no position to contradict. But if we attend closely to his words, we do not need to suspect him of being an out-and-out liar to see that his account of the final days of John Atherton was very far from being a piece of neutral reportage. It was in fact an ambitious damage-limitation exercise, as well as a work of religious and political propaganda, and an essay in (at times not so subtle) self-promotion. What is more, Bernard's text was to become the foundation stone of many later attempts to extract meaning from the shameful death of the bishop of Waterford. Some of these would reiterate the authorized version Bernard was seeking to establish; others would seek to turn it on its head.

Like so many of the characters in our story, Nicholas Bernard was an English import into the Irish Church. We do not know when or where he was born, though he became an MA of Emmanuel College Cambridge in 1624, a couple of years after John Atherton had similarly graduated in Oxford. Bernard beat Atherton to Ireland, however, and was ordained in St Peter's Church, Drogheda, in December 1626. The officiating bishop was James Ussher of Armagh, whom Bernard had met in England in 1624. Through Ussher's patronage, he acquired the deanery of Kilmore in 1627, and with his backing petitioned the bishop of Kilmore for a second living in the diocese in 1630, after the vicar of Kildrumferton had been persuaded to resign in his favour. A row ensued, of the kind we have already observed breaking out between Atherton and Laud (pp. 69–70). The solidly Protestant bishop of Kilmore, William Bedell, was certainly no admirer of William Laud, but he shared the archbishop of Canterbury's distaste for pluralism. It took a decree of Archbishop Ussher's prerogative court to overcome Bishop Bedell's opposition and install Bernard. Among Church of Ireland bishops, Bedell was virtually unique in attempting to evangelize the native Irish, and in promoting the use of the Irish language to that end. As a non-Irish speaker, Bernard could do very little to save souls in Kildrumferton, and Bedell suspected him (probably rightly) of viewing the benefice purely as a source of revenue. In 1635 Bernard acquired yet another living, the vicarage of St Peter's, Drogheda, in Ussher's own diocese of Armagh, and proceeded to arrange a complete exchange of his offices in Kilmore with the dean of the neighbouring bishopric of Ardagh. Bedell once more protested, ineffectually, against the evils of pluralism and non-residence.

Bernard's advancement, like Atherton's over the same period, was partly a consequence of his own talents, and partly down to a powerful patron. In the client-based world of the Church of Ireland, Bernard was Ussher's man through and through, becoming his chaplain and secretary, and, in later years, his biographer. It is no surprise therefore that *The Penitent Death* was dedicated to the archbishop of Armagh, nor that Ussher himself had apparently commanded Bernard to undertake writing it. The dedication was dated April 1641, but the work was not printed until much later that year, its progress through the press delayed by some 'unusual miscarriage'. Yet, as he explained to his readers, Bernard considered this to have been a fortunate mishap. For in the interim there had appeared 'a scandalous rhyming pamphlet', as well as 'diverse scattered written papers full of mistakes (some pretending to have their original from myself)'. These, he feared, 'may likely have come to thy view as mine'. The pamphlet we are already thoroughly familiar with. The manuscript papers seem not to have survived, though the mention of them provides further evidence of the very public splash created by the fall of the bishop of Waterford. Bernard therefore was obliged to assume the role of spin-doctor, correcting these false stories in order to 'vindicate' the bishop. Yet he made clear at the outset that there was to be no question of his exonerating Atherton's conduct. Even the bishop's deportment at his trial was thoroughly reprehensible: 'his carriage then is by all condemned'. Bernard wanted to tell a different story, one that described how 'afterwards he judged and condemned himself, and so we trust is not condemned of God'. There was potentially a lot at stake here. 'Let God have the glory, thou [the reader] the benefit, the Church cleared of scandal', and the author would rest content. Despite culminating in the violent death of its protagonist, Bernard's is a book designed to supply a happy ending.[2]

Before we get there, however, there is intense psychological drama, a race against the clock to produce the depth and quantity of repentance needed to save Atherton's soul, if not his neck. The *Penitent Death* is a work that straddles several genres familiar to pious readers in the mid-seventeenth century. On the one hand it is a 'conversion narrative', an account of how the life of an inveterate sinner is eventually transformed by an awareness of the free offer of God's forgiveness, part of a tradition of biographical and autobiographical writing which culminates in another work with a provenance in prison, John Bunyan's *Grace Abounding to the Chief of Sinners* (1666). On the other, it is part of the older literary tradition of the *ars moriendi*, the art of making a good death (see pp. 48–9). This was a medieval Catholic preoccupation which had received a vigorous Protestant makeover at the time of the Reformation. Puritan treatises on the manner of dying well were among the leading bestsellers of the early seventeenth century. Nor was it a peculiarly 'godly' preoccupation, as we can see from reports of a death which immediately preceded Atherton's own: that of the Lord Deputy, Christopher Wandesford, in his house on Damaske Street, Dublin, on Thursday 3 December 1640. Years later, his pious Anglican daughter, Alice Thornton, recorded how Wandesford's short last illness was 'full of divine meditations, ejaculations, and prayers'. On the night of his death, Bishop John Bramhall attended on him, and persuaded him 'that he would do well to declare in public his faith and hope in God':

> Immediately my dear father raised up himself with all his force, and steadfastly fixed his eyes to heaven. [He] then made ... a most heavenly and pathetical confession of his faith, hope and confidence in God, and that his heart did fully rely upon the all-saving

merits of Jesus Christ his redeemer, [and] in Him alone hoped for
pardon and remission of all his sins ...

This was a fine copybook specimen, washed in the dye of devout
filial reminiscence. By contrast, the particular appeal of Bernard's
Penitent Death was to combine the conventions of pious and
improving moral literature with a sensational and still topical
news story. In that sense it had something in common with a
third, often less reputable type of popular reading matter: the
'murder pamphlet'. These short relations of 'true crime', laced
with sometimes salacious details of sex and violence, poured from
the presses in the Elizabethan and Stuart decades. They were the
tabloid stories of their day. But at the same time, they were
frequently deeply moralistic texts, and indeed were sometimes composed by clergymen. Even the heavy-duty topic of predestination
was sometimes to be found within their pages. A felon's refusal to
make a declaration of guilt could be taken as a sign of preordained
damnation, for example, though usually the story climaxed satisfy-
ingly with a penitent speech from the gallows. Quite often in such
works, the crime of murder is revealed by miraculous means, occasionally by apparitions of the victims themselves. Yet, as we shall see,
the figure of Mother Leakey is allotted precisely no part in Bernard's
account of the fall and redemption of Bishop Atherton.[3]

When we enter the world of *The Penitent Death* we are plunged into
the heart of an intense working and emotional relationship between
two men, the spiritual equivalent of the boxer and his trainer
preparing for the big fight. Bernard visited the castle three times a
day, and implemented a strict regime there. At the outset, he
advised Atherton to lay aside comfortable clothing, to keep his
chamber dark, and to fast. He also instructed him 'to have his
coffin made, and brought into his chamber'. All of this was a kind
of spiritual mood-music. The first serious step towards recovery was
for Atherton to itemize his sins, and the bishop set to with pen and
ink to record all the wickedness that he could recall, 'in thought,
word, and deed, of omission, or commission against God or man'.

Soon there was a rough draft, which Atherton went over again 'with marginal aggravations', noting the circumstances of time and place, and names of persons he had wronged. Had it managed to survive, this would be quite a document. At this early stage, Atherton was concentrating hard on the 'miserable condition' in which he stood. He imagined himself on the day of judgement, with Christ reciting his sins before men and angels, and he visualized the prospect of hell 'with his wide mouth enlarged to receive him'. He could not yet feel any genuine contrition: his conscience was smitten, 'but still his heart and affections were hardened'.

Monday, and part of Tuesday, was spent in this 'wrestling with God for repentance'; the clock was ticking. On Tuesday afternoon, Atherton unloaded his conscience to Bernard in a flood of tears, 'casting himself down to the ground, taking me by the hand, and desiring me to kneel down by him and pray for him'. The next day, Wednesday, the bishop asked Bernard to keep a solemn fast with him, and between nine in the morning and three or four in the afternoon they sat together without interruption. 'I pray, deal truly, freely and impartially with me. Look not upon me as one that hath had some honour in the Church, from which I am worthily fallen, but as the most abject, base person in the world.' It is hard to imagine words less like those of the Atherton of old. After confessing 'all his sins he could remember from his youth till now', Atherton asked Bernard if he could now see any signs of true penitence in him, and whether he judged him to be in a state of pardon. If so, he begged him 'to pronounce it to him in Christ's stead'. But Bernard was no popish priest, with the power to absolve from sin in the confessional. The best both of them could do was pray 'that God would ratify it in heaven, and seal it inwardly to his soul'.

Mid-week witnessed a serious setback. A new-found sense of his own unworthiness made Atherton begin to fear there was no possibility of salvation for him. As both Catholic and Protestant writers of the time recognized, the 'temptation to despair' was always one of the devil's strongest weapons against the dying. Puritan believers in predestination, ever on the lookout for 'signs' of their status in eternity, were particularly susceptible to it. If Atherton could feel no confidence in God's willingness to forgive him, then all Bernard's efforts with him had struck the rocks. It looked as if it was going to be touch and go.

By Thursday afternoon, Atherton was calmer, 'the storm in his conscience being somewhat allayed'. In the morning he had taken communion with Bernard, and had begged him to stay to dinner. There had also been something of a domestic scene. After hearing her husband's 'discourse of death' and 'thankfulness to God for his punishment', Mrs Joan Atherton 'fell into a passion'. John tried to calm her, remarking that 'he trusted God, who had forgiven the sin, would also in time abate the scandal, and provide for her also'. Joan's response to this, if any, is not recorded. Looking ahead to a life as the widowed mother of five disgraced daughters, she may have been less inclined than her husband simply to trust in the gifts of a benign providence. Later on that day, Atherton's coffin was finally delivered to his cell. He was displeased it had taken so long to arrive, but the delay was a happy accident, for 'now he looked on it with [as] little consternation of mind, as on his bed he must sleep in'. There was a further *memento mori* that evening: news of the sudden, unexpected death of the Lord Deputy, Christopher Wandesford. For Atherton, this was an occasion to thank God that he, unlike Wandesford, had been given advance notice of the day of his departure. If he had not, he 'must undoubtedly then have sunk down to hell'. Wandesford's death, however, also gave rise to a rumour that Atherton might be able to secure a reprieve, at least until a replacement was in office. But the prospect 'moved him not'.

The bishop of Waterford was no stranger to temptations, yet he was learning to put them behind him. The thought of escape had earlier crossed his mind, but he now was able to give thanks for his 'strict imprisonment'. He had also considered petitioning to be beheaded rather than hanged. This was a recognized mark of status which a bishop might claim, and (if done properly) a swifter and less painful end than being turned off the ladder on a rope. Now, however, he considered a dog's death to be too good for him. He had also given thought to where his body might be buried—the final and most permanent indicator of status in this intensely hierarchical society. The most important people were buried inside churches; lesser souls in the churchyard outside. Yet even the churchyard 'he thought was too much honour for him'. Fearing that his friends might procure for him a better place than he deserved, he sent for the clerk of his old Dublin church of St John's. He was to make sure that he was not buried in the church, or in any usual place in the churchyard, but that his grave was fixed 'in the furthest corner, where some rubbish used to be cast, and where none could be remembered ever to have been buried before'. He was, he thought, as unworthy of the society of the dead, as of that of the living.[4]

As well as looking forward into eternity, Atherton was still reviewing his former life. He recounted several little incidents to Bernard, leaving it to his discretion to judge whether 'the knowledge of them might be useful to others'. They are certainly useful to us, struggling as we have been with the enigma of Atherton's character and personality. Some of them concern his relationship with his parents. The bishop knew that he had sinned against the fifth commandment. Ever since he had come of age he had been guilty of 'disrespect and neglect of his mother.' His father, of course, had died when he was a young child (p. 60). Yet he was clearly able to remember him, recalling a single and rather sad episode. Long ago, John Atherton senior had foretold that his son would one day be hanged. Intriguingly, Bernard adds that this 'hath been assured me also by one who had it from an ear-witness'. Perhaps we should not read too much into this disturbing little anecdote; we cannot, much as we would like to, psychoanalyse the dead. Yet it is hard to resist wondering whether the self-destructive urge so evidently a part of the bishop's adult make-up was not somehow rooted in a childhood failure to secure paternal approval. Atherton now sincerely regretted what had been a long-standing mental and verbal habit of his: 'his often wishing, would he were hanged, if this, or that be so'. Stuck in his mind was a particular unpleasant memory on the same theme. Once in his youth, 'in anger and by way of revenge, scaring his mother', as they rode together past a common gallows, he had threatened to hang himself on it with his horse's bridle. We might remember here the coolly fatalistic response Atherton made to Elizabeth Leakey's warning, as reported by the 'scandalous rhyming pamphlet': 'what must be, shall be: if I must, I must die / Marriage, and hanging, come by destiny.' This was in fact an old proverbial saying, recorded as early as the beginning of the sixteenth century, but in the light of all these morbid anecdotes, the placing of it on Atherton's lips may have been more than just a flight of the author's fancy.[5]

There were other, more mundane matters on the bishop's conscience too: drunkenness, frequenting of plays, viewing 'immodest pictures', reading 'naughty books'. He named some of these licentious texts, and wished they were burnt, but, frustratingly, Bernard does not tell us what they were. Yet it seems that, even in the prime of his transgressions, Atherton had not been utterly without feelings of remorse. His conscience had sometimes held him back from sinning 'two or three days together', and in times of sickness or fear of death he would discover 'a very hell within him'. He had even once gone so far as to compose 'a large prayer in the confession of his sins', though, prudently, he had done so in Latin, 'lest any of his servants overhearing him should understand'. Always, however, he had returned to his old ways, 'like the dog to his vomit'. Yet in these last few days the unmistakable signs of a 'true change' were starting to manifest themselves. He sent alms anonymously to the poor, and attempted to make recompense to those he had wronged, paying off his smallest debts and 'sending for some that were mean persons, and asking them forgiveness'. He also immersed himself in works of pious literature. John Foxe's *Book of Martyrs*, with its famous depictions of 'the manner of some godly men's deaths', became a particular inspiration and comfort, as Atherton began to plan the choreography of his own final performance.

On the night of Friday 4 December, the last that he would spend on earth, Atherton sat down to pen a letter to his daughters—a legacy of sound and loving parental advice of the kind which he himself had never perhaps received. A couple of days before, he had composed a similar valedictory letter to his wife, and Bernard printed as an appendix the texts of both letters as evidence of the bishop's 'growth in that time'. The letter to Joan urged his 'dear wife' to mark well 'these last words of him who these twenty years and upwards hath been your husband'. It conceded that 'in my suffering, you suffer both in your credit and estate, and what else soever concerns this world'. But if Joan were to turn to the Lord with all her heart, 'I doubt not but that God will have mercy on you, and prove a husband to you, and a father to my children'. From such starchily conventional pieties there is little we can infer about the inner realities of what must surely have been an often strained and difficult marriage. Who knows how much of a revelation the news of Atherton's infidelities and depravities may have been to his long-suffering wife? Yet Atherton begged Joan to 'misconstrue not these my dying advertisements': they proceeded 'from true affection', and he trusted that they would meet again in heaven.[6] The letter to his children regretted that he would not be able to see them 'well preferred' as he had wished. 'What share will come to your lot' was now wholly in the hands of God. Yet their father bequeathed them his blessing, along with a full inventory of wise counsel: never to go to sleep without making peace with God for the offences of the day; to be constant always in prayer; to be content with whatever God would afford them, 'poverty or riches'; to be obedient to their mother; to 'prefer an honest man that fears God' above all other qualities. Atherton appended an instruction to both letters to 'cast not away this loose paper', but to preserve it as a jewel, 'the legacy of him who can now give no other'.[7] The letters were handed over during a last tear-filled family farewell, at which (once again) his wife proved to be 'the more passionate'. Later, he sent for his servants, and 'gave them each several admonitions with tears, who all wept as if they had been his own'. His final charge to Bernard that night was that if he were asked to preach at his burial on Sunday, he should 'speak no good of me, only what may abate the scandal'.

On the morning of the day of his execution, Saturday 5 December, the bishop of Waterford was, almost literally, a new man. When

Nicholas Bernard arrived to accompany him on his journey to the gallows, Atherton greeted him with exciting news: 'Oh! God hath heard me about four or five of the clock this morning. For the space of an hour and a half I have had that sweetness in my soul, those refreshments in my heart, that I am not able to express.' As they waited for the time to draw nigh, the bishop of Waterford and the dean of Ardagh shared 'many heavenly discourses' together. But if Atherton was going to be able to speak effectively at the place of execution, the body as well as the soul required refreshment: he called 'for a little salt-butter, and brown bread, and the smallest beer'. In these last hours Atherton found himself beginning 'to yearn upon his children', prompting Bernard later to reflect that 'grace, though it be supernatural, yet doth not dry up nature'. The few objects he had still about him—his gloves, staff, belt, and seven or eight books—he gave away to friends as tokens of remembrance. His last act, as his arms were pinioned behind him on the orders of the sheriff of the county ('a papist'), was to present Bernard with the signet-ring from his finger. This was handed over with such expressions of affection, 'as it draws tears from me in the now remembering it'. And with that, the appointed party climbed into the coach, and began the short journey from which all but one of them would return later that day.

Bernard's account of what happened at the place of execution is already familiar to us in its essentials. Atherton denied 'the main thing in the indictment', and passed a few trenchant comments on the procedure of his trial. Yet he also forgave his accusers, and made a frank confession of general and particular sins. There were some offences 'the declaring of which publicly would rather increase the scandal he had given than repair it'. These he had repented of privately before God. But he freely owned up to his neglect of public preaching and catechizing, as well as of domestic prayers within his own family. A few years earlier, he told the onlookers, during a period of sickness, he had become sensible of his neglect of pastoral duties, and had resolved to be more diligent in future. But because the assize judges were at that time meeting in Waterford, he worried that people would think he had changed his ways solely out of fear, and so he carried on as before. After this lost opportunity, he became even worse, and so he 'fell into those vices, which had brought him to this shameful end'—an ambiguous remark which casts some doubt over Bernard's earlier insistence that Atherton consistently denied the sodomy charge. When he had finished what he wished to say, Atherton asked the crowd to pray with him. He recited three of the psalms, and delivered an extempore prayer on the theme of God's forgiveness. The crowd found this so moving, according to Bernard, that 'never was I compassed about so with tears and sobs in my life'. Even 'the very papists, and some priests [that] I saw', knelt down and wept openly.

Atherton was buried at around ten o'clock that evening, in accordance with his wishes, in an obscure part of the churchyard of St John's. Bernard recited the burial office for him, laying his body to rest 'in sure and certain hope of the resurrection'. Some two or three hours earlier, the verger of Christ Church had come to the minister's lodging to tell him that 'there was a rumour of a sermon, and an expectation of my saying somewhat of him'. The church of St John's was already filled to the doors, and 'with abundance of papists also'. Reluctantly (or so he says) Bernard agreed to make 'some short declaration' there.

We do not know exactly what was said. When the sermon was printed in 1641, Bernard took the opportunity to enlarge it with 'seasonable additions, which the shortness of the warning and lateness of the night would not then permit'. We can, however, easily believe that the report of a 'scandalous and ignominious death' had led it to be a packed-out occasion. The churchwardens of St John's subsequently had to pay the considerable sum of nine shillings to repair broken pews, implying a congregation which was expanded to over-capacity, and perhaps behaving raucously.[8] Characteristically, funeral sermons praised the lives of their subjects, yet any attempt to do so in Atherton's case was quite clearly inappropriate. Instead, Bernard's oration covered some of the ground he later elaborated in the *Penitent Death*, stressing the scope and depth of the bishop's repentance. 'Let him die in your thoughts for his life, but let him live in your memories by his penitent death.' Whether at funerals or elsewhere, Protestant preachers always spoke to a text.

Bernard's was from the Acts of the Apostles 26: 17–18: 'I send thee to open their eyes, to turn them from darkness to light, from the power of Satan unto God, that they may receive forgiveness of sins.' The principal doctrinal point which Nicholas Bernard wished to get across concerned 'the dignity of preachers, Christ's messengers'. Their task was to convert men and women, to open their eyes. The supreme importance of preachers could be measured in the countless glowing terms by which they were described in scripture: watchmen, shepherds, ambassadors, salt of the earth, light of the world. Naturally, Bernard did not wish his hearers to think that such reflections proceeded from 'any pride in magnifying our calling'. Atherton, he reported, had intended at his execution to make 'a large exhortative speech to the diligent performance of his function in preaching and catechising'. But thinking that few of his own faith would be present, and fearing that the papists 'would but deride him', he had decided to leave it out. Bernard now made good the omission, reminding the congregation that at their ordination ministers (and indeed, bishops) were presented with a Bible, along with a solemn charge to preach its message. This was in fact 'the sum of the office'. Yet preachers needed to be ever more diligent in performing this duty. Apart from anything else, 'the sight of those of the Romish clergy in every corner, who travel sea and land to make their proselytes' ought to 'whet our resolutions to be more industrious'. John Atherton was both a salutary reminder of what could happen when preachers took their eyes off the ball, and an inspiring example of the effects their labours could achieve. 'He that was hated at his condemnation, is loved at his execution. Such as were grieved at his life, are comforted at his death. He began with his own tears, he departs with the tears of others.' It was an oratorical tour de force. Bernard heard afterwards that many papists who came to his sermon were much affected by what they had heard: 'one who came casually thither fell into tears in the very church, and was converted'.

The last grains fall to the foot of the hour-glass, and Nicholas Bernard draws to a close in the pulpit of St John's, a preacher

preaching passionately about the pre-eminence of preachers. It is
time for us to take stock. I have let Bernard tell his story about
himself and Atherton, with minimal interruption or contradiction,
and we can probably all agree that it is a very moving and edifying
tale. As was noted at the outset, we have little opportunity either to
confirm or to contradict the exact substance of any of it. But we can
examine a little more closely just what messages Bernard intended
his readers to carry away from the eighty or so pages of text that he
devoted to the case of the bishop of Waterford. It is time, as
historians like to say, to interrogate the source.

If John Atherton is the chief protagonist of the *Penitent Death*,
there is little doubt that Nicholas Bernard is himself the hero: the
tireless, dedicated master-confessor, who in an exciting race-
against-time shapes and perfects the wayward bishop as a peniten-
tial work of art. It is fair to wonder whether Bernard's rapid
appearance at Atherton's cell door was prompted entirely by pastoral concern for a lost soul, or whether the career-savvy dean of
Ardagh had sensed a once-in-a-lifetime opportunity, a chance to
make a name for himself on the back of what must have seemed the
criminal trial of the decade. A few months later, when the Irish
rebellion bloodily erupted, Bernard rushed to set his name to some
of the first news pamphlets reporting on events—it suggests an
almost compulsive desire to be seen at the thick of the action.[9] In
the *Penitent Death*, other voices, other presences, are routinely
suppressed, though an against-the-grain reading of Bernard's text
shows them to have been there nonetheless. We hear briefly of an
unnamed friend of Atherton's who wrongly feared that 'the party to
whom he had given up himself [i.e. Bernard] was too mild'; of a
second friend who advised him to read a story from John Foxe the
night before his execution. There was another unidentified layman,
whose 'discourses' (Bernard grudgingly conceded) 'had some work
on him for the present'. In addition there were the 'divers divines,
with others that came to visit him', and the 'many that came unto
him', whom Atherton advised not to follow his example by
deferring their own repentance. Atherton's incarceration in
Dublin Castle was clearly not the exercise in dark and solitary

contemplation, or the uninterrupted dialogue of master and pupil, that a cursory reading of Bernard might suggest. Nor was the dean of Ardagh above a bit of direct self-justification when the occasion called for it. In the course of his oration on the necessity for the people to hear preaching, Bernard incongruously remarked that it was 'possible for some urgent cause, the maintenance out of one place may be employed for the upholding of God's service in another'. Bernard, who was every inch as much as Atherton the shamelessly non-resident pluralist, could hardly have argued otherwise.

Yet it would be ungenerous to regard *The Penitent Death* as solely an exercise in authorial self-aggrandizement. Bernard's initial approach to Atherton may have come about on his own initiative, but the account was published at the request of Archbishop Ussher, and for some fairly obvious reasons. The word 'scandal' buzzes around Bernard's texts like a bluebottle in an enclosed room. The all-too-public disgrace of one of its bishops risked weakening the Church of Ireland's already compromised mission to spread the gospel in a benighted island. Bernard wrote defensively of 'the expected calumny of the adversaries', the papists who would crow over the church's discomfiture. Small wonder that Bernard was careful to emphasize that from the scaffold Atherton had desired his name of infamy 'might rest only upon himself, and not be imputed to his profession', or that he lost no opportunity to point out how papists themselves had been deeply moved by the bishop's demeanour (and by the eloquence of his own sermon). If they sought to make capital from the case, they could expect to be repaid in kind: 'let not the papists object this scandal to our Church, lest we return them such foul stories from that Holy See, which we have no mind to raise'. It was the logic of mutually assured defamation. In any case, 'a Church ought not to be judged by the lives of a few professors, but by the doctrine professed'. There had been a Judas among the Apostles.

The papists, however, were not the only ones Ussher and Bernard had to worry about. The scandalous pamphlet that hastened the publication of the *Penitent Death* was not, after all, the work of a

Catholic author. As we have already seen (pp. 106–7), the disgrace of Atherton was an open goal to the root-and-branch opponents of Protestant episcopacy, or, as Bernard called them, 'such hateful birds, as ... defile their own nests by imputing it as an aspersion to the whole profession'. The reaction of such fault finders was depressingly predictable: 'let there be one gross offender in the ministry, he shall be ever gazed at, but they remember not the many glorious martyrs and unblemished preachers, who have shined in that firmament also'.

Nicholas Bernard castigated others for exploiting Bishop Atherton's unhappy fate for their own partisan ends, but he was engaged on precisely the same mission himself. His aim was to exonerate episcopacy in spite of the unworthiness of one of its representatives—but not episcopacy in the mould of William Laud or John Bramhall. In that sense at least, he and the author of *The Life and Death of John Atherton* were singing from the same hymn sheet. His attempted rehabilitation of the bishop of Waterford represented part of the revenge of what it is tempting to call 'Old' Church of Ireland over 'New' Church of Ireland. In Bernard's story some past controversies within the church are resurrected to telling effect. Among the sins of which Atherton accused himself was his unfairness to 'those whom he had prosecuted too bitterly in the High Commission Court'. Another failing was 'his too much zeal and forwardness, both in introducing and pressing some church-observations, and in dividing himself from the house of Convocation, *Anno* 1634, in opposition to the *Articles of Ireland*'. In other words, during the struggle over the introduction of the English articles and canons he had sided with the modernizers Bramhall, Laud, and Wentworth against Ussher and the venerable Calvinist tradition of the Irish Church (see p. 67). His motivation had not been so much an ideological one, as a desire 'to please some men's persons'. But these dignitaries had 'notwithstanding (with just cause) now forsaken him'. We might remember here that in the first week of December 1640, John Bramhall had made a pastoral visit to the dying Wandesford in Damaske Street, but not, it seems, to his old acquaintance and ally incarcerated in Dublin Castle.

Atherton's tragedy in fact revealed the complete moral bank-
ruptcy of Wentworth's priorities for the church. 'How able and
active this our Brother was in the recoveries of...dues, ye all
know', but in the process of regaining the rights of the Church he
had veritably 'lost himself'. The gaining of souls, 'the rights of
Christ', had been shamefully neglected. Bernard assures us that, if
Atherton had had longer to live, he would have 'given over all law
business, and have wholly employed his time in preaching'. In
Bernard's account, in fact, it is this neglect of preaching, rather
than any sexual or moral degeneracy, which troubles the bishop of
Waterford's conscience most acutely. Preaching was the essence of a
bishop's vocation, and the model of the preaching bishop was,
naturally enough, Archbishop James Ussher himself. In a marvel-
lously ingratiating dedication to his master and patron, Bernard
portrays Ussher as the template, the very 'picture' of what St Paul
looked for in a bishop: 'by which, if others in this age had been so
drawn, I believe the office had never been so much as questioned'.
There is an implied contrast here, not just with the disgraceful
Atherton, but with Archbishop William Laud, the spot-lit target
of anti-episcopal sniping across the three kingdoms, a bishop who
had once written that 'the altar is the greatest place of God's
residence on earth, greater than the pulpit; for there 'tis *Hoc est
corpus meum*; but in the other it is at most *Hoc est verbum meum*, This
is my word'.[10]

Atherton—in Bernard's account of him—was not just a walking
indictment of Laudian policies and priorities, but an actual convert
from Laudianism to a more authentic form of Protestant belief. The
theological message of *The Penitent Death* is that God's free and
unmerited gift of forgiveness is the only source of human salvation,
and that all those predestined to be saved can truly develop a sense
of 'assurance' that God has forgiven their sins. There is no truck
with 'Arminian' notions that human beings might possess the 'free
will' to accept or reject God's saving offer (see p. 31). Near the start
of his roller-coaster week of spiritual discovery, Atherton declares
that, 'whatsoever he had before uttered', he now 'utterly condemned
that doctrine of free-will naturally in man to have any saving

good'—or so at least Bernard claimed. It is a kind of doctrinal parable: Atherton was the prodigal son, who had finally given up the glittering seductions of Laudianism for the home farm of solid Calvinist orthodoxy.

Nicholas Bernard's audacity certainly deserves our admiration. Faced with the most disgraceful episode in the recent history of the Church of Ireland, he spun it around to fight a spirited three-cornered battle against malignant papists, Laudian ceremonialists, and presbyterian fanatics alike. Atherton's journey of discovery had become thinly disguised propaganda for a 'third way' in the Church—a path between root-and-branch radicalism on the one hand and the discredited status quo on the other. It was a route down which many of King Charles's Protestant subjects seemed willing to travel at the start of the 1640s. The English parliament was receiving a wave of petitions from the counties at this time, critical of Laudian 'innovations' but upholding the institution of episcopacy itself.[11] Ussher left Ireland never to return in April 1640. But in London, the archbishop of Armagh was lobbying hard for the retention of bishops, and for a vision of the Church—episcopalian, Calvinist, evangelical, unambiguously anti-Catholic—which he and many others could still remember from the reign of James I. It was not in the end to be. The Protestant bishops were driven out of Ireland by the Catholic uprising which started in 1641, and which continued to hold sway until Oliver Cromwell and his lieutenants reconquered the island in 1649–52. In England, meanwhile, the king's victorious opponents, radicalized by Civil War, formally abolished episcopacy in 1646.

With the return of Charles II in 1660, bishops were restored in both kingdoms. Ussher himself had died in 1656, and his replacement at Armagh in 1660 was none other than the aged John Bramhall, a triumphant survivor of all that had transpired and conspired against him over the past two decades. In another irony, the post was held in 1685 by Michael Boyle, the nephew of Atherton's predecessor at Waterford, and a kinsman of the earl of Cork, when the accession, and then deposition, of the Catholic King James II plunged Ireland into a further round of war and rebellion, from which parts of it have still not completely recovered.[12]

⁂

Once again we are running ahead of ourselves; we are not quite finished with our forensic interrogation of Bernard's *Penitent Death*. In spite of his grand political objectives, and his generously expansive treatment, there are some notable absences from Bernard's text. Indeed, the two themes which are perhaps the most interesting and significant features of the entire Atherton story are ones he entirely fails to mention. The first of these, of course, is the sodomy itself. The crime for which Atherton was condemned to death is nowhere mentioned by name, and any reader unfamiliar with the background to the case would be hard pressed to guess exactly what it was. Apart from the passing remark that at his trial and execution the bishop maintained his innocence of 'the main thing in the indictment', there is only one possible, and very indirect, allusion to the nature of his offence. Bernard states that Atherton had thanked God for the gift of a week's preparation; otherwise he feared he 'should still have lingered, like Lot in Sodom'. The allusion is to the book of Genesis (chapter 19) where, despite the warning of angels to take his wife and daughters and leave the doomed city, Lot delays, and is only thanks to the mercy of God ejected from the city before fire rains down upon it. Lot, of course, was an innocent man in that wicked place. Yet in no real sense does Bernard seek to portray Atherton as the victim of a miscarriage of justice. On the contrary, it is the bishop's acceptance of his just desserts which provides the starting point for a sequence of personal and political redemptions. Bernard must have worried that any overt attention to the alleged sodomy would simply over-freight his carefully calibrated moral equations. The crime was so 'detestable' and 'abominable' that it was 'amongst Christians not to be named'. Bernard took Sir Edward Coke's observation to heart in its most literal construction (p. 89).

As all readers of this book will have noticed, the other screaming silence in the *Penitent Death* is that of our friends, the

Leakeys. The rumours beginning in 1636, and given wide circulation in the pamphlet of 1641, that the ghost of Atherton's mother-in-law had returned with a message of repentance for the incestuous bishop, and that his sister-in-law Elizabeth had carried it across the sea to Ireland, are entirely air-brushed out of the picture Bernard creates. As an orthodox Protestant divine, he might simply have rubbished the tales of revenance as a fraud or superstition, or even rejected them as a demonic delusion. His reasons for choosing quietly to ignore them must remain his own. They were, of course, part of a very different narrative about the bishop from the one Bernard was constructing. They spoke of a refusal to repent and of an inexorable divine vengeance bearing down, rather than of a heartfelt response to an offer of divine mercy. There is, however, one curious little aside to be found in the *Penitent Death*, containing the most oblique of hints about the rumours from Somerset.

> About three weeks ... before the complaint was put in against him in Parliament, the man who had before been the corrupter of him in his youth, whom he had not seen in twenty years before, came casually out of England into this kingdom and visited him, the sight of whom did so affright him, as if some ghost had appeared to him. He said his very heart misgave him, and his conscience apprehended him as some presage, or messenger of a prescient vengeance drawing nigh.

It is the kind of clue we have encountered before in our pursuit of John Atherton: fascinating, intriguing, and frustratingly intangible. Who was the mysterious man, and in what way exactly had he 'corrupted' Atherton in his youth? Why, after twenty years, did he choose to visit him in Ireland in the early summer of 1640? What did they discuss? Is it even possible that there was no such man and no such meeting? That the incident was invented by Bernard to plant in his readers' minds a plausibly naturalistic origin for rumours they might have heard concerning a ghost, a threat of divine retribution, an unexpected visitor from England, and a long-buried secret? Perhaps. But if Nicholas Bernard was prepared to obfuscate about this, how much of the rest of his narration was honest reporting, how much of it tendentious myth-making?

A work like the *Penitent Death* is a document of its time. But it is also a document existing in time, preserved over decades and centuries in studies and libraries, and becoming part of the present reality for each new and curious reader. Within a few years of its first publication, the clock of history was already taking its toll, reducing the number of those with first-hand knowledge of Bishop Atherton, and thus with independently formed views of the significance of his life and death. Joan Atherton did not long outlive her husband, and was buried, in the same churchyard of St John's Dublin, in January 1642. The mighty earl of Cork and the humble Alexander Leakey both died in 1643. Archbishop Laud perished under the headman's axe in 1645, pursued to the very last by Sir John Clotworthy, who stood on the scaffold and taunted him. Clotworthy himself died in 1665, four years after Nicholas Bernard. Elizabeth Leakey quietly passed away, in Minehead, in 1656.[13] Atherton, in other words, was becoming a figure from history, long before he appears to us in that same problematic guise.

In the later decades of the 1600s, a century split in half by the trauma of civil war and revolution, a number of commentators looked back across the divide and remembered the story of Bishop Atherton. They did so with varying motives and intentions. At first glance it is perhaps surprising that Irish Catholic writers seem to have displayed relatively little interest in the Atherton case, largely confounding Bernard's fears that they would use it to undermine the ever tenuous hold of the Church of Ireland on the people of the island. The 1641 rebellion, and subsequently, the bloody Cromwellian reconquest, had of course intervened as great watersheds between the present and a still recent past. It may also be the case that Bernard's skill in refiguring Atherton as a model of repentance and Calvinist assurance made him appear rather unpromising material for Catholic polemic.

One commentator who did see such potential, however, was a Galway priest named John Lynch, author of a number of historical works written during his exile in France in the 1650s and 1660s. Lynch's *magnum opus* was his *Cambrensis Eversus*, published in Latin at St Malo in 1662. The title (which means 'the Welshman Overthrown') reveals the fact that his opponent was not a contemporary Englishman, but a Welsh priest who had already been dead for over four hundred years, Giraldus Cambrensis, or Gerald of Wales. Gerald's famous *Topographia Hibernica* was full of observations about the customs and behaviour of the Irish, observations that Lynch considered outrageously libellous. He was particularly enraged by the Welshman's suggestion that blindness and deformity were widespread in Ireland as a result of the unnatural sexual practices of the populace there. According to Lynch, there was no evidence at all for the medieval Irish being 'plunged by sensualism into unnatural crimes'. Moreover, any subsequent outbreak of 'that preposterous lust' should be laid firmly at the door of others. For 'Ireland was ignorant of these crimes, and it was not till lately, and many centuries after the death of Giraldus, that laws were made to repress them'. What Lynch had in mind here was the sodomy statute of 1634, implying, with debatable logic, that the absence of repressive legislation proves the non-existence of the problems it is framed to redress. Indeed, Lynch went further, and argued that sodomy's importation into the island could be precisely dated: it was an exotic seedling first brought over and planted in Irish soil by John Atherton, the 'Pseudo-Bishop' of Waterford. We are likely to have our own views about the notion that sodomites, like snakes, were simply unknown in Ireland before modern times. It represents, in fact, a turning on its head of the argument sometimes made by Protestant propagandists that it was the Jesuit colleges on the continent who were responsible for introducing homosexuality into England.

Nonetheless, Lynch's diatribe supplies a revealing picture of how, a decade and more after his death, the Protestant bishop of papist Waterford was remembered in some Catholic circles. Atherton, a man 'who was himself guilty of all kinds of lust', severely punished fornication, adultery, and incest in others, 'though his heart was polluted by those very crimes of which he affected so stern a hatred'. This much we have heard several times already, but the *Cambrensis Eversus* managed to bring a new twist to its discussion of Atherton's sexual hypocrisy. According to Lynch's information, Atherton himself had 'originated' in the Irish parliament the law making sodomy a capital crime, and thus was 'caught in the snare which he had laid for others'. More than this, 'he was the first person committed of having violated his own law, and was executed for the offence'. It was poetic justice of the highest and most perfect order.

It is in fact just plausible that Atherton's may have been the first judicial execution for sodomy in Ireland (John Child's came four months later). However, the loss of the records of early seventeenth century assize courts for Ireland (just as for Somerset) makes it impossible to assert this with any certainty. The idea that Atherton was the driving force behind the Sodomy Act seems much less likely. For a start he was not a member of the 1634 parliament, though it is conceivable that the parliamentary legislation might have been discussed in Convocation where Atherton did sit. As has been suggested already (pp. 89–90), it is likely that the sodomy bill was brought forward as part of a general government-sponsored reform programme, rather than as a moral crusade on the part of any one individual. Yet, however it originated, the notion that the bishop of Waterford had been thoroughly hoist with his own petard was clearly much too appealing an idea to resist. Of all the myths accumulating around John Atherton, the shelf-life of this particular one was to prove remarkably enduring.[14]

If Catholic writers were surprisingly reticent, numerous memories and traditions about Atherton were crystallizing in the hands of Protestant authors in the decades after his death. The case was picked up for example by Henry Hickman, an English minister who was ejected from his parish for nonconformity at the Restoration, and who took charge of an exiled English Church at Leiden in the Netherlands. In the course of a long-running literary duel with the unreconstructed Laudian propagandist, Peter Heylin, the

Calvinist Hickman sought to demonstrate the hazards of 'Arminian' doctrine. If he so wished, he claimed, he could produce many instances of those 'who whilst they were profane, were Arminians to the full', but who abandoned this fallacy after a God-given experience of conversion. If anyone questioned this, he would simply refer them to 'the history of the life and death of the executed Irish bishop, published by Dr Bernard'. Hickman had clearly understood the not-so-subtle theological sub-text underpinning Nicholas Bernard's narrative.

Some other writers were more concerned, however, with the morals that could be gleaned from the profaneness of Atherton's life. At some point in the 1660s or 1670s a Scottish clergyman called Alexander Clogie wrote a manuscript entitled *Speculum Episcoporum*, the mirror of a bishop. The bishop in question was William Bedell, at one time Nicholas Bernard's disapproving superior in the see of Kilmore (see pp. 128–9). Clogie, Bedell's son-in-law, portrayed him in the memoir as nothing less than a Protestant saint. But it is his interest in the fate of another bishop that concerns us here: the long-suffering Archibald Adair of Killala (see pp. 84–5). Having described Adair's unjust punishment before High Commission, Clogie was sure that his readers would wish to know 'what becomes of this poor, deprived and imprisoned bishop at last'.

> I will tell you. One of his grand-jury-men, that was fiercest against him was one D. Adderton, sometime preacher at St John's in Dublin, but then bishop of Waterford. This prelate was by the just judgement of God accused, arraigned and condemned for iniquities far above all that is left upon record concerning Sodom, and executed in the public place of shameful death, the popish sheriff Walsh insulting over him, and rejoicing that his tree did bear such desired fruit, adding that *he hoped ere long to have it bear more of the same kind*, to the great scandal of religion.

These details were not derived from Bernard's book, which does not name the sheriff, or quote any of his words. Clogie conceded that Dr Bernard 'believed that God gave him repentance unto life', and that he had preached a good sermon at his funeral. But his own primary concern was with the extraordinary turn-about whereby the former bishop of Killala, 'that was cast out of his bishopric and deprived of his episcopal dignity for inconsiderable trifles', had subsequently been promoted to fill Atherton's own position. Just as in the hands of the Catholic John Lynch, Atherton was again the perfect foil for a 'providentialist' anecdote, demonstrating the inexorable justice of the Almighty, if not the fact that He possessed a sense of humour. Clogie had one more biographical detail to relate about Atherton. He claimed that after the bishop's execution 'his poor wife went for England to petition for the £800 (her portion) which a great courtier was reported to have received for procuring that tragical promotion for her husband'. In other words, Atherton had bought his bishopric, or got someone to buy it for him. As we saw in the manœuvrings over Huish Champflower, John Atherton was not necessarily incapable of committing the sin of simony (pp. 68–70). But there is surely no truth to this particular rumour. Waterford and Lismore in 1636 was hardly a saleable commodity—the problem for Laud and Wentworth was getting someone suitable to take it on any terms. Nonetheless, the suggestion that there was something highly irregular about Atherton's promotion to the episcopate is an interesting reflex—perhaps he had not really been a proper bishop at all.

The charge was repeated a few years later in a published biography of Bedell, which drew heavily on Clogie's manuscript. This was the work of another Scottish minister, Gilbert Burnet, a renowned historian of the Reformation, then based in London. Burnet's book was published in 1685, shortly after the accession of the Catholic James II to the English throne. Its author was soon to go into exile on the continent, returning after the Revolution of 1688 and eventually becoming bishop of Salisbury. In his account of Adair, Burnet informed readers that his restoration was to a bishopric 'which came to be vacant upon a dismal account, which I would gladly pass over if I could, for the thing is but too well known'. Nonetheless, he gamely recounted Atherton's misdeeds. Having acquired Waterford by 'a simoniacal compact', the bishop successfully 'covered his own unworthiness, as all wicked men are apt to do'. Burnet chose to gloss Atherton's capital offence with the familiar tag used by Edward Coke—'a crime not to be named'. But in case there was any doubt, he added a clue for all those who knew their Bible: it was the sin 'that God punished with fire from heaven'. Like Clogie, Burnet was rather tepid in his endorsement of Bernard's book, noting merely that Atherton had 'expressed so great a repentance that Dr Bernard ... had a very charitable opinion of the state in which he died'.[15]

Yet in the main, the authors who remembered Bishop Atherton in the last decades of the seventeenth century were not so interested in fighting old ideological battles as in drawing uplifting moral conclusions from the pattern of his life and death. The tone was set within a few years of Bernard's passing by a writer who had certainly known Atherton personally, and quite possibly Bernard as well, the diarist, antiquarian, and Irish auditor-general, Sir James Ware. Ware's last work was a history of the bishops of Ireland, arranged diocese by diocese. His biography of Atherton was brief and to the point. The bishop had been condemned and executed 'for a crime not to be named'. But while in prison he had displayed true penitence 'with many tears and sighs, deploring the sins of his previous life'. This emphasis on the admirable repentance, rather than the earlier depravity, was precisely the impression Bernard had wished to leave ('Let him die in your thoughts for his life, but let him live in your memories by his penitent death'). In fact, by the middle years of Charles II's reign, Atherton's demeanour in the shadow of the gallows was acquiring the status of an approved pattern for emulation. So, for example, he was brought to the attention of Henry Jones, a young Welshman condemned to death in March 1672 for the unnatural murder of his own mother. As Jones sat awaiting execution in Monmouth gaol, he received a letter from a minister which advised him to consult 'such soul-searching books as may help to awaken, direct, comfort and further you in the way of salvation', and specifically those that 'treat of conversion, repentance, and the last things'. The minister thought Jones would do particularly well to get hold of 'such books as have been set forth of penitent malefactors, as Bishop Ather-ton ... and others, who being cast into prison for great crimes, were through divine mercy brought to repentance'. Dying well was an art that had to be learned, and one could pick up handy hints from the masters of the craft: 'Bishop Atherton found that...shutting the windows, making the room somewhat dark, was helpful to humiliation'.

Whether or not the unfortunate Henry Jones found solace in emulating the bishop's self-inflicted 'humiliation', there is little doubt that Atherton's story held a particular appeal for members of the clergy. A Shropshire minister, Robert Foulkes, himself tried and executed for infanticide in 1679, consciously modelled his own pattern of repentance on Atherton's, and an account of his death was published which lifted verbatim several phrases from *The Penitent Death of a Woefull Sinner*. 'Dr Bernard's Sermon at the funeral of John Atherton' was one of the 'bundles of pamphlets in quarto' found in the possession of the renowned nonconformist minister, Thomas Manton, on his death in 1677. A quarter of a century before, Manton had helped a fellow presbyterian clergyman, Christopher Love, to prepare for execution after his part in a failed attempt to restore Charles II to the throne. Love began his scaffold speech in 1651 with the very words that had come into Atherton's mind on his journey to Oxmantown Green ten years before: 'I am this day made a spectacle unto God, angels and men...'

Not all condemned prisoners were as spiritually adept as the godly Love. Most were common criminals, murderers, and thieves. Like Nicholas Bernard, seventeenth-century English ministers often ventured into the prisons in order to 'save' condemned felons, looking to bring them to an understanding of their own wickedness, and an assurance of their forgiveness in Christ. Many of those involved in this work must have dreamt of producing an 'Atherton' from the unpromising raw material to be found in Newgate and the county gaols. The bishop's heart-rending valedictory letters to his wife and children struck such a chord with a young clergyman from Plymouth, Abednego Seller, that in the later 1670s he copied them word-for-word out of Bernard's treatise into his commonplace book. At almost exactly the same time, another Plymouth minister was labouring, with mixed success, in the prison at Exeter to bring two convicted murderesses to a humble recognition of their own unworthiness, and their total dependence on God's mercy.[16] The minister's name was John Quick. By a remarkable coincidence, some extraordinary matters about the former bishop of Waterford had happened to come to his attention, and he too was writing them down. None of this would be made public until some years after Quick's own death. For the moment, the papers lay locked in his study, a manuscript time-bomb, waiting for its moment to explode into print (see Chapter 7).

When Atherton's story was retold in the later seventeenth century, there often seemed to be an inclination, not to forget, but certainly to forgive. This was the attitude taken by Anthony Wood, the indefatigable antiquarian who in 1691–2 produced a huge biographical register of authors produced by the University of Oxford, the *Athenae Oxonienses*. The *Athenae* included Oxfordians who had become bishops, as well as those who had published books. Though Atherton was hardly the most distinguished of this group, Wood's short biography struck a strikingly generous note. To Wood, Atherton was simply 'the unfortunate bishop of Waterford in Ireland'. He noted the 'great sufficiencies in the canon law and ecclesiastical affairs' which had brought Atherton to the attention of Thomas Wentworth. Remarkably, he also claimed that as bishop of Waterford Atherton had 'behaved himself for some time with great prudence'. His crime, naturally, was 'not now to be named', and he had been degraded and executed for it (something which, as we know, was not entirely technically accurate). For further particulars, Wood referred his readers to Dr Bernard's book, which he recommended as being 'very worthy of perusal'.[17]

From an Irish Protestant perspective, Atherton's case was revisited in 1689 by Sir Richard Cox, a County Cork lawyer, and later Lord Chancellor of Ireland, who completed a two-volume history of the island while sheltering in England from the pro-Catholic regime of James II's Lord Deputy, the earl of Tyrconnell. Atherton's was a 'tragical end', and his punishment, 'for a crime not to be named', had scandalized those patrons whose expectations he had managed to satisfy for a time. Nevertheless, 'his unparalleled repentance, and the most pious manner of his death, hath obtained for himself the pity of all good men, and undoubtedly the mercy of God'. This was precisely the kind of thing Bernard would have wanted to hear. Interestingly, Cox rejected the claim of Gilbert Burnet that Atherton had acquired the bishopric of Waterford through simony. The diocese was at the time so poor that it was 'too small a temptation to so great a sin'. More likely, as 'a bustling man of active parts', Atherton had seemed an appropriate instrument 'to promote some designs that were then on foot...for the recovery of the ancient possessions of his see'—an assessment that seems pretty much spot on. Cox's cautious defence of Atherton shows how the case could still lend itself to political purposes in the closing years of the seventeenth century, the first great age of party politics. Burnet was a Whig, one of those who enthusiastically supported the deposition of James II during the Glorious Revolution of 1688, and hailed its negative implications for the 'divine right' of kings. By contrast, 'Tories' had accepted the regime change with heartache and reluctance. Cox was one of the latter. He privately called himself 'an anti-Whig', and hated the 'canting, lying and hypocrisy' he associated with their tactics and views.[18]

Nonetheless, it was the death not the life of the bishop of Waterford which still attracted most attention in the closing years of the century. In 1690, Atherton's story was selected for inclusion in a work entitled *The Wonders of Free-Grace: Or, A Compleate History of all the Remarkable Penitents that have been Executed at Tyburn and Elsewhere for these Last Thirty Years*. This was a kind of greatest hits album of good deaths on the gallows, 'a faithful account of the ends of dying penitents legacied out for the use, example and improvement in piety of those they left behind them'. The story of Atherton's dramatic conversion was by now famous enough to demand admittance, despite falling a full twenty years outside the chronological limits the compiler had set for himself. No writer's name is attached to the text, though the work was published by the printer and pamphleteer, John Dunton, who may well have undertaken the editorial work himself. (Dunton's is another name which will recur in our story.) Despite its inevitably gory subject matter, the tone was intended to be uplifting. The book aimed to teach that God's love extended to the greatest of sinners, and that 'none need despair of the sufficiency and fullness of his mercy and free-grace, or give way to unseasonable doubtings in their souls'. Atherton's confession was 'most Christian-like', his penitence 'extraordinary'. Once again, his offence was not identified outright, though a reference to 'unnatural concupiscence' offered rather more of a clue than Bernard had deigned to provide. Nor did *The Wonders of Free-Grace* follow Bernard in reporting Atherton's protestation of innocence of the main charge. Instead, having been condemned for unnatural lust, the bishop felt 'a true sense of his so highly offending'. Nonetheless, the author did imitate Bernard's lead in one crucial respect: 'we humbly conceive the untimely fall of this unfortunate gentleman will not be interpreted to the prejudice of that Church, of which he sometimes was an unworthy member, since his falling away was visibly retrieved to his own comfort, and the glory of the Christian profession'. Rather than sticking odorously, the mud had been washed away to leave the institution of episcopacy looking, if not whiter than white, then at least a thoroughly serviceable garment of faith.[19]

Half a century after the event itself, the accepted meaning of John Atherton's imprisonment and execution had been thoroughly transformed. We can only marvel at how an incident fraught with extreme danger for episcopacy and the established Church seems to have been so effectively defused, and turned to the advantage of the authorities. Moreover, all traces of Mother Leakey's ghost, of the insolent attempts of humble Somerset folk to insert themselves into the calculations of the great and the good, appeared to have been wiped from the record. Those who derived their knowledge of the story from Bernard of course had no choice in the matter, for he, as we have seen, suppressed virtually all suggestions of a supernatural doom hanging over the bishop of Waterford. History repeats itself, but historians repeat each other. At the end of the seventeenth century, the story of Bishop Atherton seemed tagged and locked: the scandal of a debauched clerical life obliterated for ever

by the compelling account of an exemplary penitent death. But
the channels of transmission from the past to the present sometimes take unexpected turns, or can run for years below the surface,
undetected by the self-appointed arbiters of taste and memory. In
the opening years of the eighteenth century, Nicholas Bernard's
cosy monopoly of public recollection was to be rudely invaded. The
case of Bishop Atherton was to become, for a time at least, once
more a matter of pressing topical concern, and Mother Leakey's
ghost was to return with a vengeance.

INTERLUDE
In a London Coffee House

JANUARY 1710, a brisk Thursday afternoon among the clientele of Slaughter's Coffee House in St Martin's Lane near Covent Garden—a mixed bag of gentlemen, clerks, merchants, artisans, and artists. Around the wooden tables at which the patrons sit in lively groups, bewigged and hatted, the air is thick with tobacco fumes, the acrid scent of bitter coffee, and intermittently loud political argument. Some have come in to enjoy a warm dish of coffee or glass of port, in respite from the chill January air; others to indulge a competitive passion for the game of chess. But here, as at nearly all of the hundreds of coffee houses scattered throughout the city, the main business is the circulation of news, and a chance to consult the periodicals, pamphlets, and journals which the proprietor makes freely available to all those paying their penny entrance fee.

As always, there is particular interest in the latest edition of *The Tatler*. This thrice-weekly periodical started life less than a year ago, but is now regularly selling around 3,000 copies in London and further afield—a tribute to its wide-ranging and eloquent journalism, its simple double-sided single sheet format, and its budget cover price. Rather than snippets of news or commentary, each issue carries a single penetrating essay, written by one 'Isaac Bickerstaff'. The cognoscenti know this to be the pseudonym of the politician and playwright, Richard Steele, who directs his literary operations from another coffee house, the Grecian in Devereux Court. The Grecian is a favoured haunt of members of the Royal Society, Isaac Newton among them, and in fact the *Tatler* essay for Thursday 12 January has an improving scientific theme. 'I have lately applied

10. A coffee house in 1710, from Edward Ward's *Vulgus Britannicus*

myself with much satisfaction', Bickerstaff informs his readers, 'to
the curious discoveries that have been made by the help of micro-
scopes'. There follows a sequence of rhapsodic reflections on the
breathtaking allure of the infinitely tiny, 'the myriads of animals
that swim ... in the several vessels of a human body'. *Tatler* essays
are usually read out aloud in this company, though many of the
coffee-drinkers at Slaughter's prefer the red meat of social and
political satire to the delicacies of philosophical enquiry. This particular issue is thus turned over and handed round more promptly
than usual for the purpose of scrutinizing the advertisements it
carries on its reverse. Today there is a good second-hand coach for
sale, as well as cosmetics promising to wash away 'morphews,
pimples and freckles', and medicines pledging to cure the colic or
help prevent cataracts. But it is the listings of new publications
which excite most interest among this voraciously literate crowd.
Those who enjoyed the first edition of 'the poetical works of the
Honourable Sir Charles Sedley' can now treat themselves to the
second. For connoisseurs of music there is a collection of 'fifty-two
minutes and rigadoons, for violins, hautboys and bassoons'. The
pious are catered for with all 'sorts and sizes of bibles and common-
prayers, fit for churches and families'. The more controversially
inclined can mull over the arguments of a new tract, *Priestcraft in
Perfection*, which attacks the Church of England's authority, outlined in the twentieth of the Thirty-Nine Articles, to decree its own
rites and ceremonies.

But perhaps it is none of these inducements that really catches
the eye, and asks to be read out with snorts of wonderment to the
men seated around the table. That honour goes to the notice of
another printed work, published this very day, and being sold by
J. Harding at the Post Office in St Martin's Lane, only a few yards
away from the coffee house where the company finds itself. The
volume in question is this:

> The Case of John Atherton, Bishop of Waterford in Ireland, who
> was Convicted of the Sin of Uncleanness with a Cow, and Other
> Creatures; for which he was hanged at Dublin, December 5 1640.

With a Full Account of his Behaviour after his Condemnation, and the Letters he sent to his Wife and Two Daughters the Night before his Execution. To which is added, The Sermon Preached at his Funeral the night after his Execution, in St John's Church, Dublin; with some farther Account of his Life. The whole written by Nicholas Bernard, Dean of Ardagh, at the Command of Archbishop Ussher, and to him Dedicated. Printed for E. Curll at the Dial and Bible against St Dunstan's Church in Fleet Street... Price 1s.

It may be that there is no immediate rush from the tables to the door, but the bookseller Harding probably does well enough from the aroused curiosity of customers emerging from Slaughter's. Almost seventy years after his death, the bishop of Waterford is once again news, or perhaps simply prurient entertainment.

Yet among the first readers of the pamphlet printed by Curll, there is one at least who is most emphatically not amused. When the next edition of *The Tatler* arrives at Slaughter's on the Saturday following (14 January), the patrons discover that a second advertisement has been placed, nestling incongruously between those proclaiming the merits of *The Young Accomptant's Remembrancer*, and publicizing an 'unparalleled powder for cleaning the teeth'. But this advertiser has no wonder product to promote. He is offering nothing less than the unvarnished truth, and at no charge to the seeker:

Whereas in a pamphlet lately printed, entitled *The Case of Bishop Atherton*, it is said in the preface that he confessed the crime for which he unjustly suffered: he constantly denied that foul crime all along, and with his last breath; and the chief witness against him, who was afterwards hanged, confessed at the gallows, that what he had sworn against the said bishop was utterly false. And the whole kingdom of Ireland, especially the county wherein he lived, have ever since been and are at this day possessed with an opinion of his innocence. NB. All who appeared against him came afterwards to disastrous deaths. Any person that has a mind to be satisfied of the truth of this, may enquire at Seneca's Head near Somerset House in the Strand.

With fanfares duly blown, a resounding clash of stories is about to commence once more around the memory of Bishop John Atherton.[1]

6

Athenianism

LONDON in the first decade of the eighteenth century was a good place and time to be a publisher and seller of books. Twenty years after the (almost) bloodless revolution which had sent the Catholic James II into brooding exile on the continent, and established his Protestant daughter Mary and her canny Dutch husband William on the English throne, the presses were busier than they had ever been before, even in the wonder year of 1641. The capital ballooned in size through the later seventeenth century; its population reached about 600,000 by 1700, making it the largest city in Western Europe. As it did so, demand for reading material of all kinds shot up, and soon outstripped the ability of the authorities to regulate it. In 1695, the Licensing Act, which had required all printed works to seek government approval before publication, and which had limited printing to the university presses and the masters of the London Stationers Company, was finally allowed to lapse. The result was an avalanche of books, newspapers, journals, and pamphlets, the latter so numerous, complained Jonathan Swift in 1710, 'that it will very well employ a man every day from morning till night to read them'. The early eighteenth century has long been known as 'the Augustan Age', in recognition of the self-conscious neo-classicism of its leading authors. It was a time of undoubted literary giants—of Swift himself, Daniel Defoe, Alexander Pope. But the broad reading public, the habitués of coffee houses and taverns, also had a craving for the low-brow, the scurrilous, the salacious, and sensational. Such tastes were catered for in huge quantity by the army of hack printers and publishers who were already known as the denizens of 'Grub Street'. This was an actual location, just to the north of the old city wall, in the parish of

St Giles, Cripplegate. But Grub Street (like Fleet Street in a later generation) was more than merely a spot on the map—it represented an idea about writing, a place of the imagination. It is into the world of Grub Street that our story now takes us, on the trail of one of its most colourful and enterprising citizens: the bookseller Edmund Curll.[1]

At the time he turned his attention to making money out of the story of John Atherton, Edmund Curll was still a young man, but already a well-established, if somewhat disreputable character on the London publishing scene. Apprenticed to a London bookseller named Richard Smith, Curll had gone into business as a printer on his own account in 1706. By the start of 1710, he had moved to new premises at the sign of the Dial and Bible in Fleet Street, and had notched up an impressive if eclectic catalogue of publications. These included volumes of poetry, part of an edition of Shakespeare, the *Commentaries* of Caesar, some pious sermons, and a catechism, as well as the probably pornographic *The Way of a Man with a Maid*, and a series advertising quack cures for venereal disease (the cures themselves were on sale at Curll's shop in the Strand). Pornography would remain a staple of Curll's business throughout his career, and would land him briefly in prison in 1725, after his publication of *Venus in the Cloister; or, The Nun in her Smock*, a translation from a notorious seventeenth-century French original.[2] By this time, Curll had become infamous for his bitter and long-running feud with the poet Alexander Pope, which began after he published an unauthorized edition of one of Pope's verses. Pope retaliated by slipping a powerful emetic into Curll's drink, and later denounced him volubly in the *Dunciad* (1728), a sweeping satirical attack on the 'dunces' of Grub Street. Curll himself, however, managed to make considerable sums of money from the *Dunciad*, producing his own pirated edition, as well as a series of 'keys' explaining the work's allusions.

As this reaction suggests, Edmund Curll was by instinct and rehearsal an opportunist, ever on the lookout for the chance to judge and exploit his market. He was, moreover, an inveterate plagiarist and purveyor of literary shoddy goods, notorious for rearranging graphics and altering title-pages to make old publications appear as if they were fresh new books. This was precisely what he attempted with his 1710 publication of *The Case of John Atherton*, which was in essence a straight reprint of Nicholas Bernard's *Penitent Death*. The 'cow and other creatures', which the title-page declared to have been the cause of Atherton's downfall, were shameless and sheer invention, with no basis in any known seventeenth-century source. These animals were not in fact referred to at all in the short 'advertisement', or new preface, which Curll added to the reissued text. Their prominence on the cover, and in the advertising copy, was undoubtedly intended to draw in the voyeuristic casual reader, under a guise of outraged moral sensibility. 'Uncleanness with a cow' is very likely to strike us, in spite of ourselves, as a comical phrase, and it may well have raised smiles in the coffee houses and taverns of Curll's London. Yet at the same time bestiality was a crime which was still taken very seriously in the late seventeenth and eighteenth centuries, a transgressive act threatening to blur the very boundaries between the possessors of immortal souls and the brute beasts of the field. As we have seen (p. 145), Nicholas Bernard was coy in the extreme about identifying the exact offence for which Atherton was condemned, and this left considerable latitude for the exercise of the Augustan sexual imagination. After all, was not the crime of sodomy formally defined in law as 'buggery committed with mankind or beast'?[3]

The introductory remarks in Curll's edition were credited to one 'D.L.', though it is quite probable that Curll had written them himself. A new preface would have been entirely unnecessary, this writer protests, were it not for the fact that some persons were likely to criticize the timing of the reprint, and regard the revival of the story 'as directly levelled to asperse the episcopal order'. In fact, however, the intention was quite otherwise. For had 'that pious and learned prelate' Archbishop Ussher entertained any such thoughts, he would simply never have 'commanded the writing and making public the fact'. In any case, as Bernard himself had demonstrated, 'the scandal of any one person, though ever so ignominious' cannot reasonably reflect upon a community as a whole.

Curll's interest in Bishop Atherton grew directly out of an earlier publishing venture. In 1699 a pamphlet had been printed in London describing the 1631 trial for sodomy of the earl of Castlehaven, its publication prompted by the arrest of a group of men for the same offence in the previous year. In 1708, this most action-packed of old scandals was surveyed again in a pamphlet entitled *The Case of Sodomy in the Trial of Mervyn Lord Audley*, published under the imprint of John Morphew. Curll seems to have had a direct hand in this, for the work was advertised along with the Atherton tract as one of the books 'printed for and sold by E. Curll at the Dial and Bible'. The preface by 'D.L.' underlines the connection (and the likelihood of D.L being Curll himself): 'having about two years ago published from an ancient original manuscript the trial at large ... of Mervyn Lord Audley, earl of Castlehaven', he was struck by similarities and differences with the case of the Irish bishop, 'guilty of the same unnatural crimes'. Castlehaven had denied his guilt to the last. But Atherton, though he 'behaved himself some-what indecently upon his trial', subsequently confessed his crimes 'with the greatest abhorrence', and 'freely opened the inmost recesses of his soul'. With cavalier disregard for accuracy, the two cases were declared to be 'the only ones which were ever proved criminal in this part of the world'. The reason for reprinting the Atherton story now was that if these examples were known, they might serve to 'deter such persons as are unnaturally vicious from committing the same offences'.[4]

What any of this might have to tell us about changing attitudes towards sin and sodomy at the turn of the eighteenth century is a question to which we shall return. But it was the particular spin which Curll placed on Bernard's account which provoked an immediate and hostile response. As we have seen, an anonymous advertiser in *The Tatler* was within days promising to assure anyone who cared to listen that Atherton had suffered unjustly. He had protested his innocence to the end, and opinion throughout Ireland, but particularly in Waterford itself, had believed his word on this.

Still more strikingly, an implacable providence had pursued his accusers and persecutors: 'all who appeared against him came afterwards to disastrous deaths'. Enquirers who wished to know more were directed to the sign of Seneca's Head in the Strand. This marked the premises of the bookseller and printer, Peter Varenne, about whom it has not proved possible to discover very much. He was the publisher of a 1718 tract on the cure of syphilis, which establishes a link, of sorts, with Curll. It is not beyond the bounds of possibility that Curll himself arranged for the outraged public condemnation of his own work, as a means of drumming up publicity. Yet the appeals to opinion in Ireland seem to point us in another direction. Two generations after Atherton's death, a belief in his innocence of the crime of sodomy was clearly gaining ground in some Irish circles. An example is the extraordinarily free English translation of Sir James Ware's history of the Irish bishops, which appeared in Dublin in 1704. This completely refocused the entry on Atherton around the claim that he died for a crime 'which he always denied to have committed'. In the process, it sharpened up a passing suggestion in Bernard's *Penitent Death*: 'the person who swore to the points against him, at his own execution some time after, confessed he had falsely accused him'.[5] These bold attempts to exonerate the bishop of Waterford herald the arrival onto our stage of yet another impassioned re-inventor of the life of John Atherton: the Reverend John King, Anglican clergyman and rector of the parish of Chelsea.

Born in 1652, John King was Edmund Curll's senior by some twenty or thirty years. In his youth, King had been the curate of Bray in Berkshire, but he had inherited none of the famously flexible principles of an earlier incumbent of that parish, said to have boasted after remaining in office during all the vicissitudes of the Reformation that he had 'kept true to my principle, which is, to live and die the Vicar of Bray'. King, by contrast, was a clergyman—we might more aptly say, a Churchman—of firm and unbending Anglican convictions, and he demonstrated this to the full in the work he published anonymously in London in the Spring

of 1710: *The Case of John Atherton, Bishop of Waterford in Ireland,
Fairly Represented*. In the obligatory 'epistle to the reader', King
revealed that the bulk of what he had to say about the matter had
been written some time before, but that he had held off publishing
it 'in expectation of further light into the matter out of Ireland'.
Meanwhile, however, under the titillating title of *Cases of Unnatural
Lewdness*, Curll had rushed out a joint second edition of *The Trial of
the Lord Audley* and *The Case of Bishop Atherton*, and had advertised
it in the *Post-Man* on 18 March. In King's view, this made it high
time to put the world straight about the unhappy history of John
Atherton.[6]

The man of God, John King, moved in a different sphere from
the servant of Mammon, Edmund Curll. 'I know not the editor, nor
what motives he had to engage him in this undertaking', the rector
of Chelsea piously sniffed. But whether or not it was he who had
placed the notice in *The Tatler* on 14 January, King was nonetheless
not so far removed from Curll as he liked to think: both were part of
the same fellowship of advocacy and persuasion at the bar of a fickle
'public opinion'. The instruments, methods, and even the abetting
agents were similar. King's pamphlet was, for example, sold from
the premises of Curll's collaborator John Morphew near Stationers'
Hall. Yet from the outset, King was keen to underline the differences between his own unimpeachable integrity and the bad faith
and corrupt practices of the editor of the 'late partial edition'. His
readers were, for example, provided with proper paginated references for his numerous quotations from other sources. King apologized that in a few places they would come across matter labelled 'as
I have been informed; as is the common opinion; as I have received
from good testimony'. But he assured them that in all such cases he
was able to produce private letters, 'or oral testimony of persons of
credit'. This was, they were to understand, no loose compendium of
gossip, but a thoroughly researched work of history.

There was also the issue of motivation. King claimed to be moved
only by a desire 'to vindicate the episcopal order from the sly
insinuations of this publisher'. Curll's motives, by contrast, were a
mystery to him: 'the reprinting of the case of this unfortunate

bishop near seventy years after he is dead and gone, and when the matter ought to have been buried in oblivion, and quite forgotten, is not a little surprising'. Perhaps it was simply a matter of money, of a cynical calculation that so scandalous a story 'would not fail of meeting with a gainful account in this evil age'. King certainly did not believe Curll's disclaimer that he had no desire to 'asperse the episcopal order', nor his pious intention to publicize the Castlehaven and Atherton cases in order to deter others from the same offence. 'It looks an odd way of Reformation, to bring such unnatural crimes to light, and expose them to the knowledge of thousands who would never have so much as dreamed they had been committed in a Christian country, by persons of such high degree and quality, had not the story been reprinted.' Rather than deter, reporting of such transgressions was more likely to encourage emulation in an age which had become 'too prone, by report, to unnatural vices'.

Curll's hypocrisy was easy enough to expose. The cow (a word which, King noticed, had been placed on the title-page in offensively large capital letters) was not to be found in any of Bernard's editions. Yet this scandalous insertion had been carried 'far and near in the wings of an advertisement'. Nor had Bernard's original title-page in 1641 anywhere indicated the ecclesiastical status of the woeful sinner (an interesting observation which I confess had escaped my attention before this point). But Curll had identified Atherton straight off as 'Bishop of Waterford' (again in eye-catching upper-case). It was King's charitable opinion that Nicholas Bernard had suppressed details about the offence for which Atherton was condemned 'out of tenderness and modesty'. Indeed, he confessed that when he first read Bernard's book, 'I was so far from learning from his relation what the crime was . . . that I was forced for satisfaction to enquire of a learned man who had been born and bred up in the kingdom of Ireland'. The most serious instance of Curll's dishonesty, however, was the preface's assertion that Bishop Atherton had confessed himself to be guilty of the crime of sodomy. On the contrary, as King repeatedly insisted, *The Penitent Death* clearly stated that he had 'denied the main fact'. This much was confirmed by Sir James Ware, 'whose authority in Irish affairs is great'. (In fact, as we have seen, Ware says no such thing: it was the insertion of his eighteenth-century translator.) King found himself obliged to concede something we have discovered already: that Nicholas Bernard at times handles the issues in curiously round-about and ambiguous terms, reporting, for example, Atherton's acknowledgement that his vices had justly brought him to his shameful end. But in King's view, no admission of sodomy could legitimately be inferred from such a vague 'general confession'. King stopped short of pronouncing himself convinced of Atherton's complete innocence, just. Nonetheless, he was openly sceptical about the safety of the sodomy verdict. As Bernard made clear, Atherton was 'particular and full in his confession of his other and less sins', yet this one he seemingly denied to the end. Was it at all likely, King invited his readers to ask themselves, that such a crime could have been committed by a man of advanced age, one who had been 'married above twenty years', one of his 'years education and function', who had behaved himself for many years (quoting Anthony Wood) 'with great prudence'? To the rector of Chelsea it seemed to be 'almost incredible'.

Yet if Atherton was in point of fact not guilty, how was his trial and condemnation to be explained? We find ourselves back in the murky waters into which we have dipped before, and against the dark under-current of conspiracy. King was again careful not to assert categorically that there had been a plot, or to claim to be able to reveal its inner workings. But the probability of a conspiracy was the impression he undoubtedly wanted his readers to take away. Nor was this merely his own eccentric speculation. The expatriate Irishman who enlightened King as to the true nature of Atherton's alleged offence had also told him that 'he thought there was a great conspiracy against him, that he had in the judgement of most men hard and severe measures . . . and was not guilty of that brutal fact, for which he was executed'. It was, King considered, 'a truth beyond all contradiction' that innocent people occasionally fell foul of plots and confederacies. Clergymen 'of a blameless life' had sometimes suffered in this way, 'forced to bear their cross, as their Lord and Master did before them'. To illustrate the point, he launched into an extended digression concerning two relatively recent instances of it. There was the case of Robert Hawkins, minister of Chilton in Buckinghamshire, who in 1668 fell out with religious dissenters in his parish over their payment of tithes. After Hawkins (quite justifiably) took them to court, they schemed with a corrupt justice of the peace to plant stolen property in his house and accuse him of the theft. A more high-profile case was that of the current bishop of Rochester, Thomas Sprat, demonstrating that Atherton was not the only bishop to have been the target of low political intrigue. During a Jacobite invasion scare in 1692, plotters had contrived to forge the bishop's signature on a paper declaring his support for the restoration of James II. Both nefarious schemes had come unstuck, prompting King to reflect on the many instances of plots and conspiracies in history which 'by providential means have been timely detected'.[7] Others, however, had undoubtedly succeeded, and such, if the dying confession of his chief accuser was to be believed, 'was the lamentable case of that poor unhappy man, Bishop Atherton'.

King was able to mount an impressive circumstantial case in support of these assertions. That Atherton was a man who made enemies, he did not seek for a moment to deny. 'He was of a proud, passionate, and litigious temper'. His expertise in the law also encouraged him to be active in the recovery of his dues—'a fault of the first magnitude in a clergyman in some men's opinions'. It was not necessarily so in King's. When Atherton succeeded to the bishopric, it was 'scandalously impoverished by usurpation upon its lands', so that for all the noise and clamour about his going to law 'there was a great deal (and too much) to be offered for his justification in so doing'. The great men from whom he successfully recovered church lands nonetheless developed an animus against him. There were likely other motives too: 'that he fared the worse for his patron the earl of Strafford's [Wentworth's] sake, whom that parliament of Ireland hated and complained of quickly after, may reasonably be supposed'. It was distinctly curious, King thought, that the information against him in parliament had arrived so suddenly, without 'any suspicion on his side of such a storm falling on his head'. (He chose to ignore Bernard's strange anecdote about the mysterious stranger who visited Atherton three weeks before his arrest.)

Whenever Protestant Englishmen of King's generation thought about plots and plotting, particularly in Ireland, it was hard for them not to imagine Catholics at the thick of the intrigue. In Atherton's case, many of the pieces seemed to fit. The high sheriff of the county, who showed such cruelties to the bishop at his execution, was 'a bigoted Roman Catholic' with a great influence in empanelling the jury which condemned Atherton on dubious evidence. Looking back from the viewpoint of 1710, the disordered state of Ireland in Atherton's day seemed to King a quite astonishing one: 'popery was very rampant, and there was no test or law to keep papists out of the parliament or places of trust'. (Catholics were finally excluded from public office by a series of penal laws beginning in 1691 after the Protestant victory at the Battle of the Boyne.) There could be no doubt that the Romanists 'were glad of the opportunity of showing their contempt and spleen against a Protestant bishop'. There was, of course, the significant problem that John Atherton had himself at his execution acquitted the Catholics of playing a direct part in the proceedings against him, and 'seeing the town clerk of Waterford, he desired to be recommended to his friends there'. Nonetheless, in the face of evidence to the contrary, King remained convinced that 'the papists were his avowed enemies, and might stand behind the curtain, and prompt others who acted openly in this tragedy'.

Who were those others? King had one intriguing anecdote to relate about this, which is not to be found in Bernard or other surviving seventeenth-century sources.

> There is a particular story of a received and credited tradition, that upon a certain time the unfortunate bishop being at a certain great man's house (which anciently belonged to the bishopric, and as he apprehended of right did so still), upon his taking leave, he thanked the great man for his civil treatment, and hoped to return him the same in the same place. Which made the other turn from him with great indignation, and from that time (as it is supposed) was his ruin meditated, and carried on until accomplished.

King was too discreet to name names here, but there can be little doubt that the 'great man' in question was Richard Boyle, earl of Cork, or that the supposed incident took place at his familial seat of Lismore Castle, which until the late sixteenth century had been the palace of the bishops of Lismore.

An ability to produce such 'traditions' underlines the fact that the rector of Chelsea's attempt to rehabilitate John Atherton was a joint Anglo-Irish operation. From the time he became acquainted with the story of Bishop Atherton, and certainly from the moment he determined to refute Curll's tendentious assertions, King was eagerly looking across the sea to Ireland for information about the case. Some of this arrived very late in the day. In an appendix to his pamphlet, King revealed that 'since the fore-going account was sent to the press, I have received two letters from persons of undoubted credit', documents which 'afford a fuller discovery of the opinion of the people who are most competent judges of the truth'. He printed the letters, dated 20 and 27 March 1710 respectively, though he was curiously reticent about revealing who his informants were. Their identities were, he remarked, 'not material', and he could not in any case identify them without their express consent. Remarkably, however, the originals of the letters survive, bound into a first edition of Bernard's *Penitent Death*, now preserved in the British Library. They show the writers to be Thomas Milles, the current bishop of Waterford, and one of his officials, Alexander Alcock, the chancellor of the diocese. Milles was (almost inevitably) an English export to Ireland, and a relative newcomer both to the island and the diocese, having been consecrated bishop there in April 1708. Alcock had been around much longer, holding various posts in the diocesan administration since 1692. His letter was the fuller and more interesting of the two, and had been solicited by Bishop Milles after King wrote to the latter for information and assistance.[8]

The message coming from these Hibernian allies was exactly what John King had wanted to hear. Milles assured him that ever since arriving at Waterford he had found 'all the creditable, sensible people of the city and diocese' to be of the opinion that Atherton was innocent of the capital crime. It was, he suggested, 'universally believed among them that he was brought to his death by the contrivance and conspiracy of a certain number of men, who were set on work to prevent further trouble from the said bishop about lands in dispute between them'. In printing this passage, King committed a slight but significant act of censorship. Milles's original letter declared that the men had been set on work 'by a great man in that county' (Cork?), who had 'resolved to have him taken out of the way'.

Alexander Alcock's lengthier summary of local opinion about the case is a very intriguing document. Gossipy, unsubstantiable, and opinionated, it provides an illuminating snapshot of how Bishop Atherton's troubles looked to those in the diocesan hierarchy of Waterford and Lismore, men still struggling with some of the same problems he had faced three-quarters of a century before. Alcock began by admitting to Bishop Milles that documentary evidence relating to the case was now unlikely to be forthcoming, 'there having been a general sweep made of almost all records whatever in the war that immediately succeeded the bishop's execution'. With the passage of time there were also 'but very few people now alive in this city that remember so much as to have seen him'. These were in any case all papists 'who reckon his misfortune to be so great a blemish to our Church, that . . . they would rather contribute to the blackening of his character, than discover anything which they think may be offered to the public in his vindication'. It appears that the 'creditable', 'sensible' people, among whom belief in Atherton's innocence was reportedly universal, may not have been entirely representative of the population as a whole. There was another problem. Since so many local great families, reacting against Atherton's vigorous assertion of the rights of the bishopric, had been involved in his prosecution, it was very likely that lesser folk would be loath to pass on what they knew, 'believing it may draw down the displeasure of some of the friends and relations of those families upon them'. Nonetheless, Alcock had gathered whatever he could from the ancient inhabitants of the town, popish as well as Protestant. Though reluctant to have their names made use of, or to sign any depositions, most of them were, he found, quite ready to declare their belief in the bishop's innocence. Alcock had not managed to get hold of the pamphlet recently published in London, but he had seen the advertisements in the newspapers, which 'fix his crime to be committing bestiality with a cow'. This claim struck the people of Waterford as notoriously false: 'all agree that it was not that, but too much freedom with his own steward, viz one Child by name, for which he was put to death'.

Local memory had got that much right, at least. It also furnished Alcock with the identities of several of those who were believed to have given evidence at the trial. The chief prosecution witness was a menial servant of the bishop, 'who had the character of being a most profligate wicked fellow', and thus easily suborned to give false witness. It was not possible to say what had happened to him after the verdict was given, other than that 'he was observed to go off with a good purse of money for England, which was supposed to be given him as the reward of his perjury from the prosecutors'. Another witness was Howell Powell, a substantial Waterford man, 'upon whom the bishop had formerly been somewhat severe in his court'. There was also one White, the popish sheriff of the city, who 'seized the bishop with so much violence as he came from prayers in the cathedral, and would not permit him to go into his palace to bring some papers from thence, swearing he should never see the inside of that house again'. But the fiercest of his persecutors was said to be a counsellor at law named Butler, at that time recorder of Waterford (the official presiding over civil and criminal courts in the town). He was a man 'of great interest as well as fortune', from whom the bishop had recovered some lands. In consequence, Butler was believed 'to be chiefly instrumental in suborning the servant that swore against him'.

It is hard to know quite what weight we should place on this handed-down local knowledge, assuming that Alcock reports it accurately. Henry White certainly was one of the sheriffs of Waterford in the summer of 1640. It seems unlikely that he could have arrested the bishop emerging from the cathedral—Atherton was attending the parliament in Dublin when the bombshell fell, though, conceivably, the bishop may have returned to Waterford during his short period of bail. Butler was a young lawyer who had entered Gray's Inn in London in 1635, but it looks as if eighteenth-century Waterford tradition (like some later historians) was conflating him with the more imposing figure of Piers Butler, son of Lord Cahir, with whom Atherton had been engaged in notoriously bitter land litigation through the late 1630s (see p. 81).[9]

In any case, the main thrust of Alcock's information was not to delineate the precise details of a conspiracy, but to reveal how Atherton's enemies had all been made to pay the price of their perjury at the hands of a higher justice. After Powell's involvement in this business, people noticed that 'nothing prospered with him'. His wife was often heard to say that she expected naught but 'God's curse and vengeance' to descend on him and his family for the false oath he had taken against the bishop. Sheriff White meanwhile fell from a great fortune into poverty. He and his wife were reduced to living on charity, and she had died not many years ago, 'in a poor and mean cabin in the suburbs of this city'. But it was against Butler that the hand of divine providence revealed itself most implacably. Soon after the trial and execution, Butler 'became distracted', and remained so until his death. He was to be found 'frequently screeching out and crying, that he saw Bishop Atherton before him', and begging the by-standers to take him away. Vengeance stalked the Butlers into the second generation. His eldest son, 'reputed a man of good sense and understanding', turned mad. His second son was hanged. The third died prematurely after his marriage, and the fourth (shades of Atherton himself?) 'had a bastard or two by his brother's wife'. Nor was this all. The house where the Butlers dwelled, 'though as large and good as most in the city', had ever since remained desolate and uninhabited. 'And this upon the apprehension, as I have been told, of its being haunted by the bishop's ghost.'[10] On this last point, Alcock protested that 'I believe I need not tell you that I give as little credit to stories of this nature as any need to do' (he was talking to his bishop, after all). But it clearly demonstrated the conviction of Atherton's innocence to be found among the common people of Waterford: 'they thought his very ghost was sent from t'other world to clear him of the guilt'. As for the untimely deaths of those involved in the prosecution, Alcock was inclined to believe the stories. He had heard the late dean of Waterford declare that he had got it from one Mr Lynn, 'a great and intelligent man in our county', but one whom no one could suspect of being 'any way partial in the bishop's vindication'.

Alcock's letter thus tells a distinctively different story about the bishop of Waterford from those we have heard up till now: a tale of an innocent man brought unjustly to his death by malignant scheming enemies. It has some elements in common with the narratives that had long been in circulation about the bishop: secret crimes going unpunished at the time of commission, but inviting inevitable revelation and revenge; a ghost as the visible instrument of divine retributive justice. But it turns all these on their head to portray John Atherton not so much as the penitent sinner, but as the man more sinned against than sinning. At this juncture we need to ask ourselves, not whether this version is any more true than those which preceded it, but why it exercised such an alluring appeal for the rector of Chelsea, the bishop and chancellor of Waterford, and all those who shared their view of the world.

To John King's way of thinking it was notorious that 'the ministers of Christ are the constant objects of some men's invective tongues'. What united this triumvirate of Augustan Churchmen was a touchy and defensive clericalism, almost a persecution complex. All three were 'high-flyers', adherents of an Anglican High Church grouping that was on the march in the first decade of the eighteenth century, in the Churches of both England and Ireland. The triumphant taste of victory at the restoration of monarchy and episcopacy in 1660 had long since turned sour in the mouths of Anglican clergymen. The deposition of James II, a papist, but nonetheless a divinely anointed king, had thrown many of them into agonies of conscience. The Toleration Act of 1689, which accompanied the 'Glorious Revolution' placing William of Orange on the throne, had given Protestant dissenters—Presbyterians, Baptists, and the like—the right to worship in their own churches, and signalled forever the end of

Anglicanism's official monopoly over English religious expression. The coercive power of the Church, expressed through the church courts, was from this point onwards fatally weakened, and significant numbers of English people may have given up the habit of regular churchgoing altogether. The lapse of censorship in 1695 encouraged the appearance of what seemed in some quarters to be a flood of anti-clerical, rationalist, and heretical or 'deistical' literature—what Convocation complained of in 1711 as a 'deluge of impiety and licentiousness, which hath broke in upon us'. Despite its continued established status and its enormous legal privileges, the position of the Church of England looked to some of its defenders to be under severe threat. 'The Church in danger' was their watchword. In Ireland, meanwhile, though Catholic political power had been suppressed after its resurgence under James II, the Church of Ireland was still making few converts. It had, moreover, lost even the nominal adherence of Irish Presbyterians and other dissenters. Protestants of Scottish descent, particularly numerous in Ulster, had broken permanently with the religious establishment. 'The Church of Ireland of the early eighteenth century', according to one modern historian, 'was an institution torn between an exalted vision of its potential role and a circumscribed, demoralizing, and in places, sordid reality.'

Yet there were remedies at hand, or so those nostalgic for the rigid Anglican orthodoxies of the 1660s and 1670s were able to persuade themselves. In part, the remedies were political: in an age of increasingly sharp party divisions, High Churchmen openly aligned themselves with the Tories against the Whigs, in the belief that they would support the exclusive judicial and financial privileges of the Established Church. With the episcopate split between Tory and Whig sympathizers, they also looked to the revival of Convocation as an instrument of restored social and religious discipline. Sin and sodomy aside, it is possible to see why the figure of Bishop Atherton—champion of episcopal rights and pugnacious delegate in Convocation—had his attractions for Anglican high-flyers. Another High Churchman, the Oxford scholar Thomas Hearne, noted in his diary at around this time that Atherton had been 'a man of admirable natural parts, great elocution and equal learning'. He added wryly that he was 'not at all unqualified for a bishop, excepting his want of honesty'.[11]

By 1710, the Reverend John King was already a seasoned campaigner in the culture wars of the early eighteenth century. In 1701, in response to a pamphlet by the American nonconformist minister Increase Mather, he had published a tract attacking 'factious and turbulent spirits' among the dissenters, and claiming that the institution of episcopacy was directly established by Jesus Christ. Thomas Milles too had some High Church 'form'. After his arrival at Waterford in 1708, he introduced altar-pieces, and the separation of sexes in church, and he was mocked by the dean of St Patrick's Dublin, Jonathan Swift, for 'his crucifix that he wears continually at his breast'. Just like the Laudian bishops of the preceding century, Milles regarded Protestant 'fanatics' as a far greater threat to the Church than papists, and he attracted attention and complaints for keeping Catholic servants. In Waterford itself, he requested the city recorder to have a new dissenting meeting-house destroyed. Milles was not the only provocatively High Church bishop in Ireland at this time to draw criticism. In 1709, Joseph Addison, literary collaborator of the *Tatler* founder Richard Steele, identified several of the Irish bishops as men who 'inflame the inferior clergy'. John Pooley of Raphoe, for example, was in his view 'a man of ungovernable passions, inflamed with the most furious zeal and generally passes for mad'. Yet in the mind of John King, Pooley evoked memories of Atherton—not unfavourable to either—by virtue of his attitude towards the material well-being of his see. As bishop of Cloyne before his translation to Raphoe in 1702, Pooley 'was always at law for recovery of rights from sacrilegious hands'.[12]

Was Atherton then being reinvented as a saintly martyr for High Church principles? We cannot go quite so far, but there is something decidedly curious about the intensity with which John King and his collaborators had reacted to the reanimating of this long-dead clerical scandal. It seems on the surface of things to be the most spoon-rattling of storms in teacups. We need to look more closely at the timing, however, in order to understand why the reputation of Bishop Atherton might seem a matter of genuinely topical concern in the first months of 1710. Bishop Milles's manuscript letter congratulated the rector of Chelsea on his efforts to see 'the episcopal order vindicated from that reproach which the reprinting this case, in so partial a manner, was likely at this time to have cast upon it'. Chancellor Alcock was less restrained, fulminating against 'that wicked party' who are currently 'raking up all the kennels and sinks of scandal they can think of, that thereby they may throw dirt on the clergy of the established Church'. The Oxford diarist Thomas Hearne similarly believed that Curll's reprint of Bernard was designed 'to do disservice to religion, and to bring a disgrace upon the episcopal order'.

On 12 January 1710, the very day that Curll's outrageous advertisement appeared on the back of *The Tatler*, articles of impeachment were presented in the House of Lords against the Reverend Henry Sacheverell. The legal proceedings that followed raised religious tensions in England to a temperature they had not reached since the Glorious Revolution of 1688. They also unleashed a torrent of impassioned pamphleteering, to which the Atherton controversy was an unacknowledged but unquestionably linked tributary. The Sacheverell trial was the High Church movement's great crisis and, briefly, its moment of greatest triumph.

Henry Sacheverell was a hard-drinking and overbearing Oxford clergyman, whose provocative anti-Whig sermons in the early 1700s had made him the darling of the High Church party, and the bugbear of their opponents. On 5 November 1709, the anniversary of the Gunpowder Plot, Sacheverell was invited to deliver a sermon at St Paul's, London, and took as his text St Paul's Second Letter to the Corinthians 11: 26: 'in perils among false brethren'. It was conventional on such occasions to compare the deliverance of 1605 with that of 1688. But Sacheverell took the opportunity to link the Gunpowder Plot with Charles I's execution at the hands of 'fanatics' in 1649, and proceeded to rant against dissenters at what should have been a comfortably and uncontroversially anti-Catholic event. More particularly, he denounced the 'false brethren in our government', who tolerated atheism and deism, and he came very close to saying that the Toleration Act of 1689 had no validity. Printed versions of the sermon were soon selling in the tens of thousands, and members of the Whig government—particularly the Lord Treasurer, the earl of Godolphin, who had been personally attacked—decided that they had to act. The decision was taken to impeach Sacheverell before the House of Lords, just as Thomas Wentworth had been three-quarters of a century before. His offence was 'high crimes and misdemeanours'; specifically, slandering the administration by accusing it of aiming to undermine the Church and constitution. The trial opened on 27 February, and a verdict was reached on 20 March, the day Bishop Milles wrote his letter to John King from Waterford. In the interim, on the 'night of fire' of 1–2 March, High Church mobs had sacked and burned dissenters' meeting-houses across the capital.

Sacheverell was convicted on a small majority verdict, but it was a decidedly hollow victory for the Whig government. Due in part to the intervention of Queen Anne, the sentence was extraordinarily light: a three-year preaching ban. Tory supporters hailed the outcome with delight, and Sacheverell set off on a triumphal tour of the country during which he was feted by his lay and clerical supporters. His host in Cheshire was the bishop of Chester, William Dawes, patron and friend of the rector of Chelsea, John King. The general election of November 1710 saw the routing of the Whigs, and the beginning of a Tory reaction which would last until the death of Queen Anne, and accession of the Hanoverian George I, in 1714.[13]

These then were the circumstances in which any allusion to the disgrace of an almost-forgotten Anglican bishop could come to seem as if it were part of a sustained conspiracy against the Church. Ironically, in reopening the Atherton case Edmund Curll almost certainly had no such motive. In 1710 he actually wrote two pamphlets defending Sacheverell, and he attacked the Whig Bishop Burnet (no supporter of the rehabilitation of John Atherton, as we have seen) for the part he had played in the Sacheverell affair. The fraternity of Grub Street, like much of the nation, was deeply polarized in its response to Sacheverell. One of Curll's fellow

printers and pamphleteers, while professing himself a loyal Churchman, rushed into print to attack the November 1709 sermon as 'a
virulent piece of scandal', and to characterize Sacheverell himself as
resembling 'the crack-brained Don of Manchea [Don Quixote], in
quest of imaginary giants and monsters that would ravish or eat up
his Dulcinea, his ideal mistress (what he calls the Church)'. The
pamphlet's author was John Dunton, and at this juncture he joins
the lists of those who aspired to draw meaning, inspiration, or
advantage from the story of a sinful and penitent bishop. In due
course, Dunton will also direct our attention back towards that
flickeringly intermittent, but undoubtedly decisive presence in
these stories, the ghost of Old Mother Leakey.[14]

John Dunton (1659–1732) was the son of a Huntingdonshire
Anglican clergyman. Over the course of his career he played variously
the roles of bookseller, printer, traveller, pamphleteer, and autobiog-
rapher. He was a legend in own estimation, and to some limited extent,
that of posterity too. He was a man who claimed to have published over
600 separate works, who dabbled in (Whig) politics, and who experi-
mented with new journalistic and literary forms (Figure 11). We have
met with him once already. In 1690, he was the publisher of *The
Wonders of Free Grace* (pp. 155–6), which set a summary version of
Bernard's account of Atherton alongside the stories of sixteen other
'remarkable penitents' who had ended their lives on the gallows.
Interestingly, advertisements for the work, placed among the end
papers of Dunton's other publications at this time, spoke only of the
'life and death' of the other penitents, but took care to mention that
Bishop Atherton had been 'executed for B—ry.'[15] The self-denying
ordinance about Atherton's offence imposed by Nicholas Bernard had
passed its sell-by date. As was so clearly the case with Curll, the
suspicion arises that Atherton's 'remarkable penitence' provided a
good excuse to talk openly about his sodomy, and to sell more copies.

In 1691, Dunton began the undertaking which, of all his many
publishing ventures, was the most successful in his own day, and the
most significant for establishing his reputation in the longer
term. This was the *Athenian Mercury*, a periodical which appeared

ATHENIANISM *was John Dunton's thought.*
And in these features to Perfection brought:
For Knight and Gucht that Mystick Art did find
To paint John's PROJECTS *person, and his Mind.*
They with the likeness, warmth and Grace do give
And make his Picture seem to think, and live:
And's Heraldry he from the Muses farms.
For PEGASUS *shou'd be a Poets Arms.*

11. John Dunton in 1705

twice-weekly and ran through till 1697. The unique and innovative feature of the *Mercury* was its question-and-answer format, in which it anticipated the modern agony column. Readers were invited to send in queries on any topic to Smith's Coffee House, where they would be answered by a college of learned experts, the members of 'the Athenian Society' and self-styled 'men of genius'. The 'Society' was in fact a fiction, despite the appearance in 1692 of a laudatory 'Ode to the Athenian Society' by the young Jonathan Swift, and of an elaborate *History of the Athenian Society*, penned by one of Dunton's authors, Charles Gildon. There were actually only three Athenians: Dunton himself, and two of his brothers-in-law: a teacher of mathematics, Richard Sault, and Samuel Wesley, Anglican minister, and father of the future Methodist leaders John and Charles. Dunton had met Wesley a few years earlier, when the latter was a young student of divinity, and struggling to get into print a collection of whimsically eccentric verses ('To my Gingerbeard Mistress', 'On a Cow's Tail', 'A Dialogue between a Chamber-Pot and a Frying-Pan').[16] Between them the trio of 'geniuses' endeavoured to satisfy an eclectic array of concerns emanating from both male and female readers: 'Are coffee and tobacco prejudicial to procreation?' 'A lady who was near marrying hath broke it off with me. What ought I to do?' 'What matter is the sun made of?' 'Why have women longer hair than men?'

Not insignificantly for the purposes of our story, a recurrent preoccupation of *Mercury* readers was the legitimacy of belief in ghosts and spirits, and the volume of queries on this topic prompted the production of a special issue at Halloween of 1691. Earlier that year a correspondent had posed the nail-head-hitting question, 'do the deceased walk?', and was rewarded with a masterly piece of bets-hedging: 'I cannot see it irrational to conclude that it may be either the spirits of such persons, who yet in love with their bodies after their separation, do wander up and down restless and dissatisfied; or that the devil...assumes such likenesses in his pride, as if he boasted over that mortality which he has been the cause of.'

Although the trio of Athenians parcelled out questions between them according to specialism, matters relating to apparitions and the supernatural seem to have been no one's particular preserve. Dunton's own position on ghosts is difficult to pin down. In 1709 he had ambitiously planned to demonstrate in the course of a treatise of 'news chiefly respecting the invisible world' that 'there is no such thing as the apparition of a deceased person'. But a few years before this, he had given a very different impression in his book *The Dublin Scuffle*, an extended and self-exculpatory account of his quarrel with the Dublin bookseller, Patrick Campbell, largely written 'at Pat's coffee-house in Dublin, as people were dinning my ears with news'. With his friend George Larkin, Dunton had gone to call in Dublin on a young gentleman, Mr Harman, and the conversation drifted, via a discussion of allergies and sleep-walking, to the topic of haunted houses and thence to apparitions. Harman asked 'what I thought of a spectrum's assuming a human shape?' Dunton assured him that it was possible: an acquaintance of his, Mary Gossam, had been visited by one Joseph Chambers, wearing 'that very night-cap which she put on his head when she had laid him out'. Not to be outdone, Larkin added that he himself had seen an apparition of a dead woman in Staffordshire in his youth, and that 'he looked on the denying of spirits and their appearing to persons after death, to be the next degree to atheism'. Whatever the demurs of Chancellor Alcock of Waterford, a credulous attitude towards possible appearances of the dead was by no means unknown in polite circles in Ireland at the dawn of the eighteenth century.[17]

In spite of his relentless energy and eccentric versatility, Dunton never recaptured the success he had enjoyed with the *Mercury*, and perhaps because of this, he continued throughout his career to use the 'Athenian' brandmark in connection with other publishing projects. One of these was a 1710 compendium of his journalistic writings entitled *Athenianism*, a term which he chose to define as 'a search after novelties'. Dunton used the volume to announce the planned publication of his collected works 'in six hundred distinct treatises', an undertaking which he modestly promised would supply the world with 'a compendious view of universal learning'. For the moment, however, what he had to offer was a healthy appetizer of sixteen new 'projects' (ever one of Dunton's favourite words). Not all of them were entirely new. One, 'The He-Strumpets: A Satyr on the Sodomite Club', had first been published in 1707, as a commentary on a group of men (whom Dunton numbered at forty) arrested for sodomy in London. The circumstances of the case, and Dunton's satirical gloss on them, supply a revealing snapshot of how perceptions, and indeed practices, of male sodomy had apparently changed since the Castlehaven and Atherton cases of the pre-Civil War era. Whereas the sodomite of the early seventeenth-century had been defined primarily by the act itself—a sodomite was a person who had committed sodomy—his early eighteenth-century successor was much more likely to be identified by the tell-tale signs of his own distinctive nature. As a leading expert in the field comments, 'what had once been thought of as a potential in all sinful human nature had become the particular vice of a certain kind of people'. Thus Dunton's 'he-strumpets' are betrayed by their effeminacy of apparel ('men worse than goats / who dress themselves in petticoats'), and by particular forms of address ('*Sukey*, for so 'tis said you greet / the men you pick up in the street'). They have their own haunts within the city, plying their trade 'near the Exchange' and at a club 'hard by the Stocks [i.e. stock-market] / where men give unto men the pox'. The impression, supported by much other evidence, is of an emerging homosexual subculture, a world of illicit sex and sociability in 'molly houses' (male brothels), and of periodic moral panics about the existence of such places, fuelled by groups such as the recently established Society for the Reformation of Manners.[18]

Yet if some sins were acquiring new meanings in the metropolitan world of the early eighteenth century, others were still reassuringly familiar. The eleventh of Dunton's 'projects' concerned the case of four dissenting ministers 'lately silenced in their congregations for whoredom', whom he identified only as J.L., J.C., D.C., and D.L. (not the D.L. of Curll's preface).[19] Their stories were predictably sordid ones, involving the seduction of maid servants, attempted abortions and bastard-bearing, the picking up of common

whores and strumpets, as well as the 'unnatural waste' of seminal
fluid, something Dunton sententiously labelled as 'potential murder'. Dunton's fervid moralizing struggles to disguise the strong
streak of prurience and voyeurism running through his lengthy
account. It comprises an introductory essay, an anonymous 'secret
narrative' purporting to have been sent to Dunton about the cases, a
letter to the four clerics urging them to repent for their sins, and an
interminable 'sermon', in which the author hectors the miscreants in
turn. Dunton was sensitive to potential accusations of exploitation
and opportunism, and he protested that when people fell into such
'abominable lewdness' there was a moral obligation to expose them,
otherwise the effect was passively to condone their actions. This was
especially so in the case of ministers of religion 'that should set
others a good example'. Understandably enough, in the febrile
political atmosphere of 1710, and believably, from the author's perspective as an Anglican Whig with a circle of nonconformist friends
and connections, Dunton stressed that he was not looking to make
ideological capital or to score denominational points. It was no part
of his design 'to expose or scandalise the body of dissenters', people
who 'are generally very pious and very modest'. Nor did members of
Dunton's own Church have anything to feel smug about, for (and
here our interest starts to be piqued) no Anglican could feel totally
secure from such temptation 'that calls to mind the lewd conversation and tragical ends of Bishop Atherton, Dr C—er, Mr. Foulkes,
or that ever read the book entitled *The Century of Scandalous Priests*,
published by an order of the House of Commons in the year 1643'.
Of the mysterious Dr C—er and the stars of the parliamentarian
compendium of 1643 we hear no more (the scandal of the latter was
in any case as much theological as moral).[20] But the cases of
Atherton and Foulkes were explored by Dunton at some considerable length, both to reassure the fornicating four that 'you are not
the only clergymen that have been thus daring in sin', and also to
urge them to make as full, public, and heartfelt a repentance as these
two had done.

   Foulkes has crossed our path already (p. 153), a minister executed
in 1679 for murdering the bastard child he had conceived in adultery

with a young gentlewoman over whom he had been appointed guardian. Since Foulkes had modelled his prison cell repentance on Atherton's own, it is unsurprising that Dunton saw the cases as effectively interchangeable, and he freely inserted 'and Mr Foulkes' into the extensive passages which he plagiarized from Bernard's *Penitent Death*. In so ponderously equating the 'b—y' practised by Bishop Atherton, and the infanticide committed by Mr Foulkes, with the more humdrum sexual sins of the dissenting ministers, Dunton was shamelessly milking his theme. But he could expect his readers to share with him an inherited understanding that sin in its most grievous manifestations was not an *á la carte* selection, but a comprehensive set menu, in which one course led inexorably to the next. It may indeed have been the particulars of the Foulkes case that prompted Dunton to lecture the disgraced ministers about the inevitable consequences of fornication, and the common fate of bastard children. 'How many of them (to hide the infamy and shame of their birth) are by the hands of the very mothers of them strangled or drowned, or otherwise destroyed as soon as they are born! . . . How seldom is there an assize with us, wherein there are not some or other arraigned for such facts as these, the murders of bastards!' The complaint was not long after echoed (or simply copied) by Richard Steele in the pages of *The Guardian*, a successor periodical to the *Tatler* and *Spectator*: 'there is scarce an assizes where some unhappy wretch is not executed for the murder of a child'.[21] These reflections ought to be ringing very distinct bells for us. They serve to bring back into our field of vision a painful aspect of the Atherton case that seemed to have dropped out of sight after the revelations of 1640. Dunton's remarks here were unconsciously prescient. Even as he composed them, infanticide, incest, and the supernatural were very shortly to impose themselves on his attention, as they are about to return assertively to ours.

⁂

As *Athenianism* was being prepared for the press in 1710, a seventeenth 'project' was at the last minute added to the volume. Its title is worth giving in full, exactly as Dunton printed it:

The Apparition-Evidence: Or, *A miraculous Detection of the unnat-*
ural Lewdness of Dr John Atherton, *(formerly Bishop of* Waterford *in*
Ireland) *by a Spectrum, (the same Prelate whose extraordinary Peni-*
tence I recommended in the Eleventh Project *of this Book to the four*
dissenting Parsons accus'd of Adultery,—) attested by Sir George
Farwel, *Knight, the Reverend Mr.* Buckley, *and other Persons of*
Quality, who heard the whole Examination: Intermix'd with a Pro-
phetick Account *of the manner of Bishop* Atherton's *untimely End*
many Years before he was Executed: —The whole being an Original
Manuscript, *(and very great Rarity) never printed before.*

An explanation is clearly called for. Dunton informed his readers
that, since he had written his remarks on the dissenting parsons,
and recommended to them for imitation the penitent behaviour of
Bishop Atherton, a manuscript had been unexpectedly sent to him,
with the intention that it be printed as part of the work in hand.
Dunton was not prepared to name his source, saying only that he
was 'a citizen of great integrity now living in London'. Nonetheless
the document seemed to him 'a new call from heaven' for the four
dissenters to make their repentance public, as well as 'a further
confirmation of the account I gave in my eleventh project'. In
fact, as we shall see, it was a great deal more than this. It is nothing
less than the main crossing-point of our entire migratory herd of
stories, a narrative hinge between past, present, and future. But as
Dunton pledged that he would produce the whole account as he
had been sent it, 'without the addition or alteration of one word',
I propose for the moment simply to follow his example. Readers
will have a chance to catch their bearings and form their own
impressions of the tale, or rather tales, that Dunton has to tell. At
the start of the next chapter, we can resume our task of making
connections, assessing plausibility, and scratching for meaning out
of the hard soil of the historical record.

The Apparition Evidence

The providences of God ought to be observed and recorded, especially
when they be singular, and have extraordinary circumstances in them.

What I now write I heard from persons of quality and great veracity, who were present at the examination, and had relation and conversation with two of the parties concerned in this history.

Dr Bernard, dean of Ardagh, that wrote the history of Bishop Atherton's repentance (which in truth was very great and rare, a wonderful instance of the mighty power of divine grace) did not in the least touch at the crime for which he suffered. We may guess at the reasons. First, he would not bespatter his order, it being a very foul reflection on the hierarchy, that one of that eminent character should be branded for such heinous crimes, and have his fingers dipped in the blood of his own innocent bowels. Secondly, better next to its never having been committed, never to have sin remembered more. In truth, all sins should be forgotten and forsaken. But that miraculous Work of God in detecting it, and thereby bringing that proud, incestuous and bloody prelate into a most bitter, evangelical repentance, and, as a rational charity must needs oblige us to believe, into the blessed state of grace and of eternal glory; I say such a miraculous work of God ought to be had in everlasting remembrance. 'The works of the Lord are great, and sought out by all them that have pleasure therein.'[22]

There be three scenes of this tragedy, and we shall pass over to them in their proper order. At Minehead, in the county of Somerset, in the year of our Lord 1636, or thereabouts, there lived an ancient gentlewoman, the widow of one Mr Leakey. Of what quality her husband was I cannot tell, but his and her only son was a merchant in that town, that drove a considerable trade between it and Waterford, and some other ports in Ireland, and was reputed worth about eight or ten thousand pounds estate. This gentleman had but one child by his wife, of both which we shall hear more by and by.

Mrs Leakey, the old gentlewoman, was of a free, pleasant, and cheerful temper, exceeding good company, and would render herself by her carriage and discourses, by her expressions and conversation, exceeding acceptable and delightful to all sorts of persons, in so much that they would often say to her, and to one another, 'that it was a thousand pities such an excellent good-natured gentlewoman should die.' And in the midst of all their mirth she would ordinarily tell them, 'as pleasing as my company is now to you, you will not care to see and converse with me

*when I am dead, though I believe you may.' However, die she does, and
being dead and buried, some time after, she is seen again by night, and at
last at noon-day, in her own house, in the town and fields, at sea and
shore. I shall give you some eminent instances. A doctor of physick, who
lived at Minehead, having been in the country to visit a patient, as he
returned home towards the evening, meets in the field, travelling on foot
to the town, an ancient gentlewoman. He accosts her very civilly, falls
into discourse with her, and coming to a stile, lends her his hand to help
her over; but finds and feels her's to be prodigiously cold, which makes
him eye this gentlewoman a little more wistly [i.e. attentively] than he
had done before, and observes that in speaking she never moves her lips,
and in seeing never turns her eye-lids, nor her eyes. This and some other
circumstances affright him, and suggests to his fearful mind that it might
be Mrs Leakey, of whom there was a general talk in the town, that she
was dead, and yet walked again, and was seen of many. Whereupon,
when he comes to the next stile, he passes over but never turns back to pay
her his former ceremony and respect of his hand, which so incensed this
old hag that she grew as froward and sullen as the doctor, and kept
silence, and gave him no more mouth-speech, since he was become as
mute as a fish towards her. And when they came to the next stile, she got
before him, and sat just in the middle of it, so that when he came to it his
way was blocked up. Hereupon he turns aside, and goes to a gate,
thinking to cross over that into the highway, but when he came thither,
she sits astride over that also. But yet somehow or other he got over, and
coming to the towns-end, the spectrum gives him a kick on the breech,
and bids him be more civil to an ancient gentlewoman next time.*

*But this was a petty and inconsiderable prank to what she played in
her son's house and elsewhere. She would at noon-day appear upon the
quay at Minehead, and cry 'a boat, a boat ho! A boat, a boat ho!' If any
boatmen or seamen were in sight, and did not come, they were sure to be
cast away; and if they did come, 'twas all one, they were cast away. It
was equally dangerous to please and displease her. Her son had several
ships sailing between Ireland and England: no sooner did they make
land, and come in sight of England, but this ghost would appear in the
same garb and likeness as when she was alive, and standing at the main
mast, would blow with a whistle, and though it were never so great a*

calm, yet immediately there would arise a most dreadful storm that would break, wreck, and drown ship and goods. Only the seamen would escape with their lives; the Devil had no permission from God to take them away. Yet at this rate, by her frequent apparitions and disturbances, she had made a poor merchant of her son, for his estate was all buried in the sea, and he that was once worth thousands, was reduced to a very poor and low condition in the world. For whether the ship were his own or hired, or he had but goods on board it to the value of twenty shillings, this troublesome ghost would come as before, whistle in a calm at the main-mast at noon-day when they had descried land, and then ship and goods went all out of hand to wreck; in so much that he could at last get no ships wherein to stow his goods, nor any mariner to sail in them: they knowing what an uncomfortable, fatal and losing voyage they should make of it, did all decline his service.

In her son's house she has her constant haunts by day and night. But whether he did not, or would not own if he did see her, he always professed he never saw her. Sometimes when in bed with his wife, she would cry out, 'husband, look there's your mother!', and when he would turn to the right side, then was she gone to the left, and when to the left side of the bed, then was she gone to the right. Only one evening, their only child, a girl of about five or six years old, lying in a truckle-bed under them, cries out 'O help me, father! help me mother! For grandmother will choke me!' And before they could get to their child's assistance, she had murdered it, they finding the poor girl dead, her throat having been pinched by two fingers which stopped her breath and strangled her. This was the sorest of all their afflictions. Their estate is gone, and now their child is gone also; you may guess at their grief and great sorrow.

One morning after the child's funeral, her husband being abroad, about eleven in the forenoon, Mrs Leakey the younger goes up into her chamber to dress her head. And as she was looking into the glass, she spies her mother-in-law, the old beldam, looking over her shoulder. This cast her into a great horror. But recollecting her affrighted spirits, and recovering the exercise of her reason, faith and hope, having cast up a short and silent prayer unto God, she turns about and bespeaks her. 'In the name of God, Mother, why do you trouble me?' 'Peace', says the

spectrum, 'I will do thee no hurt.' 'What will you have of me?', says the
daughter. 'Why', says the spectrum, 'thou must go over to Ireland, and
visit thy uncle, the Lord Bishop of Waterford, and tell him, that unless he
repent of the sin whereof he knows himself guilty, he shall be hanged.'
'Mother', says she, 'this is a sleeveless errand that you send me about. My
uncle is a great man, and if I should deliver him such an idle message,
I should but render myself ridiculous. Pray, Mother, what was the sin
whereof he was guilty, and must repent, or he must be hanged?' 'Why',
says she, 'if thou wilt know, it is murder. For when he lodged at my
brother's house in Barnstaple, he, being then married to my sister, got my
brother's daughter with child, and I delivered her of a girl, which as soon
as he had baptised, I pinching the throat of it strangled it. And he smoked
it over a pan of charcoal, that it might not stink, and we buried it in a
chamber of that house. Now tell him that this is the sin, of which if he
don't repent, he shall be hanged.' 'O, but Mother', replies the young Mrs
Leakey, 'there's no body will carry me over, for if any of our family or
goods be in a ship, you appear and raise a storm, and they be all cast
away.' To this the spectrum retorts, 'thou shalt go, and return home
again in safety, and I will not trouble thee. And I give thee thirty days
for thy voyage. But see that thou deliver the message to the bishop that
I have told thee.' Upon this the daughter takes heart and bespeaks her,
'Pray, Mother, where be you now, in heaven or in hell?' At which words
the spectrum looks very stern upon her, but gives her no answer, and
immediately vanishes out of her sight.

A while after this, her husband returning home, she relates to him all
this dialogue, and the commission [which] was given her, and demands
his advice in it, who tells her, he would have her go. But this young
gentlewoman before she would pass over into Ireland, does first of all
consult with some godly ministers about it, to whom she discovers all
these passages, and they, considering the whole, advise her to go to
Waterford. She crosses over in the next vessel, and goes straight to the
bishop's palace, where she meets his lordship in the hall, and delivers him
the message she was enjoined, who makes no other reply than this: 'that if
he were born to be hanged, he should not be drowned'. Not being invited
to drink or stay in the palace one night, she taketh the very first
opportunity of a ship sailing to Minehead, and returns home again in

a very few days to her own house. And being known to be come back from Ireland, she is apprehended by the warrant of some justice of the peace, and brought to the sessions at Taunton, and being examined, giveth this account unto the bench which I have here written. Sir George Farrel, knight, living at Hill Bishops near Taunton, was one of the justices upon the bench. Mrs Bruen, a widow, one of his daughters, was also present in court, and Mr Buckley, then a minister near Taunton (afterward, when I was of Kingsbridge, he was rector of Thurlestone in the South Hams of Devon) heard the whole relation. From these two last persons, Madam Bruen, and Mr Buckley, I had this relation, and this circumstance more. That the justices having examined Mrs Leakey upon oath, sent her deposition up to Whitehall to the Council Table, Charles I being then king. But this deposition being no legal evidence, no witness in law, the business was let fall, and the bishop, however he might be suspected, was not at all prosecuted for this time.

And now we must shift and change our scene, and remove from Mine-head in Somersetshire, to Barnstaple in Devon. The town clerk of Barnstaple about the year 1639 was one of those whom the world called puritans. He had an apprentice of about sixteen years of age, a sturdy stugged [stocky] boy, stout enough: his name was Chamberlain. He complains often to his master that the house was haunted, and that he was frighted with apparitions. Sometimes he should see a young gentle-woman about eighteen or twenty years old, all in white, with her hair dishevelled, leading a very little child up and down the room, which seemed as if it were new born. Otherwhiles she would carry it in her arms, but very dejectedly and disconsolately, and would look upon him in a very doleful and sorrowful manner. Ordinarily there would come an old man in his gown, and sit upon the bed by him, staring him in the face, but speak never a word. These apparitions were very troublesome and afflictive to him. His godly master has him to several worthy ministers, who do converse with him, and advise him to speak to it. And one of them to encourage him to do it, watched some nights with him, but upon sight of the spectrum was so affrighted himself, that he could not speak, nor would suffer young Chamberlain to speak neither. But one night as he was sitting up writing some instrument (engrossing a deed) he came to a place which was interlined and blotted, and just then comes into the room (as he thought) his master, who sits him down by him, wedging him in, so that he could not in any wise get out. He reads the blurred paragraph over and over, but not being able to make any sense of it, he takes it up, and bespeaks, as he supposed, his master: 'Sir', says he, 'would you be pleased to read this to me, for I can't tell what sense to make of it'. But there is no answer given him. He, supposing his master was busy in meditation [i.e. prayer], conceived it good manners not to interrupt him, till having tired himself to pick sense out of this blotted passage, which he could never do, he takes it up the second time, and bespeaks his supposed master. 'Sir', says he, 'would you be pleased . . .' And with that, casting his eye upon him, soon discovers his mistake and finds that it was the spectrum that had so long troubled him.

He would now have given his life for a halfpenny, but plucking up his spirits, necessity and despair making him valiant, he boldly asks him, 'Sir, why do you trouble me?' To which the apparition replies, 'don't be afraid, I'll do thee no harm.' 'Well, what is it that you would have?' 'Why', says the spectrum, 'do thou go into such a room in the house, and dig there up the planking, and thou shalt find four boxes, one upon the other. In the first there is all sorts of wearing apparel, of silks, satins and velvet (unless my memory fails me) for men and women. In the second, abundance of good table and bed linen, very choice and fine, of holland and damask. In the third there was a sum of money in gold and silver ready coined, and two silver pots, one full of gold, which together with all the rest of those buried goods the apparition very liberally bestows upon him. But the other pot he commands him upon pain of death not to look into it, but to take it and carry it into Wales to Mrs Betty, his master's daughter; and when he landed in Wales, at such a place as the apparition assigned him, he would meet him, and deliver him a further message for her, and he should despatch all in ten days time. But he bade him look to it that he did not so much as peep into that silver pot he was to carry over to her, for it was as much as his life was worth. Young Chamberlain fairly promises to perform all that is enjoined him, and at parting the old spectrum tells him, 'in the fourth and undermost box, there be two cups of precious stones, encased in gold, take them also, for I freely give them to thee, and so good night.'

Chamberlain is glad to be so fairly rid of this troublesome company, betakes himself to his rest, and the next morning acquaints his master with his last night's adventure. His master bids him do as he was commanded, and he had promised. Accordingly, he gets into the parlour where he was directed, breaks up the boards of the planking, and finds all that the spectrum had discovered to him. He had in money near twelve hundred pounds, besides the goods, pots and cups, of which we shall hear more news anon. Never did any fellow's teeth water more upon a sweet bit, or his fingers itch to meddle with prohibited wares, than Chamberlain's eyes did to be looking into the forbidden silver pot. But the fear of the spectrum's menaces awed him and kept him much against his will within bounds, though a thousand times a day he would be peddling about it, to see what was in it. However, at last he takes his opportunity, with his pot gets into a boat, crosses over the Bar of Barnstaple and the Severn into Wales, and arrives at the place appointed for his interview with the old apparition, which was about two miles and a half from the shore. At the first meeting, the spectrum is very froward and angry, and tells him very chidingly, 'Sirrah, thou hast an earnest longing to be looking into this pot.' 'Not I', says Chamberlain. 'Nay, Sirrah, but thou hast', says the spectrum, 'and therefore do not lie unto me, but get thee presently unto thy master's daughter, and deliver her this message which I now tell thee, and give her the pot.'

What this message was—though he was earnestly importuned by Madam Fortescue, the widow of John Fortescue of Spriddlestone, in the parish of Brixton and county of Devon esq., from whom I had this relation in the year 1663, having been minister of that parish and outed of it by the Act of Bartholomew the year before, to whom Chamberlain was steward for his manors in the town and parish of Cullompton in the said county of Devon—yet he would never discover it. And craved that lady's excuse because he had married her [i.e. Mrs Betty's] sister, and it would but cast dung and reproach upon his wife's blood and family. But to go on with my story, Chamberlain had a very scrupulous conscience, and moves this case to the Devil, 'But what and if Mrs Betty will not take the pot?' 'Then', says he, 'leave it with her, and tell her from me, that it were better she had taken it, for she shall hear further from me.'

Of this Mrs Betty, by the way, she was the dearest of her father's children, who was exceeding fond of her, but she having got a great belly without an husband in her father's house, her godly parents very severely reproved her for her grievous sin against God and her own soul, and the scandal to religion, and infamy to their family. She, after she had gotten it away, as you before heard, quits her Father's house, withdraws herself from her relations, and lives privately there in Wales, for about seven years time, upon a portion that she had left her either by an aunt or grandmother.

Well, Chamberlain the next morning, between five and six, comes to her house, knocks at the door, and down comes a young gentlewoman of about twenty-seven, with her breasts naked, hair dishevelled, in a very forlorn and disconsolate condition, and asks him what his business is. To whom Chamberlain replies, 'Mrs Betty, I am commanded to deliver you such a message from a spirit that hath appeared to me', and he tells her what was given him in charge, and delivers the pot. She refuses to take it; he tells her she must; she says she will not, but he must carry it to him from whom he had it. Chamberlain then replies, 'Mrs Betty, if you do not, it will be so much the worse for you, for I am ordered to leave it with you'. With that, fetching a deep sigh and smiting her breast, 'Ah!', says she, 'it was not for nothing that I have been troubled all this night, I was born to be miserable.' And so without enquiring for her parents, or inviting him in to drink, she takes the silver pot and gets up into the chamber.

Chamberlain, having now discharged his trust and errand, immediately returns to the seaside, where finding a boat ready for Barnstaple, he enters into it. And before it launched off from land, Mrs Betty comes down into it also, and sits just against him. But all the time they were passing over never speaks a word to him, nor he to her. As soon as they arrive at Barnstaple, he goes to a tavern, and she to her father's house, whom seeing, and her mother, she falls down upon her knees and craves their blessing. Great is the joy in the whole family at the presence of this stranger, but having sat and discoursed with them about a quarter of an hour, she rises, and takes a key and hammer that hung in the parlour and goes up stairs, unlocks a chamber door, and then locks it again upon her, where she was heard beating out a board in the window, and then nail it fast again. What she took thence is not known, but having despatched her business, she opens the door, locks it again, comes down, puts the hammer and key in their places, and having sat and discoursed with her parents a quarter of an hour more, she then begs their blessing, and departs, no entreaty or importunity being able to detain her a night; no, not so much as to drink with them. But over to Wales she will go again, where indeed she returns, and lives about some fourteen months, and then falling sick, she calls her maid to her, telling her she would make her her heir, and leave her £700 after her death, which was now near at hand, provided she would solemnly promise and swear to her, that as soon as she was buried, she would take the first opportunity to go over to Ireland, and carry that silver pot (but she must not look into it) unto her uncle the lord Bishop of Waterford, with her dying message to him, that if he did not repent of the sin he knew himself to be guilty of, he should be hanged. The maid engages to her mistress to perform her will, who a few hours after died.

Mrs Betty being dead, and her last will being noised abroad, a justice of the peace near unto that place, being informed of this unusual gift and charge, sends out his warrant to bring this maid and the silver pot before him, and being examined, she gives this relation of her mistress's last will and injunction on her, as I have related. The justice commands the cover to be taken off the pot, and looking into it, finds the skeleton and bones of a little new born infant. This surprises his worship and all the spectators. Presently news of this is sent up to his majesty King Charles I and the Privy Council, who dispatch an order to the council at Dublin to seize the bishop of Waterford. This and some other circumstances jumping in at the same time caused his arraignment, condemnation and execution. But as he had been a sinner above many, so was he an extraordinary penitent. The relation of his repentance was writ and printed with his funeral sermon, which was preached by Dr Bernard, but as I said at first, without any the least notice taken or mention made of his crimes which I have now from faithful and credible witnesses inserted into this paper.

As for the great treasure which the Devil so freely bestowed on Chamberlain: in those unhappy civil wars, the Cavaliers, i.e. the king's soldiers in those parts plundered him of all, excepting five broad pieces, which he reserved, and his two cups, of which there is this remarkable story and providence:

Mr Chamberlain had by his wife, his master's daughter, two children. With these he and she travel from Barnstaple to Cullompton. The children were put in a pair of panniers, one in each, and the two cups tied upon the saddle between them. As they were travelling in a fair summer's day in July 1650 over Black Down in the way to Collumpton, about noon, the sun is overcast with a very dark and thick cloud, and on the sudden it falls a thundering very grievously and terribly, and a great thunderclap strikes in between the poor children. Which done, the dark cloud vanishes, and the heavens clear up again as bright as before. Only poor Mrs Chamberlain, all in terror and horror, supposing her children to have been destroyed by it, cries out 'O my children! My children!' But coming up to them, she and her husband find them very merry, laughing and playing without any hurt. Then they look for their two cups of precious stones encased in gold, but they find them gone. The same hand that gave them him ten years before did now taken them away, no one having been a jot better for the Devil's gift. There went a report abroad in the country, that the Devil took these cups out of Mr Chamberlain's hand, but it was not so, but as I have now recorded, and here related unto that worthy Lady Madam Fortescue, for whose manors, as I said before, he was steward, and from whose mouth I had this remarkable providence, he having acquainted her with all these passages and particulars.

7

The Narratives of the Reverend
John Quick

'Thus, Reader, I have obliged you with a great (and perhaps matchless) rarity'. Our thanks are due to the ever-modest John Dunton. The return of Mother Leakey's ghost, conjured out of silence and neglect by an opportunist Grub Street hack, brings together many of the competing stories set in train by the disgraceful life, and the ambiguous death, of John Atherton seventy years before. It also raises a set of larger questions about the workings of individual and collective memory, and about the significance of ghosts for the way the people of the later seventeenth and early eighteenth centuries understood the world in which they lived. As we have been finding throughout this book, ghosts provide important clues about the societies that imagine them, for, as a historian of classical Greece has written, 'through their excesses, the dead reveal, like fingerprint powder shaken over a table, where desires, fears, and angers are most acute among the living'.[1]

The narrative printed in Dunton's *Athenianism* is likely to strike the modern reader as a 'ghost story', or rather several ghost stories, in something close to the commonly understood sense of the term. But, crucially, it also claims to be a true relation of events, and it abounds in names, places, and dates. It both confirms and confuses a great deal of what we have established already about the alleged haunting in Minehead. The first part of the *Apparition Evidence* positively resonates with familiar echoes for us, corroborating much of what we know Elizabeth Leakey and her fellow witnesses to have sworn to before the Somerset justices in February 1637 (pp. 1-6). There is the old woman's promise to return after her death; the claim of crippling losses by sea (now directly attributed to the intervention of the spectre); Alexander Leakey's belated discovery of the facts; the uncanny death of a child. Most crucially of all, there is the decisive encounter between Elizabeth and her mother-in-law's ghost, culminating in the charge to carry a message into Ireland. Here the very phrases put in the protagonists' mouths are sometimes virtually identical to those of the earlier document—'in the name of God', 'I will do thee no hurt', 'be you now in heaven or in hell?' But there is also an abundance of contradictory detail. The first victim of the ghost's malice is now a little girl not a teenage boy, the Leakeys' daughter rather than their nephew. Atherton is married to Mother Leakey's sister, not to her daughter, and the incestuous adultery is committed with a niece not a sister-in-law. The sexual liaison which seemed to have taken place in Huish Champflower in Somerset is relocated to Barnstaple in Devon. The second part of the narrative, the Chamberlain or Barnstaple episode, appears to be only partly compatible with the revelations of the first part, and begins to point us in all sorts of different directions. If we are to take it seriously, as we surely must, it challenges us to wonder whether what we thought we had discovered about the murky past of Bishop John Atherton represents anything like the whole story.

What, then, are we to make of the *Apparition Evidence*? In the first place, we have on our hands, not so much a whodunnit, as a who-wrote-it. Having printed the relation 'without any remarks of my own upon it', Dunton went on to pronounce that no one in their right senses could reasonably doubt its veracity. But if anyone was curious to lay eyes on the original manuscript, he directed them towards 'my worthy friend Mr Daniel Waghorn in Noble Street'. From him they could discover both 'by what credible hand' the narration had been sent to Dunton, and where the original was now reposited. In spite of these helpful pointers, some later commentary would suspect Dunton himself of having been the author. We can understand why. The early eighteenth century, the era usually considered to have witnessed 'the birth of the novel', was one where writers liked to play with masks of authorial identity, and with fictitious 'truth devices', like prefatory letters. One thinks here of Defoe's *Robinson Crusoe*, or of Swift's *Gulliver's Travels*. The boundaries of fact and fiction were frequently blurred, in a way which seemed profoundly alien through much of the twentieth century, but is perhaps rather less perplexing in the current age of 'reality' TV shows. Despite its undoubted basis in recorded events, the language of the *Apparition Evidence* is overtly and unapologetically theatrical: it is a 'tragedy' in 'three scenes', which the author is required to 'shift and change'. We can see some of the same play with ideas of fiction and truth going on in another 'secret narrative', the one supposedly sent to Dunton about the four adulterous ministers. If these clergymen were to repent, its author tells us, 'you may then, if you please, take this *Secret Narrative* for a romance'. Their shameful actions, the text insisted, did constitute a true narrative, 'though I had much rather they were a fiction'. It seems as likely as not that Dunton himself wrote the 'secret narrative', or at least that he heavily reworked it. Surely the same could be true of the *Apparition Evidence*? Another possible candidate for authorship is suggested by one of the very few modern scholars to take any notice of the text: might it not have been the work of the playwright, John Gay, author of *The Beggar's Opera*? Gay was born in Barnstaple—his great-grandfather was mayor of the town in 1638. He went to school with a member of the Fortescue family mentioned in the narrative, and he was active on the London Grub Street scene by 1710. Publishing the tale at the point when his literary career was about to take off could well have represented a 'means of laying the ghosts of a childhood he now wished to disown'.[2]

But before going any further with this, I should confess that these are smokingly red herrings. Because for once in this story there is a solidly verifiable revelation, although, ironically enough, the credit for it must go to that least reliable and trustworthy of sources, our old friend Edmund Curll. In the spring of 1711 Curll reprinted his edition of Bernard's *Penitent Death of a Woeful Sinner* under the title *Some Memorials of the Life and Penitent Death of Dr John Atherton* (the cow so prominent on the title-page of the earlier

imprint was now quietly let out to pasture). He also appended to it
'a letter to the author of a pamphlet entitled *The Case of Bishop
Atherton Fairly Represented*', a rebuttal of John King. Curll (through
the person or persona of 'D.L.') again insisted that he had not the
least intention of undermining episcopacy ('for which I have the
highest veneration'), and he protested that he had no desire 'to enter
into a large controversy about the death of this unfortunate gentleman'. John King's suggestions that he was—heaven forfend—
motivated by money, were simply 'mean subterfuges as deserve
not the least notice'. Yet Curll was not prepared to let the rector
of Chelsea get away with calling him a liar for saying that Atherton
had confessed his principal offence. Had not the bishop owned up
to the *effects* of reading bad books and viewing immodest pictures,
'which confession, Sir, can refer to nothing else but the sin of
uncleanness'? What is more, had not Nicholas Bernard himself
admitted that he could not remember word for word what Atherton
had said at his place of execution, and had he not broken off his
reporting of the bishop's words 'with an &c'? If King had been in a
position to produce the bishop's last speech he would undoubtedly
have printed it, and that would have been that. But since he could
not, Curll himself would definitively settle the issue by reproducing
'the true copies of two original papers' which had recently been sent
to him. One of these was a short document attested and signed by a
Mr John Price, apparently an eyewitness of Atherton's execution. It
contained a very much briefer account of what was said on that
occasion than Bernard had supplied, but it was quite explicit on one
point: the bishop had said 'that I was guilty of the charge laid
against me' (see p. 99). As to whom this John Price may have
been, Curll had nothing to say, and it has not proved possible to
discover any more about his identity. But he was clearly no friend to
the bishop, or to the men and causes that he served. John Atherton
was in his view a 'fit tool' of Lord Deputy Wentworth. Both of
them, Price disdainfully observed, were 'zealous sticklers for altar
worship'.

What we do know, however, is that Price's statement had been
acquired, and perhaps even solicited, by the author of the second

paper, 'the late Reverend Mr John Quick', a 'minister of the Gospel
lately deceased in September 1706', and a man whose acquaintance
we have made already in passing (pp. 153–4). The copies of Price's
and Quick's papers from which Curll printed his account survive in
the British Library, among the manuscripts gathered by the great
eighteenth-century collector, Sir Hans Sloane. These make clear
that Quick wrote down and dated his own testimony in London in
1690. The document was, of course, the 'apparition evidence' with
which we are already familiar, and Curll, like Dunton, printed it in
full. He billed it as 'a true and amazing relation of the notorious
uncleanness, incest, sodomy and murder committed by Doctor John
Atherton . . . with the discovery thereof by the most apparent,
undoubted and prodigious apparition that was ever heard of, enough
to convince the greatest atheist'. True to form, Curll could not resist
pushing the envelope here—the relation had precisely nothing to say
about the matter of the bishop's sodomy. Nor, since Dunton had
already printed it, was it quite the journalistic scoop he made it out to
be. Whether Curll had (nefariously or otherwise) got hold of a
manuscript which was originally sent to Dunton, or whether multiple copies of it were circulating in London, we cannot now presume
to say. Collaboration seems the most likely explanation. In the
back-stabbing world of Grub Street, the old-hand Dunton and the
newcomer Curll were on remarkably good terms with each other.
The younger man was in fact one of a number of booksellers directly
involved in the publication of *Athenianism*.[3]

The identification of a clergyman, the Reverend John Quick, as
the author of the Minehead and Barnstaple 'ghost stories' certainly
makes sense of the several autobiographical snippets woven into the
narratives. The author claimed to have heard the details of the first
relation from various sources 'when I was of Kingsbridge', and to
have learnt those of the second from interested parties in Brixton,
Devon, in the year 1663. But it also raises a host of new questions.
Why was a minister so interested in this material in the first place?
How much of it was recorded verbatim from his sources, and how
much of it was his own invention? Why, if he considered it to be
such a 'miraculous Work of God', did he make no attempt to

publish it in his own lifetime? The most important clue here is the one crucial fact which the author of the *Apparition Evidence* chose to reveal about himself. He had been minister of the parish of Brixton, but was then 'outed of it by the Act of Bartholomew'. John Quick was the victim of a political purge. The event defined his essential identity for him over the vast majority of his adult life. And, since roughly 2,000 other clergymen shared the same fate, it changed forever the face of religious life in England.

John Quick was a native of Plymouth in Devon, born there in 1636, the year that John Atherton ascended to the bishopric of Waterford, and Susan Leakey's ghost was first seen drifting among the alleyways and warehouses of Minehead. His life was one of pious, puritan devotion: 'God wrought a saving change on his heart in his youth', so the preacher of his funeral sermon tells us. After graduating from Oxford, Quick was appointed by the town corporation of Exeter to preach in the parish of Kingsbridge-with-Churchstow on the south Devon coast: the vicarage had been confiscated from its Anglican vicar after the parliamentarian victory in the Civil War. This was on 3 November 1658. The Lord Protector, Oliver Cromwell, had died exactly two months earlier, and in less than eighteen months time the English experiment with republican government would ignominiously collapse, and the old order would start to re-establish itself.

For John Quick, this turnaround heralded a quarter century of troubles. Shortly after the Restoration of Charles II, he was removed from Kingsbridge (presumably by the return of its old vicar), but he managed to become curate at Brixton, not too far from his native Plymouth. In the meantime, a political reckoning had begun. Restored bishops and clergymen, and dogmatic royalists in Parliament, were fastidiously calculating the dues of the abused and battered Church of England, after its years of suffering and insult. There could be little or no common ground with the various radical Protestant sects and independent churches which had proliferated during the years of civil war and interregnum—the Baptists, Quakers, Congregationalists, and others. But had other counsels prevailed, an accommodation might have been possible with the more moderate Presbyterians and old-style puritans. These were people—Quick was one of them—who at least believed in the ideal of a single national church. Yet militant Anglicanism was in no mood to be accommodating. Between 1661 and 1664 a series of repressive measures known collectively as the Clarendon Code (after Charles II's chief minister, the earl of Clarendon) re-established the complete monopoly of the Church of England. For many 'godly' ministers there was an impassable sticking point: the Act of Uniformity, which was passed by Parliament in May 1662 and due to come into effect on 24 August, St Bartholomew's Day. This required them to declare publicly their 'unfeigned assent and consent' to all the rites and ceremonies contained in the Book of Common Prayer. In parish after parish, puritan clergymen found they could not in conscience do so, and the deprivations began. It did not escape notice that 'Black Bartholomew' was the anniversary of an earlier and still more dreadful event, the massacre of Huguenots by Catholic mobs in sixteenth-century Paris. The new law, Quick was later to write, deserved comparable remembrance as 'that unrighteous Act, which slew in one day two thousand able and faithful ministers of the gospel'.

John Quick himself would not subscribe to it, but nor would he quit his post. He carried on preaching at Brixton till December 1663, when the bishop of Exeter's officers arrived at the church, removed him out from the pulpit, and carried him off to gaol. Even there, he preached the gospel to his fellow prisoners, though the bishop, Seth Ward, tried unsuccessfully to prosecute him for doing so. Quick emerged from incarceration, in March 1664, with surprisingly robust health and with a life-long empathy for prisoners—something he would later put to good use in pastoral work among felons much less sophisticated and biddable than Bishop John Atherton. In 1672, King Charles issued a 'declaration of indulgence' towards dissenters, and Quick was licensed to preach in his native Plymouth. But a backlash the following year found him once again in prison for three months. He was apprehended, he later recorded, 'without any written order or warrant, excepting that of loud "damn yee's" and "sink yee's", with a pistol cocked at his naked breast'. After his release, he moved to London, taking charge of a Presbyterian congregation in Covent Garden, and, briefly, of an English church at Middleburg in the Netherlands. In the early 1680s, he was back in London as pastor of a community with its meeting-house in Smithfield. A persistent nonconformist, Quick was fined and imprisoned briefly for a third time in 1682.

The Glorious Revolution and the Toleration Act of 1689 finally brought respite from persecution, and Quick spent his last years as a respected pastor, preacher, and writer—a 'sober' nonconformist of the type of which John Dunton evidently approved (Dunton in fact published one of his treatises in 1691). His portrait looks out at us, sallow-faced but keen-eyed, from the title-page of his 1692 *Synodicon in Gallia Reformata* (Figure 12). This was the work for which he was best known in his own day, a scholarly history of the persecuted Huguenot Church in France, for which Quick felt a particular affinity. There were other, unremarkable publications in these years: a couple of funeral sermons, a catechism, *A Serious Inquiry into that Weighty Case of Conscience, whether a Man may Lawfully Marry his Deceased Wife's Sister*. A projected *magnum opus, Icones Sacrae Anglicanae. Or the Lives and Deaths of Severall Eminent English Divines*, was completed by 1700, but the by then ailing Quick failed to raise the subscriptions which were needed to see such a substantial work into print.[4]

This then, in brief, is the story of our story-teller, John Quick—a life rendered eventful by the times through which it was lived, but otherwise neither extraordinarily distinguished nor remarkable. But there was rather more to John Quick than an unswerving devotion to duty, and an unbending Calvinist orthodoxy. All throughout his life he remained fascinated by the idea that God spoke directly to his faithful on earth, if only they would attend to the signs around them. The 'providences' of God pointed the way in an uncertain world. Any idea that the Protestant Reformation had done away with the notion of the miraculous is unlikely to survive an encounter with the outlook of John Quick.[5] His history of the Huguenots, for example, emphasized the 'very many illustrious events of divine

Effigies Reverendi Viri IOHANNIS QUICK
5ti Evangely Ministri An. Ætat 55°.

12. The Reverend John Quick

providence relating to those churches'. Addressing a congregation in 1682, Quick seemed almost to put the Bible and continuing divine interventions on an equal footing with each other as sources of revelation: 'understand what God is speaking to you by his Word and providences'. The concern emerges most strongly in what is the first, and by some way the most interesting, of Quick's published writings: *Hell Open'd, or The Infernal Sin of Murder Punished*, published in 1676. The work is a kind of 'murder-pamphlet-plus': a racy narration of a shocking recent poisoning case in Quick's native Plymouth, combined with a profound theological meditation on the nature of repentance, and the abundance of God's mercy. It displays all of the flair for narrative that Quick uses to good effect in the *Apparition Evidence*. Indeed, its lively facility for scene-painting ('the streets are crowded; the mayor, magistrate and under-sheriff can hardly pass for the throngs'), as well as the frequent directions and entreaties to its 'Reader', may well have insinuated themselves unbidden into the style and structure of the book you hold in your hands.[6]

At the heart of *Hell Open'd* is an intense account of Quick's conversations in Exeter gaol with the two women convicted of murdering the wife and daughter of a Plymouth dyer named William Weeks. (They used arsenic placed in a 'dish of pottage'.) As such, it supplies a fascinating companion-piece to Nicholas Bernard's description of the last days of Bishop Atherton, and it is no great surprise to discover that summary versions of both pamphlets were included in the 1690 compendium, *The Wonders of Free Grace*. Yet whereas Bernard's penitent was an Oxford MA and a doctor of divinity, Quick's charges were two illiterate female servants: Mrs Weeks's maid, Anne Evans, and her grandaughter's nurse, Philippa Cary. The results too were more mixed. The maid quickly succumbed under the pressure of Quick's alternate threats of hell-fire, and promises of heaven, and she became a tearfully model penitent. But the nurse insisted to the very last that she had not instructed Evans to place 'ratsbane' in her mistress's supper.

This circumstance disturbed Quick deeply: why would a sinner facing imminent divine justice stick in a lie about such a matter? In the end, a combination of providential signs and his own reasoning convinced him that no travesty of justice had in fact taken place. Murdering one's employer in this period was the crime of 'petty-treason', and women convicted of it were subject to a horrible punishment: burning to death. As a promoter rather than perpetrator of the deed, Cary was sentenced to be hanged. The executions took place in Plymouth in March 1676. The young Anne Evans was fastened to a stake, a halter placed tightly around her neck. Yet God showed mercy towards her, allowing her to expire from strangulation before the pyre was lit. Despite the skill and experience of the executioner, the fuel would not take light till she had been dead a quarter of an hour. But then the wind shifted, blowing smoke into the face of Cary, about to be dispatched on an adjacent gallows. To Quick's way of thinking this was an unmistakable message from the Almighty: 'the smoke of my fury and flames of my fiery vengeance are now riding upon the wings of the wind towards thee'. When Cary was turned off the ladder, 'she went out like the snuff of a candle, leaving a stench behind her' (Figure 13).

A belief in portents, in signs, and in the supernatural detection of heinous crime—these things were not a barrier between the educated minister and the hapless servants, but rather a bridge into the spaces of a shared mental world. After the burial of Mistress Weeks, Anne Evans refused to stay any longer in the house, 'for that she was sure she would appear again as a spirit'. Quick meanwhile speculated that the presence of a spectre, invisible to all but the woman herself, might well be responsible for Philippa Cary's perplexing refusal to confess. Perhaps the spirit forbade her to admit to this murder, 'lest some other might out also'. It would not have been the first time such a thing had happened. Quick recalled an aged minister, 'a very holy man of God', telling him that in his youth, when serving a cure in Dartmouth, he had been summoned to the bedside of a dying man 'under very much trouble of conscience'. The man told him that around seven months earlier he had unexpectedly met a comrade, a sailor, whom he thought to be away at sea. '"I am dead", quoth this spectrum ... "took sick shortly upon my going to sea, and died this day and about an hour since"'. The

13. A poisoning in Plymouth, from John Quick's *Hell Open'd*

apparition gave him some instructions about his will and legacies, but threatened to tear him in a thousand pieces if he ever spoke about 'that business between thee and me, that thou well wotest [knowest] of'. In his last hours, the man was desperate to unburden his conscience to the Dartmouth minister, but found he could not do it: 'Oh Sir, do you not see him? Look how terrible he is! There he is just against me. O, how doth he threaten me!'

In this instance, the presence of a menacing ghost ensured the concealment of wrong-doing, but Quick knew it did not generally turn out this way. Addressing young people and servants among his readers, he sternly admonished them not to commit any sin 'presuming on secrecy or impunity...For there is nothing hid but shall be revealed.' Of all types of sinner, murderers had presumed most upon secrecy, and yet 'how miraculously have they been detected? Dreams, apparitions, and mere circumstances have detected and convicted them.' This was no mere platitude of the pulpit, but something Quick knew to be true from the testimony of people he trusted. The insight brings us sharply back to the starting point of this chapter: the apparition evidence, and the bothersome ghosts of Barnstaple and Minehead.

We may need to remind ourselves here of what we have learned. John Quick attributed his knowledge of the extraordinary activities of Mother Leakey's ghost in Minehead to two named persons, Mrs Bruen and Mr Buckley. They had both been present in the sessions at Taunton, when Elizabeth Leakey had been brought for examination before a group of JPs, who included Mrs Bruen's father, Sir George Farrel. These were the 'persons of quality' and 'unquestionable authorities', who, in Dunton's and Curll's glosses on the story, rendered all aspects of it entirely creditworthy. We may not wish to go quite so far as this, but we should note that all these persons were certainly real enough. Sir George Farrel (or Farwell) was a landed gentleman with his seat at Bishops Hull, a mile or so to the west of Taunton. His father was an active member of the Somerset bench of justices; he himself rather less so, though he is to be found attending the Quarter Sessions at Bridgwater in 1646, and undertaking various business on behalf of the JPs in the mid-1640s. His last appearance was at the Taunton Sessions in July 1647, 'the said Sir George Farwell dying shortly after the session'. A funeral monument in Bishops Hull church describes him as 'excellently accomplished', and the father of no less than twenty children. These included Mary, the wife of Charles Brune of Athelhampton, Dorset. Mary's own funeral monument records that she died in 1697, at the venerable age of 80. Mr Buckley, rector of Thurlestone in Devon, was without any doubt the John Buckley who served as vicar of Bradford in the archdeaconry of Taunton between 1635 and 1660, and who in 1662 (unlike John Quick) subscribed to the Act of Uniformity before Bishop Ward of Exeter. Quick must have heard their stories, either individually or in one memorable joint session, in 1660 or 1661, shortly before his ejection from Kingsbridge. This was, of course, nearly a quarter of a century after the events they purport to describe. Whether he made notes on what he had learnt at the time, we cannot say, though it seems most likely that he did. But he finally recorded them in the form they have come through to us in 1690, almost another third of a century later.[7]

Memories fade and mutate, and reinterpret themselves in the light of subsequent experience. It is conceivable that Quick's informants were confusing their memory of the examination of Elizabeth Leakey with the interrogation ordered by Laud, and undertaken by Bishop Piers in early 1637. But on the face of it this seems very unlikely. Their account is insistent on the presence of George Farwell in a sessions held at Taunton, and that it took place after the younger Mrs Leakey returned from a fruitless journey to Ireland to confront the errant bishop of Waterford. This chimes with what the scurrilous pamphlet of 1641 had to say about the trip. The evidence is starting to mount up that Elizabeth Leakey really did undertake such a mission—with motives that may have been frankly mercenary ones, or might have been, both culturally and psychologically, considerably more complex. Sadly, no record survives of any such examination held at Taunton in 1637 or 1638. But, as we have already had occasion to note, silence from the extant documents is seldom in itself decisive evidence. There is good survival in this period for the records of Somerset quarter sessions, where JPs heard criminal cases, but not for those of petty sessions, where two or more justices sat less formally without juries to expedite a range of matters pertaining to local government and law enforcement. It is starting to look very likely that Elizabeth Leakey told her story about the ghost in formal judicial settings on several different occasions, and that her evidence may have become more free and forthcoming as she grew in practice and confidence. For all that she protested to Archbishop Laud's commissioners that the apparition's message was for Atherton's ears only, or at a pinch, for the King's, it is a distinct possibility that the suggestions of incest and infanticide were eventually aired in open court, and that they subsequently seeped out through the gossip networks of local society. What Elizabeth and others may have been saying off the record, to neighbours, or to the 'godly ministers' who advised her to make the trip to Waterford, is another matter again. If untrue, these stories were seriously defamatory. Yet the bishop of Waterford, immersed in Irish politics and litigation, simply chose to ignore them. When they arrived, literally, on his doorstep in 1637 in the person of his sister-in-law, he appears to have swatted them away with a sardonic comment about his hanging fate.

Whether Atherton ever actually said that 'marriage and hanging come by destiny', or that 'if he were born to be hanged, he should not be drowned' (this was another well-worn proverb), his apparent failure to make any effort to scotch the rumours looks in retrospect like a serious mistake. This was particularly so if Quick's information was correct, and the full content of the apparition's message was forwarded to the Privy Council on the back of Farwell's examination. At the time of his greatest public triumphs, it seems that a swarm of vengeful rumours was buzzing around the head of the bishop of Waterford, waiting for their opportunity to sting. In those hours of painful self-revelation in the holding cell of Dublin castle, did Atherton say anything at all about incest and infanticide to his new friend Nicholas Bernard? If he did, Bernard clearly calculated that the weight of scandal was already too great for the Church of

Ireland to bear. So much was assumed by John Quick, who, like many of his profession in the mid-seventeenth century, was already acquainted with Bernard's mildly famous book. Like all alert readers of it, Quick had noticed that its author 'did not in the least touch at the crimes for which he suffered'. As a Presbyterian victim of episcopal coercion, we can expect Quick to understand but not to approve this reticence. Yet, though he mentions obliquely 'some other great crimes jumping against him at the same time', Quick seemed genuinely to have believed that the crime for which Atherton was put to death was not sodomy, but his part, many years before, in the callous murder of an infant. It had required no less than a 'miraculous work of God' to bring this to light, and to reduce that 'proud, bloody and incestuous prelate' to the evangelical repentance for which Bernard wanted him to be remembered.

Quick was thus already familiar with the ghosts of Atherton's past when he became acquainted with the second half of the story. This was in his former parish of Brixton, in 1663. Again, the informant, Madam Fortescue, seems to be real enough. The Fortescues of Spriddlestone were a cadet branch of a rather distinguished south-west gentry family. Yet this part of the narration takes us one step closer to the alleged supernatural and providential experiences themselves. For John Fortescue's steward of Cullompton, known to us only as Chamberlain, claimed in his youth to have been himself the recipient of spectral messages concerning the crimes of the bishop of Waterford.[8] The Barnstaple portion of the *Apparition Evidence* is in every way more perplexing than the preceding Minehead section, whose difficulties are considerable enough. They are in agreement with each other, however, about some seemingly important points. Both identify the mother of Atherton's bastard child as his niece, and both locate the transgression itself to a house in Barnstaple. We know already of course that the Leakeys did have Barnstaple connections: remember Elizabeth's sister-in-law, the impossibly puritan-sounding Lordsnear Leakey (custodian of the golden chain), who had remarried in Barnstaple to a man named John Knill in the summer of 1630 (pp. 21–2). But this does not seem to be the household in question, which is clearly identified as that of Mother Leakey's brother, the town clerk of Barnstaple and 'one of those whom the world called puritans'. Here we can fill in a few of the blanks, for the town clerk of Barnstaple in 1639 was a man called Robert Lane, a native of Somerset, who had taken up the office in 1628 and was to hold it till his death in 1653. Judging by his will, he does indeed seem to have been of the 'godly' persuasion, for there is much emphasis there on the 'everlasting happiness which Jesus Christ my saviour has purchased for me and all his elect in the kingdom of heaven'. Lane did have a married daughter named Elizabeth, who was still alive at the time of his death. He had evidently quarrelled with her over a legacy she believed was due to her from her maternal grandfather, for the dying man swore he had done her no wrong, despite her having 'scandalised' him in several different places. According to Quick's narrative, 'Mistress Betty' had lived in Wales 'upon a portion that she had left her either by an aunt or grandmother'. But it seems on balance unlikely that Elizabeth could have been the Mrs Betty of Chamberlain's account, who was in any case supposed to have died in 1640.

There is, to put it mildly, a fair amount of confusion in the air as we try to reconcile the two separate accounts of Atherton's misconduct contained in Quick's narration. For a start, the chronology simply doesn't work: the apparitions are said to start appearing to Chamberlain in 1639, and Mrs Betty was supposed to have left her father's house in big-bellied disgrace about seven years earlier. Yet by that point, Atherton had been settled in Ireland for three years, and he had been securely ensconced in Huish Champflower for around seven years before that. It is tempting to suspect the Chamberlain narrative of being in some sense a 'copycat' ghost story, piggy-backing for its own purposes onto an already well-established local tale. Yet the idea will not quite go away that Atherton was somehow connected with a godly family in Barnstaple. There is an intriguing little aside in Bernard's *Penitent Death*, one which it has been difficult to know what to do with up until this point. As the end approached, and as Atherton still struggled to convince himself of the reality of God's forgiveness, he began to reminisce to Nicholas Bernard, saying that 'he could remember in his youth, before his soul was stained with sin, when he lived for a time in some conscionable way in a certain religious family, he had some flashes of such sweetness that was of more worth than all the joy he had since'. Could this refer to a period of boarding with a godly household in Barnstaple, and if so, was this the place where the staining of Atherton's soul in earnest began? Might there even have been another transgressive incident, before the documented incest with the younger Susan Leakey? There is another, still wilder, possibility. The most alert readers may remember the licence that Atherton was granted by the Christ Church chapter in November 1630, to return to England for the space of a year 'about some special affairs of his own' (p. 66). Could it be that Chamberlain's chronology was right after all, and that the Barnstaple adultery was a repeat offence, contracted during this extended visit? It seems rather unlikely, but in the end, as with so much in this case, we simply cannot say for certain.[9]

We should perhaps in any case ask ourselves a bracing question: whether the relentless search for a core of irreducible 'fact' in the stories surrounding Bishop Atherton might be to risk missing the point. Surely it is the fantasy, rather than the reality, of John Quick's recycled narratives that invests them with their emotional power, and their considerable historical interest? How was it that, within a generation of the death of Mother Leakey, the stories about the activities of her posthumous spirit had acquired such lush and elaborate embellishment? And why was a Protestant minister, of a deeply puritan stamp, so enthusiastically promoting accounts of the doings of restless souls, when his predecessors of a generation or two before (see pp. 44–6) would instinctively have suspected iniquitous popish fraud, if not the damnable delusions of Satan?

The two or three decades following the restoration of the Stuart monarchy in 1660 were without doubt a golden age of British ghosts. The pamphlets and chapbooks of the popular press frequently carried reports of 'strange news' from various parts of the land. At the same time, learned ministers were putting together hefty compilations of apparition narratives, certified intrusions from the 'invisible world'. Ghost stories travelled freely between the two genres. The enthusiasm for them was not universal, and some old notes of caution continued to be struck. In a work of 1677, the cleric and schoolmaster John Webster mocked the idea that 'the souls of the godly and wicked, do rove up and down here upon earth, and make apparitions'. Invoking the authority of a raft of 'true sons of the doctrine of the Church of England', Webster urged his readers to be wary of 'feigned fables' and 'satanical illusions'. Twenty years later, the earl of Burlington's chaplain, John Roe, published a tract to demonstrate that apparitions of the dead were 'directly contrary to the sense of the scripture', 'useless and unnecessary', and 'inconsistent with common reason'. But Roe would not quite go so far as to say that apparitions were by definition impossible. Webster too was far from being a complete sceptic. He had heard at first hand several compelling accounts of the appearance of persons after their death. Following the lead of the Renaissance occultist Paracelsus, he speculated that these were—not souls—but the 'astral spirits' of deceased persons, substances which required a longer time than the body to surrender their vital force.[10]

For numerous other clergymen, however, the meaning of belief in ghosts was changing radically in the years after the Civil Wars. Although 'popery' remained an important ideological enemy (and a genuine political threat right up to the defeat of the last Jacobite rebellion in 1746), the idea that the common people retained popish hearts under a mere veneer of Protestantism seemed increasingly less plausible as the generations passed. After the middle of the seventeenth century, reported sightings of ghosts sounded much less like an alarming indication of the Reformation's failure to take root than they had done at its start. The wars themselves had opened a Pandora's box of radical political and religious ideas, and in some quarters at least, the fear of popery had been replaced by a new and alarming threat to religious stability: the spectre of disbelief. One name above all was associated with cynicism and scepticism about religion, that of the political philosopher

Thomas Hobbes (1588–1679). In his masterpiece of 1651, the *Leviathan*, Hobbes did not actually deny the existence of God, but he radically reduced the extent to which it was at all possible for humans to discern his will. He also suggested that biblical incidents and expressions demanded to be understood in metaphorical terms. One example was the word 'spirit', which should usually be interpreted, he argued, to mean doctrine or zeal. Hobbes marvelled at 'how we came to translate *spirits* by the word *ghosts*, which signifies nothing but the imaginary inhabitants of man's brain'. Small wonder then that in the hands of some orthodox religious writers 'Hobbism', 'atheism', and 'Sadducism' were employed as virtually interchangeable terms (the Sadducees were the ancient Jewish sect who denied the existence of angels and the resurrection of the body). Small wonder, too, if attested appearances of ghosts were increasingly leapt upon as proof of the existence of a normally invisible world of spirits, and hence of the benign interest taken in his creation by God himself. From the 1670s onwards, authors of short pamphlets reporting the appearance of ghosts more often than not gloatingly introduced the story by suggesting that 'atheism' and 'infidelity' were at last getting their comeuppance. Dunton's *Athenian Mercury* was happy to get in on the act in October 1691, pronouncing that the credibility of the stories in its Halloween special issue would undoubtedly 'conduce to the reducing of the many proselytes of Sadducism and Hobbism amongst us'.[11]

This same motive was still more emphatically centre-stage in a series of lengthier and more serious works, which were being compiled through the second half of the seventeenth century by clergymen and philosophers such as Henry More, Joseph Glanvill, Richard Bovet, Richard Baxter, and John Beaumont. In these books, apparitions of spirits are usually discussed as part of the larger controversy over the reality of witchcraft, the judicial persecution of which was grinding to a close in England in the Restoration decades (the last witch was hanged in England in 1685, and legislation punishing witches was finally repealed in 1736). Nonetheless, these authors were not in the main inclined to regard appearances of ghosts as typically the handiwork of witches.

There was, of course, an inevitable degree of ambiguity about the status of any supernatural vision. As Richard Baxter admitted, 'tis hard to know when it is a devil, and when it is a human soul that appears ... uncertain to us whether it be a good angel, or the soul of some former dear friend'. Yet the once rigidly-held orthodoxy that any apparition could only be a devil or an angel, and never the soul of a departed person, was now being fundamentally relaxed. Here, for once, the doctrinal certainties of the intelligentsia had started to fall in line with the common-sense outlook of ordinary people. The Cambridge philosopher and theologian Henry More was among the first to point out the sheer implausibility of Protestantism's inherited doctrine on the question of ghosts. Everybody knew that the typical duty-roster of the returning spirit lay in 'detecting the murderer, in disposing their estate, in rebuking injurious executors, in visiting and counselling their wives and children, in forewarning them of such and such courses'. All of these were decidedly odd activities 'for a devil with that care and kindness to promote'. Yet if such spirits were actually good angels, why would they lie and claim to be the souls of dead humans?[12]

When placing ghost narratives before the reading public, however, writers such as More knew that they could hardly just report the hearsay stories of the people. They were well aware that this would carry little weight with the sceptical sophisticates they wanted to shake out of their disbelieving complacency. The ghost stories circulating in seventeenth-century England often originated with unexplained noises in rural cottages, or with mysterious shapes appearing in front of frightened chambermaids and farmboys. But by the time they arrived fully formed on the printed page they had usually been through an exacting process of 'verification'. Such accounts almost invariably referred the reader to 'persons of credit' in the relevant locale—individuals, usually male, of superior social standing, who were in a position to swear to the truth of the circumstances. Seventeenth-century England was a society in which 'social status and reputation were critical in endowing truth-claims with authority'. In those cases where the ghost's appearance was in some way connected to the perpetrating of a crime (a considerable portion of the total), writers often emphasized that statements had been made in front of justices. Testimony given in court was sometimes printed verbatim. In many of the narratives, it was evident that the advice and assistance of local clergy had been called on, and as often as not, it was these selfsame clergymen who sent a full account of the happening to an author whom they knew was collecting material of the kind for publication.[13]

All of this poses an interesting question for us: why didn't John Quick, or some other Somerset or Devon person of 'quality', make any effort to spread knowledge of the Mother Leakey tale through the medium of print? The *Apparition Evidence* possessed all the elements likely to appeal to the anthologizers of contemporary ghost stories: it involved the dramatic appearances of a spirit, 'enough to convince the greatest atheist', the providential exposure of a serious crime, the stamp of authenticity supplied by credit-worthy persons, the involvement of magistrates, the imprimatur of a reputable clerical scribe. The rhetorical flair with which Quick constructed his narratives, and his profligate use of the first person plural, suggests strongly that he intended to share his account with a wider readership. Yet it remained, as we have seen, locked away in manuscript until it was finally published, in the most curious of circumstances, four years after the death of the author, and very many years after the alleged events themselves. At a time when many dozens of ghost stories were achieving national renown, courtesy of the books, pamphlets, and periodicals of the London press, the one that we are most concerned with had to remain obscurely local and uncelebrated, unauthorized and un-authorized in the wider world.

The oversight is particularly conspicuous in view of a striking and unusual fact about the provenance of printed ghost stories in the later seventeenth century. A remarkably disproportionate number of them originated from the south-western counties of England, and from Somerset in particular. One of the leading collectors was Richard Bovet, a gentleman from Wellington near Taunton, whose *Pandaemonium* (1684) abounds in ghost stories from the county. His contemporary, John Beaumont, author of a theological *Treatise of Spirits*, spent most of his life practising as a doctor at Ston Easton, halfway between the Somerset cathedral cities of Bath and Wells. Joseph Glanvill, whose *Saducismus Triumphatus* ('Sadducism triumphed-over') was a still more renowned work in the genre, was from 1666 rector of the former abbey church in Bath, and later the pluralist incumbent of two other Somerset parishes, Streat and Walton. Still more intriguingly, Glanvill was, like John Quick, a native of Devon, brought up in a puritan family. In fact, both men were born in Plymouth in 1636, that foundational year for the Atherton–Leakey stories. They went up to Exeter College, Oxford, within a year of each other in the early 1650s, and they must have known each other well. In later years, when both were serving as ministers in the south-west, Glanvill was widely known to be collecting accounts of providential apparitions, and considerable numbers of them were sent to him at first or second hand by local clergymen. In these circumstances, we have to wonder just why the account of the Minehead–Barnstaple apparitions managed to stay so resolutely out of the limelight.

The explanation appears to be more design than accident, for it is probable that an attempt was made in these years to bring the Barnstaple story to a wider audience. In 1682, the rural Devon parish of Spreyton was convulsed by a series of supernatural events. A letter describing them, 'from a person of quality in Devon to a gentleman his friend in London', was issued as a pamphlet in May the following year, and in 1684 Bovet published a second version, drawing on 'fresh testimonials' of its veracity. Among those able to confirm the report was 'the reverend minister of Barnstaple': a man named John Boyce was vicar there between 1675 and 1687. At around the same time, a letter from Boyce about the case was being forwarded by Andrew Paschall, rector of Chedzoy in Somerset, to his friend Mr John Aubrey in London. Aubrey (best remembered today for his gossipy *Brief Lives* of eminent contemporaries) was a man, like Glanvill and Beaumont, much interested in natural philosophy, and he was a fellow member with them of the fledgling Royal Society. He was also an aficionado of ghost stories, and published many of them (including 'The Demon of Spreyton') in his 1696 volume on a variety of mysterious phenomena, simply called *Miscellanies*. Boyce had sent the Spreyton narrative to Paschall in the first place as he knew that he would be interested in it: his friend had entreated him some time before 'to enquire into a thing of this nature, that happened in Barnstaple'. Before this, Paschall had already received from another source an account of this Barnstaple haunting: 'it fills a sheet or two, which I have by me'. What is more, he had sent it on to Joseph Glanvill 'who is collecting histories for his *Saducismus Triumphatus*'. Paschall had 'desired to have it well attested, it being full of very memorable things'. But Glanvill reported back that 'he could meet only a general consent as to the truth of the things, the reports varying in the circumstances'. In a subsequent letter to Aubrey, Paschall remembered that he had also promised to send Dr Henry More 'an account of the Barnstaple Apparition'. It is possible, of course, that Barnstaple in the middle decades of the seventeenth century was a particularly haunted place, and that Paschall's interest was in an entirely different ghost story from that of Chamberlain and Mother Leakey, one equally full of 'memorable things'. But on balance it seems much more likely that Restoration England's leading specialists in the supernatural, Joseph Glanvill and Henry More, knew all about the stories still circulating in Barnstaple concerning a spectral exposure of the crimes of John Atherton. Yet they decided to do nothing with them.[14]

Inaction, like silence, is never simple to explain. Perhaps we should take Glanvill entirely at his word: the Barnstaple apparition could not be authenticated to his exacting standards. But another possibility is suggested by the response which, as we have seen, the discussion of Atherton's case provoked when it emerged into daylight at the start of the next century—for some at least, the religious politics of the story made it just too hot to handle. The miraculous exposure of a hitherto unpunished murder was a thoroughly standard element of the apparition narratives of the time. But both the victims and the perpetrators were generally persons of little account in themselves, blank canvasses onto which the providential patterns of the Almighty could be lovingly painted. No other ghost story of the seventeenth (or any?) century revolved around suggestions of sodomy, incest, and murder committed by a bishop of the Established Church.

Ghosts were not a narrowly denominational issue in the later seventeenth century, and a concern to confound 'atheism' by demonstrating the reality of the spirit world could unite Protestants of varying hues. More and Aubrey were Anglicans, as was Glanvill, who had left his puritan childhood behind (Beaumont may have had Catholic leanings). Bovet's background seems to have been in radical dissent. Richard Baxter was an eminent Presbyterian minister. All were equally persuaded that, with the permission of God, the souls of the dead might be allowed to return with important messages for the living. Nor was this just the eccentric conviction of a handful of networked enthusiasts. When Henry More claimed that examples of 'the appearing of the ghosts of men after death are so numerous and frequent in all men's mouths, that it may seem superfluous to particularise in any', the exaggeration was slight and pardonable. Even the sceptic Roe conceded that it was commonly believed by people that God could 'send an apparition to make a discovery of some strange murder'. John Quick's erstwhile persecutor, Bishop Ward of Exeter, was as convinced as anyone that it was 'generally the case of secret murderers' to find themselves tormented by the ghosts of their victims.

Yet inter-confessional tensions were not entirely absent in these years from the business of relating ghost stories. When editing Glanvill's posthumously published *Saducismus*, Henry More took care to describe a man who claimed to have had 'conference' with a spirit as one 'of a sober, honest and sensible genius', no wild sectarian 'but an orderly son of the Church of England'. Another of Glanvill's visionaries, by contrast, had once been 'a constant frequenter of the Church', but 'fell off wholly to the non-conformists' about a year before the apparition appeared. This raised the suspicion that the motivation behind the story 'may be to make him to be accounted an extraordinary somebody amongst the dissenting party'. In the end, Glanvill accepted his testimony, though he did so with the sarcastic observation that while his defection showed 'a vacillancy of it his judgement, yet it does not any defect of his external senses'. Although personally on good terms with some nonconformists such as Baxter, Glanvill vigorously opposed the toleration of dissent, and would have been horrified had he lived to see its legal enactment in 1689. On the other side of the divide, Glanvill's college contemporary John Quick was no narrow sectarian. He was happy to praise the efforts of the conformist ministers who, 'moved by charity', cooperated in the ministry to condemned felons. Towards the end of his life, he looked back wistfully to a time of remembered 'sweet harmonious love and union' between the Anglican and Presbyterian ministers of the south-west. Yet the bitterness engendered in him by the events of the early 1660s had simply never gone away. Years later, Quick was still railing against the Act of Uniformity, 'a law which condemned us without a hearing, that cast us out of our freeholds without a trial, a law that found us innocent and made us guilty'. He also remained much concerned with the reputations of those who had suffered under it. Quick took particular exception to the account of one such minister, George Hughes of Plymouth, written by the Oxford antiquarian Anthony Wood. The passage was a product of Wood's 'Billingsgate rhetoric', his 'peculiar spleen' against all puritans and nonconformists. Wood, we should remember, also penned a surprisingly forgiving portrait of Bishop Atherton (p. 154).

It is no surprise, then, that Quick's reading of the Minehead and Barnstaple ghost stories was fundamentally conditioned by his own life-experience as a dispossessed survivor, a victim of arbitrary episcopal power. Like the town clerk of Barnstaple in his story, Quick had been 'one of them called puritans'. His interpretation of Bernard's *Penitent Death* retained precisely the kind of sharp political edge that its author had hoped, by careful editing and omissions, to have smoothed permanently away. To Quick, it was the story of how a 'proud, bloody and incestuous prelate' had been brought to a 'most bitter evangelical repentance'. There was no real mystery as to why Bernard 'did not in the least touch at the crimes for which he suffered'. He simply 'would not bespatter his order, it being a very foul reflection on the hierarchy, that one of that eminent charge should be branded with such heinous crimes'.[15] Quick, however, operated under no such inhibitions. In his hands, the *Apparition Evidence* was some way from being a piece of crude anti-episcopal or anti-Anglican invective. But it was nonetheless an uncompromising statement of faith: faith in how the immense justice of God could sweep all before it, showing no concern for the dignity of high ecclesiastical office, and securing redress for the forgotten victims of its unaccountable holders. It is understandable if the story did not much recommend itself to those for whom the restored Church of England was the surest bulwark against vice, scepticism, and irreligion, and who may have hoped that all memory of it would quietly fade away.

In focusing so much on the 'political' meanings of the story we are in danger of forgetting a rather significant fact. John Quick was only in a secondary sense the 'author' of the apparition narratives published in 1710. Behind his lively phraseology and talent for dramatic pacing lie the words of Mrs Bruen, Mr Buckley, and Mrs Fortescue, and behind them, the words and actions of Mr Chamberlain and of the younger Mrs Leakey herself. There are surely many other voices there too, though we cannot now ascribe names to them. More than two decades had passed since the alleged happenings before Quick, then a fresh-faced and idealistic young minister, heard his account of them from people who themselves had been young when the events had taken place. Moreover, these were not just any two decades, but crucible years of war and revolution. These were times when the head rolled from a king's shoulders, and when it seemed, to some at least, that the expected Kingdom of God, and earthly rule by his 'saints', was at last in prospect. When they had finally run their blood-stained course, the 1640s and 1650s amounted to a formidable cultural and historical barrier—a watershed of personal and collective memory as profound as that of the Second World War has been for the generation of our parents and grandparents. The phrase 'when I was a boy, before the civil wars' recurs regularly in the writings of John Aubrey. One of his childhood recollections was of the fashion 'for old women and maids to tell fabulous stories night times and of sprites, and walking of ghosts'. The same habit was written about less fondly in 1655 by the witchcraft sceptic, Thomas Ady. He was a man exasperated by the invincible ignorance of the old wives 'who sit talking, and chatting of many false old stories of witches, and fairies, and Robin Good-fellow, and walking spirits, and the dead walking again'. Though Aubrey contended that the wars had made the phantoms vanish, and that 'now children fear no such things', it is in fact highly unlikely the practice of telling ghost stories in company had died out anywhere by the end of the century. In 1725 a Newcastle clergyman was writing resignedly that 'nothing is commoner in country places than for a whole family to sit in a winter's evening round the fire and tell stories of apparitions and ghosts'.[16]

All of this should remind us that the agenda of the learned clergymen involved is not the whole story here. By the time that Quick was finding ways to make sense of the material, the narrative of Mother Leakey had already become in some sense a folk tale, an oral tradition passing from one generation to another. It was a tale rooted in a distinct locality, and in a particular set of expectations about how an apparition should behave: expectations which were not necessarily those of the theological 'experts'. Bruen, Buckley, and the others may have been the sources for the story, but they are also the channels through which other memories, interpretations, and imaginings, emanating from the vicinities of Minehead and Barnstaple, are able to lay claim to our attention. We cannot recreate the processes of transmission, but if we examine a little more closely the motifs and devices of the stories, we can judge what they might have to tell us about the importance and workings of the supernatural world in the popular imagination. The apparition narratives have at their centre some 'real' events, and they were told and retold by real people, not generated by some kind of amorphous folk consciousness. But at the same time it is by no means ridiculous to see them as in some sense collective compositions, cautionary tales drawing on deep wells of hope and anxiety in the culture of the English people.[17]

Take, for example, a feature of the Barnstaple story that, on the surface of things, has nothing at all to do with the crimes of Bishop Atherton: the boxes of fine linen, precious cups, and gold and silver coins which the apparition of the old man so generously bestows on young Chamberlain. If the uncovering of murder was the ghostly predilection *par excellence* in early modern England, the detection of buried treasure ran it a close second. A ballad published in 1675 (to be sung to the tune *Summer Time*) made it in fact their defining activity: 'You have heard of spirits for to walk, / Though many be you ne'er did see, / And with some men do seem to talk / About their hidden treasury'. 'Treasures you know ought not to be concealed', wrote the clergyman John Norris in 1695, 'and so great is the disorder when they are, that ghosts oftentimes think it worth while to come into our world on purpose to have them disclosed.' In pamphlet accounts, ghosts regularly direct people towards the whereabouts of stashes of cash. Even when they do not do this, there was often an expectation that hidden treasure must be involved somehow. The appearance of an apparition at a house in Southwark in the early 1660s, for example, led to conjecture that 'there has been much money hid, either in the garden or about the house, which as yet cannot be discovered'. After the spirit of the murder victim Roger Carter returned near Stamford in Lincolnshire in 1679, reports persisted among neighbours that 'Old Mr Carter had hid moneys, and that being not as yet discovered, was the cause his restless soul could find no fixed abode'. Treasure-seekers did not always wait for the dead to take the initiative. In 1680, in Mother Leakey's old hometown of Bridgwater in Somerset, rumours that there was hidden treasure in the house of John Crapp led to the assembling of a party of fortune hunters. They armed themselves with divining rods, and took their instructions from a woman who claimed she was in contact with a spirit who would tell them where to look. Having spent two nights in the house, however, they 'did not find any spirit appear unto them', and the whole group ended up on a charge in front of the mayor. Valuable documents as well as money were also sometimes brought to light by supernatural means. In one of Aubrey's ghost stories, the whereabouts of a repudiated marriage settlement is revealed to a woman in Salisbury 'hid behind a wainscot in the chamber'. Just what it was that Mrs Betty felt compelled to recover from behind a window panel in her father's house in Barnstaple must, however, remain forever a mystery.[18]

The discovery of a hoard of buried gold (like dreams of winning the lottery in more recent times) is an obvious wish-fulfilment fantasy. But just as we delight in reports of lottery-winners made miserable by their millions, so there was sometimes a satisfying twist (for others) in the tales of supernatural enrichment. Chamberlain's effortlessly acquired wealth, we should remember, was short-lived. The coins were looted by Cavaliers, and the precious cups disappeared during a mysteriously unseasonal thunderstorm in July of 1650, 'no one having been a jot better for the devil's gift'. This suggestion, that the apparition of the old man who appeared to Chamberlain in Barnstaple and Wales may have been none other than the devil himself, is a reminder of how careful people needed to be in the matter of spectres and their promises. Chamberlain should have known better. When Thomas Godard of Marlborough in Wiltshire was offered money by the ghost of his father-in-law in November 1674, he is reported to have said: 'in the name of Jesus Christ, I refuse all such moneys!' In the Spreyton case to which I have referred already (p. 222), a ghost orders a young man to carry an unpaid legacy of twenty shillings to his sister living near Totnes in Devon. But she utterly refuses to receive the gift 'being sent her (as she said) from the devil'.[19]

Chamberlain's travails with the gold-encased cups bring out another characteristic which Quick's narratives share with other apparition stories of the period: a rootedness in place, and a concern with features of the landscape and topography. The devil reclaimed his gifts from Chamberlain as he and his family were travelling from Barnstaple to Cullompton 'over Black Down'. The steep wooded escarpment and deep valleys of the Black Down Hills, straddling the Somerset–Devon border between Wellington and

Taunton to the north, and Honiton and Axminster to the south, were a recurrent location for the sighting of spectres. A pamphlet of 1690 recounted how a gentleman travelling to Taunton in September of that year had a vision of one or two hundred people, of all sorts and conditions, as he travelled over Black Down. It could be no coincidence, the author believed, that this occurred near the very place where many of those executed after the recent Monmouth Rebellion had been buried. (The rebellion, aiming to replace the Catholic James II with Charles II's bastard son the Duke of Monmouth, was comprehensively crushed at Sedgemoor near Bridgwater in July 1685.) But long before this, so Richard Bovet reported in 1684, Black Down was considered to be a place where apparitions of fairies or spirits 'most ordinarily showed themselves'. A homebound traveller there about fifty years before had seen 'a great company of people, that seemed to him like country folks', yet who vanished when he came close to them. It looks in 1690 as though responses to a recent (and traumatic) political event were being grafted onto a much older pattern of beliefs about the area.[20]

This, too, may help us make sense of some of the contours of the *Apparition Evidence*, and a number of its apparently incongruous or irrelevant details. Take the business with the doctor of physick and the stiles on the outskirts of Minehead, an episode which culminates in Mother Leakey sitting astride one of them to block his entry to the town, and kicking him in the breeches for his discourtesy. A modern folklorist has commented on the common tendency of local legends 'to confer glamour on the neighbourhood by offering some striking anecdote about one or more of its conspicuous features'. The sites selected were commonly (in a favourite jargon term of anthropologists) 'liminal' ones—that is, they delineated boundaries between places, and, implicitly, between the visible and invisible worlds. It is therefore not simply coincidental that stiles appear in a number of other ghost narratives from this period. In a relation sent to Henry More from Dr Ezekias Burton, a ghost makes its appearance at a stile in Guildford. Thomas Godard of Marlborough also encountered his father-in-law's spirit 'at a stile near Godre's grounds in Ogburn'. Some of Mother Leakey's other peculiarities can be paralleled in printed narratives. The motif of supernatural asphyxiation occurs in the case of the 'Demon of Spreyton', and the presence of whistling spirits is reported by several authors. Baxter gives an account of a haunting at a house in Lutterworth, Leicestershire, in 1646. Multitudes flocked to the site, 'and whatever time anyone would whistle, it was answered by a whistle in the room'. Mother Leakey's whistling was not of course so whimsical and random, but maliciously destructive, heralding the imminent ruin of her son's ships. As we have seen (p. 40), ship-sinking and storm-raising in the seventeenth century was pre-eminently the work of witches, and there seem to be very few cases where it is attributed to the agency of a departed spirit. In 1672, however, a pamphlet claimed that a ship returning from Newcastle, the inappropriately named *Hope-well* of London, had inexplicably foundered a few leagues from Spurn Point by Grimsby, after an apparition in the shape of a man had menaced the ship's master.[21]

Such similarities are instructive, suggesting the ways in which the integration of stock motifs helped to give shape to a strange story, and allowed both tellers and hearers of the tale to place it within a familiar frame of reference. But at the same time we need to be wary of ironing out the unique and distinctive features of the Atherton–Leakey–Betty story. Suggestions of sodomy do not appear in any of the other seventeenth-century apparition narratives I have been able to consult, nor, more surprisingly, do claims about incest. The central disclosure of the *Apparition Evidence*—the murder of an infant and the hiding of its body—does, however, resonate strongly elsewhere. Infanticide was a difficult kind of murder to detect, and though the legal record produces numerous cases of infants discovered buried beneath floors, or under the stairs, or hidden in boxes, it was widely supposed that other tiny skeletons might lie undetected for years, if not indefinitely. For these reasons, new-born child murder was, as we have seen (p. 125), the 'sin which cries for vengeance', a secret crime against which God would work miracles, 'rather than it shall be undiscovered'. The callous calculation and perverted religiosity of Atherton's alleged complicity in the murder lingers indelibly in the mind—his baptizing the child, and then smoking it 'over a pan of charcoal, that it might not stink'. There may be no connection of any kind, but it is interesting to note that a notorious murder case in a North Somerset village in 1624 involved the attempted preservation of the body to prevent it from smelling. Ironically enough, the victim in this case was a clergyman, the curate of Cleeve, and his murderers were hanged (as Susan Leakey the younger may or may not have been) at the Taunton assizes.

In the course of Quick's narrative, Mother Leakey is revealed as (or transmuted into) something she has not before been in our story: herself the perpetrator of the unspeakable crime, the woman who chokes the new-born baby to death. But because murderesses of this sort cannot rest at ease, she returns to confess her guilt and implicate her accomplice in the infanticide. That those with the responsibility for delivering children might take the opportunity to do them harm was an evident source of social anxiety at this time.[22] In Holborn, London, in 1679, an apparition in the shape of one Mrs Adkins haunted the house where she had lived in her lifetime. She had been a midwife, known for her 'extraordinary subtlety and private policy', and for her habit of uttering 'dark syllogisms' which her neighbours did not then understand. At first silent in her appearances, she eventually commanded a terrified maid to take up two tiles from the hearth and bury whatever she should find there. The effort yielded up the bones of two infants, conjectured to be 'children illegitimate or bastards, who to save their mothers' credits had been murdered and buried there'. The opinion of 'divers chirurgions' (surgeons) was that they had lain there a considerable quantity of years. Yet the message for readers was clear: that whatever the passage of time, an omnipotent providence would eventually reveal what had been hidden, that 'restless ghosts and airy forms from their dire mansions' would ever be 'compelled to rouse and discover their vile deeds'.[23]

We have now spent quite long enough attempting to disentangle the knotted narratives of the Reverend John Quick. They do not supply us with a very much clearer picture of exactly what happened in the Atherton and Leakey families in Somerset and Devon at the start of the 1620s, though they leave us in no doubt that within a few years of Atherton's departure for Ireland, if not before, claims were being made locally that a child had been murdered and its body hidden away. What they also provide, however, is considerable insight into the complex and multi-layered processes by which local traditions and popular 'folklore' might come into being. Fragments of family history and dimly remembered judicial testimony combine with long-established popular beliefs about whistling apparitions and buried treasure, and together they begin to anchor themselves on familiar places in the neighbourhood landscape. We are somewhere near the beginning of a pattern of 'folklorization' of memory. But the people whom we have to thank for the survival of these stories did not see it in anything like these terms. To John Quick and his informants, the narratives were true 'relations', properly attested descriptions of real happenings. The later purveyors of the tales, Dunton and Curll (if we take at face value what they had to say about them), believed exactly the same. Yet by the time the *Apparition Evidence* was finally printed in 1710–11, the world was changing. The fundamental meaning of ghost stories, the 'truth-value' they could command among the circles of the educated, was not what it was when Quick had first harvested the stories in the early 1660s. Enlightenment was in the air, and scepticism was on the march.

We now find ourselves back again where we began this chapter: in the London world of the coffee house and the periodical essay, at the close of the first decade of the eighteenth century. Over the course of 1711 and 1712, Joseph Addison made a number of literary contributions to *The Tatler*'s successor publication, *The Spectator*, choosing the subject of ghosts and spirits. Addison was no 'Hobbist', denying the very possibility of apparitions; they were, after all, grounded in 'the reports of all historians' and in 'the traditions of all nations'. But his pen nonetheless dripped with amused disdain for the superstitious beliefs of the common people, the 'ridiculous horrors' he found prevailing in all parts of the country. Things had no doubt been worse in the past. 'Before the world was enlightened by learning and philosophy', there was 'not a village in England that had not a ghost in it', 'scarce a shepherd to be met with who had not seen a spirit'. Yet in some places not much had apparently changed. A gentleman friend in the country had told him 'with a great deal of mirth' that his house had the reputation of being haunted, and that reports of noises in the long gallery meant 'he could not get a servant to enter it after eight o'clock at night'. A ruined abbey nearby was also reported to be haunted. Walking there late one evening, Addison found it a solitary and echo-filled place: 'I do not at all wonder that weak minds fill it with spectres and apparitions.' Such foolishness was also to be found closer to home; indeed, in Addison's own London lodgings. 'I remember last winter there were several young girls of the neighbourhood sitting about the fire with my landlady's daughters, and telling stories of spirits and apparitions.' Seating himself in the corner of the room, where he pretended to read a book, Addison managed to overhear 'several dreadful stories of ghosts as pale as ashes that had stood at the feet of a bed, or walked over a churchyard by moonlight'. There was a little boy in the company, so rapt with attention to each tale 'that I am mistaken if he ventures to go to bed by himself this twelvemonth'. His presence prompted Addison to reflect on the negative effects such narratives could exercise on young minds. 'Were I a father, I should take particular care to preserve my children from these little horrors of imagination'. He went on to quote approvingly the opinions on education of the late philosopher, John Locke. It was his conviction that once they were inculcated into a child's mind, illogical associations, such as that of the dark with evil spirits, could manifest themselves in a lifetime's worth of irrational fears.

These were far from being eccentric or unusually 'modern' opinions. A treatise defending apparitions, written in 1722 by a clergyman in the rather out-of-the-way posting of St Kitts in the Caribbean, complained that educated opinion was now 'apt to speak irreverently of apparitions, by calling them the creatures of a fearful and credulous mind'. In the same year, a publication laying down rules for the education and conduct of young women had a stern message for parents and governesses: 'permit not servants or others to terrify her with stories of apparitions, witches, ghosts etc.' Three years later, a Newcastle clergyman called Henry Bourne surveyed popular 'opinions and ceremonies' in his *Antiquitates Vulgares* ('Antiquities of the common people'). Like Addison, Bourne did not deny there might really be such things as apparitions, but he had no doubt that the vulgar people's habit of telling ghost stories to each other 'makes them many times imagine they see things which really are nothing but their own fancy'. He ventured to assert that 'almost all the stories of ghosts and spirits are grounded on no other bottom but the fears and fancies and weak brains of men'. Traditions of particular places frequented by spirits, and of haunted houses, were to be found almost everywhere in the land: 'there are few villages which have not either had such an house in it or near it'. But such tales were, at root, mere residues of 'the ignorance and superstition of the Romish Church'.

For all his sneering condescension towards the people, Bourne has a good claim to stand among the founding fathers of folklore studies. A more flamboyant and famous commentator on popular beliefs about ghosts at this time, however, was the Whig journalist, and pioneer of the modern novel, Daniel Defoe. In 1727 Defoe produced *An Essay on the History and Reality of Apparitions*. Weighing in at 395 pages, it was a hefty essay. Nor was it Defoe's first foray into the subject. In 1706, he had published a best-selling account of a reported haunting in Canterbury, *The True Relation of the Apparition of Mrs Veal*. Once again, Defoe was no rationalist or sceptic, pooh-poohing the very notion of apparitions. In fact, he devoted the greater portion of his 1727 book simply to relating apparition narratives. But he also made a clear effort to distinguish his own appraisal of these events from that of the hoi polloi. Defoe's philosophy was a more or less straight inversion of the old Protestant orthodoxy: the majority of apparitions were not devils, but a kind of angelic spirit. They were certainly 'not such as are vulgarly called ghosts; that is to say, departed souls returning again and appearing visibly on earth'. This was an instance of 'the bewildered imaginations and dreams of ignorant people, who never know how or by what rules to judge of such things'. Defoe did not even think at the end of the day it was very material whether all his stories were true or not: much more important were the moral lessons they sought to impart. This was a long step away from the obsession with authenticity and verification to be found in the writings of Baxter, More, and Glanvill (and indeed of John Quick). It looks like a concession to the sensibilities of an ever more sophisticated readership, and a move towards the more self-conscious 'fictionalizing' of ghost stories in new and developing literary genres. A rather more practical imperative was pressing in the same direction at this time. The Stamp Act of 1724 imposed a higher rate of taxation on papers and pamphlets dealing with 'publick news, intelligence or occurrences' than on those containing history, biographies, or literature. There was thus an obvious incentive for ghost stories to relocate themselves from the former category to the latter, to change from being matters of fact to becoming pleasures of the imagination. In Henry Fielding's mid-eighteenth-century novel, *Tom Jones*, when the eponymous hero is mistaken for a ghost, the effect is definitely intended to be comic. The credulity of the onlookers creates a revealing association in the author's mind: in his bloodied and bandaged state Tom looked as dreadful an apparition as was ever to be found 'in the imagination of any good people met in a winter evening over a Christmas fire in Somersetshire'.[24] We should perhaps not exaggerate the extent to which the supernatural had become marginalized and downgraded in England by the middle years of the eighteenth century. Historians are teaching us that, even among educated people, private beliefs may have remained much more open to the idea of interventions from the spirit world than a study of the 'public discourse' would suggest.[25] Nonetheless, in the world of print at least, ghost stories no longer commanded automatic attention as vehicles of moral meaning and expressions of divine purpose. The sublime was becoming the ridiculous.

It looks, then, as though our investigation of the transmission of stories about Mother Leakey and Bishop Atherton has been complicated by a succession of spectacular historical mistimings. The Atherton trial itself took place just as the approaching convulsions of civil war operated to relegate a potentially headline-grabbing scandal to the small print and the inside pages.[26] Still juicier details about the case were emerging at the very moment when the imposition of a restored Anglican hegemony made their publication impolitic and unpalatable. What purported to be the full story finally emerged into the daylight in the years when sworn oral testimony about ghosts and apparitions was simply no longer being treated by a swathe of the educated classes with the attention and respect it had commanded in the generation before. The beginning of the eighteenth century, so scholars have argued, witnessed a growing mental gulf between the culture of the 'vulgar' people and that of the social and educational elites. The authority of custom, folk memory, and oral tradition was gradually being eroded—pushed aside as a source of reliable knowledge about the past by the advent of recognizably 'modern' historical scholarship, and an increasingly instinctive disdain on the part of rulers for the habits and viewpoints of the ruled.[27] In such a climate, it might seem that we have finally reached the end of the road in the company of Mother Leakey and Bishop Atherton, figures seemingly without much to offer in the brave new world of enlightenment and industry that was about to dawn. Or if not, that at least we have reached a fork in our journey, with one signpost directing us down a winding lane towards 'Folklore', and the other pointing us in the direction of a broad thoroughfare marked 'History'. The repeatedly intertwining stories of the vengeful ghost and the reprobate bishop can, it would appear, at last be properly disentangled into the distinctly different ways of thinking about the past with which we are familiar today: reality and myth, fact and legend. Yet matters are never quite so straightforward. As we start to accelerate forwards through the eighteenth, nineteenth, and twentieth centuries, the ways in which Atherton and Leakey were to be remembered—in England, Ireland, and in Scotland too—will have further surprising transformations to undergo, and some interesting lessons to teach us about the nature of historical memory in our own times.

8

Atherton and Leakey: History and Folklore

I N the summer of 1730, Jonathan Swift, dean of St Patrick's in Dublin and author of the world's most famous fictional travel-ogue, experienced a vision of Bishop John Atherton. We should not let ourselves get too excited, for the vision was a strictly literary and satirical one. It came in the course of Swift's *An Excellent New Ballad*, a work which vented justified spleen at a fellow clergyman of the Church of Ireland, the dean of Ferns, Dr Thomas Sawbridge. Sawbridge had been indicted for raping a young woman, but he was acquitted—according to Swift, because he had managed to buy the girl off. Like so many of his predecessors in high office in the Church of Ireland, Sawbridge was a transplanted Englishman. This prompted the Irish-born Swift to offer sarcastic thanks to 'our brethren of England, who love us so dear' that they had sent over this holy priest 'for the good of our Church'. If, God forbid, Sawbridge ever ventured to become a bishop, whom would he most resemble? There was only one answer to that: 'I only behold thee in Atherton's shape, / For *sodomy* hang'd, as thou for a r—pe.'

Nearly a century after his death, therefore, the memory of Atherton remained green in Irish church circles, and coyness about the exact nature of his offence seemed to be becoming a thing of the past. Swift's sharp but passing reference fits a pattern which will become increasingly clear to us as we continue our journey through into modern times. No matter how many years had passed, a sodomite bishop was too powerful a symbol either to be allowed to rest in peace, or to be assessed neutrally as an oddity of a vanished past. In fact, Atherton's hold on the imagination of subsequent generations repeatedly reminds us how easily 'history' can become a political resource-pack, a storeroom of weapons for fighting the battles of one's own age. Swift's animus against Sawbridge certainly had a sharply political as well as a moralistic edge. The poet was a staunch Tory, but Sawbridge was a Whig, and an ardent adherent of the German Hanoverian dynasty which had acquired the British throne after the death of the last Stuart, Queen Anne, in 1714. He was the type of man, suggested Swift, 'griev'd that a *Tory* should live above ground'.[1]

Within only a few years of this allusion, Atherton's corpse was once again being resurrected as a proxy participant in the factional battles between Whigs and Tories that energized mid-eighteenth century politics in both England and Ireland. In 1736, his story was retold by the historian and Anglican priest Thomas Carte, in the course of a biography of James Butler, first duke of Ormond (1610–88), a man who had been Lord Lieutenant of Ireland under both Charles I and Charles II. Carte was not only a stout Tory, but a Jacobite, a supporter of the exiled Stuart claimants to the throne currently occupied by the Hanoverian George II. Not surprisingly, therefore, his book was full of passionate words against all those whom he regarded as having been less than one hundred per cent loyal to the earlier Stuart king, Charles I. Into this category he placed Richard Boyle, first earl of Cork. Cork had opposed the selfless efforts of Sir Thomas Wentworth to restore the legitimate rights of the Church, as well as those of Wentworth's lieutenant, Bishop Atherton, a man 'well qualified by his talents and spirit to go through with the suit'. Carte was not afraid to assert openly something which the Reverend John King and Bishop Thomas Milles had been content merely to hint at twenty years earlier (pp. 172–4). The earl of Cork had contrived to bring about Atherton's downfall, making the bishop 'a sacrifice to that litigation, rather than to justice'. Throughout his 'exemplary preparation for death', and again at his execution, Carte insisted, Atherton flatly denied the charge against him. His trial was a blatant miscarriage of justice, turning on the evidence of a single untrustworthy witness who later retracted his accusation. It thus set an extremely dangerous precedent whereby any man might lose both his reputation and his life 'by the information of any rascal that may be suborned to accuse him'. It had also taken place at a time when just about anything was encouraged 'that would throw a scandal upon that order of men, and render episcopacy odious'.[2]

Carte was, in effect, reinterpreting Atherton's death as a political martyrdom. It was not very long, however, before this revisionist reading of events was publicly challenged. The occasion was a new English edition of Sir James Ware's history of the Irish bishops. As we have seen (p. 167), the first translation of this work silently added assertions to the effect that Atherton was innocent. The editor of the enlarged volume appearing in 1739 would have none of that. He was Walter Harris, an Irish lawyer who had decided to bring out an edition of Ware's complete works after marrying his great-grand-daughter. Harris was a confirmed Whig, and in some quarters suspected to be 'a favourer of the Presbyterian party'. He threw out in turn all the arguments of the 'anonymous author' of 1710 (John King), of the first English translator of Ware, and of Thomas Carte. He pointed out that Ware had actually said no more than that Atherton deplored his previous sinful life. As a member of the Irish Privy Council of the time, Ware had the opportunity of knowing the truth, 'and zeal enough to declare it' if he had really believed Atherton to be an innocent man. Nor in fact did Dean Bernard actually pronounce him to be so 'in plain and express terms'. Atherton himself had frequently conceded the justice of the sentence against him, and he condemned himself as 'the most base, abject person in the world', worthy of a dog's death. 'Let the reader judge', Harris asked rhetorically, 'whether these exaggerated expressions of the bishop can be construed to relate to the commission of common frailties.' Harris professed to be moved by no other motive than a regard for the truth, and defied anyone to think that he cast a blemish on the whole order of bishops by exposing the 'miserable fate' of one of their number. As to the character of the crime itself, however, he opted for muted decorum rather than Swiftian frankness. 'For what is understood by the main thing in the indictment, I refer the reader to the law books.'[3]

Harris's political agenda was a subtle and implicit one, his arguments (as befitted a lawyer) calm, logical, and forensic in tone. A very different approach characterized another republicizing of the Atherton case, when Bernard's *Penitent Death* was once again published in Dublin in 1754. The reprint was part of an anonymously compiled volume entitled *The Political Balance for 1754*. This publication purported to 'weigh' different varieties of Irish patriotism, and it railed violently against an unnamed public figure of the day, a clergyman identified only as 'the Patriarch'. It was in fact Edmund Curll's edition of Bernard which was here reproduced, rather than the original tract: the 'cow and other creatures' make their four-legged appearance (see p. 165). The new editor also added some additional marginal comments. Where Bernard's dedicatory epistle sings the praises of Archbishop Ussher of Armagh, an asterisked note exclaims; 'would to heaven all his successors deservedly had such wishes!'

There is in fact little doubt what all this was about. Ussher's successor as archbishop of Armagh in 1754 was the English-born George Stone, a smooth political operator whose striking good looks had earned him the nickname 'the beauty of holiness'. But distinctly less flattering things were also being said about Stone in Ireland, where his career was dogged by persistent rumours of a penchant for his own sex. 'His practice out-vies debauchery', claimed the pamphlet, 'as much as sodomy does fornication.' The insinuations served a specific purpose, for as with the Sacheverell case of 1710 (pp. 180–81), there was a broader and immediate political context to the summoning up of Atherton's memory. In the mid-1750s, Irish politics was convulsed by the so-called 'Money Bill dispute'. The point at issue was whether the Irish parliament required explicit royal consent to apply its surplus revenues to the paying of the national debt. This was furiously rejected by an emerging party of so-called 'Patriots', men who excoriated their chief opponent, Archbishop Stone, as a high-handed representative of 'the English interest'. Stone was likened to Henry VIII's chief minister, Cardinal Wolsey, an earlier example of a corrupt and overmighty churchman, and also to Charles I's ill-fated henchman,

Archbishop William Laud. Atherton, of course, was a much more obscure figure than either of these controversial giants of English ecclesiastical history. But the memories of him which had been kept alive (for an entirely different purpose) by Dean Nicholas Bernard allowed him to join the line-up, and to function as a serviceable historical reference point, a shorthand coding for a particularly heinous type of churchman in any age.[4]

The middle decades of the eighteenth century were a period of intense political and factional strife, but they were also an age of burgeoning historical scholarship. There was an explosion in the compilation of printed annals, chronologies, and long listings of local and national office-holders in church and state. It is intriguing to observe how John Atherton is treated, if often fleetingly, in these sources. To some, he was simply 'the unhappy bishop of Waterford', about whom no more needed to be said. A listing of Irish bishops in a compendium of 1722 observed that he had been executed, 'but for what crime I know not'. The author had clearly not done his homework, for a *Chronology of Some Memorable Accidents, from the Creation of the World, to the Year 1742* found the space to note that the bishop of Waterford had been hanged 'for scandalous crimes'. Yet there was no mention at all of this event in a work, first published in 1746, which was to become the standard history of the county and city of Waterford. The author, a local doctor named Charles Smith, evidently did not regard it as something of which his compatriots should feel proud.[5]

Another kind of publication much in vogue at this time was the 'biographical dictionary', a new type of reference work which has enjoyed undiminished popularity through to the present day. In the vanguard here was the *Biographia Britannica*, published in seven volumes between 1747 and 1766. The first volume contained a lengthy biography of Atherton composed by the energetic antiquarian William Oldys (1696–1761). This began by declaring Atherton's story to be 'a very remarkable warning-piece in history, to future ages'. Oldys's was in some ways the first properly researched life of

John Atherton, drawing on a wide range of duly acknowledged and footnoted primary sources. But at the same time it was salacious and mischievous, seamlessly blending fact and supposition for the purposes of entertainment and literary effect. Oldys thus gave full prominence to the appearances of Mother Leakey's ghost, though without endorsing the event as such: 'T'is certain that a rumour of such an apparition was very rife, and made a great alarm about that time, and long after, both in England and Ireland.' Interestingly, he claimed that there were pamphlets and accounts (plural) printed about it, 'and some few years since to be seen in the Harleian Library'. He also tells us that Dr John Quick's manuscript had been 'communicated by his son', though he cannot have studied it very closely, as he mistakenly believed it described a posthumous apparition of the bishop himself, similar to that which Chancellor Alcock of Waterford had reported in 1710 (see p. 176). This curious slip notwithstanding, Oldys posed plausibly as the scrupulous and candid historian. He exhibited a particular impatience with the equivocations of Nicholas Bernard, who in his opinion had handled Atherton's case in such a general and ambiguous manner 'that the reader is quite dissatisfied from end to end in the very first enquiry he would make'. Oldys was frankly astonished that it was possible to read through Bernard's pamphlet and sermon, 'I say, through an hundred and sixty-six pages, and remain ignorant of what the bishop suffered death for'. Oldys had few qualms about redressing this imbalance in his own account, dwelling in loving detail on what he wittily termed the bishop's 'male-practices'. He was in no doubt that the mysterious visitor out of England, who called on Atherton about three weeks before his arrest (see p. 146), was one of several men with whom he had committed the sin. He also speculated about the 'naughty books' and 'immodest pictures' the bishop had confessed to owning, and had little doubt that these concerned vices 'which were more peculiarly the product of warmer climes'. 'Unnatural' sex was regarded as a characteristically Italian vice in this period, and Oldys thought it very likely that Atherton had possessed obscene verses by the sixteenth-century poet Pietro Aretino, which were first published in 1525 along with an infamous set of pornographic engravings. Another candidate for Atherton's secret bookshelf was the sixteenth-century archbishop of Benevento, Giovanni da Casa, supposed to have written a book 'in commendation of sodomity'. Oldys was quite clearly also fascinated by the more recent allegations of bestiality against the bishop. It was his conviction that, having been 'satiated' with the 'fair' sex, and having begun 'preposterously to prey on his own', Atherton became at last 'unsatisfied even in the sphere of his own species'. As we have seen (pp. 165, 202–3), this particular charge seems to have been entirely the commercially driven invention of Edmund Curll. Yet Oldys was able to throw his own tuppence into the ring here:

> we have been informed, by a gentleman of repute, who had been long in Waterford, as well as other parts of Ireland, and conversant with many grave and intelligent persons there, that he had often heard there was a favourite but unlucky mare by which the unweary bishop got his deadly downfall.

It is difficult to know what to make of this bit of third-hand equine gossip, which inspired Oldys to ruminate on how 'the world was to be new tenanted with a race of centaurs'. It seems rather as though we might consider it an interesting example of a kind of historical 'false memory syndrome', of a treasured but bogus local tradition implanted by the publicity attached to Curll's reprinting of Bernard's tract in 1710. It is a salutary reminder that 'oral' traditions can often be shown to have their origins in printed sources. Be that as it may, the claim that Atherton had been 'hanged for bestiality' was uncritically recounted by several authors in the following decades.[6]

Reference works, then as now, are notoriously derivative things, and Oldys's account supplied the foundation for shorter entries on Atherton in the *New and General Biographical Dictionary* of 1761, and *A Dictionary of the World*, published in 1772. The latter, in fact, flatly asserted that Atherton was tried for bestiality 'and received sentence of death for committing that crime with a mare and a cow'. Yet by the time a second edition of the *Biographia Britannica* was brought out in 1778, under the editorship of the Presbyterian minister Andrew Kippis, a decidedly different tone was starting to prevail. Only one article failed to make it from the old edition into the new one. According to Kippis's introduction, Bishop Atherton had 'not the least claim, from his abilities or public actions, to a place in the work'. Moreover, 'the story of him is shocking and indelicate, and told in a manner extremely disagreeable. Doubts, likewise, have been suggested concerning parts of the facts related of him.' Kippis was pleased to report that his own inclination, which was to drop the piece entirely, had been confirmed by 'the opinion of several gentlemen, distinguished for their learning and judgement'. The entry on Atherton survived rather longer in the *New and General Biographical Dictionary*, appearing in the editions of 1784 and 1795, but it was finally dropped from that of 1798. He is conspicuously absent also from *The New Biographical Dictionary* of 1796, and from the *Universal Biographical and Historical Dictionary* of 1800. These editorial decisions are small pointers to larger changes taking place in English society, hints of a new mood of public decorum, and the development of a culture of 'politeness'. We are leaving the world of Henry Fielding, and entering that of Jane Austen.[7]

In the midst of all of this, Nicholas Bernard's original intentions had never been entirely subverted or forgotten. *The Penitent Death* seems to have been reprinted once more in England in 1742. It is a work which appears regularly in printed eighteenth-century book-sellers' and auction catalogues, often as part of the collections of deceased clergymen. It was reprinted again in 1783, in a cheap edition without Bernard's extensive scriptural footnotes. According to the preface, a new edition was desirable so that 'the chaplains of the several gaols in this kingdom may be able to furnish those unhappy persons, whom the laws of God and man have condemned to an untimely death, with a little book altogether suited to their situation'. Although it had gone through several editions before, the work had become very scarce, and as a result no copy could be found for 'the late unhappy Dr—, who most earnestly desired to see it'. The gentleman remains unnamed, but we can allow ourselves the luxury of a little speculation here. In the late eighteenth century,

'Dr' still signified a learned clergyman rather than a medical practitioner, and, as one would expect, few university-educated men of the cloth were imprisoned and executed in these years. In 1777, however, the Reverend William Dodd was hanged at Tyburn for having committed forgery. Nicknamed 'the macaroni parson' on account of his sartorial elegance, Dodd's trial and execution excited immense public interest and sympathy, and culminated in a recognizably 'good death' on the scaffold.

A hundred years and more after he ended his life on a Dublin gibbet, it seems that Bishop Atherton's manner of dying and preparing for death still had some meaning for people: marginal annotations in surviving copies of the *Penitent Death* show that eighteenth-century readers read it carefully. One of them inscribed 'NB' at the point where Atherton denies 'the main thing in the indictment'. Next to the passage where Atherton spies the scaffold and exclaims 'there is my Mount Calvary', another reader wrote incredulously in the margin 'Christ = the Bp. of Waterford / Calvary = the Gallows'. Perhaps the conventions of the puritan 'conversion narrative' were not as easily understood and accepted as once they had been.[8]

As the nineteenth century beckoned, and the events and politics of the 1630s became ever more distant and remote, it began to seem rather unlikely that anyone could again get seriously excited about Bishop Atherton and his fate. He was fast becoming an interesting historical curiosity, rather than an urgent moral symbol. Thus, a bookseller could note in his catalogue in 1788 that Dunton's *Athenianism* contained 'a remarkable story of an apparition relating to Bishop Atherton, not recorded in his Life'. A little print of the bishop's likeness, based on the image in the *Life and Death of John Atherton* (see Chapter 4 above) was produced as a curio by the stationer William Richardson in 1798, and another pen-and-ink drawing of the same subject (now in the National Portrait Gallery) was executed at around the same time. The *Life and Death* pamphlet itself was reproduced in 'type facsimile' in London in about 1815. Atherton's fate had certainly not been forgotten—the Lancashire clergyman editing the letters of Wentworth's secretary Sir George Radcliffe could harrumph in 1810 that the bishop was 'a disgrace to his order and to human nature', and that 'the story is too well known' to require any elaboration. But it seemed at last that his end could be safely alluded to without anyone suspecting a plot to undermine the government of the Church by bishops.[9] Yet, as it transpired, the story of Bishop Atherton had still not yet run its course as a touchstone of topical political interest and debate. In the summer of 1822 it was to seem as painfully relevant as ever, as the Church of Ireland braced itself for the impact of another scandal, a case every bit as explosive as the one Nicholas Bernard had worked so hard to defuse almost two centuries before.

Friday 19 July 1822 was the day that everything changed for the Right Honourable Percy Jocelyn, third son of the earl of Roden, and Anglican bishop of Clogher in the north of Ireland. The 57-year-old bishop was in London, in the back room of the White Lion public house in St James's, and in the company of a young soldier of the Grenadier Guards called John Moverley, when the two men were discovered and arrested in the act of committing homosexual offences, activities that in the early nineteenth century could still cost them their lives. At a time of growing political radicalism and pressure for parliamentary reform, the furore that ensued rocked the British establishment. The Home Secretary at the time, Sir Robert Peel, received a letter from his personal secretary warning that the event threatened to 'raise up the lower orders against the higher, and in the present temper of the public mind against the Church it will do more to injure the establishment than all the united efforts of its enemies could have effected in a century'. An open court case would have been a major embarrassment for the religious and political authorities. Yet there was to be no trial. Jocelyn broke bail and fled to France, and Moverley (with the active connivance of the government) was similarly smuggled out of the country. The sense of public outrage was heightened by the fact that, a decade earlier, Jocelyn had prosecuted his coachman for

14. The bishop and the soldier: the arrest of Percy Jocelyn, 1822

malicious libel, after allegations were made about his sexual predilections. The man was severely flogged, and sentenced to two years' imprisonment. At his trial, counsel for Jocelyn had claimed (shades of John Lynch) that Ireland was thankfully free of all such continental habits, and that there was 'no instance of its existence in the memory of any professional man'.

The Jocelyn affair released a flood of tracts, newspaper reports, and satirical cartoons, attacking the Church and political authorities (Figure 14). The most effective of these were the work of William Benbow, a radical printer and (like Edmund Curll before him), an occasional publisher of pornography. Benbow earns his place in British political history for developing the notion of the general strike, something he outlined in his 1832 tract, *Grand National Holiday*. But our concern here is with an 1823 publication, prompted by the Clogher case, *The Crimes of the Clergy*. This pamphlet was the first instalment of a planned encyclopedia of clerical vices, admirably ecumenical in the range and scope of its targets. The title-page supplied a coded key for entries: 'D. Dissenter. M. Methodist. C. Catholic. F. Fornicator. A. Adulterer. S. Sodomite.' Benbow's subjects included such worthies as 'the Reverend Septimus Hodgson, child violator', 'Parson Pigott, member of the Vice Society, and hunter of obscenity for royal amusement', 'the Reverend Augustus Beeson … boxing parson'. All of these scandals were current or recent ones, and for only one of his dozen or so cases did Benbow have to turn to the pages of the historical record. 'There are precedents for everything, if they are diligently searched for, and a precedent for the crime of Clogherism is to be found in the life of John Atherton, a wretch who will ever be remembered for his infamy.' Nonetheless, thought Benbow, Atherton was a man who had nearly been forgotten 'when the Bishop of Clogher revived his case for public abhorrence'. Unlike virtually all previous commentary on the affair, Benbow made no reference to the work of Nicholas Bernard, or to Atherton's famous penitence. Indeed, it is far from clear that he had even read Bernard, though he was clearly familiar with the contents of the libellous pamphlet of 1641 (perhaps thanks to its early nineteenth-century reprinting). Benbow embellished these with his own inventions, such as that Atherton's wealth 'enabled him to provide counsel of the first talent', or that 'it is a recorded truth, that every exertion was made by his clerical associates to stay the progress of justice'. In fact, as we know (pp. 94–5), Atherton was denied legal counsel, and it seems that his clerical allies, such as Bishop John Bramhall, dropped him like a stone. The trial, which Benbow imagined for some reason to have taken place at Cork, was one which 'excited more interest than any other before or since'—indeed, the sensation caused by the arrest of the bishop of Clogher could not match it. In contrast to most earlier retellings, Benbow's account barely paid lip service to the cliché that the infamy of one or two of its members should not be allowed to reflect badly upon the Church as a whole. In fact, he argued, the 'rotten pillars' of Waterford and Clogher had between them managed to do more harm to the established religion 'than a century passed in purity by all its ministers will be able to repair'.

The Clogher affair certainly did cast a long shadow over the Church of Ireland. For the best part of two centuries the Church's papers relating to the case remained under official interdict. When, in 1998, the journalist Matthew Parris requested to see them (as part of his research for a kind of updated 'Crimes of the Clergy' volume), it required a personal decision of Archbishop Robin Eames, Anglican Primate of All Ireland, to authorize their production.[10]

This recent and raw wound must surely help to explain why, for much of the nineteenth century, Bishop Atherton no longer appears as a public exemplar of the benefits of penitent dying. Instead he seems to have become the Church of Ireland's best-kept secret. For a small church to appoint one sodomite bishop may be regarded as a misfortune; to appoint two looked like carelessness. In the Victorian period, several Irish Anglican scholars published histories of their church, but most of them scrupulously avoided the subject of John Atherton. The most distinguished nineteenth-century ecclesiastical historian of Ireland was the bishop of Down and Connor, Richard Mant, who in 1840 published a two-volume work on the church in the sixteenth and seventeenth centuries. But although Mant devoted an entire section of his book to 'measures for improving the temporalities of the Church' in the 1630s, he nowhere so much as mentions the name of Atherton. He could hardly avoid doing so in an appended 'succession list' of Irish bishoprics, with notes of resignations, translations, and deprivations. But this merely recorded the dates of Atherton's incumbency at Waterford, with no indication of how and why it came to an end. An official *Parliamentary Gazetteer* of Ireland, published in 1846, similarly observed merely that Bishop Atherton had 'died' in 1640. At around the same time, the archdeacon of Cashell, Henry Cotton, was compiling what is still the standard historical reference guide to office-holders in the Irish Church. He concluded his entry on Atherton with the briefest of passing notes that 'his crime and sad end are too well known'.

This pattern of discreet suppression characterized many Anglican treatments of the Atherton case well into the twentieth century. In 1920, the rector of Ardmore, William Rennison, published yet more succession lists of the bishops and clergy of Waterford and Lismore. In a foreword to the volume, the current bishop of Waterford praised its 'most interesting introduction', and observed how inspiring it was to take up such a book 'in these days of stress and anxiety'. (The IRA's guerrilla war for Irish independence was just then approaching its climax.) Yet it is striking that Rennison's introduction makes absolutely no reference to what was without much doubt the most interesting thing ever to happen to a bishop of Waterford. It was not, in fact, until the early 1930s that Atherton's case was once again properly examined by an Anglican scholar. The Reverend G. V. Jourdan, canon of St Patrick's Dublin, and Professor of Ecclesiastical History at Trinity College, devoted considerable attention to it in a chapter of Oxford University Press's multi-volume *History of the Church of Ireland*. Yet in the end Jourdan did little more than endorse Thomas Carte's eighteenth-century partisan view: 'the whole affair was a concocted business on the part of the church-land-grabbers, Protestant and Romanist'. In the mean time, however, historians drawn from the rival Presbyterian tradition of Irish Protestantism had been displaying no such inhibitions, referring openly to Atherton's 'horrible crimes', and to his execution for 'gross and horrible immorality'. There was also the occasional reference in Catholic works to Atherton's 'disgraceful death on the scaffold'.[11] For John Atherton, complete historical obscurity and objective historical scrutiny seemed equally unattainable goals. For a full three centuries after his death, Atherton continued to be as divisive a figure as he had been in life: a totem of rival, even tribal, appropriations of the Irish past.

What then, readers are probably asking themselves, has happened to the other main strand in our narrative? The story about Mother Leakey was enjoyed by several of the historical biographers of the mid-eighteenth century, though without much sense that they were prepared to credit it as a 'true relation'. Such writers generally concurred with William Oldys that Elizabeth Leakey's apparition may have been merely a 'bare fancy' or 'the effect of a dream'. Thereafter, however, references to Mother Leakey's ghost largely disappear from the accounts of those, like William Benbow, who were looking to make political capital out of the crimes of Bishop Atherton. Yet despite a general growth in scepticism about the immediacy and reality of the supernatural, educated opinion in the nineteenth century had by no means lost interest in such matters. Through the nineteenth and into the twentieth century, Mother Leakey's ghost was to experience a further succession of rediscoveries and reinventions.

And here we come at last to Sir Walter Scott, the original starting point of my quest to map the long and winding pathways of the Atherton–Leakey affair (p. ix). Among critics, and general readers too, Scott's stock has fallen in recent decades, but at the start of the nineteenth century he was a literary colossus, whose historically flavoured novels and poetry delighted legions of admirers in Britain, Europe, and across the English-speaking world. There is a copy of Bernard's *Penitent Death* in the library of Scott's home at Abbotsford in the Scottish Borders, but his acknowledged awareness of the episode came from a different source: the *Apparition Evidence* in Dunton's *Athenianism* of 1710. Scott first made use of the material in *Rokeby*, an epic poem of 1813. An allusion to the superstitions of seafarers, including their belief that 'whistle rash bids tempests roar', prompted him to supply an explanatory note, beginning with the observation that 'the most formidable whistler that I remember to have met with was the apparition of a certain Mrs Leakey'. He went on to relate the tale of the ghost's whistle-blowing and ship-sinking, though he directed his readers to Dunton's original for details of how the ghost dispatched her daughter-in-law to 'an Irish prelate, famous for his crimes and misfortunes, to exhort him to repentance'. Included in Scott's fan mail in the following few years was a letter from the antiquary Charles Joseph Harford, of Stapleton in Somerset. Harford confirms for us that local traditions about the supposed haunting were alive and well in the south-west: 'the memory of Mrs Leakey recorded in Note Seven of Second Canto still remains at Minehead, and her ghost ... is heard on the pier in a storm calling for a boat'. Replying to Harford in September 1820, Scott reported that 'I am happy to hear Mrs Leakey continues to exercise her ghostly functions, though on a smaller scale than before'. He confirmed that the bishop in question was 'the unfortunate Atherton, executed for an unnatural crime', and remarked that the ghost of Mrs Leakey was in his considered opinion 'a very fine one'.

Scott did not forget the story of the whistling ghost. Over many years he had been considering the idea of compiling a volume of essays on the supernatural, and it was finally published just before Christmas 1830 as *Letters on Demonology and Witchcraft*. The volume (accompanied with twelve illustrations by the renowned caricaturist George Cruikshank) sold extremely well, and netted Scott £600. It touched on many aspects of the supernatural world, but it was the topic of ghosts that particularly attracted Scott to writing it: in correspondence with his publisher, he referred to the volume as 'the ghosts'. Throughout his life, Scott had been an avid collector of ghost stories, and his novels are replete with supernatural incident and motifs. Yet by the time he published his supernatural anthology, Scott was becoming more of a sceptic and a rationalist, observing wearily that 'tales of ghosts and demonology are out of date at forty years and upwards'. It was only in the morning of life, he wistfully remarked, that 'this feeling of superstition "comes o'er us like a summer cloud" ' (an allusion to *Macbeth*, 3. 4). As a believing Christian, Scott still conceded the possibility of apparitions, but he refused to endorse any particular instances of them: 'we apprehend a solution will be found for all cases of what are called real ghost stories'. The tone was reinforced by the serio-comic character of Cruikshank's accompanying plates. His depiction of Mother Leakey captured the moment in the *Apparition Evidence* where the spectre reminds the medical doctor of his manners by kicking him in the breeches (Figure 15). Scott's own retelling of the Leakey story showed little interest in its more political aspects. He glossed over the part of Dunton's narrative dealing with the supernatural

15. Mother Leakey and the doctor of physick, from Scott's
Letters on Demonology

detection of Atherton's crimes as 'too disagreeable and tedious to enter upon'. He was in fact far more interested in how the tale had taken root, and reported that

> so deep was the impression made by the story on the inhabitants of Minehead, that it is said the tradition of Mrs Leakey still remains in that port, and that mariners belonging to it often, amid tempestuous weather, conceive they hear the whistle-call of the implacable hag who was the source of so much mischief to her own family.

Yet Sir Walter was too canny to regard this as clinching evidence for an authentic and continuous folk tradition. Rather, it was the case that Dunton, 'a man of scribbling celebrity', had succeeded 'in imposing upon the public a tale which he calls *Apparition Evidence*'. He was 'the narrator and probably the contriver of the story'. Scott's aim was to illustrate 'the peculiar sort of genius by which stories of this kind may be embodied and prolonged'. There was something to this, of course, and Scott anticipated modern scholarship in noting the ways that authored and printed materials could lie at the heart of 'popular' memory. In attributing all to Dunton, however, he was blissfully unaware of the seminal role played by John Quick, or of the various tales of Mother Leakey which we have found circulating, in all sorts of locations, some years before Dunton's time.

The *Letters* were a hit, and the response to them of readers illustrates the remarkable hold that ghosts still had over the British imagination in the early years of the nineteenth century. Some correspondents applauded Sir Walter's cool scepticism, some conversely suspected him of defending 'superstition', while others were disappointed to find him leaning so far towards 'the Sadducee side of the question'. Critical reception too suggests a culture which was unsure about the level of attention which ghosts and ghost stories really deserved. *The Monthly Review* pronounced that now 'not a man in a million...believes in ghosts', while, contrariwise, *The Gentleman's Magazine* considered such beliefs to be 'still very general among those who have never contemplated the subject philosophically'. Scott's own mixture of philosophical distaste for the subject and a deep and enduring fascination with it was strongly characteristic of his day. We can imagine him enjoying the quick-wittedness of his exact contemporary, the poet Samuel Taylor Coleridge, who was once asked whether he believed in ghosts and apparitions, and replied 'No, Madam! I have seen far too many myself.'[12]

Coleridge in fact offers us a further intriguing hint that the legend of Old Mother Leakey was capable of impressing itself upon the greatest creative minds of the age. In the late 1790s, he and his wife Sara took up residence in West Somerset at Nether Stowey, a village between Bridgwater and Minehead in the Quantock Hills. William Wordsworth and his sister Dorothy were renting a property at nearby Alfoxden. In November 1797, according to Dorothy's letters, the idea for one of Coleridge's most enduringly evocative poems, *The Rime of the Ancient Mariner*, was conceived during a long walk together down to the sea at Watchet, a few miles east from Minehead along the Bristol Channel coast. It would be crass to pretend that it is possible to demonstrate any direct and immediate influence of local traditions about Mother Leakey on the imagery of the poem, but there is a suggestive echo nonetheless. After the eponymous mariner commits the crime of slaying an albatross, and ill fortune descends on him and all his shipmates, a spectral ship approaches them on becalmed waters. It is crewed by two ghostly figures, a man and a woman, Death and Life-in-Death, who dice with each other for possession of the ship's complement. When the woman wins the mariner himself, she is exultant: ' "The game is done! I've won! I've won!" / Quoth she, and whistles thrice.' At this, the sun falls, the 'spectre-bark' shoots off over the sea, and the ship's crew begin one by one to drop dead. Could it be that what we have here is an imaginative reworking of the whistling spectre motif, a literary debt to oral traditions about Mother Leakey, that the Coleridges may have picked up from their rural neighbours in West Somerset?[13]

These flirtations of our stories with the high literary culture of the early nineteenth century reinforce a lesson we have learned already in these pages. There does not really seem to be any such thing as a 'pure' oral folklore, uncontaminated by creative contact with written and printed sources. Walter Scott believed that beliefs about Mother Leakey were current in the Minehead of his day, and blamed the inventive pen of an eighteenth-century journalist. Yet, as we saw right at the outset of this book (p. ix), by the end of the nineteenth century, a local historian in West Somerset was crediting Scott himself with having 'immortalised' the story. This was in fact the common perception of later Victorian writers on the geography and customs of the south-west, who quite regularly took notice of the well-known local tale. One observed that the story of the whistling ghost was 'sufficiently famous to be mentioned by Sir Walter Scott'; another noted that, as a consequence of *Rokeby*, the story was 'much better known than the majority of local legends'. The critic J. Cuming Walters put it more bluntly in his *Bygone*

Somerset (1897). The village of Porlock, a stone's throw along the coast from Minehead, was now, he observed, 'chiefly noted for its legends of ghosts, that of Mrs Leakey, the whistling ghost, ridiculous as it is, having been given an importance not its due by mention of it in Sir Walter Scott's *Rokeby*'.

Walters was not alone in lampooning the story. In an 1890 guide to the landscape of Exmoor, the local antiquarian John Lloyd Warden Page recounted the tale at some length, but felt compelled to add that he considered the whole business 'absurd in the extreme'. If educated writers were often intensely interested in folklore, they still needed to distance themselves from the 'vulgar' superstitions of the people. Page, in fact, reported that there were still believers in Mrs Leakey. He himself had once seen two children run away from the imagined presence of the evil spirit which was supposed to flit between Culver Cliff, at the back of Minehead Quay, and the nearby Warren Point.[14]

But while some writers were keen to avoid bestowing any hint of respectability on Mother Leakey's ghost, the last decades of the nineteenth century also saw a concerted effort in some quarters to understand how the long-lived local ghost story had actually come about. An Exeter clergyman, the Reverend William Everitt, somehow came across John Quick's manuscript, and printed it in the pages of the journal *The Western Antiquary* in July 1886. This prompted correspondence from Alfred Wallis of Exeter, pointing out the connection with Dunton (no one now seemed to remember Edmund Curll), and from William E. A. Axon of Manchester. Axon, an antiquarian and librarian, as well as teetotaller, vegetarian, and Unitarian, had contributed the entry on Atherton to that great successor of the biographical dictionaries of the eighteenth century, Oxford University Press's *Dictionary of National Biography*, published the previous year. His article is a small model of sensible Victorian erudition. Axon disputed Carte's account, and firmly dismissed the notion of a conspiracy against the bishop, though in line with contemporary sensibilities, he went no further than to say that Atherton had been executed for 'unnatural crime'. The *DNB* entry provoked a little public interest. One gentleman from

Southport in north-west England wrote to the literary journal *Notes and Queries* (still going strong) in September 1886, rather pointlessly enquiring if the bishop was not 'a connection of the Athertons of Atherton, County Lancashire?' But to others, Mother Leakey remained a more compelling object of interest than her errant son-in-law. She appeared in an 1887 volume on myths of Somerset, under the heading, interestingly enough, 'On Witches', as well as in several collections on the themes of weather and sea-lore. In December 1889, a local antiquarian, W. George, published documents concerning the case in the Minehead newspaper, *The West Somerset Free Press*. He prefaced the piece with the remark that 'it is almost as rare nowadays to find a witness who has seen a ghost, as to encounter a person who does not know someone who has'. George transcribed the 1637 examination, and was also able to include a copy of Susan Leakey's will (pp. 18–19), which Alfred Monday of Taunton had searched out for him in the Probate Office. Since most of the mid-seventeenth century wills had gone missing, 'its discovery almost amounted to a marvel'.

   This effervescence of local pride in the story was not unconnected to the development of Minehead as a tourist resort in the later nineteenth century, particularly after the railway line to Taunton had been extended to Minehead by the Bristol and Exeter Company in July 1874. 'The queen of English watering places', as one writer put it in 1877, 'is not lacking in a tale of horror.' Lodgings for visitors were soon being advertised at nearly all the houses by the quay (the Leakeys' old stamping-ground), and Minehead's illustrious history as a seaside holiday centre was thoroughly under way. Guide books were also soon being produced. 'Minehead of Long Ago' was the subject of a picturesque chapter in C. E. Larter's volume on the town in the Homeland Handbooks series, which went through at least eleven editions in the opening years of the twentieth century. Mother Leakey's story, with appropriate nod towards Walter Scott, was told once again, an example of how former 'superstitious tendencies' supplied 'a contrast to the modern town'. Larter considered it an odd circumstance that the ghost had taken to tormenting its living relatives 'for no reason that is recorded, save a small anxiety about a necklace that had not found its proper destination after her death'. Here, at least, 'history' and 'folklore' do seem to have dramatically parted company.[15]

In the twentieth century, tales of Old Mother Leakey began to attract the attention of more self-conscious 'folklore' collectors, usually much less censorious about the 'superstitions' of a past age or their survival among the common people of the present. The folklore movement in England had got properly under way in the latter part of the nineteenth century (the term itself was coined in 1846). It received an institutional focus in 1878, with the founding of the London-based Folklore Society, which aimed to put the study of traditional British culture on a thoroughly scientific footing. In contrast to the undiscriminating 'antiquarian' collectors of previous generations, the leading lights of the Folklore Society were ambitious anthropologists, convinced that the underlying presumptions of prehistoric human society could be reconstructed from the systematic study of contemporary folk beliefs and rituals. Their approach was predicated on a doctrine of 'survivals', the theory that modern peasant culture preserved vestiges of ancient pagan customs and mind-sets. An assumption of the possibility of relatively pure oral transmission of beliefs, which we have already seen to be a deeply problematic one, was close to the heart of the endeavour.[16]

Nonetheless, the folklore movement was to a considerable extent fuelled by an anxiety that primordial popular beliefs were starting inexorably to slip away under the pressures of the modern age. Through the nineteenth century, and into the early twentieth, Somerset had the reputation of being an especially 'superstitious' county. But its old rural culture was changing in the face of improved communications and less localized agricultural production. By 1920, the Mrs Leakey legend was being described wistfully in the *Somerset County Herald* as 'a ghost story which is now not given any credence'. In a 1952 volume on the history, culture, and topography of Exmoor, the Devon schoolmaster S. H. Burton reported that he had recently visited a pub there, where he had sought to discover from the locals 'more details about such famous ghosts as Mrs Leakey'.

To his disappointment, none of them could tell him any more than he knew already, and some of them had not even heard of Mrs Leakey. There was no doubt, lamented Burton, that even in remote Exmoor 'the radio and cinema, the motor bus and the popular press are destroying the regional culture'.

An undoubted product of that regional culture was Ruth Tongue, a remarkable lady born in Somerset at the turn of the twentieth century, where her father was a military chaplain at Taunton barracks. Tongue gloried in her status as a 'chimes child' (that is, one born between midnight and one on a Friday) and she spent a lifetime collecting stories and songs from local people in West Somerset. Her 1965 volume of *Somerset Folklore* contains an intriguing account of what she called 'the Whistling Ghost of Quay-Town'. It offers some revealing insight into how the raw materials of a remembered local incident, filtered through the sieve of Dunton's published *Apparition Evidence*, had been revised and refined once more by subsequent oral tradition. The predominant theme of the story is of attempts to 'lay' the ghost. The doctor of physick has become a parson, whom the ghost attacks, not for failing to help her over the stile, but for 'trying to return her to the place she had left'. Even more remarkably, local tradition apparently maintained that all attempts to lay Mother Leakey failed, 'until at length an Irish bishop managed to banish her'. Yet this exorcism did not succeed completely, and Mrs Leakey left her 'familiar' behind: 'an evil spirit is still hanging about Culver Cliffs, which has brought more than one picnic party to an abrupt end'. The mention of a familiar (see p. 79) suggests another interesting development: the gradual transformation of Mother Leakey into the figure of a witch. Tongue was aware that a royal commission had investigated the case and had 'decided that she must be a ghost'. Yet this did not quite fit the pattern that her folklore researches had led her to expect: 'it is witches ... that whistle for the wind'.

In her later years, Tongue was taken under the wing of the professional folklorist Katharine Briggs (1898–1980), who in the late 1960s was President of the Folklore Society. Briggs's classic reference work, *A Dictionary of British Folk-Tales*, reprinted

Tongue's version of 'the Whistling Ghost', but also applied to it the established techniques of scholarly folklore studies. This involved the insights of the American folklorist Stith Thompson, and the Finnish scholar Antii Aarne, who in the early twentieth century had between them devised a system for classifying the common themes and motifs to be found in world folk tales. Thus, the Mother Leakey story was seen to exemplify motifs including D.2142.1.6 (*wind raised by whistling*); E.229 (*dead relative's malevolent return*); E. 292 (*ghost causes storms*); E. 411 (*dead cannot rest because of sin*); G. 269.8 (*ship wrecked by witch*). This kind of sorting and bottling fulfilled a need on the part of folklorists to feel that they were doing something useful and academically respectable. Yet in this, and presumably many other cases, it does not actually tell us very much about what the story meant to those hearing and retelling it, nor explain at all how it developed in the precise way that it did. There was rather greater sensitivity to the particular historical circumstances of the case in the work of another amateur south-western folklorist, and stalwart of the Folklore Society, Theo (Theodora) Brown (1914–1993), who collected materials connected with it over several years before publishing an article in 1981. Brown made some attempts to tie up the two halves of the story, though she considered the allegation of infanticide 'obviously bogus', and ended up following the well-worn John King-Thomas Carte line about the likelihood of the bishop's guilt: 'to my mind it is pretty certain that Atherton was framed by his enemies'. She had, moreover, little time for the 'endless streams of silly gossip and scurrilous ballads and tracts' about the case that have been the very life-blood of this book.[17]

Over the last couple of decades, Mother Leakey has found herself increasingly drawn out of the hands of serious folklorists, and into the strange world of popular para-psychology. There are brief entries on her in *A Gazetteer of British Ghosts*; *The Encylopedia of Ghosts and Spirits*; *Ghosts' Who's Who*, and *The Good Ghost Guide*. In the last of these she makes an appearance as 'a witch who sold fair winds to sailors'. She has in fact become such a mainstay of this type of publication that in 1985 Peter Underwood (Life President of the Ghost Club Society) wrote in the introduction to his volume on *Ghosts of Somerset* that 'in having to be selective I have chosen to omit such well-known cases as Mrs Leaky of Minehead'. The internet too, with its vast labyrinths of sites on the supernatural and the occult, helps to keep the memory of Mother Leakey going, with appearances in such locations as the paranormaldatabase.com and mysteriousbritain.co.uk. In 2002, a producer's appeal on an internet forum for information about 'true' south-west ghost stories led to the filming of a short television documentary about the case, the pilot for an ITV series thrillingly entitled *Grave Detectives*. And there have been further surprising transformations and retellings in recent years, and across continents, including a neo-Gothic poem with a Victorian setting, published in a Canadian magazine of creative writing in 1992, and an eye-opening report in the 2004 edition of the New Zealand Cornish Association Newsletter about 'the Bird-Woman of Minehead'—an old witch supposed to have the power 'to transform herself into a strange cormorant-like bird, which would fly to the top of ship's masts and screech abuse at sailors'. This creature, we are told, was still being seen well into the twentieth century.

All of this has undoubtedly helped to sustain or revive traditions about Mother Leakey in Minehead itself, with two separate links to documents about the case recently made available on the web portal 'Minehead On-Line'. In 1973, a local author commented that 'it was common, even in the early years of the present century, to hear the people of Minehead's quay town ascribe dirty weather to Mother Leakey's workings'. A hundred years later, the habit had not entirely died out. In 2003, a *Daily Telegraph* journalist visiting Minehead harbour on a blustery November day was still being told by an old sailor that 'it looks like Mother Leakey's up to her tricks again'. In January 2006, I gave a talk about the case at the University of Exeter, and received afterwards a delightful communication from a young woman in the audience. In the late 1980s her parents (who operate a coach business in Minehead) had run day-trips in a customized 'ghost bus' over the Quantock Hills. Members of the family would pop up in scary costume at various points en route, with Mother Leakey making her own appearance during a staged breakdown on the misty sea road between Minehead and Dunster. Locals and returning visitors still recall the trips fondly. Various local ghost legends were pressed into service, but 'it's always Mother Leakey that they remember'.[18]

There has been, sad to relate, no comparable relaunch of John Atherton on the opposite side of the Irish Sea. Waterford requires no assistance from this infamous immigrant son to attract visitors or sell its beautiful crystal ware. But in the later part of the twentieth century Atherton enjoyed a mini-renaissance of his own, for precisely the reasons that conspired to obscure his existence for so much of the previous hundred and fifty years. As we have seen (pp. 250–51), histories of the Church of Ireland resolutely ignored his case throughout the nineteenth and earlier twentieth centuries, taking literally the injunction of British legal commentary that sodomy was 'the crime not to be named'. But from the 1970s onwards the cause of gay rights was on the march in Europe and North America, and was beginning to look for a history of its own to lay claim to. In the academic world, studies began to appear with titles like *Queering the Renaissance*, and John Atherton's name and fate began receiving regular nods of acquaintance after a brief mention of the tracts concerning the case appeared in the late Alan Bray's pioneering book, *Homosexuality in Renaissance England* (1982). Once again, the internet has proved to be a powerful instrument of modern mythology. Atherton's death now appears in the chronological listings of countless 'gay heritage' websites, though the compilers are usually aware that he can hardly be considered a straightforward martyr for the cause. Interestingly, dozens of these sites repeat the dubious suggestion, first made by the seventeenth-century Irish Catholic writer John Lynch (p. 149), that Atherton was both the driving force behind the Irish sodomy legislation of 1634, and the first man to be executed under its provisions.

Nor has Atherton's utility as a political symbol entirely run its course. In December 1990 the claim about his authorship of the 1634 Sodomy Act was revived in the course of a debate in the Irish Senate. The speaker was Senator David Norris, a literary specialist on James Joyce at Trinity College Dublin, and a leading gay rights activist. The debate was part of an ultimately successful campaign to have the Irish Republic's laws against male homosexual acts declared unconstitutional, and in breach of the European Convention on Human Rights. Such legislation, Norris informed the senators, had arisen in the most peculiar circumstances:

> There was a sensational case in the 1630s involving an Irish peer. It was found as a result of this that the provisions of the English law did not extend to Ireland, and a campaign, a kind of primitive 'save Ireland from sodomy' campaign, was launched by a bishop in Wexford...He succeeded in having this law written into the Irish statute book, and I am very glad to be able to inform the house that he was charged with the crime himself and suffered the ultimate penalty of being executed for sodomy outside Christ Church cathedral on Christmas Day, 1637.

There are more than a few historical inaccuracies in this one short passage, but Norris had made his point. When the legislation was repealed in the summer of 1993, Norris again returned to the theme of the 'grisly appropriateness' of Atherton's fate, and he warned his country of the consequences of such sexual hypocrisy: 'let bishops beware'.[19]

As far as I know, the name of John Atherton has not yet come up in the course of the current furore over 'gay bishops' in the world-wide Anglican Communion, despite the fact that he remains the only Anglican bishop ever to be tried and executed for committing homosexual acts. Perhaps it is not so surprising: objectively considered, Atherton is not a very satisfactory role-model for gay Christians of the twenty-first century, nor is the process against him one which even the most rigid of traditionalists would probably wish to emulate. But over the three and a half centuries since they ceased to be real, living, breathing people, Susan Leakey and John Atherton have both been made to don a remarkable variety of guises, and to serve a great number of disparate causes. We can perhaps think of them as cultural punctuation marks, helping us to make sense of the historical script. Or alternatively, we can recognize how, in another sense, both of them ended up becoming ghosts, flitting in and out of the hopes and anxieties generated anew in each succeeding age. We are unlikely to have heard the last of them.

Epilogue

Mother Leakey's Parlour

APRIL 2006, a bright spring morning in Minehead, Somerset. I have returned to the location where our story properly started, the graveyard of St Michael's church, a picturesque resting place parked rather precipitously on the steep slopes of North Hill, overlooking the sprawling town below, and the choppy waters of the Bristol Channel beyond. Somewhere within a few dozen feet of where I am standing, and almost exactly 330 years before I was born, the body of Susan Leakey was lowered into the broken ground and covered over with earth, while familiar words of comfort were recited above it by the aged vicar of the town, Nicholas Browse. There is now no trace of a grave marker, if there had ever been one, no way of knowing if her bones are still lying somewhere in the hallowed earth around. Alexander and Elizabeth Leakey would certainly have been present at the burial, and perhaps others of our acquaintance too: John Heathfield, Elizabeth Langstone, Lordsnear Knill. I would like to be able to say that it is a place of ghosts. But here, in the spring sunshine, and among the freshly mown grass and serried ranks of sensible Victorian headstones, I find myself struggling to recognize any feeling of tangible connection with these long-vanished people, whose lives and longings were so very different from my own.

I make my way downhill via a warren of medieval lanes, their cottages resplendent with whitewash and thatch (Figure 16). Among such prettified remnants of the past, it is easier to fantasize about continuities and connectedness, though the reverie is quickly dispelled. In front of me, the view opens up to reveal modern Minehead's most prominent building, and a reminder of how much the world has changed. Across the sands of the seafront, I catch sight of

16. St Michael's church and church steps, Minehead

the massive 'Skyline Pavilion' of Butlins Holiday Park, with its futur-
istic gleaming-white eight-peaked roof covering the structure like a
confused entanglement of giant marquees. As Samuel Taylor
Coleridge composed his masterpiece *Kubla Khan* in that lonely Exmoor farmhouse in the summer of 1797, did he ever imagine the
presence here of such a stately pleasure-dome, drawing thousands of
visitors every year to the coast of his beloved West Somerset?[1]

On reaching the shore line, I turn left, away from Butlins and on
to Quay Street. In front of me is the little harbour where Alexander
Leakey's barques once unloaded their bales of Irish wool, and

replenished themselves with barrels of grain, and firkins of haberdashery. I am in search of modern Minehead's only concrete memorial to Susan Leakey, a long-established café-cum-curiosity shop glorying in the name of 'Mother Leakey's Parlour'. I visited here once before, near the start of my research for the book, and was thrilled to come away with a souvenir mock-up of the display board set on the pavement outside the shop, a panel which recounted for tourists the story of 'the whistling ghost of Minehead'. A childish part of me still smiles at an unfortunate error in the transcription—'a pubic enquiry was held by the bishop of Bath and Wells'. Though with John Atherton in mind, it is perhaps not so very inappropriate after all. But today, and not for the first time in the course of my relationship with Mother Leakey, I am destined to suffer disappointment. Mother Leakey's Parlour is no more, displaced by the quite evidently smarter and more spaciously functional Quayside Tearooms. A corner of the signboard above the entrance announces, with perhaps just a trace of apology or regret, that the premises were 'formerly Mother Leakey's Parlour'. Even on Minehead Quay, life moves on.

I head back towards my parked car, reflecting on what my labours to restore the lives and afterlives of Mother Leakey and Bishop Atherton have actually produced, and wondering at the end just what broader conclusions emerge out of it all. Was it worth it? The tale of Mother Leakey and the Bishop was never a very famous story, clamorously demanding to be retold once more, nor yet was it ever among the best known of ghost stories, even among exponents and aficionados of the genre.[2] The actual episodes around which it weaves itself were significant, but not of hugely evident and intrinsic importance. At times, perhaps, they helped to rattle the cages of great events, but they could not by themselves open or close them. There is more to history, of course, than queens and kings, battles and elections, or even the broad sweeps of economic and social change. We have learned in recent decades that there are very considerable advantages to be gained from placing a particular local community under the historical microscope, from examining the context to a single dramatic episode, or from exploring the mental world of a humble individual. These have all become highly respectable directions for historians to take, proving especially popular amongst those of us who work on that long period between the end of the medieval world order and the onset of industrialization, a period which we call, for want of a better phrase, 'early modern'. The best examples of such tightly focused writing firmly give the lie to any uncharitable suggestion that 'the fashion for micro-history tends to encourage micro-thinking'.[3]

But despite some family resemblances, this book has not really turned out to be a 'micro-history' in anything like the conventional sense. It is not a case study relying on a rich and compact body of local sources, nor a historical reconstruction basing itself around a single remarkable archival or literary survival. Rather, it is a thing made up of disconnected fragments and shards, widely scattered in time and place, as difficult to position in tasteful and coherent relationship with each other as the ill-assorted knick-knacks that once stood upon the shelves in Mother Leakey's Parlour. Even at the end of years of painstaking research, some of our most basic questions remain unanswered and probably unanswerable. Did Elizabeth Leakey really believe that she had seen her mother-in-law's ghost? Did John Atherton actually murder his illegitimate child? What happened in the end to the child's mother? Was the bishop justly convicted on charges of sodomy? Was his downfall the result of a political conspiracy? Attempting to write about these questions has at times been an exercise in the sheer and uncooperative difficulty of history, an exposure to the blank impenetrability of the past.

But this is not the whole story. If there have been frustrations and false trails, there have also been rewards and compensations, successful hunches and serendipitous discoveries. The project started as a leap of faith, stemming from an optimistic belief that the past will always answer a sufficient number of the questions put to it to make the conversation into a rewarding one. I have no doubt that, given time, skill, and luck, there is a good deal more that could be uncovered from the historical record about Mother Leakey and the Bishop, and the ways in which both were subsequently remembered. But I have also come to the conclusion that remembrance itself is the key to understanding their significance. More than anything else, perhaps, Mother Leakey and Bishop Atherton suggest to us the extent to which the very substance of history *is* memory—personal and collective, local and national, recorded and suppressed. Memory is the marrow of our own lives. We know from experience that it is sometimes involuntary, but also that it is often selective and creative. What I have tried to do in this book is demonstrate how the memory of a particular set of episodes might survive and mutate within the inherited historical record, at times apparently forgotten and at others emphatically recalled. We have seen how the original protagonists became over time symbols or signifiers of changing attitudes across a range of important themes in the histories of Britain and Ireland: relations between religious groupings, understandings of sexuality, meanings of the supernatural, interconnections between locality and nation. The sporadic posthumous celebrity of Bishop Atherton has a great deal to tell us about the warp and weft of narrative and memory. It illustrates the ways in which our forebears instinctively recast cautionary and exemplary stories from the past in order to address their own social, political, and cultural concerns, and invites us to ask ourselves whether we do not often do the same. The figure of Mother Leakey, meanwhile, offers us the rare opportunity to observe an entire process of 'folklorization' at work; to see how, in more than one sense, a real person can get turned into a ghost and become the repository for multiple fears, hopes, dreams, and ambitions. And around and above all, there is that most basic of human impulses: the need to tell tales.

Story and history are words that quite obviously share an etymological root. Nowadays, they can be made to seem like incompatible modes of writing and argumentation, sworn rivals for our allegiance and affection. Bookshops and libraries impose a strict apartheid upon their resident volumes: fiction or non-fiction, history and literature. But it was not always so clear-cut. Indeed, for many centuries, the only history available was what we today call narrative history, the relating of plausible and persuasive stories about the persons and places of times past. We have come across examples of them throughout the course of this book. The people of the past of course understood the distinction between truth and falsehood, between authentic history and mere 'poetry'. But, as the multiple accounts of Mother Leakey and Bishop Atherton suggest, their histories were often entwined and entangled in the netting of familiar storylines, storylines that to contemporaries made the accounts seem more creditworthy, not less: narratives of personal and societal redemption, of human perfidy, of divine judgement, and of the reordering of the moral universe.

For a time, we thought we knew better. The middle and later parts of the twentieth century saw the apparent triumph of what has aptly and ironically been called 'all-conquering history'. Professional historians convinced themselves that through the analysis of economic and social structures (preferably with copious data to quantify) it was possible to arrive at an objective truth about the natures of past societies, and not to become beguiled by whatever the actual inhabitants of those societies perceived their own motives and priorities to be. But it turns out we are not really any wiser than our fathers. In the past generation, historians have increasingly turned their backs on the notion of history as a 'science', and have come to recognize its kinship to other forms of narrative writing, and its inevitable dependence on the imaginative resources of the practitioner. In response, some have feared that we are looking at a blurring, or even a collapsing, of the crucial distinction between history and fiction.[4] But there is probably no real cause for alarm. The process of writing this book—in the conscious form of a 'story', and in close engagement with the rhetorics and language of its historical characters—has encouraged me to believe that practising history as a creative craft is not some self-indulgent dereliction of duty, but an enterprise that can take us a considerable way towards understanding meaningful truths about our ancestors. And at the same time, through a tangle of narratives about the vengeful ghost of an old woman and the grievous sins of a wayward bishop, we can perhaps all learn to appreciate that the telling of stories about the past is not just the vocation of historians. It is, to a very considerable extent, the fabric of history itself.

Notes

PREFACE

1. Glanvill, *Saducismus Triumphatus*, 2nd part, A2 2^r.
2. Published by OUP in 2002 as *Beliefs and the Dead*. The conference proceedings are gathered in Newton, *Early Modern Ghosts*.
3. The literature on the 'British dimension' of 17th-century religion and politics is large and growing. For an introduction to the issues, see Bradshaw and Morrill, *British Problem*.
4. In so doing I acknowledge the critique of philosophers who argue that historical narratives are essentially 'verbal fictions . . . as much invented as found' (White, *Tropics of Discourse*, 82), but would strongly resist the temptation to collapse any meaningful distinction between history and fiction. As readers will discover in the course of this book, some stories are truer than others.

PROLOGUE

1. The following narrative is constructed from the depositions in the State Papers: TNA, SP 16/383, 13^r–18^v. Quotation from the burial service: *Book of Common Prayer*, 310.

CHAPTER 1

1. The day on which the report was endorsed—24 Feb. 1637—seems to imply a date of 1638, as it was standard practice in England before the mid-18th century to change the calendrical year on 25 March, the Feast of the Annunciation. Previous commentary on the Leakey case has assumed a 1638 setting for the justices' investigation. Yet internal and external evidence confirms it must have taken place a year earlier. The explanation is either a scribal error or the fact that some individuals did follow the practice of dating the new year from Christmas or 1 Jan.

2. Weaver, *Somerset Incumbents*, 397; Byam, *Chronological Memoir of the Three Clerical Brethren*; SRO, DD/X/CHN; Stieg, *Laud's Laboratory*, 209, 346 (noting that Heathfield was licensed to preach).

3. Davis, *Fiction in the Archives*. There is further important exploration of this point in several of the essays in Clark, *Languages of Witchcraft*.

4. Binding and Stevens, *Book of Minehead*, 11, 32–5; Toulmin Smith, *Itinerary of John Leland*, i. 167; Brereton, *Travels*, 170; Gerard, *Particular Description of Somerset*, 12.

5. SRO, DD/X/CHN; Fry, *Wills and Administrations*, 272; *West Somerset Free Press* (7 Dec. 1889), 6; SRO, DD/SP 1634/41. On bonds and female money-lending in general, see McIntosh, *Working Women in English Society*, 90–3, 98–107.

6. Howard and Stoate, *Somerset Protestation Returns*, 1, 3, 29, 34, 58, 79, 80, 90, 151, 152, 170, 175, 213, 294; SRO, D/P bw.m 2/1/1; DD/X/CHN; Q/SR/2/94; D/B/bw 1598–1602; Q/SR/19/46; DD/SAS/C795/PR/306; D/D/cd/ 62. Curiously, the Minehead register places the burial of young John Leakey in Jan. 1635, several months earlier than the date claimed by Elizabeth Leakey in her testimony of 1637.

7. SRO, DD/X/CHN; Binding and Stevens, *Book of Minehead*, 83; Eales, 'Minehead, XVII Century Reredos', 259; TNA, E 190, 1087/12; 1087/14; 1087/15; 1088/5; 1088/6. Dorothy McClaren's study of fertility patterns in Minehead has some useful comments on the town's trade: 'Marital Fertility and Lactation', 35–6.

8. Leland, *Itinerary*, i. 167; TNA, E 190, 1088/6; Bates, *Quarter Sessions Records James I*, 273, 318; Barnes, *Somerset Assize Orders*, 1; Binding and Stevens, *Book of Minehead*, 51; Barnes, *Somerset*, 14–15.

9. SRO, D/D/cd 49; Stieg, *Laud's Laboratory*, 234. The association of the Welsh with Puritanism is curious, as the movement was notably weak and unpopular in Wales at this time. See Richards, *Puritan Movement in Wales*, 1–20. Perhaps Welsh Puritans were seeking refuge in Minehead.

10. Stoyle, *Loyalty and Locality*, 92–5; Chanter, *Literary History of Barnstaple*, 30; Gray, *Lost Chronicle of Barnstaple*, 40; Tyacke, *Aspects of English Protestantism*, 90–1; Camden, *Remaines*, 33; C. W. Sutton, 'Crompton, William', *ODNB*. For a broad introduction to puritanism and its relation to other forms of Protestantism, see Marshall, *Reformation England*, ch. 5.

11. M. Dorman, 'Piers, William', *ODNB*; Stieg, *Laud's Laboratory*, 297–300; Stokes, *Records of Early English Drama*, i. 426–9, ii. 754, 977; Barnes, 'County Politics', 103–22; Gee and Hardy, *Documents*, 528.

12. Binding and Stevens, *Book of Minehead*, 51–2; Byam and Kellet, *Return from Argier*, 31–3, 75, 76–7; Bates-Harbin, *Quarter Sessions Records Charles I*, 17–18. For wider discussion of European captives in North Africa, see Matar, *Turks, Moors and Englishmen*; Colley, *Captives*; Davies, *Christian Slaves, Muslim Masters*.

CHAPTER 2

1. Brereton, *Travels*, 164–5, 170.

2. For further discussion of this, see Clark, *Thinking with Demons*; Cressy, *Travesties and Transgressions*.

3. SRO, D/D/Ca 196 (6 Feb. 1615/16); Stieg, *Laud's Laboratory*, 248; SRO, Q/SR/16/96–7; Q/SR/15/2–3; Q/SR/7/76–7; Gaskill, 'Witches and Witnesses', 59.

4. TNA, SP 16/383, 14^{v}–15^{r}; Gaskill, 'Witchcraft and Power', 131; Barry, 'Thomas and the Problem of Witchcraft', 13; Cockburn, *Western Circuit Assize Orders*, 99. For examples of Somerset 'white' magic: SRO, Q/SR/21/9–10; Q/SR/20/46–7.

5. Shakespeare, *Macbeth* 1. 3. 3–27. For other cases of shipwrecks caused by witches, Thomas, *Religion*, 536, 560. Spectral bewitchment: Rushton, 'Texts of Authority', Gaskill, 'Witches and Witnesses', 26–9, 61–2, 64; Thomas, *Religion*, 594.

6. Quotations from 1600 edn. of *A Golden Chaine*, 515. Surveys of Protestant attitudes to ghosts: Thomas, *Religion*, ch. 19; Finucane, *Ghosts*, ch. 4; Marshall, *Beliefs and the Dead*, ch. 6. Medieval teaching on purgatory: ibid., ch. 1; Duffy, *Stripping of the Altars*, chs. 9–10.

7. TNA, SP 16/383, 15^{r}. For another case of a woman's ghost (with no Catholic association) appearing in the shape of a young girl: Gowing, 'Haunting of Susan Lay', 183. Other examples in this and the preceding paragraphs drawn from Marshall, *Beliefs and the Dead*, 234–52.

8. Shakespeare, *Hamlet*, 1. 4. 21; 1. 5. 11–13; 2. 2. 599–604; Sharpe, 'Devil in East Anglia', 247.

9. Dangerous revenants: Caciola, 'Wraiths, Revenants and Ritual' and 'Spirits Seeking Bodies'; Scribner, 'Elements of Popular Belief', 237; Schmitt, *Ghosts in the Middle Ages*, 172. Evelyn, *Diary*, 6–7; Lavater,

Of Ghostes, 191–2, 196; Bod. MS Rawlinson D 47, fol. 42ʳ; Belfield, 'Tarleton's News', 284.

10. Lake with Questier, *Antichrist's Lewd Hat*, 28; *Night-Walker of Bloomsbury*. Clothing defining personal identity: Davis, *The Gift*, 51; also Jones and Stallybrass, *Renaissance Clothing*. Crosfield, *Diary*, 17; Lavater, *Of Ghostes*, 191. D'Ewes, *Autobiography*, i. 57–61; SRO, D/D/cd 56 (2 July 1622).

11. *Strange and Fearful Warning*; Chamberlain, *Letters*, i. 391–2.

12. Hodgkin, 'Reasoning with Unreason', 218.

13. Gowing, 'Haunting of Susan Lay', 195.

INTERLUDE

1. My reconstruction here follows two contemporary eye-witness accounts of the event: BL, Sloane MS 1818, 187ᵛ–189ᵛ; Bernard, *Penitent Death*, 22–5. For the character of Oxmantown Green, see Gilbert, *Ancient Records of Dublin*, under date 1635. The bridge over which Atherton crossed the Liffey on his way to execution is now called Father Mathew Bridge.

CHAPTER 3

1. Foster, *Alumni Oxonienses*, 40; SRO, D/P bw.m 2/1/1; A. Clarke, 'Atherton, John', *ODNB*; *The Clergy of the Church of England Database* (http://eagle.cch.kcl.ac.uk); Exeter University Library, MS 105; Weaver, *Somerset Incumbents*, 21, 379; Stieg, *Laud's Laboratory*, 149–63. The names of two of Atherton's daughters are to be found in SRO, D/D/rr/210; the others in an 18th-cent. annotation to the TCD copy of Ware's *Whole Works* (1764), i. 541.

2. There is a large, and controversial literature on the political and religious situation in Ireland in the first third of the 17th cent. The sketch here draws on Clarke, *Old English*; Kearney, *Strafford in Ireland*; Perceval-Maxwell, *Outbreak of the Irish Rebellion*; Ford, *Protestant Reformation*; Canny, *Making Ireland British*.

3. Byam, *Chronological Memoir*, 15–18; Rich, *Irish Hubbub*, 51; T. Seccombe, 'Jerome, Stephen', rev. A. Ford, *ODNB*; Ford, *Protestant Reformation*, 74–7. For further discussion of Jerome's scandalous misdemeanours, see Hindle, 'Shaming of Margaret Knowsley'.

4. Ronan, 'Archbishop Bulkeley's Visitation', 57–8; Gillespie, *Chapter Act Book*, 194–9. See also Gillespie, 'Shaping of Reform', 'Crisis of Reform'.

5. TCD, MS 6404, 116ᵛ; RCB Lib., C.6.1.26/3, no. 21; Gillespie, 'Crisis of Reform', 197.

6. Gillespie, 'Crisis of Reform', 199; *Historical Manuscripts Commission, Hastings*, 60. On Convocation and the Articles, See Ford, *Protestant Reformation*, 156–64, 215; McCafferty, ' "God Bless your Free Church of Ireland" ', 187–208, which emphasizes that, in allowing for quasi-sacramental confession, the Irish canons were setting a standard for the English Church to aspire to.

7. Gillespie, *Chapter Act Book*, 162, 169–70, 180–1, 186–7, 206, 212–13, 221, 223; RCB Lib., C.6.1.7.2, 10ʳ; RCB Lib., C.6.1.26/3, nos. 21–3; McEnery and Refaussé, *Christ Church Deeds*, 265, 298; Gillespie, 'Crisis of Reform', 200–1; Boydell, 'Establishment of the Choral Tradition', 246–7.

8. Gillespie, *Chapter Act Book*, 178–9, 209–11; RCB Lib., C.6.1.7.2, fo. 13; *ODNB*; RCB Lib., C.6.1.26/6, no. 13; Bray, *Anglican Canons*, 326–9.

9. Laud, *Works*, vi. 258, 398; vii. 65, 130–1, 146; *Hastings MSS*, 60, 62; Bod. Films 1730, Strafford Papers, vi. 164, 188.

10. Laud, *Works*, vii. 156, 173, 204.

11. TCD, MS 6404, 119ᵛ,120ʳ; RCB Lib., C.6.1.7.2, 12ᵛ–13ʳ; McEnery and Refaussé, *Christ Church Deeds*, 317.

12. Brereton, *Travels*, 159–60. Power, *Cathedral and Parish of Holy Trinity*, 17. On Waterford's role in the Irish Rebellion, Canny, *Making Ireland British*, 510–15.

13. On Wentworth's policies towards Catholics, see Kearney, *Strafford in Ireland*, 43–4; Clarke, *Old English*, 116–19; Ford, *Protestant Reformation*, 214–16; Canny, 'Attempted Anglicisation', 172–4, the latter placing more emphasis on Wentworth's personal hostility to Catholicism. On the problems of impropriations, Ford, *Protestant Reformation*, 67–9. The definitive study of Cork is Canny, *Upstart Earl*, biographical sketch at pp. 1–8. The following section owes much to Ranger, 'Career of Richard Boyle', 294–321.

14. Ranger, 'Career of Richard Boyle', 295–6; Canny, *Upstart Earl*, 13; *CSP Ireland, 1633–47*, 44–5; Laud, *Works*, vi. 352–3, 375; vii. 69, 221. For the processes by which earlier bishops of Waterford and Lismore had come to grant away so much of their patrimony, see Cowman, 'Reformation Bishops', 31–8.

15. Ranger, 'Career of Richard Boyle', 320–1; Wentworth, *Earl of Strafford's Letters*, i. 378–80.

16. Wedgwood, *Thomas Wentworth*, 181; Strafford Papers, vi. 299, 330–1; Laud, *Works*, vii. 238, 249; *CSP Ireland, 1633–47*, 126; TCD, MS 6404; Kearney, *Strafford in Ireland*, 114.

17. Ranger, 'Career of Richard Boyle', 297–8, 318–25; Strafford Papers, vii. 37; *Hastings MSS*, 74–6; *CSP Ireland, 1633–47*, 160, 167–8.

18. Laud, *Works*, vii. 301–2, 309, 327–8; vi. 498; Strafford Papers, vii. 7, 19, 35–7; Barnes, *Somerset*, 86; Stieg, *Laud's Laboratory*, 170.

19. Ranger, 'Career of Richard Boyle', 324–5, 332; Clarke, 'Woeful Sinner', 144; Rennison, *Succession List*, 57; Wentworth, *Earl of Strafford's Letters*, i. 380; Grosart, *Lismore Papers*, 1st ser., iv. 71, 81; v. 43–4; Strafford Papers, vii. 71; *CSP Ireland, 1633–47*, 191; Laud, *Works*, vii. 438; McCafferty, 'John Bramhall', 144; Rennison, 'Joshua Boyle's Accompt', xxxii. 42–9, 79–85; xxxiii. 42–7, 83–92.

20. Rennison, *Succession List*, 37, 53; NLI, MS 13,237 (24); Chatsworth, Lismore MSS, vol. 20, no. 94; Grosart, *Lismore Papers*, 2nd ser., iv. 35–6.

21. Chatsworth, Lismore MSS, vol. 19, no. 69; vol. 20, nos. 11, 36, 68, 107; NLI, MS 13, 237 (24).

22. McCafferty, 'John Bramhall', 161; TCD, MS 6404, 120^r, 123^{v}–4^r; Dublin, Marsh's Library, Z 4.2.1 (6), (7), (9), (10), (21); TNA, SP 63/257/28; Shuckburgh, *William Bedell*, 149; Moody, Martin, and Byrne, *New History of Ireland*, 437.

23. TCD, MS 6404, 122^r, 123^v; Wedgwood, *Thomas Wentworth*, 239–45; Merritt, 'Historical Reputation', 7–8.

24. *Journals of the House of Lords Ireland*, 99–100; *Journals of the House of Commons Ireland*, 134–5; Kearney, *Strafford in Ireland*, 262; Rennison, 'Joshua Boyle's Accompt', xxxii. 46, 81–4; xxxiii. 44. For the groupings and manœuvrings in the Irish parliament, see Clarke, *Old English*, 125–52; Kearney, *Strafford in Ireland*, 189–98; Perceval-Maxwell, *Outbreak of the Irish Rebellion*, 67–91.

25. *Journals of the House of Lords*, 102–6, 108, 110. The bishop in favour of admitting Adair may have been Ussher. At about this time he wrote to the archbishop of Tuam, requesting suspension of the judgement against him until clear instructions had come from the Lord Lieutenant: Whitaker, *Correspondence of Radcliffe*, 252.

26. Perceval-Maxwell, *Outbreak of the Irish Rebellion*, 76–82; Kearney, *Strafford in Ireland*, 85–103, 189–90; Canny, 'Attempted Anglicisation',

174–81; Canny, *Making Ireland British*, 279–90; Clarke, *Old English*, 128–31; *Journals of the House of Commons*, 148; TCD, MS 6404, 124ᵛ.

CHAPTER 4

1. Coke, *Third Part of the Institutes*, 58–9; 25 Henry VIII. c. 6; *Statutes at Large, Ireland*, ii. 81–2. The definitive study of the Castlehaven affair is Herrup, *House in Gross Disorder*.

2. Whitaker, *Correspondence of Radcliffe*, 253, 255: NLI, MS 13, 237 (25); TNA, SP 16/461/32; Sherley, *Excellency of the Order of the Church of England*, 18–19.

3. Smyth, *Chronicle of the Law Officers*, 88–9, 106, 287; Ball, *History of the County Dublin*, ii. ch. 1.

4. BL, Sloane MS 1818, 187ᵛ–189ᵛ; Bernard, *Penitent Death*, 25–6; TCD, MS 6404, 125ʳ.

5. Dublin, Marsh's Library, MS Z 3.2.5, nos. 36, 72; NLI, MS 13, 237 (25); Grosart, *Lismore Papers*, 2nd ser., v. 127–8, 134. The significance of the Donoughmore order is emphasized by Winnet, 'Strange Case of Bishop John Atherton', 13–14, and downplayed by Clarke, 'Atherton File', 53. I follow the latter's reading (ibid. 52) of the October 1640 Act. Professor Clarke has made two intriguing suggestions about possible sources of action against Atherton, though both must remain in the realm of speculation. One is to note that the patron of Archibald Adair, the episcopal enemy of Atherton who succeeded him at Waterford, was an opposition member of the 1640 parliament, the Londonderry MP Sir Robert Stewart. The other is to suggest a copycat link with the Castlehaven case, which also involved devastating charges of sodomy and rape. The executed earl's nephew, Sir Audley Mervyn, was another Ulster opposition spokesman in the Commons. Sir Piers Crosby, a long-standing enemy of Wentworth, was married to Castlehaven's widowed mother. As Clarke himself admits, however, details of the Castlehaven case were widely known (ibid. 53).

6. TCD, MS 6404, 125ʳ; BL, Sloane MS 1818, 188ᵛ; Bernard, *Penitent Death*, 26.

7. Chatswoth, Lismore MSS, vol. 21, no. 75, *CSP Ireland, 1633–47*, 44; Kearney, *Strafford in Ireland*, 199–201; S. Kelsey, 'Clotworthy, John', *ODNB* Perceval-Maxwell, *Outbreak of the Irish Rebellion*, 94–7;

Marsh's Library, Z. 4.2.1 (21); Abbott, 'Issue of Episcopacy', 45; Wedgwood, *Thomas Wentworth*, 312.

8. *Diurnall Occurrences*, 1; Jansson *et al.*, *Proceedings in Long Parliament*, i. 36–7, 44–5, 47; Bod. MS Rawlinson C 956, 141ʳ; Baillie, *Letters*, i. 283, 286; Cressy, 'Revolutionary England', 48, 51.

9. Baillie, *Letters*, i. 316, 319. Pym's speech and Wentworth's answer is reconstructed from *Briefe and Perfect Relation*, 3–6, and Rushworth, *Tryal of Thomas, Earl of Strafford*, 107, 122–3. For broader accounts of the trial and its context (none of which mention the Atherton business), see Wedgwood, *Thomas Wentworth*, 337–79; Kilburn and Milton, 'Public Context', 230–51; R. G. Asch, 'Wentworth, Thomas', *ODNB*. For Cork's antipathy to Gwyn, see Grosart, *Lismore Papers*, 1st ser. iv. 71, 81.

10. Grosart, *Lismore Papers*, 1st ser. v. 176; Chatsworth, Lismore MSS, vol. 22, no. 31. For the argument that, at least to start with, Cork was reluctant to participate in the attack on Strafford, see Little, 'Earl of Cork', 619–35.

11. BL, Sloane MS 29, 1ʳ–3ʳ. The draft is dated 15 April 1640, though this must be an error. Prynne, *Antipathie of the Prelacie*, 368; Bod. MS. Top. Oxon. c. 378, 313.

12. The *Life and Death* thus appears between an account of a parliamentary speech of Sir Simonds D'Ewes, delivered on 2 July, and a report of the execution of a Jesuit on 26 July: *The Greke Postscripts of the Epistles to Timothy and Titus* (London, 1641; Thomason/E. 167 [4]); *A New Plot Discovered* (London, 1641; Thomason/E. 167 [7]).

13. On pamphleteering in the early 1640s, see Raymond, *Pamphlets*, esp. chs. 1, 4–5; Cressy, 'Revolutionary England', 58–64; Pierce, 'Anti-Episcopacy', 809–48. It seems certain that the collapse of censorship did not create a popular appetite or aptitude for the spreading of political news, but allowed more open dissemination of the kind of subversive opinions which had earlier circulated in oral and manuscript forms: Fox, 'Rumour', 597–620; Bellany, 'Libels'.

14. The observation about variant copies is based on a close comparison of two versions in Cambridge University Library: Hib. 7.641.5 and Hib. 7.641.123. It is possible that the episcopal portrait in the *Life and Death* is simply a copy of that in the *Bishops Potion*, but it seems more likely that the same block was reused. Although nose, eyes, and beard have been reworked, and there are some very minor variants in the folding on the sleeves, the dimensions of the two figures are identical,

and the tracts employ the same typeface: compare copies 11479 and E 165 (1).

15. In this complex and sensitive area, the late Alan Bray's classic work *Homosexuality in Renaissance England* remains the surest guide. Useful conspectus provided by Hitchcock, *English Sexualities*, quote at p. 6. Linkages between sodomy and disorder: Goldberg, *Sodometries*, 1–26; Herrup, *House in Gross Disorder*, 26–38. See also Burg, 'Work of the Devil', 69–78. Debate is likely to continue between broadly 'essentialist' (there have always been gay people) and 'social constructionist' approaches to the history of homosexuality. See the divergent approaches of Boswell, *Christianity, Social Tolerance and Homosexuality*, and Halperin, *How to Do the History of Homosexuality*.

16. Bray, *Anglican Canons*, 203, 369, 399–401; Hole, 'Incest', 185–6. For the trickle of incest cases coming before the church courts in Somerset in this period, see Quaife, *Wanton Wenches*, 177–8, commenting that, after intercourse with a stepdaughter, relationships with a sister-in-law were the most commonly prosecuted offences. The key text is Gen. 2: 24.

17. SRO, DD/SAS/C795/PR/321; Jenkins, 'Act Book of Archdeacon of Taunton', 78; Bray, *Anglican Canons*, 387–9.

18. Bates, *Quarter Sessions James I*, 104, 149, for the Huish bastardy orders, and Quaife, *Wanton Wenches*, 202–24 for the pattern more generally. Jenkins, 'Act Book of the Archdeacon of Taunton', 52; SRO, D/D/ca 235 (10 Oct 1623); D/D/Ca 229 (23 June 1623). On contested interpretations of what was meant by 'common fame', see Capp, 'Life, Love and Litigation', 80–1. On persistent excommunicacy, Marchant, *Church under the Law*, 226–35.

19. Purgation seems to have been the commonest official response to Somerset clergy charged with sexual offences: Stieg, *Laud's Laboratory*, 255; SRO, D/D/Ca 244, 34–9; D/D/cd/63 (Oct 1627); D/D/Ca 274 (30 Sept. 1630).

20. For the law on infanticide, see Jackson, *New-Born Child Murder*, 29–36. For the law in operation, Walker, *Crime, Gender and Social Order*, 148–58; Gowing, 'Secret Births', 87–115; Dickinson and Sharpe, 'Infanticide', 35–51 (quote from Grosvenor at p. 35). Contemporary stereotypes of 'murdering mothers' are analysed by Dolan, *Dangerous Familiars*, 120–70; Lake with Questier, *Antichrist's Lewd Hat*, 58–60 (and 70–8 on male child-murderers). For Barker, see J.C., *Araignment of Hypocrisie*, A1ᵛ. The case is discussed by Lake, '"Charitable

Christian Hatred"', 145–50. It is striking that the accusations against Atherton, the only known case of a bishop alleged to be involved in a child-murder, are not mentioned in any of the modern scholarship on infanticide.

CHAPTER 5

1. Bernard's *Penitent Death* comprises an 'epistle dedicatory' to Archbishop Ussher; a short address 'to the reader'; 'A Relation of the Penitent Death of the said John Atherton' (1–36), and a separately paginated 'Sermon Preached at the Burial of the Said John Atherton' (1–44). As much of the following discussion draws heavily and thickly upon this source, I have dispensed with multiple individual citations for quotations.

2. C. Diamond, 'Bernard, Nicholas', *ODNB*; Bernard, *Life of Usher*, 57. On Bedell, see K. S. Bottigheimer and V. Larminie, 'Bedell, William', *ODNB*; Ford, *Protestant Reformation*, 124–5, 216–19.

3. Thornton, *Autobiography*, 23–5. On the development of the *ars moriendi* tradition, see Beaty, *Craft of Dying*; Houlbrooke, *Death*, chs. 6–7. On murder pamphlets: Lake, 'Deeds Against Nature' and 'Popular Form, Puritan Content?'; Robson, 'No Nine Days Wonder'.

4. For the importance of burial location to Irish society, see Tait, *Death, Burial and Commemoration*, ch. 4. On the significance of particular sites within the churchyard, particularly the preference for the south side, see Daniell, *Death and Burial*, 99–100; Cressy, *Birth, Marriage, and Death*, 466; Marshall, *Beliefs and the Dead*, 301.

5. Tilley, *Dictionary of Proverbs*, 715. The saying was included in a collection of proverbs by the Lincoln schoolmaster, John Clarke, published only shortly before Atherton's death: *Paroemiologia Anglo-Latina*, 230.

6. This was a contemporary cliché, but also a genuine hope of many bereaved spouses in this period, see Marshall, *Beliefs and the Dead*, 215–20.

7. The penning of last letters of generalized advice to one's children was a fairly common practice among elite families in the 17th cent. (to wives, less so). Other than in the extraordinary circumstances of its composition, Atherton's letter seems to have been highly conventional in its themes. See Houlbrooke, *Death*, 143–5.

8. Gillespie, *Vestry Records of St John*, 145. Atherton's burial is recorded in the parish register: Mills, *Registers of St John*, 38.

9. Bernard, *A True and Perfect Relation*; *Letter sent from Dr. Barnard*; *Siege of Drogheda*.

10. Tyacke, *Aspects of English Protestantism*, 142.

11. Maltby, *Prayer Book and People*, makes the case for a broad swathe of proto-Anglican sentiment in the 1630s, anti-Laudian but also anti-puritan, though this may be rather different from Bernard's nostalgia for the Jacobean past.

12. A. Ford, 'Ussher, James', *ODNB*; Simms, 'The Restoration', 433–8.

13. Mills, *Registers of St John*, 43; SRO, DD/X/CHN.

14. Lynch, *Cambrensis Eversus*, ii. 145–7. Bray, *Homosexuality*, 20, 52, 75.

15. Hickman, *Historia*, 91. S. Wright, 'Hickman, Henry', *ODNB*; Shuckburgh, *William Bedell*, 149–50; Burnet, *William Bedell*, 143–4. The suggestion that Joan Atherton had gone to England to petition for her rights may not, however, be without foundation: a court order of 12 Aug. 1641 granted her and her daughters 'all the lands, goods and chattels' which the bishop held at the time of his death, and which as a result of his felony were forfeit to the Crown: annotation to TCD copy of Ware, *Works* (1764), i. 541.

16. Ware, *De Praesulibus*, 200. Evidence for Ware's acquaintance with Atherton is found in their joint appointment to a commission to investigate the value of lands in Nov. 1636: RCB Lib., C.6.1.26/9. *Bloody Murtherer*, 17–18. Foulkes, *Alarme For Sinners*; Manton, *Catalogus*, 60; E. C. Vernon, 'Manton, Thomas', *ODNB*; *Love's Case*, 15; Bod. MS Rawlinson D. 1110, 49^{r-v}; S. Handley, 'Seller, Abednego', *ODNB*.

17. Wood, *Athenae Oxonienses*, i. 632, 825.

18. Cox, *Hibernia Anglicana*, ii. 58–9; S. J. Connolly, 'Cox, Sir Richard', *ODNB*.

19. *Wonders of Free-Grace*, B1^{r-v}, B2^{v}, 147–60.

INTERLUDE

1. This speculative reconstruction of the scene in Slaughter's Coffee House owes a debt to the evocation of the furbishment and function of these institutions in Pelzer and Pelzer, 'Coffee Houses', 40–7; Clayton, *London's Coffee Houses*; and Cowan, *Social Life of Coffee*. Further information on Slaughter's in Shelly, *Inns and Taverns*, 108,

and Lillywhite, *London Coffee Houses*, 529–30. The view, made famous by the German sociologist Jürgen Habermas, that London coffee houses in the 18th century facilitated the emergence of a bourgeois 'public sphere' of widening participation in public and political life is perhaps implicit in my sketch, though the earlier history of manuscript and print discussion of the Atherton case warns against too great a sense of novel departures. See Habermas, *Public Sphere*. For Steele and the genesis of *The Tatler*, see C. Winton, 'Steele, Sir Richard', *ODNB*. See also Porter, *Enlightenment*, 79–80, who refers to the 'collusive sense of shared superiority' forged by the daily essays of *The Tatler* and its successor, *The Spectator*. The issues in question are 119, *From Tuesday January 10. to Thursday January 12 1709* [i.e. 1710], and 120, *From Thursday January 12 to Saturday January 14 1709.* Modern edn. (minus the adverts), ed. Bond, ii. 205–15.

CHAPTER 6

1. The standard account of early 18th-cent. London's popular print culture is Rogers, *Grub Street*. There is useful commentary in Hoppit, *Land of Liberty?*, ch. 6, and Porter, *Enlightenment*, ch. 4 (quote from Swift at p. 93). For what follows on the career of Curll, see Strauss, *Unspeakable Curll*; Hill, *Two Augustan Booksellers;* R. N. MacKenzie, 'Curll, Edmund', *ODNB*.

2. Curll himself protested that the sole aim of the work was to 'lay open the abuses and corruptions of the Church of Rome': *Humble Representation*, 7.

3. Barchas, *Graphic Design*, 13–14; Hitchcock, *English Sexualities*, 62; 25 Henry VIII, c. 6. For a discussion of attitudes towards bestiality, and some piquant 17th-cent. cases, see Fudge, 'Monstrous Acts', 20–5.

4. [Bernard], *Case of John Atherton,* 'Advertisement'; Hitchcock, *English Sexualities,* 15; Herrup, *House in Gross Disorder,* 134–7. For a parallel case of late 17th-cent. reprints of an older puritan conversion narrative tilting the balance 'from edification to titillation', see Lake with Questier, *Antichrist's Lewd Hat,* 326.

5. Nicholson, *Modern Syphylis;* Ware, *Commentary on the Prelates,* 27–8.

6. King's *Case of John Atherton* comprises 'To the Reader' (pp. 1–3); 'The Case of John Atherton' (pp. 3–35); and an 'Appendix' (pp. 37–44). Unless noted otherwise, all references and quotations in the following paragraphs are from this source.

7. Both of the cases cited by King were *causes célèbres* of the day. He seems to have been working from the following printed accounts: *Perjur'd Phanatick*; Sprat, *Late Wicked Contrivance*; id., *Second Part of the Late Wicked Contrivance*.

8. The shelfmark of this 1641 Dublin edn. is BL, G5552. G. Le G. Norgate, 'Milles, Thomas', rev. J. C. Walton, *ODNB*; Rennison, *Succession List*, 40;. Cotton, *Fasti Ecclesiæ Hibernicæ*, i. 175.

9. *Historical Remarks of the City of Waterford*, 19. For the recorder's duties, see Smith, *County and City of Waterford*, 200–2. On Butler, see Winnet, 'Strange Case of Bishop John Atherton', 13–14, and Clarke, 'Atherton File', 53.

10. For another Irish example of a house believed to be 'haunted with spirits', see Lovel, *Horrid and Strange News*. See also Gillespie, *Devoted People*, 110–12. Clodagh Tait has commented on the extent to which ancient Irish tradition seems 'low on ghosts', and speculates that an increased occurrence of ghost stories from the later 17th cent. may reflect the growing cultural influence of English and Scots settlers: *Death, Burial and Commemoration*, 154–5.

11. On Anglicanism's woes, see Hoppit, *A Land of Liberty?*, 33–4, 223–5, 230–4; Porter, *Enlightenment*, 96–122; Bennett, *Tory Crisis*, chs. 1–4; Holmes, *Trial of Sacheverell*, ch. 2. For the Irish scene, see Connolly, *Religion, Law and Power*, 171–90 (quote at p. 171), and Ford, Milne, and McGuire, *By Law Established*. Hearne, *Remarks*, ii. 93. Hearne contrasted Atherton to his advantage with the new bishop, Thomas Milles, whom he considered 'the most meanly fitted' person ever to be raised to the episcopate. Indeed, he wrongly assumed Milles had authored the 1710 vindication, and thought it 'but a poor pamphlet': ibid., 388.

12. King, *Animadversions on a Pamphlet*, A2^v, 21–9; Bolton, *Caroline Tradition*, 45–6; Norgate, 'Milles'; Connolly, *Religion, Law and Power*, 173. In 1711 Swift called Pooley 'an old doting perverse coxcomb': *Journal to Stella*, i. 354.

13. Hearne, *Remarks*, ii. 388. The essential work on the Sacheverell affair remains Holmes, *Trial of Sacheverell*. See also W. A. Speck, 'Sacheverell, Henry', *ODNB*; id., *Birth of Britain*, chs. 6–7.

14. MacKenzie, 'Curll'; Dunton, *Bull-Baiting*, 2–4.

15. See the lists of new books appended to Dunton, *Voyage* and Gildon, *Post-Boy Rob'd*. On Dunton's life and publications, see H. Berry, 'Dunton, John', *ODNB*; ead., *Gender, Society and Print Culture*; Hill,

Two Augustan Booksellers; McEwen, *Oracle of the Coffee House*; Parks, *Dunton and the Book Trade*. See also Bhowmik, 'Facts and Norms', 345–65.

16. Swift, *Poems*, i. 13–25; Gildon, *History of the Athenian Society*; Hill, *Two Augustan Booksellers*, 7–8.

17. *Athenian Mercury*, 1/16, Q. 1; 1/27, Qs 1, 29; 2/7, Q. 5; 3/4, Q. 17; 3/17; 4/7, Qs 1, 7; 4/20, Qs 2–3; 4/10; McEwen, *Oracle of the Coffee House*, 25; Dunton, *Christian's Gazette*, 79; id., *Dublin Scuffle*, 354–6.

18. Dunton, *Athenianism*, dedicatory epistle (quote at p. ix); 'Project IV: The He-Strumpets', 93–9. On changing meanings of sodomy, see Bray, *Homosexuality*, ch. 4 (quote at p. 104); Hitchcock, *English Sexualities*, ch. 5; Norton, *Mother Clap's Molly House*, ch. 2; Trumbach, *Sex and the Gender Revolution*.

19. Dunton, *Athenianism*, 219–303. The explicit references to John Atherton are at 223, 245–52, 255–8.

20. The text Dunton was referring to was White, *First Century*.

21. Quoted in Hoppit, *Land of Liberty?*, 64, who notes in fact a growing judicial reluctance to convict women of infanticide in this period.

22. The quotation is from Psalm III: 2.

CHAPTER 7

1. Johnston, *Restless Dead*, p. viii.

2. Quotations from Dunton's *Athenianism* at 360, 242, 243. On the interplay of factual and fictive elements in the imaginative writing of the period, see Davis, *Factual Fictions*; McKeon, *Origins of the English Novel*. For the alleged connection with Gay, see Noakes, *John Gay*, 73–6 (quote at p. 74).

3. [Bernard], *Memorials of the Life and Death of Atherton. Bishop Atherton's Case Discussed* is separately paginated: letter to King at 2–4, continued on p. 16; 'Amazing Relation', 4–14; Price's statement, 14–15. On Curll's relations with Dunton, see Hill, *Two Augustan Booksellers*, 18. Hill notes (p. 23) that manuscripts had a habit of 'coming into Curll's hands'.

4. On Quick's career and writings, see A. Gordon, 'Quick, John', rev. S. Wright, *ODNB*; Jackson, 'Nonconformists and Society', 44; Freke, *Funeral Sermon*; Williams, *Funeral Sermon*, quotation on youthful conversion at p. 35; Calamy, *Continuation of the Account*, 331–5; Matthews, *Calamy Revised*, 401–2. No writer on Quick has

noted, or noticed, his authorship of the 'Apparition Evidence'. The manuscript of 'Icones Sacrae' is preserved in Dr Williams Library, London. Visitors are encouraged to consult a good 19th-cent. transcription in 2 vols.: MS 38.34/5. Quick's colourful account of his 1673 arrest in Plymouth is at ii. 538–9. The work printed by Dunton was *The Young Man's Claim*.

5. Historians are, in fact, increasingly sceptical of the old idea that Protestantism turned its back on the supernatural and cleared the way for a more 'modern' outlook on the world. See the persuasive presentation in Walsham, 'Miracles'.

6. Quick, *Synodicon*, title-page; *Test of True Godliness*, 3; *Hell Open'd*, from which all references in the following few paragraphs are drawn.

7. Bates-Harbin, *Quarter Session Records*, i. 4, 10, 19–20, 28, 114; iii. 1, 11, 17, 19, 21, 22, 31, 35, 42; Collinson, *History and Antiquities of Somerset*, iii. 255–6; Weaver, *Somerset Incumbents*, 315; Clergy of the Church of England Database (http://eagle.cch.kcl.ac.uk:8080/cce/bishops/DisplayBishop.jsp?ordTenID=242).

8. A 19th-cent. local historian suggested that Chamberlain's first name was James, but it is not clear what evidence, if any, there is for this: NDRO, B 19z/1. Chamberlain does not appear in the 1674 hearth tax returns for Cullompton, though 'Esq. Fortescue' is listed for Brixton: Stoate, *Hearth Tax*, 21, 155. Quick himself is assessed on four hearths in Plymstock parish in 1662: ibid. 158.

9. NDRO, B 19z/1 (notes on the town clerks of Barnstaple by Sydney Harper); TNA, Prob 11/228, fos. 321^r–322^v; Bernard, *Penitent Death* (1641), 18.

10. Webster, *Displaying of Witchcraft*, 44, 46, 296–300, 311–12: Roe, *Certainty of Future State*, 2–3, 14.

11. Hobbes, *Leviathan*, 213. See *The Restless Ghost*, 3–4; *Strange but True Relation of Horrid and Bloudy Murder*, 2; *Narrative of the Demon of Spraiton*, 1–2; *Account of Horrid and Barbarous Murder*; Telfair, *True Relation of an Apparition*, 3; *Athenian Mercury*, 4/10 (31 Oct. 1691). For discussion of how contemporaries used and understood the term 'atheism', see Aylmer, 'Unbelief in Seventeenth-Century England'; Hunter, 'Problem of "Atheism"'; as well as the essays in Hunter and Wootton, *Atheism*.

12. More, *Immortality of the Soul.* (quotation at 296); Glanvill, *Saducismus Triumphatus*; Bovet, *Pandaemonium*; Baxter, *Certainty of the Worlds of Spirits*, (quotations at 3 and 7); Beaumont, *Treatise of Spirits*. For

discussion of the controversies around the end of witchcraft prosecution, see Bostridge, *Witchcraft*.

13. Quotation: Woolf, *Social Circulation*, 369. Involvement of clergymen with ghost stories: Bover, *Pandaemonium*, 177; Glanvill, *Saducismus Triumphatus*, 227, 228, 229, 230, 231, 235, 238, 245, 250, 260, 282, 285; Baxter, *Certainty of the Worlds of Spirits*, 20, 63, 73, 147; *Narrative of the Demon of Spraiton*, 4; *Strange and True News from Long-Ally*, 4; *Restless Ghost*, 6–7; *Strange but True Relation*, 2; *True and Impartial Account*, 6. Accounts offered to magistrates: Glanvill, *Saducismus Triumphatus*, 5, 8, 232; Baxter, *Certainty of the Worlds of Spirits*, 75, 248; *Strange and Wonderfull Discovery*, 3–7; *True and Perfect Account of a Dreadful Apparition*, 4; *Demon of Marleborough*, 8; *Strange and Wonderful News from Lincolnshire*, 4; *Strange and Wonderful News from Exeter*; *Full and Truer Relation of Barwick and Mangall*, 2. On how 'evidence' from ghosts fed into legal process, see Gaskill, *Crime and Mentalities*, 217–19, 231–4. For further insightful discussion of the 'verification' of ghost stories, and their appropriation by clerical elites in the Restoration period, see Handley, '"Visions of an Unseen World"', ch. 1.

14. S. Mandelbrote, 'Beaumont, John', *ODNB*; W. E. Burns, 'Glanvill, Joseph', *ODNB*. Bovet for some reason has been denied a place in the *ODNB*. See the brief discussions in Brown, *Fate of the Dead*, 19, Finucane, *Ghosts*, 122, and Bostridge, *Witchcraft*, 90–1; Aubrey, *Miscellanies*, 113–21, 126. Chanter, *St Peter, Barnstaple*, 99 (for Boyce). At least one of Paschall's stories did make it into Glanvill's text: a description of a haunting in his own father's house in London in 1661. *Saducismus Triumphatus*, 281–8.

15. More, *Immortality of the Soul*, 286; Ward, *Case of Joram*, 14–15; Roe, *Certainty of a Future State*, 11; Glanvill, *Saducismus Triumphatus*, 272 (incorrectly paginated), 216–17. Glanvill's controversial works included *Apology and Advice* (against Andrew Marvell), and *Impartial Protestant* (which antagonized Richard Baxter); Quick, *Hell Open'd*, 26; 'Icones Sacrae', ii. 477, 528, 482; BL, Sloane MS 1818, 178^{v}.

16. Aubrey, *Remaines*, 24, 159, 164; Fox, *Oral and Literate Culture*, 188–9.

17. Robert Darnton's alertness to the 'historical dimension' of French folk tales provides an instructive model here, though we should note his caveat that repeat retellings 'infused the tales with many meanings, most of which are now lost because they were embedded in contexts

and performances that cannot be recaptured'. *Cat Massacre*, 17–78 (quote at p. 71).

18. *Strange and Wonderful News from Northamptonshire*; Norris, *Love of God*, Preface (unpaginated); *The Restless Ghost*, 8; *Strange but True Relation*, 7; *Most Strange and Dreadful Apparition*, 3–4; *Strange and True News from Long-Ally*, 7; *Strange and Wonderful News from Lincolnshire*, 4; Trotman, 'Treasure-Seeking at Bridgwater', 220–1; Aubrey, *Miscellanies*, 63–4.

19. *Demon of Marleborough*, 4; *Demon of Spraiton*, 4.

20. *Strange and Wonderful News from Exeter*; Bovet, *Pandaemonium*, 208. For other haunted tales from the area, see Mathews, *Blackdown Borderland*.

21. Simpson, 'Local Legend', 27–8; Glanvill, *Saducismus Triumphatus*, 235, 209, 212; *Demon of Marleborough*, 1. Doctors of physic feature in another contemporary story: *Strange and True News from Long-Ally*, 8. *Demon of Spraiton*, 6; *True Relation of an Apparition*, 12–14; Baxter, *Certainty of the Worlds of Spirits*, 6, 42; *True and Perfect Account*.

22. Though an earlier generation of historians undoubtedly exaggerated the propensity of midwives to be persecuted as witches: Harley, 'Historians as Demonologists'.

23. Capp, *Gossips*, 303; Gaskill, *Crime and Mentalities*, 211, 253, 256; Malcolmson, 'Infanticide', 191–2, 195–6; C.W., *Crying Murther*; *Great News from Middle-Row*. The Holborn case was also the subject of two ballads: *Midwives Ghost*, and *New Ballad of the Midwives Ghost*.

24. *Spectator*, i. 52–4, 453–5; iii. 570–2; Cockburn, *Philosophical Essay*, 39; Essex, *Young Ladies Conduct*, 129; Bourne, *Antiquitates Vulgares*, 76–7, 84–8; Defoe, *Essay on Apparitions*, quotes at 25 and 75. My interpretation of Defoe is indebted to the perceptive reading in Handley, 'Visions', 160–4. See also Baine, *Defoe and the Supernatural*. For the Stamp Acts and the suggestion that they helped to 'divide up a previously intact discourse–narrative' into separate categories of 'news' and 'novels', see Davis, *Factual Fictions*, 95–101. Fielding, *Tom Jones*, i. 294.

25. On this theme, see Handley, 'Visions'; Davies, *Witchcraft, Magic and Culture*; Barry, 'Public Infidelity'.

26. Metaphorically speaking: the earliest newspapers didn't have headlines.

27. The classic statement of this view is Burke, *Popular Culture*. Sophisticated treatments in the English context include Fox, *Oral and Literate Culture*; Woolf, 'The "Common Voice"'; id., *Social Circulation of the Past*.

CHAPTER 8

1. Swift, *Poems*, ii. 516–20.
2. Carte, *Life of Ormonde*, i. 67–8; S. Handley, 'Carte, Thomas', *ODNB*.
3. Ware, *Works*, i. 539–41. See also ii. 362–3 where he dismisses Bishop Thomas Milles's attempt to exonerate Atherton. The charge of presbyterian sympathies is noted by the 18th-cent. owner of a copy in the Bodleian Library, Oxford (Gough Irel. 133), verso of title-page. P. Carter, 'Harris, Walter', *ODNB*.
4. *Politicall Balance*, quotes at 9 and 12. *Dictionary of National Biography*, xviii. 1297–9. For the political background, see York, *Neither Kingdom Nor Nation*, ch. 2.
5. Weaver, *Somerset Incumbents*, 379 (a manuscript compiled by an 18th-cent. archdeacon of Taunton); Hawkins, *Perjur'd Fanatick*, iii; Nichols, *Irish Compendium*, 292; *Chronology of Accidents*; Smith, *Waterford*, which discusses Atherton (but not his fate) at 147.
6. [Oldys], 'Atherton', in *Biographia Britannica*, i. 246–54. The entry is anonymous, but his authorship is confirmed by the entry on Oldys himself in *New and General Biographical Dictionary*, x. 39. For the impact of print on oral traditions, Fox, *Oral and Literate Culture*, 242–51. Bestiality: Harris, *History of Dublin*, 351; Trusler, *Historians Guide*, 7; *Treble Almanack*, 144; Beatson, *Political Index*, 170.
7. *New and General Biographical Dictionary*, i. 448–51; Brookes, *Dictionary of the World*, i. s.v. 'Atherton'; *Biographia Britannica* (1778), i, p. xx.
8. No copies of a 1742 edn. appear to survive, but it is noted by White, *Catalogue of Books*, 191, and by Rennison, *Succession List*, ix. *Penitent Death* (1783), 2. On Dodd, see Howson, *Macaroni Parson*. Marginalia: NLI, J92 ATH/1651, p. 46; J92 ATH/1642, p. 55. Frequent references to the Atherton texts in book catalogues can be found by searching 'Eighteenth Century Collections Online'.
9. Simco, *Catalogue of Books*, 89; Cambridge University Library, Hib. 8.642 (print pasted opposite title-page); National Portrait Gallery, D943 (undocumented, but dated by the NPG to late 18th/early 19th

cent.); *Life and Death* (?1815); Whitaker, *Correspondence of Radcliffe*, 253.

10. Parris, *Great Unfrocked*, 144–56; D. Huddleston, 'Jocelyn, Percy', *ODNB;* Benbow, *Crimes of the Clergy*; Prothero, 'William Benbow'.

11. Examples of Anglican reticence: Ball, *Reformed Church of Ireland*; Olden, *Church of Ireland*. Mant, *Church of Ireland*, i. 740; *Parliamentary Gazeteer*, iii. 500; Cotton, *Fasti Ecclesiæ Hibernicæ*, i. 128; Rennison, *Succession List*, 2; Jourdan, 'Rule of Charles I', 27–8; Killen, *Ecclesiastical History*, ii. 25; Reid, *Presbyterian Church*, i. 293; O'Shea, *Luke Wadding*, 172.

12. Scott, *Works*, 728; *Letters*, xii. 443–4; *Letters on Demonology*, 6–8, 34, 228–30, 232; Sutherland, *Life of Scott*, 336; Parsons, *Witchcraft and Demonology*, esp. 7–15; *Samuel Taylor Coleridge*, 632.

13. Ibid. 52–3; Holmes, *Coleridge*, chs. 7–8. On possible folkloric sources for the spectre-bark: Lowes, *Road to Xanadu*, 274–80. I was alerted to the possible Coleridge connection by Brown, 'Old Mrs Leakey', 150–1.

14. Page, *Exploration of Exmoor*, 35–8; Snell, *Book of Exmoor*, 230–2; Walters, *Bygone Somerset*, 194. See also Poole, *Customs of Somerset*, 101–2.

15. *Western Antiquary*, 36–8, 69–71, 102, 226–7; W. Axon, 'Atherton, John', *Dictionary of National Biography* (Oxford, 1885), see B. C. Hollingworth, 'Axon, William Edward Armytage', *ODNB*; *Notes and Queries*, ser. 7, 11 (18 Sept. 1886), 229; Boger, *Myths of Somerset*, 557–8; Almy, 'Weather Wisdom', 554; Jones, *Credulities*, 68–9; *West Somerset Free Press*, 6, reprinted as George, *Historical Gleanings*; Poole, *Customs of Somerset*, 101; Binding and Stevens, *Book of Minehead*, 106–7; Larter, *Minehead*, 6.

16. Dorson, *British Folklorists*. I have also benefited here from reading an as yet unpublished paper of Alex Walsham's: 'Recording Superstition in Early Modern Britain: The Origins of Folklore Revisited'.

17. Davies, *People Bewitched*, 153–8; Watson, *Calendar of Customs*, 410–11; Burton, *Exmoor*, 156–62; Tongue, *Somerset Folklore*, 6, 84; Briggs, *Dictionary of Folk-Tales*, i. 599–600; H. E. Davidson, 'Briggs, Katharine Mary', *ODNB*. See Aarne and Thompson, *Types of the Folk-Tale*. Brown, 'Old Mrs Leakey', 141–54. Theo Brown's papers, held at the University of Exeter (MS 105), contain useful notes and correspondence about the case.

18. See Underwood, *Gazetteer of Ghosts*; Spencer and Spencer, *Encylopedia of Ghosts*; Hallam, *Ghosts' Who's Who*; Brooks, *Good Ghost Guide*; Turner, *Ghosts in South West*. Underwood, *Ghosts of Somerset*, 3. The programme (made by Raw Charm Productions) was screened on HTV-West on 31 Oct. 2003. Major, 'Mrs Leakey's Ghost', 77–9; N.Z. Cornish Assoc. Newsletter, July 2004 (online at www.busby.net/nzca/vol339.html); Hurley, *Legends of Exmoor*, 26; R. Webber, 'Weekend to Remember' (www.telegraph.co.uk/travel/main.jhtml? xml); pers. comm. Roxanne Grimmett, 9 Feb. 2006.

19. Bray, *Homosexuality*, 14–15, 18, 72; Goldberg, *Queering the Renaissance*, ref. to Atherton at 54. See also e.g. McCormick, *Secret Sexualities*, 64; Aldrich and Wotherspoon, *Gay and Lesbian History*, 32. *Seanad Éireann*, 127 (12 Dec. 1990), and 137 (29 June 1993), online at www.oireachtas-debates.gov.ie.

EPILOGUE

1. The poem begins: 'In Xanadu did Kubla Khan / A stately pleasure-dome decree . . .'. *Samuel Taylor Coleridge*, 102. For an account of how Coleridge's creative process was interrupted by the unexpected arrival of 'a person from Porlock', see Lawrence, *Coleridge and Wordsworth in Somerset*, 103–4.

2. In the 17th cent. e.g. the tale of the 'drummer of Tedworth' was infinitely better known and more widely discussed, as, in the 18th cent, was the Canterbury ghost of Mrs Veal, or the London Cock Lane ghost: Hunter, 'Drummer of Tedworth'; Handley, 'Visions', 127–60, 218–31.

3. Fine examples of micro-historical approaches include Wrightson, *Poverty and Piety*; Duffy, *Voices of Morebath*; Le Roy Ladurie, *Carnival at Romans*; Davis, *Return of Martin Guerre*; Ginzburg, *Cheese and the Worms*. The disparaging quotation about micro-history is in the *New York Review of Books* (20 Oct. 1994), cited in the online *Oxford English Dictionary* (www.dictionary.oed.com, s.v. 'micro-history').

4. I have drawn here on the insights of the work in Kelley and Harris Sacks, *Historical Imagination* (particularly the essay by Patrick Collinson), and on Chartier, *Cultural History*, ch. 2, and *Edge of the Cliff*, ch. 1 (quote at p. 14).

Bibliography of Sources Cited

MANUSCRIPT SOURCES

The National Archives, London
Minehead Port Books, E 190, 1087/12; 1087/14; 1087/15; 1088/5; 1088/6.
Prob 11/228, will of Robert Lane.
State Papers, Domestic Series, Charles I, 16/383, 461.
State Papers, Ireland, Charles I, 63/257.

British Library, London
Sloane MS 29, draft treatise on the state of Ireland.
Sloane MS 1818, John Quick papers.

Dr Williams' Library, London
MS 38.34/5, transcription of John Quick, 'Icones Sacrae'.

Bodleian Library, Oxford
MS Rawlinson C 956, diary of Sir John Holland.
MS Rawlinson D 47, letter of Daniel Featley.
MS Rawlinson D 1110, commonplace book of Abednego Seller.
MS. Top. Oxon. c. 378, diary of Thomas Wyatt.
Films 1730, Strafford Papers.

Exeter University Library, Exeter
MS 105, Theo Brown Papers.

National Library of Ireland, Dublin
MS 13,237, letters to earl of Cork

Trinity College, Dublin
MS 6404, diary of Sir James Ware.

Marsh's Library, Dublin
MS Z 4.2.1, Irish High Commission papers.

MS Z 3.2.5, Irish parliamentary orders.

Representative Church Body Library, Dublin
C.6.1.7.2, Christ Church Chapter act book, 1634–70.
C.6.1.26/3, Christ Church accounts.
C.6.1.26/6, 9, Christ Church estate and legal papers

Somerset Record Office, Taunton
D/B/bw, 1598–1602, Bridgwater bailliffs' accounts.
D/D/Ca 196, 235, 229, 244, 274, ecclesiastical court act books.
D/D/cd 49, 56, 62, 63, ecclesiastical court deposition books.
D/D/rr/210, Bishops' Transcripts, Huish Champflower.
DD/SAS/C795/PR/306, 321, ecclesiastical court articles.
DD/SP 1634/41, inventory of the goods of Susan Leakey.
DD/X/CHN, transcript of Minehead parish register.
D/P bw.m 2/1/1, parish register of Bridgwater St Mary.
Q/SR, quarter sessions records: 2/94; 7/76–7; 15/2–3; 16/96–7; 19/46;
    20/46–7; 21/9–10.

North Devon Record Office, Barnstaple
MS B 19Z/1, notes on the town clerks of Barnstaple by Sydney
Harper.

Chatsworth House, Derbyshire
Lismore MSS, vols. 19–22, letters to earl of Cork.

PRINTED PRIMARY SOURCES
AND CALENDARS

*An Account of a most Horrid and Barbarous Murder and Robbery . . . with the
    most Strange, Wonderful and Miraculous Discovery of the Same*
    (Edinburgh, 1694).
ALMY, P., 'Weather Wisdom', *The Gentleman's Magazine*, 277 (Dec. 1894).
The Athenian Mercury, 1–4 (1691).
AUBREY, JOHN, *Miscellanies* (1696).
—— *Remaines of Gentilisme and Judaisme*, ed. J. Britten (1881).
BAILLIE, ROBERT, *The Letters and Journals of Robert Baillie, A.M., Prin-
    cipal of the University of Glasgow*, ed. D. Laing (3 vols., Edinburgh,
    1841).

BALL, J. T., *The Reformed Church of Ireland (1537–1886)* (1886).

BARNES, T. G. (ed.), *Somerset Assize Orders 1629–1640*, Somerset Record Society, 65 (1959).

BATES, E. H. (ed.), *Quarter Sessions Records for the County of Somerset*, i. *James I 1607–1625*, Somerset Record Society, 23 (1907).

BATES-HARBIN, E. H. (ed.), *Quarter Sessions Records for the County of Somerset*, ii. *Charles I 1625–1639*, Somerset Record Society, 24 (1908).

—— (ed.), *Quarter Sessions Records for the County of Somerset*, iii. *Commonwealth, 1642–1660*, Somerset Record Society, 28 (1912).

BAXTER, RICHARD, *The Certainty of the Worlds of Spirits* (1691).

BEATSON, ROBERT, *A Political Index to the Histories of Great Britain and Ireland* (1788).

BEAUMONT, JOHN, *An Historical, Physiological and Theological Treatise of Spirits, Apparitions, Witchcrafts* (1705).

BENBOW, WILLIAM, *The Crimes of the Clergy* (1823).

BERNARD, NICHOLAS, *The Penitent Death of a Woefull Sinner, or, The Penitent Death of John Atherton, Executed at Dublin the 5. of December 1640* (Dublin, 1641).

—— *A True and Perfect Relation of all the Severall Skirmishes, Brave Exploits, and Glorious Victories obtained by the English Protestants, over the Irish Rebels, when they raised the Siege of Tredagh* (1642).

—— *A Letter sent from Dr. Barnard, a Reverend Divine, and Parson of Tredagh to Sr. Simon Harcourts Lady in Westminster* (1642).

—— *The Whole Proceedings of the Siege of Drogheda in Ireland* (1642).

—— *The Life and Death of the Most Reverend and learned Father of Our Church, Dr James Usher* (1656).

—— *The Case of John Atherton, Bishop of Waterford in Ireland, who was Convicted of the Sin of Uncleanness with a Cow, and Other Creatures; for which he was hanged at Dublin, December 5 1640* (1710).

—— *Some Memorials of the Life and Penitent Death of Dr John Atherton, Bishop of Waterford in Ireland... To which is added, an Account of the most Amazing Apparition ever heard of* (1711).

Biographia Britannica: or, the Lives of the Most Eminent Persons who have Flourished in Great Britain and Ireland (7 vols., 1747–66; 5 vols., 1778–93).

The Bloody Murtherer, or, The Unnatural Son his Just Condemnation (1672).

BOGER, E., *Myths, Scenes, and Worthies of Somerset* (1887).

The Book of Common Prayer 1559, ed. J. E. Booty (Washington, DC, 1976).

BOURNE, HENRY, *Antiquitates Vulgares; or, the Antiquities of the Common People, Giving an Account of Several of their Opinions and Ceremonies* (Newcastle, 1725).

BOVET, RICHARD, *Pandaemonium, or The Devil's Cloyster, being a Further Blow to Modern Sadduceism* (1684).

BRAY, G. (ed.), *The Anglican Canons, 1529–1947*, Church of England Record Society, 6 (Woodbridge, 1998).

BRERETON, WILLIAM, *Travels in Holland, the United Provinces, England, Scotland and Ireland MDCXXXIV–MDCXXXV*, ed. E. Hawkins, Chetham Soc., 1st ser. 1 (1844).

BROOKES, RICHARD, *A Dictionary of the World... With an Historical and Biographical Account of its Principal Inhabitants* (2 vols., 1772).

BURNET, GILBERT, *The Life of William Bedell DD, Bishop of Kilmore in Ireland* (1685).

BYAM, HENRY, and KELLET, EDWARD, *A Return from Argier* (1628).

CALAMY, EDMUND, *A Continuation of the Account of the Ministers, Lecturers, Masters and Fellows of Colleges and Schoolmasters, who were Ejected and Silenced after the Restoration in 1660* (1727).

Calendar of State Papers Relating to Ireland, 1509–1670 (24 vols., 1860–1912).

CAMDEN, WILLIAM, *Remaines of a Greater Worke* (1605).

CARTE, THOMAS, *An History of the Life of James Duke of Ormonde* (2 vols., 1736).

CHAMBERLAIN, JOHN, *Letters*, ed. N. McClure (2 vols., Philadelphia, 1939).

A Chronology of Some Memorable Accidents (Dublin, 1743).

CLARKE, JOHN, *Paroemiologia Anglo-Latina... Or Proverbs English, and Latine* (1639).

COCKBURN, ARCHIBALD, *A Philosophical Essay Concerning the Intermediate State of Souls* (1722).

COCKBURN, J. S. (ed.), *Western Circuit Assize Orders 1629–1648: A Calendar*, Camden Soc. 4th ser. 17 (1976).

COKE, EDWARD, *The Third Part of the Institutes of the Laws of England* (1644).

COLERIDGE, S. T., *The Oxford Authors: Samuel Taylor Coleridge*, ed. H. J. Jackson (Oxford, 1985).

COLLINSON, J. *The History and Antiquities of the County of Somerset* (3 vols., Bath, 1791).

COTTON, H., *Fasti Ecclesiæ Hibernicæ: The Succession of the Prelates and Members of the Cathedral Bodies of Ireland* (6 vols., Dublin, 1847–78).

COX, RICHARD, *Hibernia Anglicana* (2 parts, 1689).

CROSFIELD, THOMAS, *The Diary of Thomas Crosfield*, ed. F. S. Boas (1935).

CURLL, EDMUND, *The Humble Representation of Edmund Curll, Bookseller and Citizen of London Concerning Five Books, Complained of to the Secretary of State* (1725).

C. W., *The Crying Murther, Contayning the Cruell and most Horrible Bu[tchery] of Mr. Trat, Curate of Old Cleaue* (1624).

DEFOE, DANIEL, *An Essay on the History and Reality of Apparitions* (1727).

The Demon of Marleborough. Or, More News from Wiltshire in a most Exact Account of the Aparition of the Ghost or Spirit of Edward Aven (1675).

D'EWES, SIMONDS, *The Autobiography and Correspondence of Sir Simonds D'Ewes*, ed. J. O. Halliwell (2 vols., 1845).

The Diurnall Occurrences, or, Dayly Proceedings of Both Houses, in this Great and Happy Parliament (1641).

DUNTON, JOHN, *A Voyage Round the World* (1691).

—— *The Dublin Scuffle . . . Also Some Account of his Conversation in Ireland* (1699).

—— *The Bull-Baiting: or, Sach—ll Dress'd up in Fire-works* (1709).

—— *The Christian's Gazette, or, News Chiefly Respecting the Invisible World* (1709).

—— *Athenianism: or, The New Projects of Mr John Dunton* (1710).

ESSEX, JOHN, *The Young Ladies Conduct: Or, Rules for Education* (1722).

EVELYN, JOHN, *The Diary of John Evelyn*, ed. J. Bowle (Oxford, 1983).

FIELDING, HENRY, *The History of Tom Jones* (2 vols., 1908).

FOSTER, J. (ed.), *Alumni Oxonienses: The Members of the University of Oxford 1500–1714* (1891).

FOULKES, ROBERT, *An Alarme For Sinners, Containing the Confession, Prayers, Letters, and Last Words of Robert Foulkes* (1679).

FREKE, THOMAS, *A Funeral Sermon Occasioned by the death of the Reverend John Quick* (1706).

FRY, E. A. (ed.), *Calendar of Wills and Administrations in the Court of the Archdeacon of Taunton* (1912).

A Full and Truer Relation of the Examination and Confession of W. Barwick and E. Mangall (1690).

GEE, H., and HARDY, W. J. (ed.), *Documents Illustrative of English Church History* (1896).

GEORGE, W. *Historical and Antiquarian Gleanings Relating to Minehead and Neighbourhood* (1889).

GERARD, THOMAS, *The Particular Description of the County of Somerset Drawn up by Thomas Gerard of Trent 1633*, ed. E. H. Bates, Somerset Record Society, 15 (1900).

GILBERT, J. T. (ed.), *Calendar of the Ancient Records of Dublin* iii (Dublin, 1892).

GILDON, CHARLES, *The Post-Boy Rob'd of his Mail* (1692).

—— *The History of the Athenian Society for the Resolving all Nice and Curious Questions* (1692).

GILLESPIE, R. (ed.), *The First Chapter Act Book of Christ Church Cathedral, Dublin 1574–1634* (Dublin, 1997).

—— (ed.), *The Vestry Records of the Parish of St John the Evangelist, Dublin, 1595–1658* (Dublin, 2002).

GLANVILL, JOSEPH, *An Apology and Advice for some of the Clergy, who Suffer under False, and Scandalous Reports* (1674).

—— *Saducismus Triumphatus: or, Full and Plain Evidence Concerning Witches and Apparitions* (1681).

—— *The Zealous, and Impartial Protestant* (1681).

Great News from Middle-Row in Holbourn: Or a True Relation of a Dreadful Ghost (1679).

GROSART, A. B. (ed.), *Lismore Papers* (2 series, 10 vols., 1886–8).

HARRIS, WALTER, *The History and Antiquities of the City of Dublin* (Dublin, 1766).

HAWKINS, ROBERT, *The Perjur'd Fanatick* (1728).

HEARNE, THOMAS, *Remarks and Collections of Thomas Hearne*, ed. C. E. Doble *et al.*, Oxford Historical Society (11 vols., 1865–1919).

HICKMAN, HENRY, *Historia Quinq-Articularis Exarticulata, or, Animadversions on Doctor Heylin's Quintquarticular History* (1674).

Historical Manuscripts Commission, Hastings MSS, iv (1947).

Historical Remarks of the City of Waterford from 853 to 1270, To which are added a List of the Mayor, Bayliffs and Sheriffs from 1377 to 1735 (Waterford, ?1735).

HOBBES, THOMAS, *Leviathan*, ed. K. R. Minogue (1973).

HOWARD, A. J., and STOATE, T. L. (ed.), *Somerset Protestation Returns and Subsidy Rolls* (Bristol, 1975).

JANSSON, M. *et al.* (eds.), *Proceedings in the Opening Session of the Long Parliament: House of Commons* (2 vols., Rochester, NY, 2000–1).

J. C., *The Araignment of Hypocrisie* (1652).

JENKINS, C. (ed.), 'Act Book of the Archdeacon of Taunton', in T. F. Palmer (ed.), *Collectanea II*, Somerset Record Society, 42 (1928).

JONES, W., *Credulities Past and Present* (1898), 68–9.

Journals of the House of Commons of the Kingdom of Ireland, i (Dublin, 1796).

Journals of the House of Lords of Ireland, i (Dublin, 1779).

KILLEN, W. D., *The Ecclesiastical History of Ireland* (2 vols., 1875).

KING, JOHN, *Animadversions on a Pamphlet Intituled Advice to the Churches of the Nonconformists in the English Nation* (1701).

—— *The Case of John Atherton, Bishop of Waterford in Ireland: fairly represented* (1710).

LAUD, WILLIAM, *The Works of Archbishop Laud*, ed. W. Scott and J. Bliss (7 vols., Oxford, 1847–60).

LAVATER, LUDWIG, *Of Ghostes and Spirites Walking by Night 1572*, ed. J. Dover Wilson and M. Yardley (Oxford, 1929).

The Life and Death of John Atherton, Lord Bishop of Waterford and Lismore (1641).

The Life and Death of John Atherton (?1815).

LOVEL, HENRY, *Horrid and Strange News from Ireland, being a True Relation of what happened in the Province of Munster, at a Castle of one of the Fitz Garrets called Ballimarter* (1643).

Mr Love's Case (1651).

LYNCH, JOHN, *Cambrensis Eversus, seu potius Historica Fides in Rebus Hibernicis Giraldo Cambrensi Abrogata*, ed. and tr. M. Kelly, (3 vols., Dublin, 1848–51).

MANT, R., *History of the Church of Ireland from the Reformation to the Revolution* (2 vols., 1840).

MANTON, THOMAS, *Catalogus Variorum et Insignium Librorum Instructissimae Bibliothecae Clarissim Doctissimiq Viri Thomae Manton* (1678).

MATTHEWS, A. G., *Calamy Revised, being a Revision of Edmund Calamy's Account of the Ministers and Others Ejected and Silenced, 1660–2* (Oxford, 1934).

The Midwives Ghost (1680).

MILLS, J. (ed.), *The Registers of St John the Evangelist Dublin 1619 to 1699* (Dublin, 1906).

MORE, HENRY, *The Immortality of the Soul* (1659).

A Most Strange and Dreadful Apparition of Several Spirits and Visions (1680).

A Narrative of the Demon of Spraiton in a Letter from a person of Quality in the County of Devon (1683).

A New and General Biographical Dictionary (11 vols., 1761–2; 12 vols., 1784).

A New Ballad of the Midwives Ghost (1680).

NICHOLS, FRANCIS, *The Irish Compendium* (1722).

NICHOLSON, ISAAC, *The Modern Syphilis:, or The True Method of Curing Every Stage and Symptom of the Venereal Disease* (1718).

The Night-Walker of Bloomsbury (1683).

NORRIS, JOHN, *Letters concerning the Love of God* (1695).

OLDEN, T., *The Church of Ireland* (1892).

[OLDYS, WILLIAM], 'Atherton, John', in *Biographia Britannica*.

O'SHEA, J., *The Life of Father Luke Wadding* (Dublin, 1885).

PAGE, J. L. W., *An Exploration of Exmoor* (1890).

Parliamentary Gazeteer of Ireland (3 vols., Dublin, 1844–6).

The Perjur'd Phanatick, or, The Malicious Conspiracy of Sr. John Croke of Chilton, Henry Larimore and other Phanaticks against the Life of Robert Hawkins, clerk (1685).

PERKINS, WILLIAM, *A Golden Chaine* (Cambridge, 1600).

The Politicall Balance, for 1754. The Mock-Patriot, for 1753. To which is added, the Case of John Atherton (Dublin, 1754).

POOLE, C. H., *The Customs, Superstitions and Legends of the County of Somerset* (1877).

PRYNNE, WILLIAM, *The Antipathie of the English Lordly Prelacie* (1641).

QUICK, JOHN, *The Young Man's Claim unto the Holy Sacrament of the Lords Supper* (1672).

—— *Hell Open'd, or The Infernal Sin of Murder Punished. Being a true Relation of the Poysoning of a Whole Family in Plymouth* (1676).

—— *The Test of True Godliness. A Sermon Preached at the Funeral of Phillip Harris* (1682).

—— *Synodicon in Gallia Reformata: or, the Acts, Decisions, Decrees, and Canons of those Famous National Councils of the Reformed Churches in France* (1692).

REID, J. S., *History of the Presbyterian Church in Ireland* (2nd edn., 3 vols., Belfast, 1867).

RENNISON, W. H., *Succession List of the Bishops, Cathedral and Parochial Clergy of the Dioceses of Waterford and Lismore* (Waterford, 1920).

—— 'Joshua Boyle's Accompt of the Temporalities of the Bishopricks of Waterford', *Journal of the Cork Historical and Archaeological Society*, 32, 33 (1927–8).

The Restless Ghost: or, Wonderful News from Northamptonshire and Southwark (1675).

RICH, BARNABY, *The Irish Hubbub, or, the English Hue and Crie* (1617).

ROE, JOHN, *The Certainty of a Future State: or, An Occasional Letter Concerning Apparitions* (1698).

RONAN, M. V. (ed.), 'Archbishop Bulkeley's Visitation of Dublin, 1630', *Archivium Hibernicum*, 8 (1941).

RUSHWORTH, J., *The Tryal of Thomas, Earl of Strafford, Lord Lieutenant of Ireland, upon an Impeachment of High Treason* (1680).

SCOTT, WALTER, *The Letters of Sir Walter Scott*, ed. H. Grierson (12 vols., 1932–7).

—— *The Works of Sir Walter Scott*, Wordsworth Poetry Library (Ware, 1995).

—— *Letters on Demonology and Witchcraft*, ed. P. G. Maxwell-Stuart (Ware, 2001).

SHERLEY, WILLIAM, *The Excellency of the Order of the Church of England under Episcopal Government* (1662).

SHUCKBURGH, E. S. (ed.), *Two Biographies of William Bedell* (Cambridge, 1902).

SIMCO, JOHN, *A Catalogue of Books and Prints* (London, 1788).

SMITH, CHARLES, *The Antient and Present State of the County and City of Waterford* (Dublin, 1746).

The Spectator, ed. D. F. Bond (5 vols., Oxford, 1965).

SPRAT, THOMAS, *A Relation of the Late Wicked Contrivance of Stephen Blackhead, and Robert Young, against the Lives of Several Persons by forging an Association under their Hands written by the Bishop of Rochester* (London?, 1692).

—— *The Second Part of the Relation of the Late Wicked Contrivance* (1693).

The Statutes at Large, Passed in the Parliaments of Ireland (8 vols., Dublin, 1765).

STOATE, T. L. (ed.), *Devon Hearth Tax Returns* (Bristol, 1982).

STOKES, J. (ed.), *Records of Early English Drama: Somerset* (2 vols., Toronto, 1996).

A Strange and Fearful Warning to all Sonnes and Executors (that fulfill not the will of their dead Fathers) (1623).

Strange and True News from Long-Ally in More-Fields, Southwark (1661).

A Strange and Wonderfull Discovery of a Horrid and Cruel Murther Committed Fourteen years Since (1662).

Strange and Wonderful News from Exeter (1690).

Strange and Wonderful News from Lincolnshire (1679).

A Strange but True Relation of the Discovery of a Most Horrid and Bloudy Murder (1678).

SWIFT, JONATHAN, *Journal to Stella*, ed. H. Williams (2 vols., Oxford, 1948).

SWIFT, JONATHAN, *The Poems of Jonathan Swift*, ed. H. Williams (2nd edn., 3 vols., Oxford, 1958).

The Tatler, 119, *From Tuesday January 10. to Thursday January 12 1709* [i.e. 1710], and 120, *From Thursday January 12 to Saturday January 14 1709*.

The Tatler, ed. D. F. Bond (3 vols., Oxford, 1987).

TELFAIR, ALEXANDER, *A True Relation of an Apparition, Expressions and Actings of a Spirit, which infested the House of Andrew Mackie* (Edinburgh, 1696).

THORNTON, ALICE, *The Autobiography of Mrs Alice Thornton*, ed. C. Jackson, Surtees Soc. 62 (1875).

TILLEY, M. P., *A Dictionary of the Proverbs in England in the Sixteenth and Seventeenth Centuries* (Ann Arbor, 1950).

TOULMIN SMITH, L. (ed.), *The Itinerary of John Leland* (5 vols., 1964).

The Treble Almanack for the Year MDCCLXXXVI (Dublin, 1786).

A True and Impartial Account of the Apparition of John Freeman, esq. to a Young lady at Dawney-court in Buckinghamshire (1696).

A True and Perfect Account of a Strange and Dreadful Apparition, which Lately Infected and Sunk a Ship Bound for Newcastle (1672).

TRUSLER, JOHN, *The Historians Guide* (Dublin, 1773).

WALTERS, J. C., *Bygone Somerset* (1897).

WARD, SETH, *The Case of Joram. Sermon Preached before the House of Peers in the Abby-Church at Westminster* (1674).

WARE, JAMES, *De Praesulibus Hiberniae Commenarius. A Prima Gentis Hibernicae ad Fidem Christianam Conversione ad nostra usque Tempora* (Dublin, 1665).

—— *A Commentary on the Prelates of Ireland, from the first Conversion of the Irish Nation to the Christian Faith down to our Times* (Dublin, 1704).

—— *The Works of Sir James Ware Concerning Ireland*, ed. Walter Harris (3 vols, Dublin, 1739).

—— *The Whole Works of Sir James Ware*, ed. Walter Harris (2 vols., Dublin, 1764).

WEAVER, F. W. (ed.), *Somerset Incumbents. From the Hugo MSS 30, 279–80 in the British Museum* (Bristol, 1889).

WEBSTER, JOHN, *The Displaying of Supposed Witchcraft* (1677).

WENTWORTH, THOMAS, *A Briefe and Perfect Relation of the Answers and Replies of Thomas Wentworth, Earl of Strafford, to the Articles Exhibited against him by the House of Commons* (1647).

—— *The Earl of Strafford's Letters and Dispatches*, ed. W. Knowler (2 vols., 1739).

The West Somerset Free Press (Sat. 7 Dec. 1889).

The Western Antiquary, 6 (July 1886–Feb. 1887).

WHITAKER, T. W. (ed.), *The Life and Original Correspondence of Sir George Radcliffe* (1810).

WHITE, BENJAMIN, *A Catalogue of a Large and Valuable Collection of Books* (London, 1780).

WHITE, JOHN, *The First Century of Scandalous, Malignant Priests Made and Admitted into Benefices by the Prelates* (1643).

WILLIAMS, DANIEL, *A Funeral Sermon Occasioned by the Death of the Reverend Mr John Quick* (1706).

The Wonders of Free-Grace, or, A Compleat History of all the Remarkable Penitents that have been Executed at Tyburn and Elsewhere for these last Thirty Years (1690).

WOOD, ANTHONY, *Athenae Oxonienses* (2 vols., 1691).

SECONDARY AND POST-1900 SOURCES

AARNE, A., and THOMPSON, S., *The Types of the Folk-Tale: A Classification and Bibliography* (Helsinki, 1928).

ABBOTT, W. M., 'The Issue of Episcopacy in the Long Parliament, 1640–1648' (University of Oxford, D.Phil. thesis, 1981).

ALDRICH, R., and WOTHERSPOON, G. (eds.), *Who's Who in Gay and Lesbian History* (2000).

AYLMER, G. E., 'Unbelief in Seventeenth-Century England', in D. Pennington and K. Thomas (eds.), *Puritans and Revolutionaries* (Oxford, 1978).

BAINE, R. M., *Daniel Defoe and the Supernatural* (Athens, Ga., 1968).

BALL, F. E., *A History of the County Dublin* (6 vols., 1902–20).

BARCHAS, J., *Graphic Design, Print Culture and the Eighteenth-Century Novel* (Cambridge, 2003).

BARNES, T. G., 'County Politics and a Puritan Cause Célèbre: Somerset Churchales, 1633', *Transactions of the Royal Historical Society*, 5th ser. 9 (1959), 103–22.

—— *Somerset 1625–1640: A County's Government During the 'Personal Rule'* (1961).

BARRY, J., 'Introduction: Keith Thomas and the Problem of Witchcraft', in J. Barry, M. Hester, and G. Roberts (eds.), *Witchcraft in Early Modern Europe: Studies in Culture and Belief* (Cambridge, 1996).

BARRY, J., 'Public Infidelity and Private Belief? The Discourse of Spirits in Enlightenment Bristol', in W. De Blecourt and O. Davies (eds.), *Beyond the Witch Trials: Witchcraft and Magic in Enlightenment Europe* (Manchester, 2004).

BEATY, N. L., *The Craft of Dying: A Study in the Literary Tradition of the Ars Moriendi in England* (New Haven, Conn., 1970).

BELFIELD, J., 'Tarleton's News out of Purgatory (1590): A Modern-Spelling Edition, with Introduction and Commentary' (unpublished Ph.D. thesis, University of Birmingham, 1978).

BELLANY, A., 'Libels in Action: Ritual, Subversion and the English Literary Underground, 1603–1642', in T. Harris (ed.), *The Politics of the Excluded, c.1500–1850* (Basingstoke, 2001).

BENNETT, G. V., *The Tory Crisis in Church and State, 1688–1730: The Career of Francis Atterbury, Bishop of Rochester* (Oxford, 1975).

BERRY, H., *Gender, Society and Print Culture in Late-Stuart England: The Cultural World of the Athenian Mercury* (Aldershot, 2003).

BHOWMIK, U., 'Facts and Norms in the Marketplace of Print: John Dunton's *Athenian Mercury*', *Eighteenth-Century Studies*, 36 (2003).

BINDING, H., and STEVENS, D., *The Book of Minehead with Alcombe* (Tiverton, 2000).

BOLTON, F. R., *The Caroline Tradition of the Church of Ireland with Particular Reference to Bishop Jeremy Taylor* (1958).

BOSTRIDGE, I., *Witchcraft and its Transformations, c.1650–c.1750* (Oxford, 1997).

BOSWELL, J., *Christianity, Social Tolerance and Homosexuality* (1980).

BOYDELL, B., 'The Establishment of the Choral Tradition, 1480–1647', in Milne, *Christ Church Cathedral*.

BRADSHAW, B., and MORRILL, J. (eds.), *The British Problem, c.1534–1707* (Basingstoke, 1996).

BRAY, ALAN, *Homosexuality in Renaissance England* (1982; 2nd edn., New York, 1995).

BRIGGS, K. M., *A Dictionary of British Folk-Tales* (4 vols., 1971).

BROOKS, J., *The Good Ghost Guide* (Norwich, 1994).

BROWN, T., *The Fate of the Dead: A Study in Folk Eschatology in the West Country After the Reformation* (Cambridge, 1979).

—— 'The Ghost of Old Mrs Leakey', in H. R. E. Davidson and W. M. S. Russell (eds.), *The Folklore of Ghosts* (Cambridge, 1981).

BURG, B. R., 'Ho Hum, Another Work of the Devil: Buggery and Sodomy in Early Stuart England', in S. J. Licata and R. P. Petersen (eds.), *Historical Perspectives on Homosexuality* (New York, 1981).

BURKE, PETER, *Popular Culture in Early Modern Europe* (1978).

BURTON, S. H., *Exmoor* (1952).

BYAM, E. S., *Chronological Memoir of the Three Clerical Brethren . . . Byam* (Ryde, n.d.).

CACIOLA, N., 'Wraiths, Revenants and Ritual in Medieval Culture', *Past and Present*, 152 (1996).

—— 'Spirits Seeking Bodies: Death, Possession and Communal Memory in the Middle Ages', in B. Gordon and P. Marshall (eds.), *The Place of the Dead: Death and Remembrance in Late Medieval and Early Modern Europe* (Cambridge, 2000).

CANNY, N., *The Upstart Earl: A Study of the Social and Mental World of Richard Boyle, First Earl of Cork 1566–1643* (Cambridge, 1982).

—— 'The Attempted Anglicisation of Ireland in the Seventeenth Century', in J. F. Merritt (ed.), *The Political World of Thomas Wentworth , Earl of Strafford, 1621–1641* (Cambridge, 1996).

—— *Making Ireland British 1580–1650* (Oxford, 2001).

CAPP, B., *When Gossips Meet: Women, Family and Neighbourhood in Early Modern England* (Oxford, 2003).

—— 'Life, Love and Litigation: Sileby in the 1630s', *Past and Present*, 182 (2004).

CHANTER, J. R., *Sketches of the Literary History of Barnstaple* (Barnstaple, 1866).

—— *Memorials, Descriptive and Historical of the Church of St Peter, Barnstaple* (Barnstaple, n.d.).

CHARTIER, R., *Cultural History: Between Practices and Representations*, tr. L. G. Cochrane (Ithaca, NY, 1988).

—— *On the Edge of the Cliff: History, Language and Practices*, tr. L. G. Cochrane (Baltimore, 1997).

CLARK, S., *Thinking with Demons: The Idea of Witchcraft in Early Modern Europe* (Oxford, 1997).

—— (ed.), *Languages of Witchcraft: Narrative, Ideology and Meaning in Early Modern Culture* (Basingstoke, 2001).

CLARKE, A., *The Old English in Ireland 1625–42* (1966).

—— 'The Atherton File', *Decies*, 11 (1979).

—— 'A Woeful Sinner: John Atherton', in V. P. Carey and U. Lotz-Heumann (eds.), *Taking Sides? Colonial and Confessional Mentalités in Early Modern Ireland* (Dublin, 2003).

CLAYTON, A., *London's Coffee Houses: A Stimulating Story* (2003).

COLLEY, L., *Captives: Britain, Empire and the World, 1600–1850* (2002).

CONNOLLY, S. J., *Religion, Law and Power: The Making of Protestant Ireland 1660–1760* (Oxford, 1992).

COWAN, B., *The Social Life of Coffee: The Emergence of the British Coffeehouse* (New Haven, Conn., 2005).

COWMAN, D., 'The Reformation Bishops of the Diocese of Waterford and Lismore', *Decies*, 27 (1984).

CRESSY, D., *Birth, Marriage, and Death: Ritual, Religion, and the Life-Cycle in Tudor and Stuart England* (Oxford, 1997).

—— *Travesties and Transgressions in Tudor and Stuart England* (Oxford, 2000).

—— 'Revolutionary England, 1640–1642', *Past and Present*, 181 (2003).

DANIELL, C., *Death and Burial in Medieval England 1066–1550* (1997).

DARNTON, R., *The Great Cat Massacre* (Harmondsworth, 1984).

DAVIES, O., *A People Bewitched: Witchcraft and Magic in Nineteenth-Century Somerset* (Trowbridge, 1999).

—— *Witchcraft, Magic and Culture, 1736–1951* (Manchester, 1999).

DAVIES, R. C., *Christian Slaves, Muslim Masters: White Slavery in the Mediterranean, the Barbary Coast, and Italy, 1500–1800* (Basingstoke, 2003).

DAVIS, L., *Factual Fictions: The Origins of the English Novel* (New York, 1983).

DAVIS, N. Z., *The Return of Martin Guerre* (1983).

—— *Fiction in the Archives: Pardon Tales and their Tellers in Sixteenth-Century France* (1988).

—— *The Gift in Sixteenth-Century France* (Oxford, 2000).

DICKINSON, J. R., and. SHARPE, J. A., 'Infanticide in Early Modern England: The Court of Great Sessions at Chester, 1650–1800', in M. Jackson (ed.), *Infanticide: Historical Perspectives on Child Murder and Concealment, 1550–2000* (Aldershot, 2002).

DOLAN, F. E., *Dangerous Familiars: Representations of Domestic Crime in England, 1550–1700* (Ithaca, NY, 1994).

DORSON, R. M., *The British Folklorists: A History* (1968).

DUFFY, E., *The Stripping of the Altars: Traditional Religion in England 1400–1800* (New Haven, Conn., 1992).

—— *The Voices of Morebath: Reformation and Rebellion in an English Village* (New Haven, Conn., 2001).

EALES, F. C., 'Minehead, XVII Century Reredos', *Somerset Archaeological and Natural History Society Proceedings*, 81 (1936).

FINUCANE, R. C., *Ghosts: Appearances of the Dead and Cultural Transformation* (New York, 1996).

FORD, A., *The Protestant Reformation in Ireland 1590–1641* (2nd edn., Dublin, 1997).

—— MILNE, K, and McGUIRE, J. I. (eds.), *As by Law Established: The Church of Ireland since the Reformation* (Dublin, 1995).

FOX, A., 'Rumour, News, and Popular Political Opinion in Elizabethan and Early Stuart England', *Historical Journal*, 40 (1997).

—— *Oral and Literate Culture in England 1500–1700* (Oxford, 2000).

FUDGE, E., 'Monstrous Acts: Bestiality in Early Modern England', *History Today* (Aug. 2000).

GASKILL, M., 'Witchcraft and Power in Early Modern England: The Case of Margaret Moore', in J. Kermode and G. Walker (eds.), *Women, Crime and the Courts* (1994).

—— *Crime and Mentalities in Early Modern England* (Cambridge, 2000).

—— 'Witches and Witnesses in Old and New England', in Clark (ed.), *Languages of Witchcraft*.

GILLESPIE, R., *Devoted People: Belief and Religion in Early Modern Ireland* (Manchester, 1997).

—— 'The Shaping of Reform, 1558–1625', and 'The Crisis of Reform, 1625–60', in Milne, *Christ Church Cathedral*.

GOLDBERG, J., *Sodometries: Renaissance Texts, Modern Sexualities* (Stanford, Calif., 1992).

—— (ed.), *Queering the Renaissance* (Durham, NC, 1994).

GINZBURG, C., *The Cheese and the Worms: The Cosmos of a Sixteenth-Century Miller*, tr. J. and A. Tedeschi (1980).

GOWING, L., 'Secret Births and Infanticide in Seventeenth-Century England', *Past and Present*, 156 (1997).

—— 'The Haunting of Susan Lay: Servants and Mistresses in Seventeenth-Century England', *Gender and History*, 14 (2002).

GRAY, T. *The Lost Chronicle of Barnstaple* (Exeter, 1998).

HABERMAS, J., *The Structural Transformation of the Public Sphere: An Inquiry into a Category of Bourgeois Society*, tr. T. Burger (Cambridge, 1989).

HALLAM, J., *Ghosts' Who's Who* (Newton Abbot, 1977).

HALPERIN, D. M., *How to Do the History of Homosexuality* (2002).

HANDLEY, S., ' "Visions of an Unseen World": The Production and Consumption of English Ghost Stories, *c*.1600–1800' (University of Warwick, Ph.D. thesis, 2005).

HARLEY, D. 'Historians as Demonologists: The Myth of the Midwife-Witch', *Social History of Medicine*, 3 (1990).

HERRUP, C., *A House in Gross Disorder: Sex, Law and the Second Earl of Castlehaven* (Oxford, 1999).

HILL, P. M., *Two Augustan Booksellers: John Dunton and Edmund Curll* (Lawrence, Kan., 1958).

HINDLE, S., 'The Shaming of Margaret Knowsley: Gossip, Gender and the Experience of Authority in Early Modern England', *Continuity and Change*, 9 (1994).

HITCHCOCK, T., *English Sexualities, 1700–1800* (Basingstoke,1997).

HODGKIN, K., 'Reasoning with Unreason: Visions, Witchcraft, and Madness in Early Modern England', in Clark (ed.), *Languages of Witchcraft*.

HOLE, R., 'Incest, Consanguinity and a Monstrous Birth in Rural England', *Social History*, 25 (2000).

HOLMES, G., *The Trial of Doctor Sacheverell* (1973).

—— *The Birth of Britain: A New Nation 1700–1710* (Oxford, 1994).

HOLMES, R., *Coleridge: Early Visions* (1989).

HOPPIT, J., *A Land of Liberty? England 1689–1727* (Oxford, 2000).

HOULBROOKE, R., *Death, Religion, and the Family in England 1480–1750* (Oxford, 1998).

HOWSON, G., *The Macaroni Parson* (1973).

HUNTER, M., 'The Problem of "Atheism" in Early Modern England', *Transactions of the Royal Historical Society*, 5th ser. 35 (1985).

—— and WOOTTON, D. (eds.), *Atheism from the Reformation to the Enlightenment* (Oxford, 1993).

—— 'New Light on the "Drummer of Tedworth": Conflicting Narratives of Witchcraft in Restoration England', *Historical Research*, 78 (2005).

HURLEY, J., *Legends of Exmoor* (Williton, 1973).

JACKSON, M., *New-Born Child Murder: Women, Illegitimacy and the Courts in Eighteenth-Century England* (Manchester, 1996).

JACKSON, P. W., 'Nonconformists and Society in Devon 1660–1689' (University of Exeter, Ph.D. thesis, 1986).

JOHNSTON, S. I., *Restless Dead: Encounters between the Living and the Dead in Ancient Greece* (Berkeley, Calif., 1999).

JONES, A. R., and STALLYBRASS, P., *Renaissance Clothing and the Materials of Memory* (Cambridge, 2000).

JOURDAN, G. V., 'The Rule of Charles I', in W. A. Phillips (ed.), *History of the Church of Ireland from the Earliest Times to the Present Day* (3 vols., Oxford, 1933).

KEARNEY, H., *Strafford in Ireland 1633–41: A Study in Absolutism* (2nd edn., Cambridge, 1989).

KELLEY, D. R., and HARRIS SACKS, D. (eds.), *The Historical Imagination in Early Modern Britain: History, Rhetoric, and Fiction, 1500–1800* (Cambridge, 1997).

KILBURN, T., and MILTON, A., 'The Public Context of the Trial and Execution of Strafford', in J. F. Merritt (ed.), *The Political World of Thomas Wentworth, Earl of Strafford, 1621–1641* (Cambridge, 1996).

LAKE, P., 'Deeds Against Nature: Cheap Print, Protestantism and Murder in Early Seventeenth-Century England', in K. Sharpe and P. Lake (eds.), *Culture and Politics in Early Stuart England* (Basingstoke, 1994).

—— 'Popular Form, Puritan Content? Two Puritan Appropriations of the Murder Pamphlet from Mid-Seventeenth-Century London', in A. Fletcher and P. Roberts (eds.), *Religion, Culture and Society in Early Modern Britain* (Cambridge, 1994).

—— ' "A Charitable Christian Hatred": The Godly and their Enemies in the 1630s', in C. Durston and J. Eales (eds.), *The Culture of English Puritanism 1560–1700* (Basingstoke, 1996).

—— with QUESTIER, M., *The Antichrist's Lewd Hat: Protestants, Papists and Players in Post-Reformation England* (New Haven, Conn., 2002).

LARTER, C. E., *Minehead, Porlock and Dunster*, The Homeland Handbooks, 18 (1901).

LAWRENCE, B., *Coleridge and Wordsworth in Somerset* (Newton Abbot, 1970).

LE ROY LADURIE, E., *Carnival: A People's Uprising at Romans 1579–1580*, tr. M Feeney (1980).

LILLYWHITE, B., *London Coffee Houses* (1963).

LITTLE, P. 'The Earl of Cork and the Fall of the Earl of Strafford, 1638–41', *Historical Journal*, 39 (1996).

LOWES, J. L., *The Road to Xanadu* (2nd edn., 1951).

McCAFFERTY, J., ' "God Bless your Free Church of Ireland": Wentworth, Laud, Bramhall and the Irish Convocation of 1634', in J. F. Merritt (ed.), *The Political World of Thomas Wentworth, Earl of Strafford, 1621–1641* (Cambridge, 1996).

—— 'John Bramhall and the Reconstruction of the Church of Ireland, 1633–1641' (University of Cambridge, Ph.D., 1996).

McCLAREN, D., 'Marital Fertility and Lactation 1570–1720', in M. Prior (ed.), *Women in English Society 1500–1800* (1985).

McCORMICK, I., *Secret Sexualities: A Sourcebook of Seventeenth and Eighteenth Century Writing* (1997).

McENERY, M. J., and REFAUSSÉ, R. (eds.), *Christ Church Deeds* (Dublin, 2001).

McEWEN, G. D., *The Oracle of the Coffee House: John Dunton's Athenian Mercury* (San Marino, Calif., 1972).

McINTOSH, M. K., *Working Women in English Society 1300–1620* (Cambridge, 2005).

McKEON, M., *The Origins of the English Novel 1600–1740* (Baltimore, 1987).

MAJOR, A., 'Mrs Leakey's Ghost', *On Spec: The Canadian Magazine of Speculative Writing*, 4/2 (1992).

MALCOLMSON, R. W., 'Infanticide in the Eighteenth Century', in J. S. Cockburn (ed.), *Crime in England 1550–1800* (1977).

MALTBY, J., *Prayer Book and People in Elizabethan and Early Stuart England* (Cambridge, 1998).

MARCHANT, R. A., *The Church under the Law: Justice, Administration and Discipline in the Diocese of York 1560–1640* (Cambridge, 1969).

MARSHALL, P., *Beliefs and the Dead in Reformation England* (Oxford, 2002).

—— *Reformation England 1480–1642* (2003).

MATAR, N., *Turks, Moors and Englishmen in the Age of Discovery* (New York, 1999).

MATHEWS, F. W., *Tales from the Blackdown Borderland*, Somerset Folk Series, 13 (1923).

MERRITT, J. F., 'The Historical Reputation of Thomas Wentworth', in J. F. Merritt (ed.), *The Political World of Thomas Wentworth, Earl of Strafford, 1621–1641* (Cambridge, 1996).

MILNE, K. (ed.), *Christ Church Cathedral, Dublin: A History* (Dublin, 2000).

MOODY, T. W., MARTIN, F. X., and BYRNE, F. J. (eds.), *A New History of Ireland, ix. Maps, Genealogies, Lists* (Oxford, 1984).

NEWTON, J. (ed.), *Early Modern Ghosts* (Durham, 2002).

NOAKES, D. *John Gay: A Profession of Friendship* (Oxford, 1995).

NORTON, R., *Mother Clap's Molly House: The Gay Subculture in England 1700–1830* (1992).

PARKS, S., *John Dunton and the English Book Trade: A Study of his Career with a Checklist of his Publications* (New York, 1976).

PARRIS, M., *The Great Unfrocked: Two Thousand Years of Church Scandal* (1998).

PARSONS, C. O., *Witchcraft and Demonology in Scott's Fiction* (Edinburgh, 1964).

PELZER, J. and L., 'The Coffee Houses of Augustan London', *History Today*, 32 (Oct. 1982).

PERCEVAL-MAXWELL, M., *The Outbreak of the Irish Rebellion of 1641* (Dublin, 1994).

PIERCE, H., 'Anti-Episcopacy and Graphic Satire in England, 1640–1645', *Historical Journal*, 47 (2004).

PORTER, R., *Enlightenment: Britain and the Creation of the Modern World* (2000).

POWER, P., *The Cathedral and Parish of Holy Trinity Waterford* (Waterford, 1940).

PROTHERO, I., 'William Benbow and the Concept of the "General Strike" ', *Past and Present*, 63 (1974).

QUAIFE, G. R., *Wanton Wenches and Wayward Wives: Peasants and Illicit Sex in Early Seventeenth-Century England* (1979).

RANGER, T., 'The Career of Richard Boyle, First Earl of Cork in Ireland, 1588–1643' (University of Oxford, D.Phil., 1959).

RAYMOND, J., *Pamphlets and Pamphleteering in Early Modern Britain* (Cambridge, 2003).

ROBSON, L. A., 'No Nine Days Wonder: Embedded Protestant Narratives in Early Modern Prose Murder Pamphlets 1573–1700' (University of Warwick, Ph.D. thesis, 2003).

ROGERS, P., *Grub Street: Studies in a Subculture* (1972).

RUSHTON, P., 'Texts of Authority: Witchcraft Accusations and the Demonstration of Truth in Early Modern England', in Clark (ed.), *Languages of Witchcraft*.

SCHMITT, J.-C., *Ghosts in the Middle Ages: The Living and the Dead in Medieval Society*, tr. T. L. Fagan (Chicago, 1998).

SCRIBNER, R. W., 'Elements of Popular Belief', in *Handbook of European History 1400–1600*, ed. T. Brady, H. Oberman, and J. Tracey (2 vols., Leiden, 1994–5).

SHARPE, J., 'The Devil in East Anglia: The Matthew Hopkins Trials Reconsidered', in J. Barry, M. Hester, and G. Roberts (eds.), *Witchcraft in Early Modern Europe: Studies in Culture and Belief* (Cambridge, 1996).

SHELLY, H. C., *Inns and Taverns of Old London* (repr., 2004).

SIMMS, J. G., 'The Restoration, 1660–85', in T. W. Moody, F. X. Martin, and F. J. Byrne (eds.), *A New History of Ireland, iii. Early Modern Ireland, 1534–1691* (Oxford, 1976).

SIMPSON, J., 'The Local Legend: A Product of Popular Culture', *Rural History*, 2 (1991).

SMYTH, C. J., *Chronicle of the Law Officers of Ireland* (1839).

SNELL, F. J., *A Book of Exmoor* (1903).

SPENCER, J. and A., *The Encylopedia of Ghosts and Spirits* (1992).

STIEG, M., *Laud's Laboratory: The Diocese of Bath and Wells in the Early Seventeenth Century* (London and Toronto, 1982).

STOYLE, M., *Loyalty and Locality: Popular Allegiance in Devon during the English Civil War* (Exeter, 1994).

STRAUSS, R. *The Unspeakable Curll: Being Some Account of Edmund Curll, Bookseller; to which is added a full List of his Books* (1927).

SUTHERLAND, J., *The Life of Walter Scott* (Oxford, 1997).

TAIT, C., *Death, Burial and Commemoration in Ireland, 1550–1650* (Basingstoke, 2002).

THOMAS, K., *Religion and the Decline of Magic* (1971).

TONGUE, R. L., *Somerset Folklore*, ed. K. M. Briggs (1965).

TROTMAN, E. E., 'Seventeenth-Century Treasure-Seeking at Bridgwater', *Notes and Queries for Somerset and Dorset*, 27/269 (1959).

TRUMBACH, R., *Sex and the Gender Revolution i: Heterosexuality and the Third Gender in Enlightenment London* (Chicago, 1998).

TURNER, J., *Ghosts in the South West* (Newton Abbot, 1973).

TYACKE, N., *Aspects of English Protestantism c.1530–1700* (Manchester, 2001).

UNDERWOOD, P., *A Gazetteer of British Ghosts* (1971).

—— *Ghosts of Somerset* (Launceston, 1985).

WALKER, G., *Crime, Gender and Social Order in Early Modern England* (Cambridge, 2003).

WALSHAM, A., 'Miracles in Post-Reformation England', in K. Cooper and J. Gregory (eds.), *Signs, Wonders, Miracles: Representations of Divine Power in the Life of the Church* (Woodbridge, 2005).

WATSON, W. G., *Calendar of Customs, Superstitions, Weather-Lore... Connected with the County of Somerset* (Taunton, 1920).

WEDGWOOD, C. V., *Thomas Wentworth, First Earl of Strafford, 1593–1641* (1961).

WHITE, H., *Tropics of Discourse: Essays in Cultural Criticism* (1978).

WINNET, R., 'The Strange Case of Bishop John Atherton', *Decies*, 39 (1988).

WOOLF, D., 'The "Common Voice": History, Folklore and Oral Tradition in Early Modern England', *Past and Present*, 120 (1988).

—— *The Social Circulation of the Past: English Historical Culture 1500–1730* (Oxford, 2003).

WRIGHTSON, K., *Poverty and Piety in an English Village: Terling, 1525–1700* (2nd edn., Oxford, 1995).

YORK, N. L., *Neither Kingdom Nor Nation: The Irish Quest for Constitutional Rights 1698–1800* (Washington, DC. 1994).

INDEX